LOUIS XI.

HISTORY

OF

CHARLES THE BOLD,

DUKE OF BURGUNDY.

BY

JOHN FOSTER KIRK.

VOL. II.

PHILADELPHIA:
J. B. LIPPINCOTT & CO.
1864.

CONTENTS OF VOL. II.

BOOK III.

CHAPTER I.

CHAPTER II.

BOOK IV.

CHAPTER I.

CHAPTER II.

CHAPTER III.

CHAPTER IV.

HISTORY

OF

CHARLES THE BOLD.

BOOK III.

CHAPTER I.

RESULTS OF THE KING'S DISGRACE AND THE DUKE'S TRIUMPH.—CRISIS IN THE AFFAIRS OF ENGLAND.—CONSEQUENT FRESH EMBROILMENT BETWEEN LOUIS AND CHARLES.

1469–1470.

On Sunday the 15th of January, 1469, the great hall of the palace at Brussels was the scene of a brief but impressive ceremony. The walls were hung with tapestry representing the achievements of Hannibal, Alexander, and other famous conquerors. A barrier ran across the lower end of the apartment. Within were rows of seats on either side of a broad passage-way, that led to a dais, or elevated platform, at the upper end, richly carpeted with cloth of gold. On the dais was placed a chair of state, where sat "the most high, *victorious*, and redoubted prince, Charles duke of Burgundy and Brabant." The nearest seats were occupied by the prince-bishop of Liége, Philip, prince of Savoy, Edmund duke of Somerset, the knights of the *Toison d'Or*, and many representatives of foreign courts — "embassies from France, England, Hungary, Bohemia, Naples, Sicily, Cyprus, Norway, Poland, Denmark, Russia, Livonia, Prussia, Austria, Milan, Venice, and other states." The members of the ducal household were ranged according to their degrees.

In the courtyard without, where the snow lay thick upon the pavement, a crowd of burghers, — men of wealth and note, — bearing fifty-two banners ornamented with different devices, had waited patiently and silently for more than an hour and a half. At length they were admitted; and, the barrier being removed, they entered the enclosure, and passed up the hall to the foot of the dais. There they laid the banners on the floor, and, kneeling, uttered simultaneously, and in a tone expressive of the deepest humility, the single word, "Mercy!" A royal charter was then read aloud, known as the "Great Privilege" of Ghent, by which Philip the Fair, king of France, in the year 1301, had conferred upon that town the right of electing its own *échevins*, or magistrates. When the reading was finished, the Seigneur de Groux, chancellor of Burgundy, rose and inquired what was the pleasure of his sovereign in regard to this instrument. "That it shall be annulled!" was the stern reply; whereupon Master Jean le Gros, chief secretary of the duke, slit the ancient parchment with a knife, in sight of the whole assembly.

The duke then addressed the deputation at his feet, consisting of the municipal authorities of Ghent and the deans of the fifty-two guilds. He enlarged upon the heinous offence committed by the citizens on the occasion of his "joyous entry." The concessions then extorted from him had been duly carried into effect. But from that time he had refused to visit Ghent, or to hold any communication with a people who had offered so gross an insult to his person and sovereignty. All their attempts to conciliate him had been contemptuously repulsed. At length they had proffered the amplest reparation, and approached him with the humblest supplications. They had consented to the re-imposition of the *cueillotte* and to the forfeiture of many of their most valued immunities. They had again barred up the "condemned" gates, surrendered their banners, and sent their representatives to make their submission publicly to their offended prince, and to solicit his forgiveness. This he now granted, promising, while they continued to be his loyal and obedient subjects, to accord them his favor and protection.[1]

[1] "Relation de l'assemblée solennelle tenue à Bruxelles le 15 Janvier, 1469;" Gachard, Doc. Inéd. tom. i. pp. 204–209. — "Privilège accordé par Philippe Roy de France à ceux de la Ville de Gand, avec l'acte de la cassation dudit Privilège," &c; Lenglet, tom. i. pp. 87–93. — Extrait de l'Hist. manuscrite des Antiquitez de Flandres, par Wiellant; Lenglet, tom. ii. p. 627. — Commines, tom. i. pp. 144–146.

The terrible punishment recently inflicted upon Liége had served as a warning to the burghers of Flanders. Every where, indeed, the success which had hitherto attended all the enterprises of Charles, and especially the triumphs which he had gained over the French king, had produced a deep impression, and caused him to be regarded as the most powerful sovereign in Christendom. In his progress through his different states, he was attended, not merely by a numerous and splendid train of his own vassals, but by a far greater number of foreign envoys than was then seen assembled at any other court.[2] His alliance was sought by all: by neighboring princes his arbitration was requested in cases of dissension. He had renewed his former relations with the duke of Brittany. His friendship with the king of England was cemented by an interchange of the insignia of their respective orders, the Garter, and the *Toison d' Or*.[3] The affairs of Gueldres, of which we shall hereafter have occasion to speak, were referred to his decision. The king of Bohemia — the famous George Podiebrad, the ablest and most enterprising of the German electoral princes, — convinced that the duke of Burgundy could alone furnish the means of resisting the invasions of the Turks, and of saving the empire from the ruin that

[2] See the "Ancienne Chronique" — evidently a journal, or itinerary, kept by successive *maîtres-d'hôtel* in the Burgundian household — in Lenglet, tom. ii. pp. 194, 196, et al. — Gachard has some remarks on this extraordinary concourse of foreign envoys at the court of Charles the Bold. Doc. Inéd. tom. i. p. 206, note.

[3] Letters-patent, in Lenglet, tom. iii. p. 99, et seq.

seemed impending over it, was desirous to secure his election as "king of the Romans," and sent an ambassador to the Netherlands to negotiate a treaty with that object, stipulating, in the event of its attainment, for two hundred thousand florins to be paid to himself as the reward of his exertions.[4] By another arrangement, concluded in the spring of 1469, Sigismund, duke of Austria, hoping thereby to secure the aid of a powerful ally against his hereditary enemies the Swiss, conveyed to Charles, for a valuable consideration, his possessions in Alsace,—subject, it is true, to the right of redemption, but with little likelihood that any claim for restitution would ever be made.

Thus the result of the events narrated in the preceding chapter had been to raise the duke to a situation of greater power and command than he had previously held, to exalt him in the estimation of the world and in his own. The effect on his rival had been, in a proportionate degree, that of depression and defeat. His high hopes, his lofty language, his great preparations, his appeals to his people, and their enthusiastic response, had suddenly ended in the abandonment of his projects, in the surrender of his rightful claims, in a shameful treaty, and in a

[4] The motives of the king of Bohemia are thus stated in the treaty itself: "Serenissimus Dominus Rex, attendens illustrissimum Principem Dominum Karolum, &c., . . . præ cæteris Imperii principibus esse ætate floridum, strenuum in armis ac justitiæ præcipuum zelatorem, multisque aliis virtutibus præditum, præterea plurimis ac maximis dominiis et principatibus abundare, in eundem Dominum Karolum direxit oculos suæ mentis," &c. Lenglet, tom. iii. p. 117.

scene of personal degradation that excited the amazement of the world. And this was a consequence, not of any trial of strength, — of an open struggle concluding in disaster, — but of his own folly and imprudence.[5] After his return from Liége, he still endeavored to retain the mask — the appearance of apathy, of contentment — which he had found it convenient and even necessary to assume. He affected to be entirely satisfied with the reception he had met with from his cousin of Burgundy. He commanded the arrest and punishment of any person who should speak of that prince in the language of disrespect; and he ordered, under the gravest penalties, that the treaty should be registered by the parliament and carried into effect by the proper officers of the crown. Meanwhile he could not bring himself to face his subjects in the capital. Even the distant echo of their mocking epigrams was more than he could support. The very magpies and parrots, swinging in their cages at the street doors, piped and screamed all day a scurrilous refrain, — "Pérette and Péronne, Pérette and Péronne!" — the former name supposed to have been that of a low-born mistress of the king, — as well as other and still viler cries; and when the police, acting under royal instructions, made a general seizure of all the talking-birds in Paris, and

[5] "Quod . . . cum tantas contraxisset copias ut oppressurus Burgundionum ducem suosque facile putaretur, nulla tamen congressione facta, nullo prælio, nullo certamine habito. in tam turpes et coronæ suæ tam prejudiciales pacis conditiones . . . descendisset." Basin, tom. ii. p. 208.

handed them over to the authorities, the malicious clerks, with due official pains, registered each culprit, with the phrases and rhymes he had been taught to pronounce: —

"Robber, scamp, away! away!
Pérette, — some drink, I pray!"[6]

That keen perception of the ridiculous which enables its possessor to lay bare the follies and weaknesses of others, makes him peculiarly sensitive to the shafts of sarcasm when directed against himself. He feels the sting in proportion to his powers of using it. He arms his persecutors with his own superior weapons. Wounds which in other flesh would speedily heal, rankle and fester in his. So it was with Louis. His feigned insensibility had withstood the piercing glances of his Burgundian foes, the terrible reproaches and dying looks of hatred and contempt cast at him by his victims at Liége. But the light sneering laughter of the Parisians forced him

6 "Larron, paillard, va, va dehors!
Pérette, donne-moi à boire."

De Troyes (Lenglet, tom. ii. pp. 77, 78.) — Basin, tom. ii. p. 209. — Gaguini Compendium, ap. Sismondi, tom. xiv. p. 283.

Does the reader remember Goldsmith's account of the colloquial abilities of the French parrots? "I could not help observing," he says, "how much plainer their parrots spoke than ours, and how very distinctly I understood their parrots speak French, when I could not understand our own, though they spoke my native language. I was at first for ascribing it to the different qualities of the two languages, and was for entering into an elaborate discussion on the vowels and consonants; but a friend that was with me solved the difficulty at once, by assuring me that *French women scarce did any thing else the whole day than sit and instruct their parrots.*" (Animated Nature, London, 1774, vol. v. p. 276.) Louis should have shut up the women, not the parrots.

into self-betrayal; till at length he had a fit of illness—the effect, no doubt, of mortification and exhaustion.

But while he felt so acutely the wounds inflicted on his self-esteem, the graver injuries which he had sustained soon roused him to fresh exertions. His condition now was not unlike that in which he had found himself at the conclusion of the War of the Public Weal. Normandy he still retained. But if Champagne were to be given up, the sacrifice would be scarcely less, the recovery far more difficult. To establish his brother in that province, would, as has been already remarked, be a virtual surrender of it into the hands of the duke of Burgundy, with the tenacity of whose gripe Louis was not unacquainted. But Charles's parting words had left the king at liberty to make, if possible, a different arrangement, without incurring the responsibility and the penalties of a direct infraction of the treaty. To profit by this concession, it was necessary that he should furnish a substantial equivalent in lieu of Champagne, and that his brother should be induced to accept of that equivalent. An appanage that ought to satisfy the claims of the heir-presumptive to the crown, might be formed of the duchy of Guienne, enlarged by the addition of some smaller neighboring fiefs, comprising the ancient heritage of the Plantagenets on the shores of the Bay of Biscay. And, in order to make this province more worthy of his brother's acceptance, Louis sent an army, under the count of Dammartin, in that direction, for the purpose of correcting the Armagnacs, who would be likely to prove troublesome neighbors, and unfit company for a young prince not sufficiently on his guard against bad examples and bad advice.

The person who at present wielded a controlling influence over the feeble mind of Charles of France, was that same Odet d'Aydie, Sire de Lescun, who, five years before, had been the instrument in abstracting him from his brother's court. This nobleman, himself a native of Guienne, was a thorough master of intrigue. He was the chief adviser, not only of the king's brother, but of the duke of Brittany. He had probably little desire to see the former established in Champagne, where, if he accompanied him, his own ascendency must soon give place to that of a more absolute will. In Guienne, which was far distant from the Burgundian dominions, and which had the further advantage of bordering on Brittany, Odet, as he hoped, would continue to play the important part which he now filled. Induced by these considerations, and by others not less weighty, which Louis had seized an opportunity of presenting to him, he signed an agreement, promising to exert whatever influence he possessed for the promotion of the royal views.[7]

But while the king was thus successful in dealing with a former enemy, his project had well-nigh failed

[7] "Je le servirai tout ainsi que si j'étais en sa maison; . . . et quand je me mêlerai des faits de mon dit sieur Charles, ce sera pour faire service au roi et non à lui." This engagement to act the part of a traitor and a spy was of course ratified by a solemn oath. Perhaps, as he balanced the treason by subsequent perjury, Lescun considered his conscience acquitted.

through the treachery of a dependent. Balue, the factotum of his master, who had been raised by him from the meanest condition, and employed in his most secret affairs, and for whom, in spite of his general unpopularity and infamous life, a cardinal's hat had been recently obtained from the reluctant pope, was detected in a private correspondence with the Burgundian court. A messenger, carrying a letter in cipher, in the cardinal's handwriting, was arrested on the frontier. It contained full information of the king's intentions in regard to his brother, and suggested the means of counteracting them, recommending, in particular, that Charles of France should be induced to leave his present retreat and remove to the Netherlands. The bishop of Verdun, a friend of Balue's, whom he had introduced into the royal councils, was implicated in the plot. Unwilling to give occasion for scandal by consigning to the brief but zealous and effectual custody of Tristan l'Hermite these two distinguished criminals, both prelates, and one a prince of the church, Louis provided them with accommodation in a pair of iron cages, where they passed eleven years in tranquil retirement, undisturbed by the tumults, unharassed by the temptations, of the world.[8]

[8] Documents relating to this affair, which made a great noise, and formed the subject of a long discussion between the French and Papal courts, are to be found in the Hist. de Bourgogne, tom. iv., preuves, p. cclviii. et seq., and Duclos, tom. iii. p. 250 et seq. — "On conserve encore la cage de Balue dans la porte forteresse du pont de Moret." Michelet, tom. vi. p. 294, note.

The populace of Paris were greatly amused and exhilarated by

After much wavering, Charles of France gave his consent to the settlement proposed for him by the king. He was invested with the title of "duke of Guienne," took formal possession of his fief, and swore fidelity to Louis, to the exclusion of all other alliances, on the True Cross of Saint-Laud.[9] A personal interview between the royal brothers followed. It took place on the 7th of September, 1469, on a bridge of boats laid across the River Sèvre, near the village of Charon. A wooden barrier had been constructed in the usual form, with a window or opening, guarded by iron bars, that allowed the two princes to see each other's face and to converse together. Charles was visibly touched at this first meeting after so long a separation. A few words of cordial greeting from the king — assurances that the past was forgotten, that there was no feeling in the royal bosom so strong as fraternal affection — completed the reconciliation. The prince insisted on passing the barrier; he threw himself at his brother's feet; they embraced "more than twenty times," and remained for an interval overpowered by their emotions, and unable to speak. The multitude that lined the shores wept in sympathy; cries of "*Noël! Noël!*" resounded from either bank; and Heaven itself gave a visible token of its approval. The tide, which, had it flowed to the full

the fate of Balue. Doggerel verses like the following were sung in the streets: —

"Maître Jean Balue
A perdu la vue
De ses évêchés;
Monsieur de Verdun
N'en a pas plus un,
Tous sont dépêchés."

[9] Acte du serment fait par Charles de France, Lenglet, tom. iii. p. 106.

height, must have cut short the affecting scene, began to ebb when still four feet below the ordinary level of high water.[10]

After some days the new duke of Guienne returned home, accompanied by two of the king's servants, who were to reside at his court in the character of ambassadors. His conscious inexperience, conjoined with the strong desire he felt to conduct his affairs in a manner that should please his brother, made the counsel of these persons an invaluable aid. They were always at hand, and their advice was implicitly followed. His old associates found themselves regarded by him with coldness and disfavor. The Burgundian envoys sent to congratulate him on his new dignity, and to inquire whether he were satisfied with the arrangement, were received with less than the customary courtesy on such occasions. He professed to owe the change in his fortunes to the spontaneous kindness of Louis, to whom his gratitude was unbounded. He declined to accept the collar of the *Toison d'Or*, which the envoys had been commissioned to present to him. The king, he said, had done him the honor to invest him with the order of Saint Michael, and there could be no higher companionship

[10] The miracle is attested by several witnesses, whose relations may be read in Lenglet (tom. iii. p. 107) and Dupont, Preuves (tom. iii. pp. 260–268), as well as by Louis himself, in a letter written at the time (Duclos, Preuves, tom. iii. p. 249), where, however, the pious transport excited by the occasion has led to a really unnecessary stretching as well as to a palpable blunder: — "La marée qui devoit être cejourd'hui la plus grande de l'année, s'est trouvé la moindre de beaucoup qu'on ne vit de mémoire d'homme, et si est retraité *quatre heures* plutôt qu'on ne cuidoit."

than that into which he was thus admitted.[11] To a proposal for a new treaty of alliance, he replied that he would willingly ally himself with those who were the king's allies, — of whom he had gladly learned that the duke of Burgundy was now one, — as, on the other hand, he must regard as enemies those who were the enemies of his sovereign. He even dismissed the envoys without the usual presents of plate — an unnecessary insult to the representatives of the prince to whose interference he was indebted for his present position.[12] His admirable docility was a great relief to Louis, who seemed now to have no cause for apprehension on the side of Guienne. The count of Armagnac, whose proximity and intriguing disposition might otherwise have occasioned inconvenience, had in the mean time been thoroughly beaten and driven from the country; while a strong force continued to mount guard over Brittany, and was inspected from time to time by the king in person. In his relations with the duke of Burgundy, Louis exhibited an excessive caution — the effect of his recent experience of that prince's untractable character. He scrupulously avoided every occasion of fresh offence. The preservation of complete tranquillity on the existing basis was apparently his sole desire. Meanwhile events were occurring elsewhere that demand our attention. The affairs of England — where elements

[11] The duke of Brittany, on the other hand, refused the order of Saint Michael — newly created by Louis, in vain emulation of the Golden Fleece and the Garter.

[12] Lettre de M. de Beuil au Roy, touchant l'ambassade du Duc du Bourgogne à celui de Guienne. Histoire de Bourgogne, tom. iv. preuves, p. cclx.

of disturbance had long been secretly at work — were approaching a crisis which was to lead, not only to new convulsions at home, but to new complications and embroilments abroad.

Our course will now lead us for a time over the highway of English history; yet the track is a rough one, and the guide-posts stand far apart — a matter, however, of the less consequence, as they are mostly false.[13] The estrangement secretly existing between

[13] Nothing is more singular than the dearth of authentic information and documentary evidence in regard to the Wars of the Roses, contrasted with the vivid glimpses we obtain at the domestic manners and social condition of the country, at the same period, through the medium of the "Paston Letters." On the waters of the great deluge floats a little family ark, sending forth, if not doves with olive branches in their mouths, yet carrier-pigeons with missives beneath their wings directed to — posterity. The faces of the stern and practical old Agnes, of the good housewifely Margaret, of politic Sir John and slashing John the Younger, are scarcely less familiar to us than those of any group in the literary 18th century. Strange, too, is the impression produced by an introduction to some famous historical character amid scenes and associations seldom connected with history or fame. What a change from the half-fabulous Fastolfe of Shakespeare and the chroniclers, contending with the "Witch" of France, and looming through a purple mist of carnage and glory, to the old curmudgeon of the "Paston Letters," getting deeds and inventories drawn, and grabbing every rood of land to which he can bolster up a claim!

But is it possible to believe that these are the only relics of any value that exist of English life and character in the 15th century? Were the Pastons the only writers or preservers of letters in that age? Did Warwick write none? Could his correspondence be brought to light, English historians, reluctant to consult the best sources of information in regard to him which we now possess — the writings of his French and Burgundian contemporaries — would perhaps be able to get some clearer notion of the man, and cease to enunciate such extraordinary judgments as that delivered by Mackintosh, who talks of "his preference of the pleasure of displaying power to that of attaining specific objects of ambition; and his almost equal readiness to make or unmake any king, according to the capricious inclination or repugnancy of the moment." The first step towards a real knowledge of the

the earl of Warwick and the sovereign whom he had himself been a principal instrument in raising to the throne, has been noticed in a former chapter. That estrangement, there can be little doubt, had its natural source in the dissimilar characters of the parties, and in the circumstances which had linked them together. They had fought side by side in a revolutionary struggle; and triumphs thus gained preclude, in a great measure, those settled relations by which opposites are harmonized and divergent tendencies constrained. The prize achieved through their common endeavors belonged exclusively to one; and he, content apparently to wear it as an empty bauble, was not, on this account, the less jealous of a companion who would fain have used it for the attainment of greater ends. Hence the occasion for open rupture on a question of foreign policy — Warwick, like the great De la Pole at an earlier period, aspiring to shape out a new course of action; Edward, with less enterprise and calculation, but with a truer national instinct, resolving to abide by the ancient landmarks. But not unconnected with these differences on matters of government, there was also on the side of Warwick — as truly represented in the earlier, though now generally discarded accounts — a private pique arising out of Edward's marriage with Elizabeth Woodville. The earl, during his dominion at the council board, had proposed to seek a suitable match for his sovereign among the branches or connections of the

history of this period should perhaps be to throw the so-called English chroniclers out of window.

royal family of France, with the view of thus ratifying and cementing that final peace between the two nations which it had been from the first his great object to establish. His project had been approved not only by the council, but tacitly at least by Edward. It was opened both to the French king (with whom, indeed, it may possibly have originated) and to Philip of Burgundy, then on the best terms with Louis, and scarcely less desirous than the latter of seeing forever closed the feud which he had formerly done so much to keep alive. It was arranged that Warwick, with some of his coadjutors, should proceed to Saint-Omer, to meet the king of France and the duke of Burgundy, for the purpose of discussing, perhaps of concluding, all the points of the proposed alliance. This, it will be perceived, was an exact imitation of the policy which, thirty years before, had been pursued by De la Pole and his party — a policy that had proved successful in its immediate purpose, but in its effects fatal to its framers and to the internal tranquillity of the realm. Edward the Fourth, however, was not so easily disposed of as Henry the Sixth. His character was different, and his training had been different. He had neither been born witless nor been rendered witless by floggings administered under the authority of an order in council. Moreover, he was a connoisseur in beauty, and indebted to his own handsome person for much of his popularity. While assenting to the politic schemes proposed for him by his minister, he had already been guided in his choice of a wife by his tastes and inclinations. A day or two before Warwick's intended departure, the gallant monarch smilingly announced to his council that he was already privately wedded — a communication received with consternation, and digested with extreme difficulty.[14]

[14] The statement of early though not contemporaneous writers, that the breach between Edward and Warwick, dated from the former's marriage, has been disputed with much ingenuity and erudition by several modern authors of distinction, including Lingard and Sir E. Bulwer Lytton. Against the array of evidence which they have produced — such as the contradiction, before noticed, of Warwick's mission to France, in 1463 or 1464, for the purpose of negotiating a marriage between his sovereign and the Princess Bona of Savoy, and the tokens he gave on more than one occasion, by his demeanor in public, of his satisfaction with the king's choice — we can oppose but a solitary piece of testimony, which, however, will probably be deemed conclusive. Although Warwick did not visit the French court in either of the years above mentioned, his coming was, as we have seen in a former chapter, expected there in 1464, and he sent thither an agent — Sir Robert Neville. (Ante, vol. i. Book II. ch. i. note 21.) Sir Robert carried with him as vouchers letters to the king and to the duke, giving a full explanation of the reasons for delaying the visit; and a letter of the same tenor was addressed to an official personage at the Burgundian court by Lord Wenlock, a member of the council, well known as a devoted adherent of the earl's, and, as it appears from his letter, one of the party that was to have accompanied him. After reminding the person to whom he writes that the intended negotiations at Saint-Omer were to have related to three subjects — *the king's marriage*, a truce, and a final peace, — Wenlock proceeds with a communication which he desires may be considered as confidential: "Or est il ainsi que, quant au mariage, le roy en a prise femme à son plaisir, sans le sceu de ceulx qu'on y devroit appeler à conseil : par raison lequel est a grant desplesir de plusieurs grans seigneurs, et mesmement à la pluspart de tout son conseil ; mais depuis que la matière est procedé sy avant qu'on n'y peut remedier, on y fault prendre pasciens maulgré nous. Or est il ainsy que la chose fut gardée sy tres cecrete, qu'on ne pouvoit scavoir la verité quant de la part de mon dit souverain seigneur, jusques à ce qu'environ cinq ou six jours pres le jour de nostre comparicion pour communiquer à Saint Omer sur les matieres devant dittes : et pour ce qu'on ne scet pas de sà, veu que ceste mariage est ainsy fait et passé comme dit est, quelle entention le roy a de sa part pour proceder sur les autres deux points, à scavoir sur tresves ou

Here was, indeed, a double source of mortification. It was not alone the plans and advice of Warwick that had been slighted and cast aside. If the king were minded to wed a subject, what fitter bride for him to have selected than a daughter and co-heiress of the great nobleman to whom he owed his crown, whose possessions were immense, who was the natural head of the aristocracy and the rival of the monarch himself in the affections of the people ?[15] These considerations Edward had strangely overlooked. He

paix, [Mark the connection here indicated between the king's marriage and the overthrow of Warwick's policy — as well as the evident intimation of all confidential intercourse having ceased !] l'oppinion de Mss[rs]. du conseil par de ca, est que mon dit seigneur le comte de Warwick ne passera par la mer jusques ad ce qu'on advertis de par le roy de la verité de son vouloir et plaisir en ceste partie." This letter, dated Reading, Oct. 3, 1464, has been printed, by Mlle. Dupont, from a manuscript in the Imperial Library. See Wavrin de Forestel, Anchiennes Cronicques d'Engleterre, tom. ii. pp. 325–327, note.

Here, indeed, it is not stated that the secret was disclosed by Edward himself. On that point. we have followed the text of Wavrin — the publication of whose work makes no very important addition to the general stock of authorities on this period of French or English history, but whose opportunities for obtaining information give value to some of his occasional statements.

[15] This suggestion, adopted from Sharon Turner, may be supported by the following arguments : 1st. In Warwick's position nothing could be more natural than the feeling of disappointment here ascribed to him ; 2d. His early and notorious enmity to the queen is thus more fully accounted for than by any other theory ; 3d. His views in subsequently marrying one daughter to the duke of Clarence and the other to the prince of Wales, offer a strong corroboration of his having long cherished the wish of seeing one of them elevated to the throne. Sir E. B. Lytton, in his learned romance of "The Last of the Barons," while acknowledging the plausibility of Turner's conjecture, makes the original cause of the quarrel a gross insult offered by Edward to the Lady Isabella Neville. In this he has followed Hall and other chroniclers — better authorities for the novelist than for the historian. Commines, who had received the account from an English bishop, — probably a very good authority on such points, — says that Edward had jilted one English lady (name concealed), if not two.

had stooped to the daughter of a commoner; he loaded her kinsmen with titles and pensions, raised them almost to an equality in rank and station with the haughty Nevilles, and soon gave them a much larger share of his confidence.

The spirit of disaffection thus awakened found the material for intrigues and conspiracies in a similar state of things to that which had long been turned to the same account in France. Though the king had been several years married, he was still without male issue. By the rules of succession subsequently recognized, his daughter, the Princess Elizabeth, would have been considered as the presumptive heiress to the crown. But as yet there had been no example of a queen-regnant; and, in the actual condition of affairs, it might well be questioned whether a disputed title, like that of the house of York, would be suffered, even by the partisans of that house, to pass to a female branch. It was natural, therefore, that the duke of Clarence, the elder of the king's two brothers, should still cherish hopes of the succession; and these expectations, combined with the pliancy of his character and the weakness of his understanding, made him, like Charles of France, the proper tool of faction. Nothing was easier than to excite his jealousy of the Woodvilles, to draw him into an alliance with the Nevilles, and to convince him that the crown of England, instead of descending by any title of inheritance or law of Parliament, formed a portion of the dowry which the Lady Isabella, the eldest daughter of the kingmaker, would bring to the husband of her choice. The marriage, accordingly, took place at Calais, in July, 1469, without the king's consent or previous knowledge.[16]

In the same summer, while the earl and his son-in-law were still at Calais, an insurrection broke out in Lancashire. Sixty thousand men rose in arms, alleging the common grievance on such occasions — the misgovernment practised by unworthy persons who had gained insidious possession of the royal ear. Edward marched northward in person, but sent forward his main body, under Herbert earl of Pembroke. A battle ensued. The royal forces were utterly defeated. Pembroke himself, Earl Rivers, —

[16] Edward may not have been ignorant of the project, but he certainly was not privy to the execution of it. The better to evade suspicion, Warwick went first to the court of Burgundy, had an audience of Charles, and waited on the duchess, at Aire, who, though doubtless cognizant of his secret disaffection towards her brother, was far enough, as Wavrin tells us, from suspecting what he then had in his brain. (Anchiennes Cronicques d'Engleterre, tom. ij. p. 402.)

Warwick's nature, Sir Bulwer Lytton remarks, has been "happily described" by Hume as "one of undesigning frankness and openness." Looking at the salient points of the kingmaker's career, we might find reason to admire Hume's undesigning simplicity. A very different description is given by several writers, and especially by Wavrin, who had the advantage of Hume, not in beauty of style, but in a personal acquaintance with the earl. "Le plus soubtil homme de son vivant," is the epithet applied to him by the Burgundian chronicler. If this was mere prejudice, it had private as well as political grounds. On the occasion just noticed of Warwick's visit to the Burgundian court, Wavrin applied to him for information on a subject connected with his researches. In reply he was warmly invited to follow the earl to Calais, where all his inquiries would be answered. He accordingly went, was most hospitably entertained, but though he stayed several days, failed to have his curiosity gratified. He was then asked to come again in two months —when he contrived to elicit something. He then perceived that some great matter was in preparation, and a few days after his departure the marriage took place.

the queen's father, — and one of her brothers, were taken prisoners, and immediately beheaded. The king, deprived of his chief supporters, and deserted by his troops, was unable to make head against the victorious rebels, and retreating towards the south, summoned Warwick, who had so often stood by him in the hour of need, to his assistance. The earl, accompanied by Clarence, crossed the Channel, collected new forces, and marching northward, met the king at Honiley, near Oxford. At that moment Edward found himself a captive.[17]

Thus the spectacle was exhibited of two kings of England, both prisoners, Henry the Sixth being still confined in the Tower of London, and Edward the Fourth having been deprived of his liberty by his own adherents. But royal captives are always embarrassing. The singular turn which events had taken roused the Lancastrian party, still numerous though subdued. They expected and demanded the restoration of Henry, and made preparations for supporting that demand with their swords. But if the former dynasty were reëstablished, what had Warwick, ambitious of placing his daughter on the throne, and of ruling in the name of his weak son-in-law, to expect but the meed of treason? On the other hand,

[17] Hume endeavors to throw doubt on Edward's captivity, but his arguments are refuted by Lingard. In addition to the proofs adduced by this learned historian, there is a mention of the fact, as one of common notoriety, in the duke of Burgundy's reply to the French ambassadors at Saint-Omer, in July, 1470 : "Attendu que en ce tems le Roy d'Angleterre était aussi empechié ailleurs et *en la puissance et prison du comte de Warwich.*" Hist. de Bourgogne, tom. iv. preuves, p. cclxxv.

the principal Yorkist nobles, though well satisfied with the sudden overthrow of the queen's family, still regarded Edward as their monarch, and insisted on his release. The city of London — where Edward was especially popular, where he was deep in the books of the wealthy goldsmiths, and still deeper in the affections of their buxom wives — raised its powerful voice to the same purport, being urged, moreover, by a menacing letter from the duke of Burgundy, who threatened a rupture of the alliance and the loss of the all-important trade with Flanders. In this dilemma, Warwick found himself compelled to drop the prize that had so strangely fallen into his hands. He patched up a reconciliation with Edward, obtained a general pardon for himself, his adherents, and all who had been engaged in the late revolt, and soon after retired, with Clarence, to his estates, there to await, or to contrive, some new explosion that might be conducted to a better result.

Early in the following spring (March, 1470), another rebellion occurred, in Lincolnshire. This time the leaders, either acting in concert with Warwick — as the rumors of the time asserted — or merely taking their cue from what had become the evident aim of his intrigues, proclaimed their purpose of deposing Edward and placing the duke of Clarence on the throne.[18] The king mustered his

[18] See the contemporary, and, in fact, official account of the Lincolnshire rebellion printed in the Camden Miscellany (vol. i.), which throws more light on one of the most obscure passages in English history than any thing else that has yet been published.

adherents and hastened towards the scene of action. He sent letters to his brother and to Warwick, desiring them to join his standard with their retainers, protesting his disbelief in the reports adverse to their loyalty, and assuring them of such treatment as ancient friendship and nearness of blood had once entitled them to expect. This summons being disregarded, or evasively answered, another followed, in a more peremptory tone, but still holding out the promise of renewed amity and complete forgiveness of the past. At length they were commanded to appear within a certain term, with a notice that failing to comply, they would be proclaimed as traitors.[19] Meanwhile Edward's usual good fortune in battle had not deserted him. The rebels were beaten and dispersed, their leaders taken and put to death. Then the king turned his arms, enwreathed with victory, against the faithless brother and the treacherous friend, conspirators to rob him of a crown which the one was supposed to have conferred and which the other had hoped to inherit. Their efforts to raise a sufficient force to meet him in the field proved futile. They belonged now to neither of the two great parties, and neither was willing to assist them. They were forced to retreat. A price was set upon their heads. Accompanied by their wives and families and by a numerous train of followers, they fled to the southern coast, hastily collected a

[19] See the letter to Clarence, in the Chronicle of the Lincolnshire Rebellion, p. 13. — "And a like letre, undre prive seale, was sent to the erle of Warewicke."

small fleet of vessels, and embarking, sailed for Calais, where Warwick, who was "captain," or governor, of that sole remnant of the English conquest in France, expected to find shelter and security. But his deputy, the Lord Wenlock, refused him entrance, and turned the guns of the batteries on his ships. The territory surrounding Calais was no longer French, but Burgundian.[20] The duke was at Boulogne, and his vengeance, still more than that of Edward, was to be dreaded, if Warwick were suffered to land. Privately Wenlock gave his patron notice of this danger, and advised his taking refuge in France. In revenge, the fugitives, as they passed down the Channel, captured a number of Flemish coasting vessels, which they carried with them to Harfleur and other ports of Normandy, and there sold as lawful prizes.[21]

To comprehend the full importance of these events in connection with our subject, a moment's glance is still necessary at the exact relative positions of the different parties. The house of Lancaster had owed its firm establishment on the throne to the wise administration of Henry the Fourth, and to the genius, the lofty spirit, and the wonderful achievements of his son. The English are a people not perhaps more discontented than others under a good government, but impatient certainly

[20] Since 1465 — when, as will be remembered, the counties of Guines and Boulogne had formed a portion of the spoil extorted from the French king. Ante, vol. i. p. 316.

[21] Commines, liv. iii. ch. 4.—Haynin, tom. ii. p. 153. — Basin, tom. ii. lib. 3, cap. 1. — Wavrin de Forestel, tom. ii.

beyond all others under misgovernment. Their history has, in all ages down to the present time, exhibited a continual series of revolutions — the changes of public opinion being speedily followed by corresponding changes in the policy and composition of the government. The system now is that of organized and peaceful revolution: the minister resigns, the Parliament is dissolved. Formerly the minister and the dynasty were both deposed, and the contest was decided, not at the hustings or on the floor of Parliament, but on the battle-field.[22] In the 15th and 16th centuries the statesmen and political writers of the continent regarded and habitually described the English people as changeable, inconstant, turbulent, destitute of any loyal attachment to their sovereigns, and amenable to no restraint save that of superior force.[23] The national

[22] To secure a peaceful change of government under a free constitution is one of the most difficult problems which nations have to work out. Were England a small state, ostracism — which among the Greeks had exactly this object — would afford the mildest precaution possible for an incoming administration against its own sudden and violent overthrow.

[23] Even Commines, who shows a strong and peculiar partiality for the English people and their form of government, notices, as a characteristic trait, their readiness to plunge into civil war. "Veez quelles sont les mutations d'Angleterre . . . De tous les peuples du monde, celluy d'Angleterre est le plus enclin à ces batailles." (Tom. i. p. 262.) So also Chastellain: — "Le corrage du peuple est mobile et variable, et ne quiert que nouveau seigneur tousjours." (Œuvres, p. 485.) The Venetian *Relazioni* afford many citations of a still stronger character. We may be allowed to quote a few examples. "Sono facili a sollevarsi per propria disposizione contro il suo re, e desiderosi sempre di cose nuove." (Relaz. de V. Quirini.) "Non è da maravigliarsi delle frequente sollevazioni di quel regno, che spesso è stata occupato da chè ha avuto in esso più forza che ragione." (Relaz. di G. Micheli.) "Sono di poca fede verso il loro re."

creed was so suddenly, repeatedly, and violently changed; so many successive dynasties were overthrown; noble, princely, and even royal blood was shed so profusely on the battle-field and on the scaffold; so many ministers and royal favorites, some of them persons who had risen from the meanest stations, after retaining for a while absolute supremacy in the counsels of the nation, ended their career in ruin and disgrace; popular outbreaks — not the mere desperate risings of an oppressed or starving populace, or the banded efforts of feudal princes against the encroachments of the sovereign; forms of resistance to the supreme authority with which Continental nations were sufficiently familiar; but movements

(Relaz. di G. Soranzo.) "Sono universalmente tutti desiderosi di novità, . . . e tentano ogni cosa che lor viene nell' animo, come se tutto ciò che si puo immaginare si potesse esseguire facilmente. Da questo sono nate tante sollevazioni nel regno, che non sono stata viste altretante in tutto il resto del mondo. . . . Di qua è nata la mutazione della fede. . . . Di qua sono causate tante depressioni d'uomini grandi ed esaltazioni de' bassi, tante prigione, tanti esilj, tante morti, che pare cosa incredibile." (Relaz. di M. Soriano.) But perhaps the most singular proof of the universality of this opinion is to be found in the cool and unqualified assertion of it in a letter of advice addressed to an English sovereign, by the representative of a friendly power, containing also some highly philosophical suggestions as to the causes of the phenomenon. "Vostre majesté scet les humeurs des Angloys et leur voluntez estre fort discordantes, désireux de nouvelleté, de mutation, et vindicatifs, soit *pour estre insulaires*, ou *pour tenir ce naturel de la marine* [from the changeable and tempestuous sea], ou *pour en estre les mœurs corrompus;* et que les roys du passé on esté forcés de traicter en rigeur de justice et effusion de sang, par l'exécution de plusieurs du royaulme, voire du sang royal, pour s'asseurer et maintenir leur royaulme, dont ils ont acquis le renom de tyrans et cruelz." (Simon Renard to Queen Mary, Papiers d'État de Granvelle, tom. iv. p. 129.) Many similar passages might be quoted from writers of the 17th century. In fact, it was not until after the great French Revolution that "le mutin Anglais" was transformed into "the conservative Englishman."

in which men of all ranks participated, which had their origin, in fact, in the dissensions of parties, not in the hostility of classes,[24] — were of so frequent

[24] The late Mr. Buckle describes the "Fronde" as a war of parties, and the "Great Rebellion" as a war of classes. "From the beginning of the [latter] contest, the yeomanry and traders adhered to the Parliament; the nobles and the clergy rallied round the throne. And the name given to the two parties, of Roundheads and Cavaliers, proves that the true nature of their opposition was generally known." (Civilization in England, vol. i. pp. 595, 596.) But, in a strict sense, a war of classes is one which has its origin in a broad and impassable gulf between the rich and the poor, the noble and the base-born, the privileged and the oppressed, territorial suzerainty and civic immunities. Such wars belonged especially to Continental Europe, where, to say nothing of the chronic feud between the nobles and the chartered towns (and the latter are well represented by M. Guizot as virtually created by a universal insurrection), the internal fires found a frequent vent in wide-spread and devastating "Jacqueries" and "Peasants' Wars." There is nothing similar in English history, save a few obscure and comparatively innocuous explosions, like Cade's insurrection, and the Cornish revolt in the reign of Henry VII. Of course in all civil wars in which a whole nation is divided, social affinities and repulsions cannot fail to have an influence. But the lines of demarcation between the different classes of society having, in past ages, been much less strictly drawn in England than among Continental nations, that influence is in general far less discernible in its political contests.

Another notion on the same subject is thus broached by Mr. Buckle: "In England, our civil wars have all been secular; they have been waged, either for a change of dynasty, or for an increase of liberty. In France, on the other hand, at the mere name of religion, thousands of men were ready to take the field." (Ibid. p. 465.)

Surely, many wars for a change of dynasty or an increase of liberty would fall in the category of "religious wars." But by confining his attention to the 16th century, contrasting the sanguinary conflicts between the Catholics and the Huguenots with the supposed indifference of the English people to the successive changes introduced by the government into the established creed, and overlooking all indications of the different modes in which the same grand battle was fought out in different countries, the author is enabled to give some coloring to his favorite theory that religion and scepticism have respectively led to retrogression and progress. It might be asked, however, whether Laud and Puritanism, Jesuitism and Nonconformity, had not at least as large a part in the Great Rebellion and the revolution occurrence, and so often successful in overturning the government, that to the eye of the foreign observer, unable to comprehend these oscillations, the spectacle presented was that of a society destitute of the elements of coherence and stability. Nor was the impression less remarkable on the minds of those who had a nearer view of the scene. The influence on the national literature is very striking. Here we find the explanation of the prominent place which the drama occupies in the literature of England, and of the fact that what is strictly to be called Historical Tragedy is, in modern times, peculiar to that literature. Shakspeare, his predecessors and contemporaries, witnessed the strongest workings of human passion and the most pathetic scenes of human suffering in conjunction with the dignity of rank, the grandeur of state affairs, and the general action of the national mind. "Sad stories of the death of kings," sudden and strange vicissitudes in the career of ambition, and violent fluctuations of fortune in the contests of parties, absorbed the imagination of the poet and the attention of the people. Mere narrative was unequal to such themes for a public so familiar with the reality; and — as among

of 1688 as any hostile feeling between the yeomanry and the nobles.

But discussions of this nature are not very profitable. Setting out with a pet theory, and jotting down every statement — or misstatement — casually met with, or even industriously hunted up, that may seem to support it, can hardly be considered a proper method of historical analysis and research. It is a method by which almost any opinion may be easily proved — and as easily disproved.

the ancient Athenians — the national history was best taught and best remembered in the bold and lifelike representations of the stage.

During that portion of the 15th century which comprised the reigns of Henry the Sixth and succeeding monarchs down to the accession of Henry the Seventh, English history exhibits a rapid succession of violent and bloody convulsions. In that period the throne was twice lost and twice regained by each of the rival houses that laid claim to it. Thirteen pitched battles were fought between Englishmen and on English soil. Three out of four kings died by violence; eighty persons connected with the blood royal were reckoned as having perished in war or by the hand of the executioner or of the assassin; and the great majority of the noble families became extinct or sank into obscurity. It is usual to represent the Wars of the Roses as simply a struggle between two great aristocratical factions, of which the people was an unconcerned spectator. But similar phenomena to those which produced this impression belong also to most of the struggles, warlike or peaceful, of a later day. It is because in England the different elements of society have always been more completely interfused — because the aristocracy has been divided from the commonalty, and the inhabitants of the towns from the rural population, by lines less stringent than in other countries, that in nearly all its political contests the nobles have stood forth as the leaders and active partisans on either side, while the great body of the nation has seemed to be simply an arbiter of the quarrel, appealed to, openly or tacitly, by both parties, and giving its sympathy and support to each in turn. But whoever might fight the battles, the war in all cases has had its origin in the heavings and tossings of the popular mind. In the present case this influence is especially clear in the beginning of the conflict — where its presence has been especially denied.[25] The incapacity of the third monarch of

[25] The received theory in regard to the origin and nature of the Wars of the Roses (Mr. Buckle would have considered the name alone as a sufficient indication of their character) is thus stated and supported by Macaulay — that great master of the art of *expression*, whose language never conveys less, or intimates more, than was clearly intended. After noticing the expulsion of the English from France in the reign of Henry VI., he goes on: "Cooped up once more within the limits of this island, the warlike people employed in civil strife those arms which had been the terror of Europe. The means of profuse expenditure had long been drawn by the English barons from the oppressed provinces of France. That source of supply was gone; but the ostentatious and luxurious habits which prosperity had engendered still remained; and the great lords, unable to gratify their tastes by plundering the French, were eager to plunder each other. The realm to which they were now confined would not, in the phrase of Comines, the most judicious observer of that time, suffice for them all. Two aristocratical factions, headed by two branches of the royal family, engaged in a long and fierce struggle for supremacy." (History of England, ch. 1.)

Such views as these tend to destroy the continuity of history, and to render the study of it useless. That Commines, notwithstanding his sagacity and his appreciation of English freedom, should have thus thought, is not extraordinary, when we consider the medium through which he looked — the haze of feudal power and feudal strife by which he was surrounded. Yet he cannot, correctly speaking, be regarded as an "observer" of the causes which led to the struggle in England. The first mutterings of the storm began with the accession of the infant Henry VI. From 1422 to 1455 it raged in the Parliament and in the government, one minister after another being deposed and attainted. In the latter year the sword was publicly drawn. Ten years later, and when the house of York seemed to be firmly established, Commines, then not nine-the Lancastrian line, the consequent anarchy in the government, the king's marriage with a French princess,—entailing the surrender by treaty of French provinces of which the English had still retained possession,—the open efforts of the queen and of those who were in power to close the war by a complete recognition of the house of Valois as the rightful sovereigns of France, destroyed the popularity of the descendants of John of Gaunt, and led to their expulsion from the throne, and the restoration of the elder line of the Plantagenets in the person of Edward the Fourth.

From the moment of his accession, this prince, as we have seen, had proclaimed his intention of effacing the disasters and disgraces that had fallen on the English arms. He treated Louis as a usurper; he renewed the old alliances with the disaffected vassals of the French crown; he obtained grants from the Parliament for the purpose of raising an army; and his personal gallantry and prowess, and undoubted military talents, seemed to promise a career of glory in the same field of enterprise that had been trodden by the most illustrious of his

teen years of age, was riding behind his master at Montlhéry, his eyes, it is true, keenly observant, but his brain, as he confesses, filled with youthful illusions. Moreover Commines was a foreigner—a circumstance which in that age made an immense difference in the opportunities for observation. He gathered his notions of the civil war in England, as he himself tells us, from exiles—a class whose distorted vision has been amply noticed by Lord Macaulay. It does seem to us remarkable that a great modern writer, one, too, so seldom at a loss for an original explanation of the facts of history, should have been content in the present instance to adopt a conception so shallow.

predecessors. We have seen, also, the anxiety with which Louis had all along watched these prognostics of another invasion, his efforts to avert it, his preparations to meet it. At the outset of his reign he had furnished some slight aid to the exiled Lancastrians; but their consequent renewal of the war had been short and disastrous — ending in the capture of Henry, the flight of his queen and son, and the bloody deaths of their principal adherents. Louis had declined to sanction any further enterprises of the same nature, until assured of better chances of success. Instead of incurring the risk of hastening, by fresh provocations, the catastrophe which he dreaded, it became his policy to make a party for himself among those who were now in the ascendant, to win, if possible, from the house of York an acknowledgment of his rights, at the worst to sow divisions in its councils and among its supporters. We have seen to what extent he had succeeded. The government of Edward had repelled all his approaches. No peace was to be obtained — only the renewal from time to time, for a limited term, of the existing truce. Edward — England — was still his enemy. Warwick was his friend and sole ally, and as such he now sheltered him in his dominions, and was prepared to lend him effective support in regaining the ascendency which he had lost.

The duke of Burgundy, on the other hand, a Lancastrian by descent, — whose court was the refuge, whose bounty was the support, of the exiled chiefs of the party, — had nevertheless connected himself by the strictest bonds of alliance with the reigning dynasty. This connection was based not merely on the common interests of the two princes, but on the common interests of the two countries. Charles, as he himself expressed it, had formed an alliance not with the king alone, but with the kingdom, of England.[26] He maintained a direct correspondence with the corporations of London and other great towns. He wrote and spoke the language with entire facility. He boasted that he was "more English than the English themselves."[27] He calculated on the possible chances of his one day inheriting the crown.[28] Only in the event of a single contingency — that of Warwick's obtaining the ascendency which he coveted — was the alliance in danger. England was the duke's friend; but Warwick was his enemy. And this enemy — no longer a private but a public enemy, having proclaimed himself as such by his spoliation of the duke's subjects — was now also a rebel against the authority of his sovereign, — the duke's ally, — and was concocting plans for his overthrow under the protection and with the assistance of the French king, who had so lately sworn peace and friendship towards the duke on the True Cross of Saint-Laud.

Here, then, were sufficient grounds and motives for

[26] "Avec le Roy et le *royaulme.*" —Commines, tom. i. p. 255; and letter of Charles to the magistrates of Calais, Hist. de Bourgogne, tom. iv. preuves, p. cclxxxix.

[27] "Par St. George, lequel me cognoit estre meilleur Anglois, et plus desirer le bien de iceluy royaume, que vous et tous les autres Anglois ne sont." French translation of an English letter, in his own handwriting, to the magistrates of Calais, Hist. de Bourgogne, tom. iv. preuves, p. cclxxxix.

[28] See postea, Book III. ch. 2, note 41.

complaint and outcry. The seizure of the Flemish ships, — the personal wrong to the duke of Burgundy himself, — though it must be put forward as the chief basis of his demands, was the least important part of the affair. That was an act already accomplished, without the knowledge or connivance of the king; and so far as he had become responsible for it by the sale of the captured property in his territories, it was in his power to repair the injury by a disavowal, accompanied by pecuniary compensation to the owners. But the continued presence of Warwick and his adherents on the French soil, the protection afforded them, their preparations for a new enterprise against Edward, which, if successful, would wrench England from the alliance of the duke of Burgundy, and throw her into the arms of her ancient foe, formed the real subject of quarrel, and admitted of no redress — unless, indeed, Louis were ready to abandon one of the main objects of his policy at the moment when there was a chance for its accomplishment.

The clamor which Charles raised was loud and prolonged. He addressed letters to his ambassadors in France, to the king, to the royal council, to the Parliament of Paris, to the Constable, — as governor of Normandy, — and to his subjects at home, setting forth the particulars of Warwick's piratical exploit, and denouncing the shelter given to the earl and his companions in France as a complicity in the insult and a flagrant violation of the late treaty.[29] Copies

[29] Hist. de Bourgogne, tom. iv. preuves, pp. cclxi. - cclxxii. — Lenglet, tom. iii. p. 146 et seq. — Gachard, Doc. Inéd. tom.

of these letters were circulated in the Flemish cities, and read aloud in the public assemblies, as a means of giving notoriety to the affair.[30] The mild replies of Louis — stating that he had already ordered an inquiry into the circumstances, with a view to causing reparation to be made; that he desired above all things to maintain his present amicable relations with his cousin of Burgundy; that his own ships and those of Warwick were to be employed, not against Charles, but in an expedition against England, the ancient enemy of France — formed no interruption to the torrent of the duke's invectives. To a letter addressed to two of the royal council, commissioned to conduct the inquiry and make restitution, he attached a characteristic postscript with his own hand: "Archbishop, and you Admiral, the vessels which you tell me are intended to be used by the king against England have attempted nothing except against my subjects; but, by Saint George! if some provision be not speedily made, I will take the matter into my own hands, without waiting for your motions, which are too tardy and too arbitrary."[31] Accordingly he ordered reprisals to be made, and confiscated the property of the French merchants resident at Bruges.[32] But he had no desire to have his injuries

i. pp. 226–231.—That Louis was himself well aware that any countenance he might lend to Warwick would be a violation of the treaty, will presently appear from letters of his own.

[30] See an order to this effect in a letter to the bailiff and *échevins* of Ypres, Gachard, Doc. Inéd. tom.. i. p. 231.

[31] Hist. de Bourgogne, tom. iv. preuves, p. cclxxi.

[32] Ibid. pp. cclxxii.–cclxxiv. ccxc. et seq.

redressed, since they afforded him a justification — if any were needed — for openly assisting the English monarch, and taking those measures for his defence which Edward himself, strangely indifferent to the warnings he received from his ally, had wholly neglected. A fleet collected in the ports of Holland and Flanders was stationed off the coast of Normandy, to guard the Channel and prevent Warwick's departure or intercept him in his passage. Charles maintained his own post in Picardy, sending an envoy to Calais to watch the temper of the garrison, to confirm Wenlock in his fidelity to the reigning sovereign, and to exact both from the governor and the inhabitants a renewal of their oaths of allegiance.[33]

This clamorous, stormy method of procedure was much disrelished by Louis. His own tastes — the delicacy of his nerves — led him, on most occasions, to prefer the quietest and gentlest methods of dealing with embarrassments and of avoiding perils. He had sent the Sire du Plessis, his confidential secretary, to confer with Warwick, but excused himself from granting him a personal interview. He even declined, at first, from conscientious scruples, to accord him any assistance until he should have sent the captured vessels beyond the limits of the French territory.[34] Finding it, however, useless to insist upon

[33] Commines (who was himself the envoy), tom. i. p. 236.

[34] "Veu le traité de Péronne, le Roy ne peut parler à Monsieur de Warwic, ne lui donner faveur, tant qu'il ait la prinse des subjets de Monsieur de Bourgogne, avec luy ès Pays du Roy, . . . et pour ce que le Roy lui prie qu'il envoye ladite prinse . . . . hors les Pays du Roy." Instructions, &c., Lenglet, tom. iii. p. 124.

this point, he professed himself ready to supply the earl with money and ships, but wished him not to delay his departure when the whole English nation was so impatient for his return. "Monsieur du Plessis," he wrote, "you know the desire which I have for Warwick's return to England, as well because I wish to see him get the better of his enemies — or that, at least, through him the realm of England may again be embroiled (*ou à tout le moins que par son moyen le Royaume d'Angleterre fût en brouillis*) — as to avoid the questions which have arisen out of his residence here. . . . For you know that these Bretons and Burgundians have no other aim than to make this a pretext for breaking the peace and reopening the war, which I would not see commenced on such a ground of quarrel (*laquelle je ne voudrois point voir commencée sur cette couleur*). . . . Wherefore I pray you take pains, you and others there, to induce Monsieur de Warwick, by all the arguments in your power, to hasten his departure; but I beg that this may be urged in the softest manner possible (*par toutes les plus douces voyes que pourrez*), and so that he shall not perceive that we have any other end in view than his advantage."[35]

In the same spirit of gentleness, the king despatched a special embassy to the Netherlands, for the purpose of assuaging the resentment of his fiery cousin by mild remonstrances and specific promises of satisfaction. The envoys had an audience of the

[35] Letter dated Amboise, June 22, 1470. Duclos, tom. iii. preuves, pp. 292, 293.

duke, at Saint-Omer, on the 15th of July, and were not a little surprised at the style of their reception. Charles, surrounded by his nobles, was seated on "a rich and pompous throne," raised five steps above the floor — "higher than ever king or emperor was accustomed to sit." He did not even lift his hat as the representatives of his sovereign bent the knee before him, but acknowledged their presence merely by a slight inclination of the head and a gesture permitting them to rise. When the purpose of their mission had been stated, Hugonet, a member of the ducal council, in the absence of the chancellor, commenced the delivery of a speech characterized by the formality and prolixity which among public functionaries were then regarded — strange as it may seem to the modern reader — as the essential features of oratorical argument. But Charles, though in general patient and even punctilious in the observance of forms, was not now in a mood to suffer his meaning to be obscured by far-fetched allusions or a circuitous phraseology. He cut the orator short, and himself descanted, in briefer and more direct terms, not much flavored with courtesy, on the injuries he had received and the little prospect he saw of their being redressed. The king affected to be his friend, yet had given and was still giving his countenance and support to the duke's enemy. The envoys, in answer, pointed to the offers made by Louis as furnishing an adequate remedy. "Remedy!" Charles repeated; "I tell you there is no remedy possible." "What!" replied the ambassadors, raising their eyes to heaven in well-affected astonishment and grief, "has it been found possible, Monseigneur, to reconcile two nations after a long war and profuse shedding of Christian blood, and shall not a petty dispute like this admit of being settled? The king desires to avoid all occasions of dissension and disturbance. He offers you friendship, and peace, and reparation for every wrong. It will not be his fault if trouble ensue. Monseigneur! the king and you have a Judge, who is above you both." The covert threat, still more the hypocritical tone of this reply, put Charles beside himself. Starting to his feet, "We Portuguese," he exclaimed in a voice of thunder, — while his dark eyes, flashing fire, and his dark skin, beneath which the crimson flood coursed in tumultuous eddies, seemed, like his words, to proclaim his southern origin and to abjure his descent from the house of Valois, — "We Portuguese, when we see our friends become the friends of our enemies, send them to the hundred thousand devils of hell!"[36] With this abrupt and startling climax, the audience terminated, the hearers remaining mute and paralyzed with astonishment.

Even his own nobles, those among them who were

[36] "Entre nous Portugalois avons une coustume devers nous, que quand ceulx que nous avons tenu à nos amis se font amis à nos ennemis, nous les commandons à tous les cent mille diables d'enfer." Chastellain, p. 495. The official report of this audience, in which Hugonet's speech is reported at length, and no doubt correctly, while Charles's remarks are softened down to a whining apostrophe, — "Oh vous Bailly de Vermandois èt M. Jacques sont-ce-cy les aimities que Monseigneur le Roy me porte!" &c., — may be found in the Hist. de Bourgogne, tom. iv. preuves, pp. cclxxiv.–cclxxxvi.

the most deeply and sincerely attached to his person and to his house, and who had grown gray in its service, were wounded by this unbecoming burst of passion. The strict alliance he had formed with England met with no approval among his vassals of this class.[37] Whatever dislike they might entertain to the present occupant of the French throne, and however ready they might be to draw their swords against him in defence of their own sovereign, they still regarded that royal and ancient house, the parent stem of so many illustrious shoots, as a thing of divine origin and appointment, the fountain of chivalry and of honor, from which their title to distinction, and their right to call themselves "noble," were derived. It seemed to them a piece of singularly bad taste thus, by an obvious implication, to consign the king of France to the "hundred thousand devils of hell."[38] By such language their prince had sullied his own *fleurs-de-lis*, the glorious emblems strewn upon his shield, the cognizance of his birth, and of his claims to the homage and obedience of his subjects.[39] "We Portuguese"! Why had he not said, at once, "We English"? Why, since he had chosen to sink his paternal origin and remember only his mother's line, had he not gone

[37] "Quoique le maistre feust ne quel ne com fait, eulx tous estoient en affection devers France, non pas vers Angleterre." Chastellain, p. 496.

[38] "Il y avoit de malvais agoust pour commander tacitement ung roy de France à tous les cent mille diables." Ibid. p. 496.

[39] "Et sambloient à ceulx qui deuil y prenoient, qu'à ly mesmes il se fist grand blasme en ces paroles, considéré encore qu'il estoit subgect du roy, et honoré et paré des armes des fleurs de lys, la gloire et splendeur de son front et le plus cler de ses tiltres." Ibid. ubi supra.

still further back, tracing his descent from that Lancastrian race which had brought unnumbered woes to France, proclaiming himself, not merely a foreigner on the French soil, but the enemy of the French name? But such, doubtless, was his real meaning.[40] He had forgotten the sentiments in which he had been trained; he desired to revive the horrible and parricidal conflict which still cast its shadow on *their* recollections of the past, but which was known to *him* only by tradition.

What, in fact, had embittered Charles's feelings, and given a deeper tinge to the pride and harshness of his character, was his perception of a strong though silent aversion to his policy and a growing estrangement to his person among all classes of his subjects. His ardent energies, his indefatigable labors, the triumphs and successes which had raised him in the consideration of his equals, had failed to win for him the cordial coöperation, the strenuous devotion, which he demanded as a debt from all who acknowledged him as their prince. Among the nobles of his household, at least among the younger members, the rigorous discipline and severe routine of service and attendance which he had thought proper to establish, the irksome tasks, the wearisome forms, the long audiences at which it was necessary to sit, mute and rigid, "as if at a sermon," the sharp reprimands that were sure to

[40] "Et en ce, quand il se nommoit Portugalois, fut murmure aussi de ses propres gens, pour ce que tacitement contempnant le nom de France, dont il estoit, ne se osa nommer Anglois là où le cuer luy estoit; mès se renommoit de la feue de sa mère, ancienne amie d'Angleterre et contraire à France." Ibid. ubi supra.

follow every act of negligence or sign of inattention had produced a feeling of discontent that waited only for an opportunity to display itself in open mutiny or desertion.[41] If such were the feelings towards him of the class whose general instincts and habits were his own, still less could the fiery, impatient, and imperious prince be an object of sympathy or affection to the burghers of the Netherlands, a slow, stolid, and phlegmatic people, fond of pleasure and of ease, with whom Charles had nothing in common, save a stubbornness of temper, that served only to give intensity and force to the mutual repulsion of characters so opposite. By them he was regarded with fear; every upward step in his career inspired them with fresh alarm. They bent before the sway of his vehement and impetuous will, but with a coldness and moody reluctance, more exasperating to a temper such as his than direct contradiction or violent resistance. A few weeks before the scene just noticed, when he

[41] "Le duc de soi mesmes en estoit assez cause, par trop estre roide et dur à ses gens en diverses manières non apprises, par espécial aux nobles hommes, lesquels il maintint et voult asservir en estroites servitutes; comme de l'audience où il falloit estre enclos trois fois la sepmaine, comme à ung sermon; . . . et se d'aventure il chéit à mesprendre à qui que ce feust, en cas encore dispensable, si convenoit il encore porter correction volontaire; et parquoi beaucoup de gens de bien s'en tannèrent, et en devindrent tous frois." Chastellain, p. 479. In December, 1468, the duke had laid down some new regulations for the purpose of securing greater care and expedition in the minor details of his government, at the same time informing his nobles that any of them who found their duties irksome were at liberty to retire from his service. All professed their willingness to conform to his commands; and Charles then courteously thanked them, acknowledging the onerous nature of the labors imposed on them. See Gachard's note to Barante, tom. ii. p. 327.

had spoken in terms so uncivil of the king of France, he had addressed an angry invective to the deputies of Flanders, remarkable, among other reasons, because it seems to have been preserved in the exact words in which it was delivered, undiluted by the chroniclers or the official reporters, too careful in general to smooth away whatever was characteristic in the expression or the form.

The duke had made a demand upon the provinces for an annual subsidy of a hundred and twenty thousand crowns, to be continued for three years. It had become a matter of vital importance that he should have always on hand a body of troops ready for any sudden emergency. His great enemy, the king, had a permanent force sufficient to meet any unforeseen attack; sufficient, also, should he be so disposed, to allow of his making such an attack on a neighbor. What was to prevent Louis from seizing, by a *coup-de-main*, the towns on the Somme, or ravaging at pleasure other exposed portions of his rival's territory? Already such an assault had been menaced, and, had it been made, might well have proved successful. The present calm was but a warning, to those who studied its signs, of the necessity for fresh preparations. Accordingly, Charles issued an ordinance "for the levy of a thousand lances," amounting to five thousand combatants, to be regularly paid and drilled, and kept ready for active service, under officers of his own appointment. The greater portion of the expense he proposed to defray from his treasury, or the revenues of his domain; but he called upon his wealthy subjects in the Netherlands to aid him to the extent already mentioned. The forms under which alone such a grant could be obtained, afforded sufficient room to both parties, the sovereign and the people, for the display of their peculiar characteristics. Charles had no power, such as had recently been exercised in France, of imposing a tax without the previous consent of the subject. Neither was there in the Netherlands any legislative body, like the Parliament of England, to whom applications for money were addressed by the sovereign, and by whose single vote they were granted or refused. He was the common ruler of many distinct states, and was compelled, when he needed money, to present what was technically termed a "request" to each of the provinces separately — a system indicative, not of a strongly limited prerogative or of a lofty popular freedom, but of the crude relations between a feudal prince and that class of his subjects on which the vestments of feudalism sat uncouthly and uneasily. Even if, for his own convenience, he summoned the Estates of all the provinces simultaneously, they did not merge into a national assembly, like the States-General of France. They were still so many different representative bodies; each must be consulted and treated with apart; while each was careful to couple its assent to the proposed measure with the stipulation that all the others should concur.[42]

[42] The name of the "States-General" subsequently crept into use in the Netherlands; and, in the 16th century, it suited the purposes of William of Orange and his party to represent the assembly thus

On the present occasion most of the provinces had already acceded to the grant, when the Estates of Flanders — the wealthiest and most important of them all — were convened, first at Lille, where the matter was opened to them by the chancellor of Burgundy, and afterwards at Bruges, where they received letters from Charles, urging the necessity for their compliance. They appointed a deputation, headed by Jean Sersanders, the pensionary of Ghent, to wait on the duke at Middelbourg, and present what they styled a "Remonstrance," specifying three "points" which they required to have settled before giving their

called as a constitutional body invested with legislative functions. But this was a view which could not and did not stand the test of historical investigation; and the admission of it by modern writers shows a misconception of the theory on which the government of the provinces was built — a matter on which we shall hereafter have occasion to remark. Despotic as was the character of Philip II., he had reason in asserting at the outset of the troubles that he had trod in the footsteps of his predecessors, and had made no innovations. In the questions discussed at that time, the *legal* right — and it was the legal right alone that was then openly called into controversy — lay on the side of the king. Take, for example, one point, which gave rise to greater clamor and excitement than any other, and the real nature of which seems not to have been apprehended even by the more recent historians, native or foreign. The dismission of Granvelle from his place in the council was demanded on the ground that he was a foreigner. The sole pretext for this objection to him was a provision in the ancient charters of the duchy of Brabant excluding foreigners from appointment to office. Now Granvelle held no office in the duchy of Brabant. He held no office in any of the provinces. The council was simply a part of the sovereign's household, in the composition of which he was entirely unrestricted. Former sovereigns had never hesitated to place foreigners in the council. Never before had the practice been objected to. It need hardly be added that, as a native of Franche-Compté, Granvelle would in any case have been entitled to nomination. With reason might Philip exclaim, "They will say next that I too am a foreigner."

consent. They complained, first, that whereas the chancellor had given them to understand that the money was to be raised by *all* the duke's provinces — which would have included Burgundy — it now appeared, by his own letters, that only his provinces *here* (*son pays de par deça*) — by which were meant the Netherlands — were to be called upon to contribute. Secondly, they required that the proportion should be previously fixed in which each province was to be assessed. And thirdly, they desired a specific declaration that the fiefs and arriere-fiefs, which by the terms of the recent ordinance were to furnish the troops, should be exempted from the payment of the tax.[43] After a brief conference with Hugonet and another member of his council, Charles turned towards the deputies, and thus addressed them: —

"I have listened to your declaration and remonstrance, the gist whereof lies in three points, which, for the sake of brevity, I abstain from reciting.

"And as to the first point, touching the discrepancy you allege between the proposition as made by my chancellor and the tenor of my letters, it seems to me that there is *none*, but that my chancellor and I have understood it in the same way; for, by my provinces *here*, are meant Holland, Zealand, Flanders, Brabant, Luxembourg, Limbourg, Hainault, Picardy, the *Châtellenie* of Lille, the Boulognais, and the county of Guines, which are those that have

[43] Gachard, Doc. Inéd. tom. i. pp. 216–219.

been always accustomed to furnish me with subsidies and aids, — and not my province of Burgundy at all.[44] Besides *that* has no money; it takes after France (*il sent la France;*) but it has plenty of good soldiers, the best I have in all my provinces, who have served me well, and are a powerful aid, for they amount to a third of my army.

"Then, as to your demand for an assessment, apportionment, and so forth, — when you have consented and acceded to my request, then this shall be regulated with the advice of my council. Nor is there any reason why it should be done first; for if you refuse your consent to the grant, there will be no apportionment required. But it seems that you make this demand out of subtlety and malice, and that neither you nor those that have sent you have any will or intention to please me or to conform to my request. And you act in this as you have always done — you Flemings! For neither to my father nor to me did you ever grant any thing in a free and liberal spirit. True it is that you have always granted what was asked, or even more; but it was done so tardily and uncheerfully as showed there was no heartiness or good-will in the doing of it — as is the way with you still; your Flemish skulls are so thick and hard, and you persist always in your

[44] We have here an instance of that want of clearness which, according to Chastellain, was sometimes noticeable in Charles's speeches before he had become warmed by his argument. He means apparently to say, "There has been no discrepancy; for my chancellor, in speaking of all my provinces, never intended, any more than myself, to include Burgundy, but only these provinces, which are," &c.

stubbornness and perverse opinions. And yet you had better bethink you whether others be not as wise as you, and have not heads as well! I am half of France and half of Portugal, as I would have you remember, and know well how to encounter such heads as yours — ay, and *will* do it too!

"'Tis but a little matter, a grant of six score thousand crowns a year, for three years, from all my provinces; I shall have but a thousand lances, making but five thousand combatants; and yet this will pay but a third part of the expense; and the rest I must pay out of my domain, or else they will have to fast eight months of the year. And I am not doing it for myself alone, but for the protection, security, and defence of my provinces, to preserve them in tranquillity and peace; for it is better to provide in time against any sudden incursion or assault by our enemies than to expose ourselves to be invaded, chased away, trampled upon; and it is to provide against such dangers and pressing occasions that I propose to keep on hand these thousand lances, which, as I have told you, make not a third of my army, Master Jean Sersanders! And there is a great necessity for my doing it, seeing the great appearance there is that I shall be at war with some of my neighbors — and I can name *him*. 'Tis the king of France, who is so fickle and so inconstant, that no one knows what he intends, or how to protect one's self against him; for *he* has his troops always ready; and therefore it is that *I* also wish to have these thousand lances ready, which may perhaps be enough to meet any sudden attack, if no greater danger should arise — for to resist the whole power of the king of France it would *not* be enough. And I marvel much at your manner of acting, and how you should dare to make any communication or speak to me of the discharge of my fiefs and arriere-fiefs, knowing, as you do, the tenor of my ordinance, and how I intend that every one should govern himself by that, and that, if any one be called upon for more than is there specified, he need but to come to me and it shall be remedied.

"I tell you I have no cause to be content with it; and I would have you know that on no account will I rescind my ordinance. And who are they, of all my provinces, who require it of me, save you — Flemish heads? Is it Holland, or Zealand — provinces acquired by my father, which were never before called upon in this manner, and which are not so wealthy as my province of Flanders? Certes, no! but what is more, the good towns there, the burghers and the merchants, render me service. Is it Brabant? No, again! for there I have the service of the fiefs and arriere-fiefs; and the towns, besides, have raised a good number of lances, and the burghers and merchants serve me too. And so in Hainault, Picardy, and my other provinces — which have as great and as many privileges as you. And, what is more, very great seigneurs, my cousin of Saint-Pol and my cousin of Marle, for example, let me enjoy the services of their vassals. And you, forsooth, would deprive me, in my necessity, of the services of my own subjects, on the pretext of your privileges — which are all *null!* By this very proceeding you forfeit them! Ay! you will say and will insist that I have sworn to maintain them. 'Tis true! But you also — *you* have sworn to serve me and to be my faithful and obedient subjects. And yet I know there are some of you who hate me; and among you Flemings, with your hard skulls, you have always either hated or despised your prince; for when they were not very powerful, you despised them, and when they *were* powerful, and you could do nothing against them, you hated them. *I like better that you should* HATE *than despise me;* nor, for your privileges, or aught else, will I suffer myself to be trampled on, or that any thing shall be attempted against my right and sovereignty — and I have the power to resist it![45] There are those who would be willing that I should be obliged to try the chances of battle with but five or six thousand combatants — who would gladly see me defeated, slain, quartered! But before I will endure that you should deprive me of my subjects or attempt any thing against my sovereign rights, I will make such provision and resistance that you will learn by the effect that you cannot and must not do it. Your displeasure will encounter my displeasure; 'twill be like the glass and

[45] "Entre vous, Flamengs, avecq vous dures testes, avez toujours contempné ou hay vostre prince.... J'ayme mieulx que vous me hayés que contempnez; ne, pour vous privileges ne aultrement, ne me lesray fouler, ne emprendre riens sur ma haulteur et seignourie, et suy puissant assez pour y resister." Gachard, Doc. Inéd. tom. i. p. 223.

the iron crock — let the glass hurl itself against the iron, it is but broken for its pains.

"There are those, too, who know not what it is to enjoy the favor of their prince — a thing easy to acquire for one who desires to do right; for it is not a hard matter to do right, if one is in earnest about it; but to do wrong, and to apply one's self to *that*, is very hard and troublesome. Do you, then, set about doing right, and govern and conduct yourselves so sagely that you lose not my grace (for you know not what it is that you will lose!) and be my good subjects and I will be your good prince. And if any fiefs or arriere-fiefs are called upon to contribute to this grant, I will have regard to that, and will discharge them from their obligations to the extent of their assessment. And when you shall have determined to accord my request — which you *will* do, in any event! (and I do not mean to burden you further, unless some greater necessity should occur) — send some of your deputies after me to Lille or Saint-Omer, and there, with my chancellor and council, I will determine on the apportionment, and we will speak also of other matters touching my province of Flanders." [46]

The effect of this explosion — which was doubtless listened to by the "Flemish heads" with suffi-

[46] Gachard, Doc. Inéd. tom. i. pp. 219–224.

We have given a perfectly literal translation of this extraordinary address. M. Gachard remarks (Doc. Inéd. tom. i. p. 131), with great propriety and force, that having sought in vain in the events of history for something to account for the violent hatred manifested towards Charles's memory by the people of Flanders, he has found it sufficiently explained by this and similar speeches.

cient stolidity of countenance, though not without inward perturbation — was an immediate vote by the Estates in conformity with the duke's demand. Yet the subsequent proceedings were marked by the slow deliberation characteristic of "skulls so hard and thick." At every step fresh obstacles were interposed; in vain were whip and spur, coaxings and caressings, alternately applied; the dull animal refused to mend his pace; and such was the strain on the temper and patience of the rider that he at length declared himself ready to dismount and leave to others a thankless and unprofitable task.[47] This offer, or menace, — whichever it should be termed, — passed apparently unheeded; and it was not until the close of the year 1471, that the first instalment of the grant was collected and paid, and the small regular army, or standing militia, known as the "*bandes d'ordonnance*," was established and organized.

The handful of fine dust which the king had attempted to throw into the eyes of his antagonist, the latter, with a sudden and contemptuous puff, had blown away. The more need that the lunge which was to follow should be rapid and deadly. "Tell Monsieur de Warwick" (Louis had written to his agents in Normandy), "that the king will assist him to recover England, either with the help of the Queen Margaret or by whatever other means he may propose. . . . Only let him communicate his desire in

[47] See post, Book IV. ch. 3.

this respect as speedily as possible, and the king will lay aside all other affairs for the purpose of accomplishing it."[48] This was coming to the point; for events had shown that without some stronger support than he had derived from his connection with Clarence, the earl was playing a hopeless game, and the next move would probably be his last. Yet the only remaining way to gratify ambition and the thirst for vengeance lay through the lowest depths of humiliation and of infamy. He must kneel to those whom he had himself crushed and degraded, abjuring his past triumphs, sullying his own renown; he must betray Clarence as he had forsaken Edward, adopt the war-cry of a beaten enemy, and stand before the world as the very incarnation of treason and of perjury. It was not strange that he should have shown some reluctance to take the initiatory steps in this direction. But he might safely commit the negotiation to Louis, whose own experience and entire freedom from idle scruples pointed him out as the fittest person to conduct it.

The business proved, however, of a more difficult nature than the king had anticipated. Margaret and her son, the titular prince of Wales—whom Louis as he boasted, had from his love for Warwick hitherto treated as absolute strangers, "as much so as if he had never seen them" [49] — were summoned to meet him at Angers, the capital of her father's duchy. In misfortune and exile, Margaret of Anjou

[48] Instructions, &c., Lenglet, tom. iii. p. 125.

[49] Ibid. ubi supra.

still retained the loftiness of carriage and of soul joined with the feminine keenness and tenacity of feeling which had distinguished her in the days of her proud but stormy queenhood. She listened with indignant scorn to the proposal that she should adopt as the champion of her cause the man to whom, beyond all others, it owed its overthrow and abasement. The arguments employed by Louis seemed at first to have no effect on the high-spirited queen. But they were, in truth, of irresistible force, before which the strongest feelings of resentment and of pride must finally yield. To forego such an opportunity of restoring her husband to his freedom and his throne, her son to his country and his birthright, would have argued a mind not merely unpractical but distraught. Margaret at length consented to see Warwick at her feet; to hear his confession, his excuses, and his protestations; to bid him rise and show himself henceforth as faithful and attached as he had before been disloyal and hostile. But a harder trial still awaited her. It was not enough for Warwick that he had secured the means of wreaking vengeance on an ungrateful sovereign. The monarch whom he was about to restore might prove not less unmindful of the claims of the kingmaker than Edward had proved. The throne, again occupied by a Lancastrian prince, would be surrounded by men who had shed their blood in the defence of that house, who had been its constant and trusted adherents alike in disaster as in triumph, and who had lost power, possessions, and native land for its sake alone.

No exploits of one who from mere selfish instincts had at this late hour become its partisan, would be sufficient to counterbalance such services and such claims. Some securer basis was wanting for the supremacy which he aspired to hold. The newly-formed alliance must be strengthened by a closer bond. Having so recently effected the marriage of one daughter with the heir of York, he now sought as a husband for the other the heir of Lancaster. The wily Louis seems to have kept back this part of the plan until Margaret should have so far conquered her aversion as to regard Warwick in another light than as the most detested of her enemies. But the horror with which she received the proposal showed how small was the change which had been effected in her sentiments by a reconciliation wrung from her necessity. She saw, she said, neither honor nor advantage, for herself or for her son, in such a match; by a like sacrifice, could she have stooped to it, she might already have obtained from the usurper himself the recognition of the youthful prince as next in succession to the crown. The struggle lasted for more than a fortnight. Louis displayed his accustomed tact, and his knowledge of the female character, by exchanging the language of argument for that of entreaty. He appealed to Margaret not merely as queen of England, but as his own kinswoman and a princess of France. Warwick, he said, was of all men the one to whom he himself was most beholden. The fortunes not only of the house of Lancaster, but of the house of Valois, depended on his success. At last, overcome by the importunities of all around her, the queen gave way. Her son was affianced to the Lady Anne — the marriage to take place when her father had replaced the crown of England on the head from which his hands had torn it. It was further agreed that in default of issue from this union, the Duke of Clarence should inherit, and that he and Warwick should administer the affairs of the kingdom during the minority of the prince of Wales.[50]

For several weeks after these arrangements had been made, and the preparations for the intended enterprise completed, the blockade maintained by Charles's fleet gave no opportunity for the attempt. At length a storm dispersed the Flemish ships, and compelled them to seek refuge in their own ports. Before they had time to reassemble, Warwick, with his company, had put to sea and crossed the Channel in safety. He landed at Dartmouth on the 13th of September. In a few days more than sixty thousand men had collected round his standard — the same standard that had gone down before him on so many bloody fields. With forces increasing at every step, he marched directly against Edward. That prince, having quitted the capital, where lay his surest support, to suppress a new insurrection in the north, chose this part of the kingdom, where his enemies were

[50] "Mannere and Guiding of the Earl of Warwick at Angeirs," in Ellis's Original Letters, 2d series, vol. i.— Chastellain, p. 501.— Basin, tom. ii. lib. iii. cap. 2.— "Aujourd'hui," wrote Louis on the 25th of July, "avons fait la mariage de la Reine d'Angleterre et de lui [Warwick]." Duclos, tom. iii. p. 294.

strongest, as the scene of what must prove a decisive conflict. His infatuation can only be explained by his blind belief in his own invincibility in actual battle, or a Sardanapalus-like incapacity for exertion until his blood had been stirred by the trumpet-call of an approaching foe. He is said to have expressed the wish that his brother of Burgundy would guard the sea, not to prevent Warwick's departure from France, but to cut off his return. For himself, he desired nothing more than the opportunity of meeting his enemies in the open field.[51] But even this opportunity had been lost by his supineness. His soldiers deserted him in great numbers. His nobles had begun to listen to secret overtures from Warwick. The red rose was assumed, the war-cry of Lancaster was heard, in his own camp. His crown was already lost, and his person was in danger. He fled precipitately to the eastern coast, and with seven or eight hundred followers, the remnant of his army, embarked at Lynn, on board of some Flemish trading vessels, which carried him to the coast of Holland, there to solicit the protection of an ally whose counsels, had he heeded them, would have saved him from this sudden reverse of fortune.[52]

Less than a fortnight had intervened between the landing of Warwick and the flight of Edward, and the revolution seemed to be complete. The earl met with no resistance at his entrance into London, where his first act was to open the prison doors which he

[51] Commines, tom. i. p. 243

[52] Commines, liv. iii. ch. 5.—Chastellain, pp. 488–493.

had himself closed on the unfortunate Henry. Was it a reality or a shadow that came forth to occupy the throne? Six years before, that pale, meek figure, divested of crown, sceptre, and regal apparel, bound with ropes like a convicted felon, had followed him through the streets, amid a jeering multitude, to be immured in the Tower; and now, pale and meek as then—innocent and imbecile as when, half a century ago, in feeble infancy, presented to the people of two great realms as their common sovereign—it passed through the same streets, behind the same proud soldier, amid a silent, wondering throng, to be invested anew with the trappings of royalty, to play the same puppet-like part on a stormy and crowded stage.[53] The grim ghosts of slaughtered Talbots, Somersets, and Cliffords, of the many thousands that on French and English ground had died in defending the rights of the son of Henry the Fifth, would have formed the fittest cortége in this triumph of their phantom-king.

But in the eyes of the French monarch—a person not much given to idle moralizings—this pageant was a substantial as well as glorious sight. So sudden and complete a victory surpassed his hopes, and filled him with a transport of joy such as he had never before experienced.[54] Margaret and her son, the wife and daughter of Warwick, all the exiled adherents of

[53] "Y avait ung roy assis en chaière; autant y eust fait ung sac de laine. . . . Estoit une ombre en une paroit. . . . Le roy y estoit subgect et muet comme ung veau couronné." Chastellain, p. 487.

[54] "Se bagnoit le roy Loys en roses, ce lui sembloit, d'oyr ceste bonne aventure." Chastellain, p. 486.

the house of Lancaster, were invited to Paris, where they were sumptuously entertained, and welcomed with a grand ovation, with solemn processions and salvoes of artillery. The same rejoicings and thanksgivings were ordered in all the great towns of the kingdom. Louis himself went on a pilgrimage to the shrine of Notre Dame de Celles, in Poitou, there to acknowledge in private his obligations to the dear patroness who had bestowed on him this transcendent mark of her favor. A splendid embassy was despatched to London, to felicitate Henry on his restoration, and to arrange with Warwick a treaty of peace and of alliance against the common enemy. A similar treaty was formed with the prince of Wales, acting as the representative of his father. Proclamation was made that all Englishmen, with the exception of "the rebel and usurper Edward of March, his adherents and accomplices," should henceforth be admitted into France without passport or safe-conduct. English merchants, visiting the French markets, were to enjoy the same immunities and privileges as native-born subjects. Fairs were established at Caen, in Normandy, for the purpose of promoting the growth of commercial relations between the two countries. On the other hand an embargo was placed on the existing trade with Flanders, the king's subjects being forbidden, under the severest penalties, to visit the Netherlands, and the subjects of the duke of Burgundy refused entrance into France.[55]

[55] De Troyes, Lenglet, tom. ii. pp. 87, 88.—Hist. de Bourgogne, tom. iv. preuves, p. cclxxxvii. et al.—Chastellain, p. 487.

These were preliminary steps to that vigorous and effective stroke which Louis now had in contemplation. Two years ago he had thrown away his opportunity, lost the flood-tide of fortune, and been caught in shallows and quicksands, which had well-nigh swallowed him, and from which he had escaped in sorry and unenviable plight. By his own patience and skill he had evaded the worst consequences of that disaster, and now, by a surprising turn of luck, he was in a better situation than ever for making a bold and determined move. His preparations, indeed, were not yet complete; for the suddenness of Warwick's success in England, by which the enemy's position had been turned, — leaving him assailable on what had hitherto been his strongest side, — had outstripped the calculations of the king. He was eager to repair this delay. At the moment of receiving the happy tidings, he wrote to the count of Dammartin, — whom he had learned to consider as his right arm in every enterprise of war, — desiring his immediate presence, in order that they might confer upon the means of "preventing the duke of Burgundy from setting himself up as king in the realm of France." The count's arrival being somewhat delayed, Louis wrote again, a few days later, in this impatient strain: "*Monsieur le Grand Maître*, I am all amazed and mortified at having no reply from you touching these good news. It seems you are no longer in the same mind with respect to Burgundy, while I, for my part, see therein the sole Paradise of my imagination (*n'ay autre Paradis en mon imagination que celuy-là!*) . . . On Monday I go to

Tours, and shall therefore write nothing further at present; but I have a greater hunger to speak with you than I ever had for talking with confessor about the salvation of my soul. Written at Loches, October 28," 1470.[56]

At Tours, whither he was on the wing when this missive was despatched, the king had summoned at short notice an assembly of nobles, prelates, and representatives of the principal towns, by whose voices he might be assured of the general concurrence of his subjects in the measures he proposed to take. Whether from press of time, or from the fear that some extraneous matter, some question touching his own administration, might be introduced into the discussion, he had preferred, instead of leaving to the burghers themselves the election of their deputies, to nominate certain conspicuous members of that class as those who were to take part in the proceedings.[57] It was not therefore a formal meeting of the "Three Estates," but rather what is known in French history as a "Convocation of Notables." Yet substantially it was the same assembly as had on a former occasion given publicity to his appeal and aroused the nation to his support. From this body he was now to obtain his release from the obligations of the treaty of Péronne. Many of the nobles present had bound themselves to maintain that treaty, and to oppose and punish any attempted violation of it by the sovereign. But they were called upon to consider

[56] Cabinet de Louis XI., Lenglet, tom. ii. p. 256.

[57] Commines, tom. i. p. 211.

whether the very nature of its provisions, the circumstances under which it had been signed, and the subsequent conduct of the other party, did not justify Louis in repudiating the agreement, and relieve *them* from the responsibility of enforcing it. The history of the transaction, till now suppressed and forbidden even to be whispered, was openly rehearsed. On Cardinal Balue, whose later and verified treason made him the convenient scape-goat for such a charge, was laid the blame of the unfortunate visit to Péronne, he having conspired with the duke of Burgundy, and by false representations induced the king to accede to the proposal for an interview. The "dishonest treatment" which Louis had met with from the duke was "notorious throughout all Christendom." "The gates of the castle and the town had been closed upon him," and "many strange and unseemly words in the tone and with the meaning of menaces, threats, and intimidations," had been addressed to him by the duke and by certain of his people, "such as would have been a reasonable cause of alarm in the most self-possessed man in the world."[58] Under the influence of constraint and fear the king had signed — he knew not what. Whenever his ministers had remonstrated against any extravagant concession, the answer of the duke's servants had been, "Monseigneur *wills* that it should be so." Nevertheless the king had

[58] "Furent dites au Roy et à ses Gens, par le dit Duc de Bourgogne et ses Gens, plusieures estranges et mal gracieuses paroles, sonnans et denotans menaces, peur et craintes, et dont le plus constant homme du monde eust eu cause raisonnable de doubter."

intended the faithful observance of the treaty, and had promulgated his ordinances to that effect. But the duke, on the other hand, had not only violated many of its provisions, but had failed in his allegiance and broken his obligations as a French vassal and a prince of the blood. He had never taken, and had refused to take, the customary oath of fealty and homage for his possessions in France. He had confiscated property of the king's subjects residing in the Netherlands to the amount of four hundred thousand crowns. He had conspired with the self-styled king of England, Edward of March, against the tranquillity of the realm. Under the pretext of making lawful reprisals for the seizure of his vessels by the earl of Warwick, an injury for which he had been offered and had refused reparation, he had sent an armed fleet against the ports of Normandy, which had obstructed navigation and committed many depredations along the coast. A great number of minor cases were recounted, in which he had maltreated the king's subjects, usurped his functions, and defied his authority. And finally, instead of seeking redress in a lawful manner, for his own grievances, real or pretended, he had, not merely by his acts, but in express words, abrogated and renounced the treaty which he had extorted from his sovereign by treachery and force.[59]

After a full deliberation, it was pronounced by the concordant voices of the whole assembly, "with-

[59] Lenglet, tom. iii. pp. 72–81.

out the least discrepancy or diversity of opinion," each member consulting "his own judgment and his own conscience," that the king was discharged, "in law, in honor, and in reason," from the obligations of his oath. The princes and nobles who had given their seals and pledges for the execution of the treaty were, in the like solemn manner, released from their engagement. The duke of Burgundy, it was further declared, had, by his illegal and rebellious acts, incurred the forfeiture of all his fiefs. The sovereign was bound by the vows made at his coronation to punish his disobedient and refractory vassal. All the nobles present tendered individually, and "without being requested so to do," their assistance for this purpose. A royal proclamation was thereupon issued, setting forth these facts; and an usher of the Parliament carried a summons to the duke to appear before that body at Paris, and answer to the charge of *lèze-majesté* preferred against him by the unanimous voice of the nation.[60]

These intimations of a hostile design were not given before the plan had been formed for carrying that design into effect. On the side of Louis all was now in readiness. The state of things that had arisen at the beginning of his reign, when he had stood alone

[60] Lenglet, tom. iii. pp. 68–72. —Dumont, Corps Diplomatique, tom. iii. p. 428. — Ordonnances des Rois de France, tom. xvii. p. 353. Commines, tom. i. pp. 211, 212. — Mademoiselle Dupont's note on this passage in Commines is erroneous. The summons of which Chastellain speaks was sent to Philip the Good. The mention of the duke of Orleans as present, on that occasion, among the Knights of the Toison, is itself a sufficient proof of this.

against a band of powerful assailants, had not only ceased to exist, but seemed to be completely reversed. The princes and nobles, instead of being leagued with the duke of Burgundy against the king, were leagued with the king against the duke of Burgundy. Among all those who had taken part with Charles in the War of the Public Weal, or who had countenanced that movement, he had no longer a single ally. All were arrayed against him, all had offered their coöperation in reducing him to submission. England — that is to say, Warwick — promised to contribute four thousand men, who were to land at Calais, and thence make incursions into the neighboring counties of Boulogne and Guines. The duke Nicholas of Lorraine, of the house of Anjou, grandson of René, nephew of Margaret, — to whom Louis, by way of cementing his alliance with this family, had offered the hand of his daughter, the Princess Anne — was to prevent the feudal levies of the two Burgundies from marching through his territory to the assistance of their sovereign, or divert them from the attempt by an attack on Franche-Comté. The duke of Guienne, eager to display his zeal in the service of a brother to whom he was so greatly beholden, had raised the ban and arriere-ban of his province, and brought five hundred lances to the king's support. Even the duke of Brittany — what with the French forces mounting guard on his frontier, what with his fear of being left in complete isolation, when even England had fallen away and joined with her ancient enemy — dared not remain neutral or entirely inactive, and sent a small force, under the Sire de Lescun, to serve against his old ally. Dammartin, with the main bulk of the army, had taken his station near the borders of Picardy, and was preparing to overrun that province and capture the towns which had been mortgaged to Philip by the treaty of Arras, subsequently redeemed by Louis, and again surrendered to Charles by the treaty of Conflans. But there was no one who showed such an eagerness to secure the triumph of the king and the ruin of the duke of Burgundy, as the Constable Saint-Pol, the vassal and former comrade of Charles, whose sons were still in the service of that prince, and who risked the forfeiture of his estates by taking part against him. He assured the king that a general spirit of disaffection existed in the Netherlands, which could not fail, at a conjuncture so favorable, to break out in open rebellion. He pretended to have derived his knowledge on this subject through secret channels of intelligence, and to have formed such relations with influential burghers in Ghent and other Flemish cities as would enable him to set the revolt in motion whenever the moment should arrive. In Picardy, the chief seat of his seignorial power, he could act more openly and directly. His influence both with the nobles and the towns would facilitate the conquest of that province; and he offered, with the aid of four hundred lances which Louis placed under his command, to get possession of Saint-Quentin, one of the most important places on the Somme, strongly fortified, and capable with a proper garrison of becoming one of the strongest bulwarks of the French territory.[61]

It seemed to be the general belief that all was over with the duke of Burgundy; that this prince, lately so powerful and triumphant, was about to be overwhelmed by an irresistible tide flowing in on him from every quarter. The malcontents among his own servants shared in this belief. Several of the younger nobles — among others, his half brother Baldwin, one of the bastard sons of Philip the Good — fled secretly to France, where they were received by the king with open arms, provided for in his service, and encouraged to publish the vilest and most incredible calumnies against the master whom they had deserted. Charles, on his part, perhaps with as little foundation in truth, accused the fugitives of having formed a conspiracy against his life.[62] The war of letters and manifestoes was prolonged by a correspondence, full of violent recriminations, between the duke and the count of Dammartin and others of his old associates in the War of the Public Weal. The latter were charged with perfidy and ingratitude in having abandoned an ally to whom they owed the restoration of their confiscated estates: the former was reminded of his shameful treatment of the king, in disregard of his plighted faith and honor.[63] This public interchange of abusive epithets

[61] Commines, tom. i. p. 210. — Duclos, tom. iii. preuves, p. 295.

[62] Chastellain, p. 479 et seq. — Hist. de Bourgogne, tom. iv. preuves, p. ccxcviii. et seq. — Duclos, preuves, tom. iii. pp. 297–306. — Basin, tom. ii. lib. iii. cap. 4, 5. — Gachard, Analectes Beligques, pp. 66–70.

[63] Cabinet de Louis XI., Lenglet, tom. ii. pp. 237–241.

and slanderous denunciations among princes and other persons of the highest note — as piquant and exciting then as it is now devoid of all interest or flavor — served as the prelude to more active hostilities. The train was fired according to the preconcerted plan. Burgundy was invaded on different sides, by detached bodies of troops, villages were burned, the surrounding country was laid waste. Hainault suffered a similar irruption from bands composed in part of natives of Liége, collected on the frontier and headed by their old leader, Raes de Heers.[64] Early in December, the Constable, as he had promised, made himself master of Saint-Quentin. No resistance was offered by the inhabitants: the officers who had exercised authority in the name of the duke of Burgundy were dismissed; a strong garrison occupied the town, and the command was intrusted to men who were personally devoted to Saint-Pol, and whose fidelity to *him* was unaffected by the allegiance which they might owe to any higher potentate or prince, whether he were styled duke of Burgundy or — king of France.

Meanwhile Dammartin, after the seizure of several less important places, appeared with all his forces before Amiens. This town, intersected by various channels of the Somme, natural and artificial, was then the seat of a considerable trade, and was amply protected by a citadel and other fortifications. Like most of the other towns, however, it was unpro-

[64] Gachard, note to Barante, tom. ii. p. 367.

vided with a garrison, and the inhabitants were known to be favorable to the reëstablishment of the royal authority. Charles, who was at Arras, advanced with such troops as he was able to muster, in the hope of relieving the place, or at least of securing its fidelity and prolonging the defence. But the royal army was far superior to his own, and reënforcements, including large quantities of artillery, were daily arriving from Paris. The duke could not venture to enter the town, where he would probably have been cut off from any chance of succor. Having waited till Dammartin had crossed the river, he was then obliged to retreat hastily to Dourlens. Amiens then surrendered to the king's lieutenant. Roye and other places quickly followed its example. But Montdidier, which was defended by a small garrison, and Abbeville, where Philippe de Crèvecœur had assembled three thousand lances, rejected the summons to surrender, and were left unassailed. These exceptions did not prevent Louis from making proclamation in the capital that the whole of Picardy had been reunited to the crown.[65] The customary rejoicings were ordered, and thanksgivings duly offered in the churches. Yet the king was secretly alarmed at the ease and rapidity with which these successes had been gained. He was thrown into a state of nervous trepidation on hearing that Dammartin had crossed the Somme. It was, he said, the greatest act of folly of which he had ever heard. To give

[65] De Troyes, Lenglet, tom. ii. p. 89.

battle in the enemy's territory, in the midst of a hostile population, would be to risk the total destruction of the army,—that army on which he had expended all his resources and on which depended his salvation. His general had neither followed his instructions nor even answered his letters; and Louis raised a hue and cry, as if the chancellor of his exchequer had absconded, carrying with him the contents of the treasury.[66] There were other and more substantial causes for his uneasiness. The contingent promised by Warwick had failed to make its appearance. Flanders gave no sign of intending to throw off the yoke of its legitimate sovereign. There was something suspicious, too, in the conduct of Saint-Pol and other great nobles, loud as they were in their professions of loyalty and of devotion to the cause they had so recently embraced. What, for example, was the meaning of these messages they were continually sending to the duke of Burgundy? The navigation was becoming critical. It was time for Louis to shorten sail, take soundings, and keep a sharp lookout for sunken rocks ahead. Dammartin accordingly, having garrisoned the other towns, retired with the bulk of his forces to Amiens, where he made preparations for defence. The king, with a

[66] "Je vous envoye la double des lettres que j'ai écrites au Comte de Dammartin ; il ne m'a point fait de réponse, . . . ne je n'ai onc nouvelles de lui. . . . Je ne vis onc si haute folie, que d'avoir fait passer la rivière aux gens qu'il a. . . . Je vous prie, envoyez-y quelques gens pour sçavoir comment il s'y gouverne, et m'en faites sçavoir des nouvelles deux ou trois fois le jour, car je suis en grand mal aise." Letter to the Admiral of France, Duclos, tom. iii. p. 306.

powerful reserve, stationed himself at Beauvais, some forty miles in the rear, keeping with him the dukes of Bourbon and Guienne, and other great vassals of the crown.

CHAPTER II.

PLOTS AND PURPOSES OF THE FRENCH PRINCES.—COUNTER-REVOLUTION IN ENGLAND.—RENEWED CONFEDERACY AGAINST LOUIS.—PERFIDIOUS NEGOTIATIONS.—FINAL WAR BETWEEN LOUIS AND CHARLES.

1471-1472.

THE situation of the duke of Burgundy, at this juncture, was one of greater difficulty than danger. Feudal France, openly arrayed against him, could have no real desire to accomplish the ruin of a prince whose alliance had been its main protection against the encroachments of an anti-feudal king. It was indebted to the fears and the weakness of Louis for its comparative immunity from his aggressions, for the graciousness of his regards, and for his lavish benefactions. Were he once relieved from external causes of embarrassment, a change would be speedily made in the management of his domestic affairs. Offices and pensions would be swept away; economy would succeed to prodigality; the grandee must give place to the *rotûrier;* there would be punishments as well as rewards; and where now the royal looks were sweet as summer, they would fall blighting and blasting like the winter's frosts. It was necessary that he should be kept in perpetual troubles and embroilments. The trammels of the treaty had been taken off only in order that he might plunge into fresh difficulties — in order that he might expend in war energies so mischievously exerted in the intervals of peace.[1]

On the other hand, the growing power of the duke, the very fact that he alone among the vassals of the crown was able single-handed to maintain a contest with the sovereign, had weakened the sympathies and excited the jealousy of his old allies. They were not unwilling that his haughty confidence in his own isolated strength should meet with a rebuke. But they were ready to return to his support, when he should have acknowledged his dependence on their aid, and accepted of the conditions which they annexed to their offers.

Though Charles had been twice married, his daughter Mary was still his only child. To her, at her father's death without male issue, would descend that great inheritance, those rich and populous provinces and towns, for which he was envied by all the princes of Christendom. Such a prize was naturally the

[1] "Desiroient plustost la guerre entre ces deux grans princes que paix . . . mais leurs fins n'estoient pas telles que le Roy entendoit, mais tout à l'opposite. . . . Craignoient que ces tres grans estatz qu'ils avoient ne fussent diminuez . . . que s'il n'avoit debat par le dehors, qu'il falloit qu'il l'eust avec ses serviteurs. . . . C'estoit pour maintenir plus seurement leurs estatz, et que le Roy ne brouillast parmy eulx, s'il estoit en repos." Commines, tom. i. pp. 209, 210, 216.

object of many longing glances; but though it must fall, sooner or later, to the keeping of another, it was guarded by its present possessor with a jealous care. It was his winning card, to be played only at the crisis of the game, when it might insure a complete victory. Or, rather, it was a powerful loadstone which he held, — moving it now in this direction, now in that; drawing towards him whatever was susceptible to its magnetic influence, but carefully withholding it from actual contact, lest it should cease to be available for future use. Its power had been tried upon the duke of Guienne, as a means of dissolving his then newly-formed connection with the king.[2] But in the first zeal of his conversion, when he had missed no occasion of displaying his loyalty and his subserviency to the wishes of his brother, the young prince had shown himself proof against the strongest allurements. In the mean time, however, a great change had taken place in his condition and prospects. Louis had now a son, an heir *apparent* to the crown:[3] Charles of France was no longer the "second person" in the realm, no longer the destined successor to a throne which he had done his best to shake from its foundations. He had now no peculiar claim on the royal favor or forbearance; and he was thrown back upon his old connections, to share in the common danger and avail himself of the common resources. He had thus fallen once more under the

[2] Lettre de M. de Beuil au Roy, Hist. de Bourgogne, tom. iv. preuves, p. cclxi.

[3] The future Charles VIII., born in June, 1470.

tutelage of the duke of Brittany, or rather of the Sire de Lescun, an adroit tactician, whose mastery over both these princes has been already noticed, and whose hand is visible in all the plots and conspiracies of the time, though we never seem to catch any satisfactory glimpse at his face or person. The king, indeed, fancied that he had secured the services of this adventurer as a secret coadjutor in his own plans.[4] But either he had paid inadequately for the assistance he required, or the passion for intrigue had exerted fresh and irresistible seductions on a breast in which it had long reigned absolute; for Lescun was now busily employed in reuniting the broken threads of a confederacy of which he had been originally one of the principal contrivers. One part of his plan was to bring about the marriage of the duke of Guienne with the heiress of Burgundy,—less, perhaps, with a view to the ulterior consequences of such a union, than as a means of elevating his own position and obtaining a wider field for the exercise of his peculiar talents. Under his direction the duke of Brittany had taken up the project and opened a negotiation with Charles. But the latter, though he did not answer the proposal with a definite refusal, had plainly no intention of acceding to it. He had other and more brilliant prospects in view, projects and enterprises of his own, interests and desires apart from those which he shared with the

[4] "Sommes de tout point amis Monsieur de Lescun et moi, et par ainsi sommes surs de ce côté." Letter of Louis to the Sire Duplessis, July 25, 1470, Duclos, preuves, tom. iii. p. 294.

other princes of France. The present conjuncture, therefore, when he was menaced from different quarters, was seized upon as an opportunity for a warning demonstration which should convince him of his need of their support, and compel him to the sacrifice of his private inclinations for the benefit of the common cause.[5]

There were also other motives at work, purposes and cross-purposes, plots and counter-plots. The shuttles of intrigue were darting swiftly to and fro, weaving their Liliputian meshes, delicate yet strong — meshes in which some, now the busiest in contriving them, would one day find themselves entangled beyond all hope of extrication. The Constable Saint-Pol, besides being a party to the general design, had taken advantage of the occasion to put in action a scheme of policy suggested by the peculiarities of his position, and by the impulses of an ambition which had perhaps been inflamed by the recent and signal success of Warwick in a somewhat similar career. He, too, aspired to hold the balance between two rival sovereigns, elevating and depressing each in turn, throwing the preponderance into whichever scale might carry with it his own hopes or interests for the time.[6] By the possession of Saint-Quentin, the strongest place on the frontier, surrounded, too, by territory of his own, he hoped to rule the battle as he listed, trace the limits of conquest on either hand, unite perhaps the disputed towns in his own grasp,

[5] Commines, tom. i. p. 217 et al.

[6] Basin (who suggests a comparison between Warwick and Saint-Pol), tom. ii. p. 380.

and form them into the basis of an independent power. If either party strove to dispossess him, he would find his protection in an alliance with the other. But this necessity he trusted to avoid by skilful management in his dealings with both, alternately playing with the hopes and anxieties of each, and ever fomenting their mutual strife. A bold and perilous scheme, depending for its success on the power to wheedle and deceive an intellect so shrewd and crafty as that of Louis, to intimidate and coerce a spirit so fearless and inflexible as that of Charles.[7] Yet as long as these princes continued hostile to each other, it might be possible for one who possessed a keen glance, a cool head, and steady nerves, to move with safety along this tortuous path between steep precipices and jagged rocks; and the chances of their reconciliation might well have seemed sufficiently remote to be dismissed from the calculations.

The treacherous conduct of his former friends had no other effect upon the duke than to harden him in the determination to pursue his own course, irrespective of theirs. Their secret overtures brought no concession; their advice that he should be on his guard against the disaffection existing among his subjects was answered by an intimation that they were ill acquainted with his affairs, that it behooved them better to have an eye on the machinations of

[7] "Il cuydoit, pour la situation où il estoit . . . les tenir tous deux en craincte, par le moyen du discord où ilz estoient, auquel il les entretenoit: mais son entreprinse estoit tres dangereuse: car ils estoient trop grans, trop fors et trop habiles." Commines, tom. i. p. 227.

their own servants, who had given them wrong counsel, and to remember their obligations to an ally who had ever been so faithful to his.[8] Against the Constable Charles conceived "a marvellous hate," which struck deep roots in a soil naturally too prolific of such plants.[9] He confiscated whatever property of Saint-Pol lay still within his reach; but he was compelled to adjourn to a more propitious moment his hopes of an ampler revenge. At present he could act only on the defensive; the entanglements were many, requiring a prudent handling; and in prudence he was less deficient than has been commonly supposed. It was towards England that his eyes directed their most anxious glances. Its defection would involve not merely an addition to the other hazards of the war — the possible loss of a battle or of a strip of territory, to be repaired at some future day — but a serious blow, permanent in its effects, at the vital interests, the commerce and industry, of the Netherlands. His anger against Edward was not decreased on learning that that prince, now an outlaw and a mendicant, was come to seek assistance at his hands and an asylum in his states. He would rather have been told that his brother-in-law was dead,[10] that the Easterlings, who were then at enmity with the English, and whose ships Edward had narrowly escaped in his flight, had succeeded in intercepting him. The stadt-

[8] Commines, tom. i. p. 221.

[9] "Conceut une merveilleuse hayne contre luy, qui jamais depuis ne luy partit de cueur." Ibid. p. 218.

[10] "Eust beaucoup mieulx aymé sa mort." Ibid. p. 249.

holder of Holland, Louis de Bruges, Lord of Gruthuse,[11] had received the exiled monarch, at his landing, with all courtesy and respect, and sent notice of his arrival to the duke. The latter, while he ordered that Edward should be suitably lodged, and assigned a pension of five hundred crowns a month for his support, would not compromise himself openly by inviting him to his court. He lost no time in despatching a new embassy to Calais — where the well-known Neville crest, "the rampant bear, chained to the ragged staff," had been hastily assumed by all the inhabitants from the governor downwards — and sent letters to Wenlock and the magistrates, written in English and with his own hand, proclaiming his intention to maintain the alliance intact, reminding them of his Lancastrian descent, declaring his readiness to recognize whatever dynasty the nation might itself establish, and warning them not to imperil the safety of their town and the true interests of their country by lending their countenance to the pernicious schemes of Warwick, and suffering troops to be landed sent from England to the assistance of the French king. "I shall be sorely grieved," he wrote, "if the ambition of a single man should give occasion for dissension and hostilities between me and a people and kingdom to which I have ever shown myself so strongly attached. But if you cannot endure my

[11] The same nobleman whom we saw giving prudent counsel to Charles in his troubles at Ghent (ante, Book II. ch. 1), and honorably distinguished for his patronage of letters and the early Flemish printers.

friendship, by Saint George, who knows me for a better Englishman and a more hearty lover of that kingdom than you or any other English, you and all those who desire to put it to the proof shall learn by the result whether I am descended from the blood of Lancaster or partake of its qualities. I had rather show it by my friendship than my enmity; but take me as you desire to have me; for such, to the fullest extent, you will find me."[12]

This mixture of menace, flattery, and remonstrance, or rather perhaps the considerations to which it pointed, did not fail of the due effect. Calais was then the emporium of the trade in wool, the most important branch of commerce between England and the Netherlands.[13] The mercantile community of England had a deep stake in the preservation of the alliance, and its voice even then was too potential in such matters to be disregarded by Warwick, who thus found himself compelled to remain neutral in a contest in which his own interests were not less concerned than those of his ally. For the struggle for supremacy between the French king and the duke of Burgundy, revived by the late change in the government of England, involved the question in what

[12] Hist. de Bourgogne, tom. iv. preuves, p. cclxxxix., where the letters are in French, apparently contemporaneous translations. See also Commines (who was again an envoy), tom. i. p. 251 et seq.

[13] Commines notices the great activity of this trade at Calais, and its importance to the commercial interests of London (tom. i. p. 255). In 1558, after the capture of Calais by the duke of Guise, the *entrepôt*, or, as it was called, the "staple," of the trade in wool was removed to Bruges. Guicciardini, p. 355.

hands that government was to rest. Louis had formed the combinations which had led to the overthrow of Edward; and now Charles, with a policy not unworthy of his rival, was laying plans for the overthrow of Warwick. Efficient instruments for this design were ready to his hand. The dukes of Somerset and Exeter, hereditary chiefs of the Lancastrian party, having enjoyed for several years the hospitality of the Burgundian court, were about returning to their native country, to the enjoyment of their rightful honors and estates. They owed the termination of their life of exile and dependence, and the triumph of their cause, to a revolution effected by the man who, beyond all others, had been the object of their hatred. This circumstance had occasioned little change in their feelings towards him. Or rather, jealousy was now superadded to a deeply-rooted enmity. Warwick, if no longer an open foe, was equally detested as a rival; they had the same interest as ever in unseating him from his position, and they readily entered into an engagement with the Burgundian prince to exert their influence for that purpose. After their departure Charles began to lend a favorable ear to the urgent and incessant supplications addressed to him by Edward to assist him in an enterprise for the recovery of his crown. In the face of his late professions, he could not openly support or countenance a hostile expedition against England, and he issued a proclamation forbidding his subjects to take part in it. But privately he gave his approval, supplied the requisite funds,[14] and hired a fleet of vessels from the Easterlings to convey Edward and his followers, with such recruits as might be secretly enlisted, to the English coast.[15]

Having no longer any immediate danger to apprehend on this side, and leaving the different schemes he had devised for extinguishing the source of danger to work out their appointed end, Charles took the field, towards the close of February, 1471, prepared to try his strength with the king of France and commit their quarrel to the arbitrament of war. Though the forces of the two Burgundies had been prevented from coming to his assistance, his army numbered not less than thirty thousand combatants, perfectly equipped, comprising all the different kinds of troops which made up the feudal array and which were deemed essential to its full efficiency, and furnished with a variety of weapons, most of them long since superseded by that single instrument which scatters death so widely on modern fields of battle. Fourteen hundred wagons carried the artillery and warlike munitions. The passage of the Somme was effected at Picquigny, a small but fortified town, which was quickly taken by assault, the castle, though of great

[14] Fifty thousand *florins à la croix de Saint-André*—equivalent to 5,175,000 francs of the present currency of France. Commines, tom. i. p. 257, note.

[15] Commines, tom. i. pp. 256, 257.—Edward had one or more interviews with his brother-in-law, at Aire, January 2–4, and at Saint-Pol, January 6. His sister, the duchess of Burgundy, paid him a visit about the same time. Ancien Chronique, Lenglet, tom. ii. p. 197. And see Haynin, tom. ii. p. 158.

strength, being surrendered by the garrison, whose numbers were inadequate for its defence. Resolved, if possible, to bring the contest to an immediate and decisive issue, the duke held his course straight towards Amiens, and met with no serious resistance till he arrived before its walls. Twenty-five thousand troops — including twelve hundred lances, "the best in France," and four thousand archers of the bands established by the ordinances of Charles the Seventh, and denominated "frank-archers," were assembled in that place, under the command of Dammartin, the Constable, the Admiral, and other great officers of the crown; a vast number of the nobility, with their feudal retainers, had gathered around the royal standard at Beauvais; and the king was earnestly entreated not to refuse the battle offered on such advantageous terms, or miss so fair an opportunity for crushing the rebellious vassal who had presumed to cope with him as an equal.[16]

But now, as ever, Louis declined to stake his fortune and his hopes on a single cast of the die. In the present instance, it was not merely that he would not venture the risk of a defeat, — and to one who stood upon such slippery ground a single defeat would be inevitable ruin; victory itself, even were it certain, offered but a questionable gain. Instead of confirming the doubtful fidelity of many of his ad-

[16] Lettre de A. Maziles, Hist. de Bourgogne, tom. iv. preuves, p. ccciii. — Haynin, tom. ii. p. 170 et seq. — Commines, lib. iii. cap. 3. — Letters, &c., in Dupont, tom. iii. preuves, pp. 275-281. — Gachard, Rapport sur les Archives de Dijon, and notes to Barante, tom. ii. pp. 371, 372.

herents, it would afford them the opportunity which they sought of forming a compact on their own terms with his assailant. It was enough that he had the means of repelling the attack, of defending the conquests he had already made. While, therefore, he exhorted his generals to show by their vigilance and their valor in defence that they had had experience in war, had fought against the Talbots, the Salisburys, and other heroes of a former strife,[17] — he forbade any encounter with the enemy in the open field. "Destroy the fauxbourgs on the side of Picardy," he wrote in substance to Dammartin; "cut down the hedges and the trees, and whatever else might shelter the approaches of the foe. Do not wait to excuse yourself hereafter by saying that you did not expect to be assailed at this point or that. Establish convoys for the safe conveyance of provisions from Paris, Rouen, and other places; maintain strict justice and discipline, and you will be in no want of supplies; above all, keep me constantly informed as to your condition." [18]

The wisdom of this policy was justified by the event. After a vigorous bombardment continued for several weeks, with a "horrible destruction" of steeples and walls, no solid advantage had been gained, nor was there the slightest prospect of bringing the siege, if such it could be called, to a successful termi-

[17] "J'ai bien esperance que vous . . . montrez que vous avez autrefois vu le Comte de Salisberi, Tallebot, l'Escalles et tous ces gens-la." Duclos, tom. iii. preuves, p. 308.

[18] Duclos, tom. iii. preuves, pp. 307, 308.

nation. An assault was out of the question, the defenders, exclusive of the citizens, being hardly less numerous than the assailants; and the manœuvres by which it was attempted to draw out the garrison and bring on a general action, led only to some partial sallies and desultory skirmishing. At length the hostile parties began to negotiate. According to Commines the first overtures came from Charles, who, wearied and disgusted with a fruitless enterprise, and enraged at the duplicity of Saint-Pol and his confederates,—made more apparent by the secret communications still constantly going on,—determined to cut short these delusive intrigues, and despatched a billet—"six lines, in his own hand"—to the king, in which he "humbled himself," expressing his regret that the treacherous instigation of those who were playing false with them both should have led to the renewal of the war.[19] Louis received these advances joyfully. A truce for three months was quickly made. Some places in Burgundy which had been captured by the royal troops were restored to Charles, but the towns on the Somme remained in possession of the king. The truce, in fact, though followed on both sides by a partial disbandment of forces, was merely a suspension of arms; and hardly

[19] Commines, tom. i. p. 225. On the other hand, Louis, in a letter written at the time (Duclos, tom. iii. preuves, p. 310), states that the overtures had been made through Saint-Pol; while Charles, in a communication to the municipality of Dijon, speaks of the proposals for a truce as having come from the opposite side. (Hist. de Bourgogne, tom. iv. preuves, p. ccciv.) These different accounts are not perfectly irreconcilable.

had it been concluded when events occurred elsewhere which could not fail to have the effect of reviving the struggle in a more determined spirit and more sanguinary form.

Somewhat less than six months had elapsed since his sudden and enforced departure from the shores of England, when Edward of York again approached them, to reassert his title to a crown, lost, if not justly forfeited, by his own wanton defiance of fortune.[20]

[20] Excepting in a few particulars, taken chiefly from sources not hitherto examined, we have exclusively adhered, in this account of Edward's expedition, to the contemporary narrative edited by Mr. Bruce for the Camden Society, and previously consulted in manuscript by Sharon Turner. Michelet, who finds it substantially the same as that given by the Burgundian chronicler Wavrin de Forestel, is obviously mistaken in supposing it to have been derived from the latter. On the contrary, the French is a mere translation, with some amplifications, from the English narrative, which was undoubtedly prepared by a person in Edward's suite and an eye-witness of the events described, and that for the express purpose of being transmitted to the Burgundian court and disseminated on the Continent. ("Plaise vous sçavoir," wrote Edward himself to his brother-in-law on the 28th of May, "que nous vous envoyons par le porteur de ceste, *une mémoire en papier*, contenant *tout au long* nostre conduite et bonne fortune, depuis le tems de nostre département de vostre pays jusqu'à maintenant." Hist. de Bourgogne, tom. iv. p. cccvi.) Accordingly, we find another, though shorter and freer translation of it in Basin (tom. ii. lib. iii. cap. 9–13), a writer of Burgundian proclivities; while a contemporaneous abridgment (of which an English translation, taken from a copy in the library of Ghent, may be found in the Archæologia, vol. xxi. pp. 11–23) has been published from a manuscript in the Bibliothèque Impériale, by Mademoiselle Dupont. (Mem. de Commines, tom. iii. preuves, pp. 281–291.) That the document at Ghent is an abridgment, and not the original "*mémoire en papier*," is proved as well by the style as by its not answering to the description in Edward's letter. The objection to all the other detailed accounts, unless Warkworth's be an exception, is, not that they emanated from Lancastrian sources, but that they were compiled long subsequently to the events.

His followers, part of them the companions of his exile and part Flemings, efficiently armed, and numbering in all about two thousand men, were divided chiefly among four large luggers, which with fourteen vessels of a lighter draught composed his fleet. It made its appearance the day after setting sail from Flushing, off the coast of Norfolk, where Sir Robert Chamberlain and others were sent on shore to communicate with known adherents of the house of York, and ascertain from their accounts of the state of the country and the sentiments of the people whether this were a favorable place for the descent. They brought back a report that the duke of Norfolk, on whose friendly disposition much reliance had been placed, was absent, and that the earl of Oxford, sent down from London, was already making preparations to resist an invasion. The ships then continued on their way till they reached the mouth of the Humber, where they were scattered by a tempest, and driven ashore at different points along the northern border of that estuary. Edward, with the Lord Hastings, and five hundred men who had sailed in the same ship, landed on the 14th of March, at Ravenspur, where seventy years before the banished Henry Bolingbroke had disembarked to establish that dynasty which the present adventurer had himself overturned. He passed the night at a "poor village," two miles from the sea, and the next morning was joined by his brother Richard, who, with his ship's company of three hundred men, had effected a landing near the same spot; by his brother-in-law Earl Rivers, who had been driven fourteen miles further up the coast; and by the rest of the party. A conference was held, and it was resolved, seemingly on a suggestion of the moment, instead of recrossing the Humber and marching directly to the south, to advance westward towards York, and to publish, on the way, as Edward's purpose, that he had come not to set up his pretensions to the crown, but merely to recover his hereditary title and estates. Scouts were sent before to disseminate this statement, to learn the condition of affairs and the temper of the inhabitants, and, by a judicious distribution of the money furnished from the coffers of the duke of Burgundy, to neutralize opposition or gain support for the cause.

The people had already begun to assemble in arms at various points along the route, less, however, with any hostile feeling to the person of the pretender, than from alarm at the prospect of a fresh outbreak of civil war in a part of the country which had been so often wasted by contending armies. Such being their disposition, it was found not difficult to content them with a declaration which offered the chance of a final and peaceful settlement of the dispute. They withdrew therefore from the towns and villages, leaving an open and deserted road to the invaders, who, "sometimes comforted and sometimes discomforted" by the contradictory intelligence that reached them, still pursued their march, till they arrived, on the 18th, before the walls of York. The magistrates and other principal citizens, having assembled within the gates, after a short parley admitted

Edward and a few of his attendants. They, too, affected to be satisfied by his professions, confirmed, according to some accounts, by his oath;[21] and his whole company were received into the city, where they lodged that night, and were hospitably entertained.

The next morning they departed towards the south, and passed unmolested the castle of Pomfret, though occupied by a garrison under the marquis of Montague, brother of Warwick, who had been sent thither for the express purpose of meeting a contingency like the present. The example given by York, the chief city of the north, insured a like reception at other places in the shire. The earl of Northumberland, the greatest landed proprietor in these parts, was privately well affected to the enterprise, but refrained from joining it, lest he should excite a division among his tenantry, most of whom were of a different way of thinking. Influenced by this inactivity and apparent neutrality of the principal nobles, the gentry also remained quiet; and the little party of adventurers passed along, through the midst of enemies and of friends, without either receiving support or encountering opposition, neither party caring to provoke a collision or give the signal for bloodshed. At Wakefield they received the first

[21] Such is the assertion, credible enough in itself, of later Lancastrian writers. The suppression of the fact, if fact it were, by the Yorkist official narrator, who does not scruple to admit the lie minus the oath, shows, if not a regard for truth, at least a perception that the time had not yet come when a talent for perjury was to be ranked among the fitting accomplishments of princes.

small addition to their numbers, and at Nottingham they were joined by "two good knights" with some six hundred followers. Here they learned from their scouts that a hostile force was gathering on their flank. By the course they had taken they had evaded the earl of Oxford, who had marched northward along the coast for the purpose of meeting them,[22] and had now turned in pursuit of them, with the duke of Exeter, the Lord Bardolph, and four thousand troops collected in the midland counties. To seek the earliest occasion of encountering his enemies, and by an exhibition of dauntlessness and vigor to awaken the sleeping courage of his adherents, was Edward's policy, as it was his instinct. He diverged, therefore, from his route, with the purpose of attacking the Lancastrians at Newark; but at his approach, their leaders, startled by this unexpected movement, took suddenly to flight, and a force which, had it merely hung upon his rear, might have embarrassed his progress and frustrated his design, was at once disbanded and dispersed.

Returning to Nottingham, he "determined to keep the next and right way towards his great rebel, the earl of Warwick," who had set out from London for his own county, to arm his retainers and confront the handful of invaders who, as if protected by a secret charm, were advancing, unobstructed and un-

[22] Oxford's preparations in Norfolk, and his purpose "to follow and pursue" Edward, "if he should arrive northward as ye weet by likelihood he should," appear from his letters to his brother and to other persons, which have been printed by Fenn.

challenged, into the heart of the kingdom. But the time was already past when a slight repulse — the mere show of resistance — might have been fatal to the enterprise. At Leicester Edward received a re-enforcement of three thousand men; his partisans, encouraged by his boldness, had begun to stir themselves; and from this point every onward step was attended with a fresh accession to his strength. Instead of meeting him in the field, Warwick, though still superior in the number of his forces, retired within the walls of Coventry, and waiting for Clarence, Montague, Oxford, and others of his party, to come to his assistance, refused the challenge to an immediate combat. Having renewed his defiance on three successive days, Edward pushed forward and occupied the town of Warwick, and here on the battlements of his foe first unfurled the royal standard and issued his proclamations as the rightful monarch of England.

And now it was seen that the power thus openly assaulted had been already covertly sapped. From the first it had been deficient in the elements of stability. The revolution on which it was based might be termed an accident in the natural sequence of events. The pretensions of the house of York, however doubtful their validity in constitutional law, had clearly a far greater vitality, a stronger force of public sentiment in their favor, than those of the house of Lancaster. The traditionary sympathies appealed to by the latter prevailed chiefly in the remoter districts of the country, among the rude population of Cornwall, Wales, and the northern shires,[23] always the strongholds of obsolescent opinions and decaying sects. The central parts of the kingdom, the towns, the trading population, were on the side of Edward. The Yorkists, whatever the characters of their leaders, represented the party of progress, which sooner or later, under one form or another, was sure to obtain the ascendency. Their opponents had gained little support by the recent change in the government. As long as Henry remained secluded from the world, imagination might invest him with the virtues of a saint, and pity create a sympathy in his behalf. When he had been again brought before the public eye, nothing was visible but his incapacity. He was merely the tool of a subtle and unscrupulous ambition; and Warwick, detested as a renegade by his old companions, was regarded by his new allies with secret aversion and distrust. Even in his own family there would seem to have been disaffection, if not actual treachery; while the duke of Clarence, defrauded even of his chance of inheriting that crown which had been promised him as the immediate reward of desertion and rebellion, had become a fit subject for the arts of seduction employed by the opposite party. Even before his departure from France, a lady in the household of his wife had been the medium of communications from his brother; [24] and since his return

[23] Turner makes the singular mistake of supposing that the Yorkists predominated in the north. He is contradicted by an express statement of his own guide — the official narrator.

[24] Commines, tom. i. pp. 241, 242.

to England, the influence of his mother, of his sisters the duchesses of Exeter and Suffolk, "and most especially my lady of Burgundy," who "at no season ceased to send her servants and messengers to the king where he was and to my said lord of Clarence, into England," with "the mediation of certain priests and other well disposed persons," had completed the conquest. Accordingly, having assembled his retainers and "such as would do for him," to the number of more than four thousand, Clarence now hastened to the scene of action, where his help was confidently expected by each of the hostile parties. In an open field, at the distance of three miles from Warwick, the brothers met, and in the presence of all their followers, drawn up in martial array, exchanged greetings hardly less affectionate than those which, as related in the last chapter, had sealed the reconciliation between the French king and the duke of Guienne.[25]

[25] "M.gr le roy et frère, venant atoute ses gens ung matin, mon frère de Clarense qui venoit ausy atout grant puissance vers luy, se trouverte au chans près l'eun de l'autre assés près d'eune ville nommée Bancbry; lors chescun mit ses gens en ordonanse, et se tira mondit s.r de Clarense, à petite conpagnie arière de ses gens, en aprochant mondit s.gr et frère, lequel se véant vient vers luy, et mondit, s.r de Clarense se mit à genous, tellement que mondit s.r et frère véant son humillité et parolles le leva et baisa plusieurs fois, et firent grant chière, et lors il crierent 'Vive le roy Eduart!'" Letter of the duchess of Burgundy to her mother-in-law, the duchess-dowager, in Haynin, tom. ii. pp. 188–193.

This letter, which has not been cited by any English historian, contains what was probably the first intelligence sent to the Burgundian court of Edward's movements after his landing. The bearer of the news, an Englishman, left London on the morning after the battle of Barnet, but while crossing the Channel was captured by the Easterlings, who, however, landed him in Zealand. The tone of the letter evinces the same ardent interest on the part of the writer in the for-

Thus betrayed, Warwick had the choice of leaving Edward to continue his march to London, — where there was little reason to expect that he would meet with a repulse, — of leading forth his troops, dispirited and weakened by desertion, to encounter an enemy now superior in numbers and confident of victory, or of himself following the example of Clarence, abandoning a cause which he was incompetent to uphold, and crowning his strange career by this last and basest act of perfidy and treason. The temptation was placed before him in the form of "divers good conditions," which might not, perhaps, have been rejected, if the arrival in the mean while of the earl of Oxford and the duke of Exeter had not cut short the opportunity for negotiation. For Edward there could be no greater hazards than those which, in a crisis like the present, must result from any apparent lack of confidence or vigor; and however indolent he might seem in a state of fancied security, he had never failed, when aroused, to exhibit these qualities in a remarkable degree. Once more he drew up his forces in battle array before the walls of Coventry, and, his challenge being still disregarded, set out, without further delay, in the direction of the capital, protecting his rear, in case of pursuit, with "a good band of spears and archers," and sending messages

tunes of her own family and in the politics of her native country which made her at a subsequent period so active an intriguer against the first Tudor sovereign. It is a fact characteristic perhaps of Charles, as well as of his wife, that the name of Margaret of Burgundy, "the persecuting Juno of the English Æneas" — is a cipher in the history of the Netherlands.

before to "his true lords, servants, and lovers," in the city, who thereupon "advised and practised how that he might be received and welcomed."

It is remarkable how much the invasion was indebted for its steady progress and complete success to the nature of the preparations made for resisting it. At the first news of Edward's landing, the Lancastrian nobles had scattered to their respective counties, to raise their retainers and bring them into the field. The duke of Somerset, his brother the marquis of Dorset, and the earl of Devonshire, had hastened to the south-west, and having collected their adherents, were awaiting on the coast the arrival of Margaret and her son, whose presence might be expected to breathe new life into the cause, and whose long continuance in France, after the triumph of their party, is one of the most singular features in the affair. It is attributed by contemporary writers to the prevalence of adverse winds. As Edward, at the same season, had made a longer voyage from the coast of Holland, it may be suspected that the winds in the Channel were under the control of the French king, in whose ships the queen and her party were to sail, and who was perhaps desirous that Warwick should have time to secure his own supremacy in the government before Margaret's advent on the scene. In this dispersion of the Lancastrian chiefs, Warwick's youngest brother, the archbishop of York, had been intrusted with the charge of Henry's person and the care of providing for the defence of the capital. Being warned of the enemy's approach, he called upon the citizens to take arms, and by way of animating their loyalty and courage, placed the imbecile monarch on horseback and conducted him in a procession from Saint Paul's through Cheapside and other principal streets. No better means could have been devised for revealing the total lack of sympathy in those to whom the appeal was addressed and the weakness of the cause which it was intended to support. No loyal cheers were raised, no hats were thrown up, no prayer of "God bless King Harry," greeted the pageant as it passed. The mayor and aldermen, who had assembled in council, and watched for some indication of the popular feeling, were now safe in deciding not to expose the city to the hazards of an assault. The archbishop, equally satisfied of his own impotence, lost no time in communicating with Edward and making terms for himself. The partisans of the house of York were suffered to take possession of the Tower; the city gates were thrown open; and on the 11th of April, a month from the day on which he had quitted Holland, the restored monarch made his entrance into London at the head of his army and amid the general acclamations of the people.

He went first to Saint Paul's, and thence to the episcopal palace, where the archbishop "presented himself to the king's good grace, and, in his hand, the usurper, King Henry." The vanquished monarch submitted to his fate without reproaches and seemingly without regret. Embracing his rival, who had merely offered his hand, "Cousin," he said, "I bid you welcome; my life, I ween, will be safe in your hands." The conqueror, half-contemptuously, bade him be at ease and feel no apprehensions,[26] and again mounting his horse, proceeded to Westminster, where, after he had "made his devout prayers," he was welcomed by his queen, who at the time of his flight had taken sanctuary within those inviolable precincts. During his absence she had given birth to a son, whom "she presented him at his coming, to his heart's singular comfort and gladness." He recognized in this ill-fated child — the future Edward the Fifth — an omen and a pledge of the security of his conquest.

Hitherto not a single drop of blood had been spilled in the progress of a revolution which seemed already to be complete. The crown had been restored to Edward as strangely and almost as suddenly as it had been restored to Henry a few months before. But this latter transfer was destined to be final; and the rivalry that had so long divided and convulsed the nation, breeding mortal strife between neighbors and kin, arming brother against brother and father against son,[27] had been too violent in its course to have a

[26] "Mondit s.gr et frère ly tendy la main, mais le roy Henry le vient embrachier en disant: 'Mon cousin vous soyés le très bien venu, je tiens que ma vie ne sera pas en dangier en vo mains, et mondit s.r et frère luy respondy qu'il ne se sousiast de riens, et qu'il povit ferre bonne chierre.'" Letter of the duchess of Burgundy, Haynin, tom. ii. p. 189.

[27] The scene in which Shakspeare represents a father slain by his son and a son by his father, in one of the battles of these wars, faithfully depicts the division that existed in the nation. Among the higher ranks, there was not a conspicuous man on either side but was nearly related by blood to leaders of the opposite faction. This alone goes far to show that there were nobler motives at work than those arising out of a mere

peaceful end. The suspense, the stupefaction, was over; the agony and tragical conclusion were at hand.

Warwick, reënforced by Montague, had, as had been foreseen by Edward, followed him closely in his march. If London should refuse him entrance, the king would be enclosed by enemies and cut off from every chance of succor or possibility of retreat; or, failing this contingency, it was hoped that his soldiers, in the certainty and exultation of their triumph, would abandon themselves to the celebration of the approaching Easter festivities, and, surprised in a state of riot and disorder, be found incapable of resisting an attack. But both expectations proved alike groundless. Far from suffering his energies to relax, Edward was still impatient for the hour when Victory should set her seal on his success. What he had already done was to recover the confidence of his

scramble for spoils. The knight who died rejoicing that he had "kept the bird in his bosom" must have believed that there were principles involved in the contest. The duke of Exeter was content to beg his bread in the streets of the Flemish towns, while his wife took her place by her brother's side in the court of England. In the middle and lower ranks the division of sentiment was not less marked. Generally speaking, the populace of the larger towns was on the side of York. Yet many deserted Edward for Warwick, regarding him as the proper chief of the party. One fruitful source of error on this subject is the idea commonly attached to the word "retainers." On the Continent, the opinions of the noble decided those of his tenantry. But this, as we have seen in the instance of Northumberland, was not so uniformly the case in England. Moreover the yeomanry and freeholders — a class that had no existence on the Continent, were accustomed of their own free choice to attach themselves to the standard of some popular nobleman, and were hence classed among his retainers — as was also the case with many inhabitants of towns, from causes to be hereafter noticed.

own party. What he had still to do was to encounter and subdue his enemies. *He* had possession of the capital. *They* were strongest in those parts of the kingdom where the influence of the capital was little felt, where the feudal principle still retained its vigor, and where, consequently, large bodies of men not unpractised in the use of weapons could be most easily collected and brought into the field. Unless he could succeed in beating in detail the forces now mustering against him, he was still in danger of being overwhelmed and crushed by superior numbers. Instead, therefore, of waiting to receive the attack, he determined to meet the approaching foe, of whose movements he had been kept constantly advised. Taking with him the unfortunate Henry, of whose person he was minded in every contingency to keep possession, he quitted London on the second day after his arrival. At Barnet, ten miles from the metropolis, his advance guard came in contact with that of Warwick, and drove it from the town. The main body of the Lancastrians lay encamped, half a mile off, "under a hedge side," on a broad and level heath. It was late in the evening when Edward came up; yet he would not allow his people to quarter themselves in the town, but removed at once into the fields, where he encamped, in the darkness, some what nearer than he had intended to the hostile army, though not immediately in its front. Commanding absolute silence to be preserved throughout the night, he snatched a few hours' repose; while the guns with which the Lancastrians were well supplied boomed at intervals, but, being aimed in complete uncertainty of the enemy's position, inflicted no damage.

Between four and five o'clock, on Easter morning (April 14), both armies were astir. The ground was covered with so thick a fog that it was impossible, even after the sun had risen, for either party to discern the disposition of the other or form any estimate of their relative strength. Nevertheless the king, committing "his cause and quarrel to Almighty God, advanced banners, did blow up trumpets," and, having first ordered his artillery to open, took his place, on foot, in the centre of his line, and charged with all his forces. His left wing, overlapped and thrown into disorder, was quickly driven from the field, the stragglers, as they fled, spreading rumors of defeat. But defeat never fell upon his arms where Edward fought in person. Whatever his defects as a politician, as a soldier and a general he had no equal in that age. His impetuosity and prowess inspired his followers with an invincible courage. Assailing his enemies "in the midst and strongest of their battle," he "beat and bore down before him all that stood in his way," and, turning first to the one hand and then to the other, followed up each fresh advantage with unwearied ardor till the field was completely won. Three hours sufficed for the struggle, the discomfiture, and the rout. The number of the slain is variously reported; but the carnage was probably great, for the cry of "Spare the people!" which, to the honor of the English name, had never been disregarded in the moment of victory throughout these civil wars, was in this battle unheeded or unheard.[28] Among those who fell on the Lancastrian side were the earl of Warwick and the marquis of Montague. The latter is said to have been slain by his brother's people, while in the act of deserting to the enemy.[29] Warwick, who, contrary to his usual practice, had dismounted and shared the perils of the common soldier, when he saw that the day was lost leaped upon his horse and made for the shelter of a wood, where, unable to find a passage, he was espied, overtaken, and put to death by his captors.[30] The bodies of both

[28] Commines (tom. i. p. 260) tells us that Edward, enraged at their former desertion of his standard and their sympathy with Warwick, had conceived a great hatred of the common people, and had determined, even before his departure from Flanders, not to grant them the customary mercy; that accordingly in the battle of Barnet no quarter was given, and the slaughter of the vanquished party was great, while on the other side not less than 1500 were slain. Warkworth, a good authority, reckons the slain on both sides at 4000. On the other hand, Sir John Paston, who was in the battle, writing a few days afterwards to his mother, says, after mentioning the men of note that had fallen, "and other people of both parties to the number of more than a thousand"—a statement followed by all recent historians. Yet this is one of the cases in which the first account is not to be regarded as the most certain.

[29] This is the statement of Warkworth, a writer with evident Lancastrian leanings. See his Chronicle, edited by Mr. Halliwell.

[30] It is a noticeable fact that the Yorkist writers are generally less unfriendly to Warwick than the Lancastrians. The official narrator says, daintily, that he was taken "somewhat fleeinge." The account in the text is that of Warkworth. It agrees substantially with that given in the letter of the duchess of Burgundy, who says, however, that Warwick's captors were leading him back, when he was recognized by another party of the pursuers and by them slain. Edward, she adds, on hearing of his capture, hastened up for the purpose of saving him, and expressed great regret for his death. (Haynin, tom. ii. p. 190.) Was the source of that regret the recollection of ancient friendship, or the disappointment of a desire to lead "his great rebel" in triumph back to London?

Warwick's attempt at flight, while

were carried to London, and exposed in Saint Paul's Cathedral, to the recognition of the populace, in order that no uncertainty might exist as to the fate of those who had borne so conspicuous a part in the strife, and whose desertion of Edward had divided the sympathy of his own adherents.[31]

On the same fatal morning on which the battle was fought a French fleet arrived off the coast of Dorsetshire, and a numerous company of ladies, knights, and gentlemen, with a small escort of troops, disembarked at Weymouth. Songs of triumph and loud gratulations were still ringing in her ears, all the misfortunes of the past were forgotten in the swelling joy and pride of an illusive present, when Margaret of Anjou once more set foot upon the English soil. The disastrous tidings brought to her on the following day occasioned a revulsion of feeling which, courageous as was her spirit and steeled by the unparalleled vicissitudes of her career, was greater than she could bear. "Her heart was pierced with sorrow, her speech was in a manner passed,"[32] she fell swooning to the

it did not save his life, seems to have been unfortunate for his fame. In the Burgundian court, at least, he had a reputation for cowardice, having in all his battles, it was said, taken previous precautions for his own safety in case of defeat. (See Chastellain, p. 485 et al.) Yet among the Burgundian cavaliers there were some, as we have already seen, and as will appear more notably hereafter, who were greater adepts in providing for their own safety than the English earl.

[31] "Pour che que mondit s.gr le roy et frère entendy que aucuns de la ville ne créoite pas que ledit Warvic et son frère fuisent mors, il fit aporter les corps lendemain, le leundy de Pasque au matin, en la dite église Saint-Pol, où il furent couchies et descouvers de la poitrine en amont à la vue de ung cescun." Letter of the duchess of Burgundy, Haynin, tom. ii. p. 191.

[32] See Polydore Virgil — who in the reign of Henry VII. collected the traditions of the Lancastrian party.

ground, and Hope fled forever from a soul which it had so long and marvellously sustained. Though surrounded by gallant and devoted followers, she proposed to abandon the struggle, and return, with her son, to the protection of her father's court — to the quiet in which hitherto she had found no repose, and which had seemed to her more intolerable than the anxieties and dangers of an earlier period. But Somerset and the other chiefs who had assembled to meet her resisted this purpose as a betrayal of their party, whose ardent loyalty, maintained throughout a long season of adversity, would be forever quenched if its leaders, at a moment like the present, should yield to the promptings of a pusillanimous despair. Far from being dismayed by the overthrow of the Nevilles, they professed to consider this as a gain rather than a loss to the cause. Its true adherents, they represented, would now come forward with greater heartiness and alacrity.[33] In the four great counties lying between the English and Bristol Channels, the whole population was devotedly attached to the house of Lancaster. The men of Dorsetshire and Somersetshire were already arrayed under the banners of their hereditary leaders; those of Devonshire and Cornwall were awaiting a summons to the field. The Welshmen were arming under Tudor earl of Pembroke; Cheshire, Lancashire, and other northern counties would

[33] Indications of the same feeling appear in the Paston Letters. Sir John and his younger brother — both taken and the latter wounded at Barnet — were far from being depressed by that defeat, and believed that their cause was now nearer to a complete triumph than it had ever been before.

speedily be roused; while even on the eastern coast, especially in Kent, there were indications of an intention to resist the usurper.

Nor would these plans for again encircling the kingdom with the flames of civil war have failed to take effect, if Edward had not watched every movement, guarded against every contingency, and thwarted every attempted combination, with a vigilance, a foresight, and a vigor that prove how great was the military genius which a deficiency in the moral elements of greatness or the lack of a loftier ambition prevented him from exhibiting with a steadier purpose, on a wider theatre of action, and with a brighter lustre to his fame. The main host of his enemies was now confined within the south-western angle of the island; and to prevent them from breaking loose, to bar their passage by whatever avenue they might endeavor to effect it, to force a battle at the earliest moment and at the remotest point, were the objects to be kept in view. If they meditated marching upon London, their shortest and easiest route lay across the table lands of Wiltshire. But as this would bring them at once into the centre of the kingdom where they could expect no reënforcements, it was more probable that they would march eastward along the coast, with the purpose of collecting their adherents in Hampshire, Sussex, and Kent. There was an equal chance, however, that they would shape their course towards the north, skirting the borders of Wales, receiving succors by the way, and anticipating, if they should succeed in reaching Cheshire unopposed, such an overwhelming augmentation of their strength as must throw Edward once more on the defensive, and deprive him of that power to follow the instincts of his intrepid nature which formed the chief advantage of his present position. Still he dared not march westward to intercept them on this last-mentioned line until by some movement of their own his conjectures should be changed into certainty. He therefore took up his quarters at Windsor, where he remained till the 24th of April, recruiting his army and waiting for the reports of the numerous scouts who had been sent to collect information. From Windsor he removed to Abingdon, and being now apprised that the Lancastrians, after proceeding to Exeter, where they had assembled the array of Devonshire and Cornwall, had set out by the northern road through Taunton and Bridgewater towards Bath, he made a rapid march to Cirencester, where he arrived on the 29th, and, in full confidence of their approach, the tidings of which were here confirmed, chose his position, three miles from the town, and prepared for battle.

Tuesday, the 30th, having passed without the enemy's making his appearance, the king, impatient of a delay which he was unable to explain, pushed forward on the following day in the direction of Bath. This movement had been reckoned upon by the Lancastrian leaders as a means of giving him the slip. He halted, however, at Malmesbury, twenty miles short of Bath, waiting for further and more exact information. His enemies, meanwhile, after giving out that they intended to march directly to meet him, had suddenly changed their course, turning aside to Bristol, where they received reënforcements of men, money, and artillery, and whence they could continue their progress northward by a different route from that on which Edward expected to meet them. The situation, as will be perceived on reference to the map, had now become exceedingly critical. On the morning of Thursday, the 2d of May, the Yorkists were at Malmesbury, the Lancastrians at Bristol. A line drawn between these two places would represent the southern base of a triangle of which the northern apex might be found either at Gloucester, at Tewkesbury, or at Worcester, according as the lines of march represented by the sides were more or less convergent. But since the more westerly line was somewhat longer than the other, forming, in fact, the hypothenuse while that was the perpendicular, it was necessary for the Lancastrians to gain at least a day's start in advance. To effect this object they again made a feint of offering battle, sending a small party to Sodbury, midway between Bristol and Malmesbury, to fix upon convenient ground for receiving the attack. Again Edward allowed himself to be momentarily deceived. He marched to Sodbury on the evening of the same day, and having selected his position, remained there during the night. Early in the morning, thanks to the vigilance of his spies, he discovered his error. The Lancastrians, having travelled all night up the bank of the Severn, were now at Berkeley, far on the road to Gloucester. To intercept

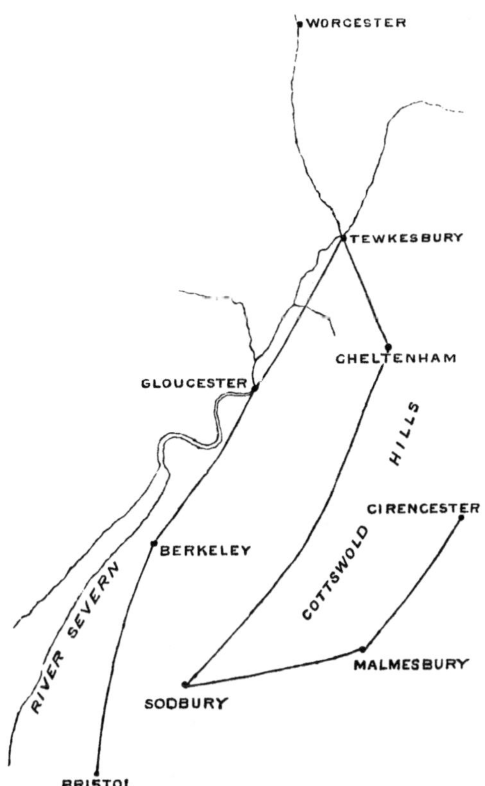
WORCESTER
TEWKESBURY
CHELTENHAM
GLOUCESTER
HILLS
CIRENCESTER
COTTSWOLD
BERKELEY
RIVER SEVERN
MALMESBURY
SODBURY
BRISTOL
BATH

them with his army before they should reach this latter point was no longer possible; and if they gained possession of the town, which was strongly fortified, they would be sheltered from an immediate attack, and would hold an excellent position for awaiting the expected succors from Wales and other quarters. There was still time, however, for a well-mounted party to carry notice of the enemy's approach to Richard Beauchamp, the newly-appointed governor of Gloucester Castle; and having despatched this warning, the king set out, with his whole army, by the nearest route to Tewkesbury, whither the Lancastrians, if they failed to enter Gloucester, would necessarily proceed, and where he trusted to come up with them.

Thus the two hostile armies were now marching in the same direction, on concentric lines, and the trial was one of endurance and of speed. The day was "right an hot" one for the season; on neither route were there any villages; and the soldiers of Edward travelled more than thirty miles without any other refreshment for themselves or their horses than what was afforded by the waters of a single brook, "where was full little relief, it was so soon troubled with the carriages that had passed it." They had, however, two advantages over the enemy. A much larger proportion of their force consisted of cavalry, and their course lay across the Cottswold, an open and level, though elevated tract of country, while that of the Lancastrians led through lanes and woods, which offered many obstructions to their progress. They lost some time, moreover, in a vain attempt to enter Gloucester, where, though the inhabitants were friendly to them, the governor was successful in preventing their admission. During the latter part of the day the distance between them and their pursuers was rapidly diminished, and the enemy's scouts began to swarm along their flank. Nevertheless, they reached Tewkesbury somewhat earlier in the evening than Edward arrived at Cheltenham, then a mere village five miles to the south-east. But all hope of making good their escape was now past. They had been on the road the whole of the preceding night, had marched since the morning a distance of thirty-six miles, and were incapable of any further advance till thoroughly refreshed by food and sleep. Here, therefore, they must stand at bay; and their leaders made choice of a position well adapted to their purpose on the hills sloping southward from the town. The ancient Saxon abbey, with its magnificent Norman church, was "at their backs; afore them, and upon every hand of them, foul lanes and deep dikes, and many hedges, with hills and valleys, a right evil place to approach as could well have been devised."

Being apprised of the enemy's intention to receive battle, Edward, after a short delay at Cheltenham, led his army two miles further towards Tewkesbury, and halted for the night. At break of day his troops were again under arms. He gave the command of the vanguard to his brother Richard, duke of Gloucester, then only nineteen years of age; the rear guard was intrusted to Lord Hastings; while the rest of the forces were led by the king in person, with the exception of a small detachment sent forward to the edge of a wood, in case an ambush had been set for an assault upon his flank. Trumpets were blown, banners unfurled, and the aid and protection of the Almighty, the Virgin Mother, the blessed martyr Saint George, and all the Saints, solemnly invoked. The cannon then opened their fire; and the whole army advanced to the attack, the lines of bowmen in front sending forth a continual flight of arrows. The Lancastrians, had they been content to avail themselves of the advantages of their position, waiting till their assailants had crossed the fences and ditches and begun to gather on the rising ground, might then by a vigorous repulse have thrown them into confusion, where confusion must have ended in rout. But they were now to experience the usual ill effects of a divided command. It was easy for the different chiefs to stimulate by their exhortations and example the courage of their men; but there was no one to direct or to restrain the ardor of the chiefs. The prince of Wales was too young to exercise any real authority. Yet his presence, and that of his mother, who had ridden through the ranks to animate the spirits of the troops, and who did not retire from the field till the battle had begun, was perhaps the reason for not investing any subject leader with the sole command. However this may have been, the duke of Somerset, whose force was posted in the front, led away either by his own impatient valor or by the restlessness of his men under the fire of the artillery and the archers, determined to leave his vantage-ground and come at once to an encounter with the enemy. He is even said to have cloven with his battle-axe the skull of one of his associates, Lord Wenlock, who opposed this rash design.[34] Descending by a slanting course through "certain paths and ways" which he had before reconnoitred, he entered an enclosed field, and falling suddenly on one end of the enemy's lines, gained a slight advantage. But the Yorkists speedily rallied. Fresh bodies came pouring to their aid. The assailants were pushed back up the hill, and were now, in their turn, taken in flank by the party which, as already mentioned, had been detached by Edward to guard against a surprise. They were soon in complete disorder. The trees and bushes, the fences, the obscure paths, which had favored the suddenness of their advance, became obstacles to their retreat. They threw away their arms and fled in different directions. But without spending time in the pursuit, the king, uniting all his forces in a solid mass, charged, with resistless vigor, the main body of the Lancastrians, whose already wavering lines were at once broken by the shock. "Such as abode hand-strokes were slain incontinent." But more were slaughtered in the chase, "flying towards the town, to the abbey, to the church;" while not a few, hotly pursued, were

[34] This is the more probable from the fact — not appreciated by modern writers — that Wenlock was no true Lancastrian, but a mere *Warwickite.*

drowned in a mill-stream that flowed through a neighboring meadow, which has retained to this day the name of "Bloody Field." [35]

About three thousand of the Lancastrians are stated to have fallen in this battle, which may properly be regarded as the last in the struggle between the rival Roses.[36] A great number of prisoners were taken in the town, and the abbey was filled with fugitives, to whom, though not entitled by any charter or ancient custom of the place to the immunities of sanctuary, the victor, when, with dripping sword, he entered the church to offer his

[35] The facts and quotations in the text for which no different authority is cited are taken from the narrative published by Mr. Bruce.

[36] The battle of Bosworth and the overthrow of Richard III. have in our view no intimate connection with the Wars of the Roses. It is true that the position and pretensions of the Earl of Richmond enabled him to rally to his standard many of the old adherents of the Lancastrian line, and in conjunction with other circumstances, pointed him out as the proper person to conduct the revolution. But it is difficult to believe that the bulk of the Lancastrian party — far greater sticklers for the cause of legitimacy and hereditary right than their opponents — should have continued for a period of fourteen years — a period following so fatal a defeat as that of Tewkesbury and the virtual extinction of the Lancastrian line; a period, too, during which the few surviving chiefs of their party were either in exile or had accepted a pardon, and during which not a solitary rising occurred — to nourish expectations of a new revival of the struggle and to centre their loyalty upon a person so little entitled to claim it as Richmond. Even from their own point of view Edward IV. must have been considered as king *de jure* as well as *de facto*. And if we look at what was of much more importance than the sentiments of a faction, — at the feelings and condition, namely, of the nation at large, — we see that the house of York had nothing whatever to fear until its own internal convulsions and crimes had inspired general disgust. In short, the revolution of 1485 bears to the "Wars of the Roses" a similar relation to that which the revolution of 1688 bears to the "Great Rebellion."

devotions, gave an assurance that their lives should be spared. But the mercy thus hastily granted was presently revoked. Among the captives were found many persons of note and noble birth. Of these the duke of Somerset and thirteen others were brought to trial, on the following day, on a charge of treason, before the duke of Gloucester sitting as Constable of England, and the duke of Norfolk as Earl Marshal. They were sentenced to death and immediately beheaded. Somerset's brother, the marquis of Dorset, and his friend the earl of Devonshire had been slain in the fight. The young prince of Wales had fallen alive into the hands of his enemies, but was put to death on the field. So much is admitted by a contemporary Yorkist writer, who was undoubtedly present.[37] The common version of this tragical occurrence is first found in works of a later date, written after the house of York had fallen by its own internal divisions and been succeeded by a dynasty that pretended to derive its title from the house of Lancaster. According to this account, the son of Margaret of Anjou, being brought before the conqueror, was upbraided with his insolence in having invaded the realm of England. Undaunted by his perilous situation, the youth made answer that he had come to recover the inheritance which was justly his. Enraged by these words of defiance from a

[37] "Edward, called Prince, was *taken* fleinge to the towne wards, and slayne, in the fielde." Historie of the Arrivall of Edward IV. in England and the finall Recouerye of his kingdomes from Henry VI. p. 30.

beaten foe, the king, without replying, struck or pushed him in the face with his gauntleted hand — a signal to Gloucester, Clarence, and Hastings, who were standing near, and by whose barbarous daggers the gallant boy was instantly despatched.[38]

From Tewkesbury Edward marched to Worcester and thence to Coventry — a central position, where his army was daily augmented by numbers that had waited for a decisive victory before joining his standard, and whence he prepared to strike another blow in whatever quarter his enemies might first gather head. But the clouds on the distant horizon broke and rolled away before his threatening glance. In some of the northern shires, risings had commenced; but the people now proffered their submission to the earl of Northumberland on condition of a general pardon. The men of Kent, under the leadership of the Bastard of Falconberg, — a somewhat famous adventurer, who had been in the pay of Warwick, but whose exploits by sea and land partook more of a piratical than a partisan character, — had advanced, during Edward's absence, to the walls of

[38] The earliest work containing this story is, we believe, the history composed by Polydore Virgil. It bears intrinsic marks of high embellishment. Its dubiousness consists, however, not, as the modern annotators insist, in the improbability that Edward, Gloucester, and Clarence should have imbrued their own hands in the blood of their youthful kinsman, — for they were all capable of this; and the latter two had each a private motive, in addition to that which all had in common, for removing him from their path, — but in the lofty language and demeanor attributed to the poor boy, or rather in the natural temptation to invest him with a halo of this kind. Warkworth's account has a simplicity and touch of pathos that look more like nature. He was killed, says that chronicler, — not asserting by whom, — "while calling for succor on his brother-in-law of Clarence."

London, and were preparing to assault them, when the news of the king's victory and approach caused their sudden flight and dispersion to their homes. Their leader was taken and executed. The few surviving Lancastrian chiefs once more abandoned the struggle, and made their escape to Scotland or to the Continent. In fact, there remained no longer any pretext for opposing Edward's title to the crown. On the 23d of May, two days after his return to the capital, his rival closed, in the Tower, a life marked throughout by the strangest contrast between internal tendencies and outward conditions. By rumor Henry's death was attributed to violence, possibly on no stronger foundation than the time of its occurrence and the obvious motives for desiring it. Those who alone had any actual knowledge of the circumstances announced it to the world as the effect of "pure displeasure and melancholy"[39] — language that might well provoke the suspicion it was apparently intended to avert.[40]

[39] "The certaintie of all whiche [the defeat at Tewkesbury and subsequent events related in the text] came to the knowledge of the sayd Henry, late called kyng, being in the Tower of London, not havynge, afore that, knowledge of the saide matars, he toke it to so great dispite, ire, and indingnation, that, of pure displeasure, and melencoly, he dyed the xxiij. day of the monithe of May." Arrivall of Edward IV. p. 38.

The date here given must be the correct one, unless — which is not at all improbable — the death was concealed for two days and purposely misdated. Warkworth says, "The same nyghte that Kynge Edwarde came to Londone, King Herry, beynge inwarde in presonne in the Toure of Londone, was putt to dethe, the xxj. day of Maij, on a tywesday nyght, betwyx xj. and xij. of the cloke, *beynge thenne at the Toure the Duke of Gloucetre*, brothere to Kynge Edwarde, and many other." p. 21.

[40] Attempts have been made to clear the house of York from this imputation — chiefly on the ground that it is unsupported by actual

All the descendants of Henry the Fourth, the founder of the Lancastrian dynasty, were now extinct.[41] The main supporters of the Lancastrian

proof, i. e. proof that can be considered as legally sufficient. But in such cases, legal proof is rarely to be found, and is still more rarely demanded, by history. That Henry's name and person should no longer serve as a rallying point for opposition must have been the immediate determination of the victor. It was with this view that he had, as we have seen, carried Henry with him to Barton; and in the preceding year, it had been thought, at the Burgundian court, one of the strangest evidences of his supineness and want of discernment, that he had not, in anticipation of Warwick's invasion, placed the captive king on board of a vessel in the Thames to be carried to Flanders or some other place of security. (See Chastellain, p. 488, where it seems to be implied that the duke of Burgundy had recommended this course.) But why, it has been asked, had he not put his rival to death at the moment of his return to London, in April, 1471? For this obvious reason, that the prince of Wales was then still alive and free, and would at once have become the object of a much stronger sympathy than had ever been felt for his father. That Henry, with his naturally apathetic mind, and after all he had passed through, should have chosen a moment so convenient to his enemies for dying of "pure displeasure and melancholy," would show a very obliging disposition on his part; and the circumstance that no symptoms of physical disease made their appearance renders the coincidence still more striking.

As to Gloucester's part in the transaction, that is of course a different question. But all the attempts to whiten the character of that prince seem to us signal failures. The belief in his guilt existed at the time, as we know from the Continental writers. Yet there is nothing stronger against him than the significant phrase of Warkworth. Shakspeare, it has been said, is guilty of an anachronism in representing the Tower as associated at that day with scenes of murder and misery. It was simply a royal residence, say the objectors. But Shakspeare may perhaps have recollected, what his critics seem to have forgotten, that to Henry at least, after his six years of imprisonment within its walls, it must have appeared a somewhat dismal abode.

41 Had the Lancastrian party really doubted that Edward IV., however invalid his previous claims, was the rightful successor of Henry VI., they would, instead of transferring their allegiance to the house of Tudor, have sought for the true heir among the descendants through a female branch of John of Gaunt. This idea, however, never seems to have been entertained in England. But among the Continental princes who might have preferred a claim

cause — those alike who had loyally adhered to it from the first and those who from motives of personal ambition had more recently embraced it — had perished with it. The revolution of the preceding year seemed to have been successful for the moment only to afford Edward the opportunity of exterminating his enemies at a single swoop.[42] A solitary figure remained upon the stage — that of the widowed, childless, desolate queen. Two days after the battle of Tewkesbury Margaret was discovered in a religious house near Worcester, and being delivered up to the conqueror, was carried in his train to London. After a captivity of five years she recovered her freedom on the payment of a heavy ransom by the French king. She then retired to Anjou. Those who saw her in her latter days were appalled at the spectral

there was one at least too eager-eyed and too ambitious of empire to overlook the possible chance of his having one day an opportunity of adding to his other titles that of "King of England." Notwithstanding the aid he had so recently given to Edward, Charles of Burgundy was no sooner informed of the death of Henry VI. than he privately obtained from his mother, the Duchess Isabella, a granddaughter of John of Gaunt, a renunciation in his own favor of her title to succeed to the throne of England; and at the same time he made a secret declaration before a notary that in abstaining for the present from a public assertion of the right thus obtained, he did not consider himself barred from putting it forth when occasion might arise. (See the documents published by M. Gachard, in his "Particularités et Doc. Inéd. sur Commines, Charles le Téméraire et Charles-Quint, pp. 5–8.) Surely Charles, though the ally of York, might have boasted that, in his regard for "legitimacy" he was more a Lancastrian than the Lancastrians themselves!

42 His own ideas, or those of his party, in regard to the complete and final termination of the struggle, may be gathered from the following extract: "It appered to every mann at eye the sayde partie was extinct and repressed for evar, without any mannar hope of agayne quikkening." Arrivall of King Edward IV. p. 38.

form and ghastly looks in which Despair had written the terrible story of his triumph over a strong and passionate heart.[43] Indebted, at the close of her troubled life, for shelter and subsistence to the charity of a former dependant, she died at the castle of Dampierre, in 1483.

Such had been the disastrous issue of the schemes concocted by Louis of France for the purpose of securing the alliance of England, or, at the worst, of prolonging the internal dissensions which had weakened the government of that kingdom and prevented it from taking its place in the front rank of his opponents. Not only had Edward recovered his crown; his power was more firmly established than ever. Henry and Warwick were both gone; the motive and the means of resistance were alike extinct. Secure in the possession of his rights, Edward was now bound by a closer tie than ever to the duke of Burgundy, who had opened the way for his restoration; while he had stronger grounds than ever for hostility to the king of France as the chief author of his recent troubles and temporary dethronement.

Louis had, in truth, experienced a cruel reverse. The bright visions in which he had begun to indulge had suddenly vanished. The "Paradise of his imagi-

[43] "Son sang calciné par tant d'agitations, affaiblit peu à peu tous ses organes; son estomac se rétrécit à un point extraordinaire, ses yeux se creusèrent, sa peau se sécha jusqu'à aller en poussière, et les regards se détournaient avec effroi à la vue d'un spectre vivant digne de pitié." Villeneuve-Bargemont, Hist. de René d'Anjou, tom. ii. notes, p. 340.

nation" had receded, and he was again plunged into Purgatorial fires, the element in which his fate had too evidently condemned him to exist. The peril that had so often haunted his uneasy mind now presented itself again in a distinct and towering form. That England and Burgundy should combine against him seemed the necessary consequence of his own futile efforts to render such a combination impracticable. Both Edward and Charles had suffered recent and unprovoked aggression at his hands, and the recoil might well be expected to prove fatal to the aggressor.

The general anticipation of this result served to set in motion all the elements of mischief and to give fresh life to the plottings and intrigues that for a while had lain idle and dormant. Once more Louis found himself abandoned, isolated, and menaced from every quarter. The duke of Guienne withdrew abruptly from his brother's court. The count of Armagnac, who had fled across the Pyrenees, boldly returned to take possession of his confiscated estates. Under the management of the Sire de Lescun all the princes of the west of France — the Foix and the Armagnacs, the dukes of Brittany and Guienne — united together in a solid league, with an avowed purpose of hostility to the king. Their emissaries were active throughout the realm in attempting to stir up discontent. The coöperation of England was invited, and the restitution of its ancient dominions in France was offered as the reward of its support. Negotiations were again opened for the marriage of the duke of Guienne with the heiress of Burgundy. In case this project should fail, it was proposed that the young prince should marry the daughter of the count of Foix, whose two sisters were wedded respectively to the duke of Brittany and the count of Armagnac. This union would have completed a family alliance between the great vassals of the crown holding contiguous fiefs on the shores of the Atlantic and the frontiers of Spain. It offered therefore many chances of political aggrandizement, and was hardly less menacing to the integrity of the kingdom and the growth of monarchical power than the Burgundian match.[44]

The mere agitation of such schemes was sufficient to fill the breast of the too sensitive Louis with anxieties and alarms. He despatched an envoy to remonstrate with his brother, to remind him of the oath he had solemnly sworn on the True Cross of Saint-Laud, and to warn him of the certain and dreadful penalty — death within the year — that attached to the violation of a vow thus taken.[45] He instructed his agent not to quit Guienne, whatever rebuffs he might receive, at least as long as Lescun remained there; to feign illness, if necessary, as a pretext for delaying his return; to keep an eye on all the move-

[44] Ambassade des Ducs de Guienne et de Bretagne à celui de Bourgogne, Hist. de Bourgogne, tom. iv. preuves, p. cccvii. — Basin. — Commines. — De Troyes. — Documents in Lenglet, tom. iii. — Duclos, tom. iii. preuves, pp. 314–316. — In the preceding summer, when the parties had been ostensibly on a most friendly footing, Louis would fain have persuaded Foix to send his daughter to the French court, promising to treat her "comme fille de Roi." See his letters to the counts of Foix and Narbonne, Duclos, tom. iii. preuves, pp. 310–314.

[45] Instructions à M. du Bouchage, Lenglet, tom. iii. pp. 160–164.

ments of the conspirators; above all, to discover means of thwarting the different projects for Charles's marriage. On this last point, the vehemence of his language, the lavishness of his promises, and the erratic flights of his fancy are equally characteristic. The envoy is exhorted to set "all his five senses" at work, and the Blessed Virgin is entreated to sharpen his wits and prosper his business. His success will put the king in Paradise. If the duke of Guienne will consent to take an unobjectionable wife,[46] his brother will never more, so long as he shall live, attempt to exercise any inspection or control over him, and he shall have as much authority as the king himself, or more, throughout the whole realm of France.[47] The daughter of the duke of Burgundy,

[46] An unobjectionable wife, in the estimation of Louis, and the person whom he was really anxious that his brother should espouse, was the spurious daughter of Henry IV. of Castile, popularly known as "la Beltrajama," from the name of her reputed father. Such an alliance would have been a fruitful source of trouble, as well as a personal degradation, to the duke of Guienne, besides kindling a civil war in Castile. Hence its doubly advantageous character in the eyes of the French king. Nor was the proposal less agreeable to Henry, who hoped by accepting it to obtain French support against the pretensions of his sister and legitimate heir, the Princess Isabella, then newly wedded to Ferdinand of Aragon. (See the negotiations on this affair in Lenglet, tom. iii. pp. 156–160.) But it was in vain that invitations were sent to the duke of Guienne from the court of Castile. He had, indeed, at one time looked in that direction with matrimonial views; but the bride whom he had sought was the Princess Isabella. He had been rejected by the lady, partly on political grounds, partly on account of his watery eyes and thin legs.

[47] "S'il veut prendre femme qui ne soit point suspecte, *tant que je vivrai*, je n'aurai inspection sur lui, et aura puissance en tout le Royaume de France autant ou plus que moi, *tant que je vivrai.* [Note the eagerness expressed in the repetition of the italicized phrase.] Brief, Monsieur du Bouchage, *mon ami*, si vous pouvez gagner ce point, vous me mettrez en Paradis."

Louis earnestly asserts, comes of a race tainted with hereditary disease. She herself is now afflicted with a horrible malady. Some say that she is dead. The king is not absolutely certain of the death, but he is positive in regard to the illness.[48]

On the other hand, Louis lost no time in making fresh overtures to the duke of Burgundy. Charles had already consented to a prolongation of the *truce;* the king thought there could be no time more suitable than the present for the conclusion of a lasting *peace,* or even of a mutual alliance, offensive and defensive, a treaty of cordial and perpetual amity between the two courts. To secure this desirable arrangement, he professed himself willing to relinquish, for the second time, his possession of Amiens and all the other towns which he had so recently and suddenly recovered. He would also abandon his protection of the count of Nevers and the Constable Saint-Pol, the two chief objects — next to the king himself — of Charles's enmity. That the latter, on his part, should withhold his support from the dukes of Brittany and Guienne, whose temporizing course had justly excited his displeasure, seemed but a mere nominal sacrifice to require from him in return. Finally, and as a means of cementing the proposed alliance, Louis — kindly overlooking the doubtful existence of his fair goddaughter, as well as her pre-

[48] "Les filles de mondit Duc de Bourgogne ont été toutes malades du mal chaud, et dit-on que la fille est bien malade et enflée, aucuns dient qu'elle est morte. Je ne suis pas sûr de la mort, mais je suis bien certain de la maladie." Letter du Roy au Sieur de Bouchage, Duclos, tom. iii. p. 316.

carious situation if she were actually alive — suggested, as the most suitable of all matrimonial connections, her marriage with his own son, a promising young prince, now upwards of a year old.[49]

Such offers as these were not to be lightly rejected. But Charles annexed to his acceptance of them two conditions of a somewhat ambiguous tendency. He required that the articles stipulating for the renunciation, by both parties, of their old alliances should be embodied in a separate instrument, bearing a different date; and he demanded the actual cession of the towns in Picardy before the treaty should be confirmed. On the former point no objection was raised; but Louis preferred to retain possession of the towns until he should have received a formal assurance, under the duke's own hand and seal, that the other portions of the agreement would be faithfully adhered to. He suggested, however, various ingenious modes of meeting the difficulty, and of satisfying Charles as to the sincerity of his intentions. He would give hostages, of such rank and in such number as might be required, for the prompt fulfilment of his obligations. His envoys should bind themselves by the most solemn oaths not to deliver the treaty into his hands, or retire beyond a certain distance from the frontier, until the towns had been given up. Or the document might be deposited, under the same pledge and on the same conditions, in the custody of the chapter of Notre-Dame at

[49] Instructione à Monsieur Craon, &c., Hist. de Bourgogne, tom. iv. preuves, pp. cccviii.–cccxi.

Paris.[50] Finding these and other propositions of a like nature wholly ineffectual, the royal ambassadors began to entertain suspicions in regard to the duke's good faith. They shrewdly doubted whether, even if he should sign the treaty, it was his intention to abide by it; and they accordingly warned their master that his rival was playing false with him. But Louis cast aside these surmises as ungrounded and frivolous. "Bring the matter to a conclusion," he wrote sharply in return. "Obtain the duke's letters in the form agreed on, and I make no doubt he will hold to them. If it concerned my life, I am resolved to trust him. Therefore send to me no more in regard to such suspicions; for, since he has declared himself by word of mouth so well affected towards me, the greatest desire I have in the world is to see the arrangement definitively settled."[51]

Several months were spent in these negotiations, but not less actively on both sides in preparations for war. The king had taken the precaution of lining all the eastern frontier of Brittany and Guienne with forces sufficient to overwhelm both provinces when the signal should be given.[52] His fears of an English

[50] Hist. de Bourgogne, tom. iv. preuves, pp. cccviii.–cccxi.

[51] Letter to the Sire de Craon and Pierre d'Oriole, Dec. 11, 1471, Duclos, tom. iii. preuves, pp. 319–323. — The whole letter is full of similar expressions of trust and eagerness, and promises of good behavior towards Charles in all time to come: "S'il plaît à Dieu et à Notre-Dame que vous ayez conclu, je vous assure que tant que je vive, je n'aurai ambassade, qu'incontinent ja ne le fasse sçavoir à Monsieur de Bourgogne," &c.

[52] De Troyes, p. 92. — Hist. de Bourgogne, tom. iv. preuves, p. cccxii. et al.

invasion had in some degree subsided. Indolence and sensuality had again thrown their chains over Edward; and neither gratitude to Charles, resentment against Louis, nor emulation of the exploits of his own warlike predecessors, could yet rouse him to fresh exertions. He contented himself with sending profuse acknowledgments of the assistance he had received from his brother-in-law, coupled with vague promises of reciprocal aid, and the removal of all restrictions upon the trade and intercourse between their respective subjects.[53] Charles, indeed, seems hardly to have counted on receiving more efficient support. It was sufficient for the moment that Warwick had been overthrown and the balance of power restored. At all events his own plans were laid without reference to the coöperation of England.[54] During the interval afforded by the truce, he was diligently employed in amassing and organizing the materials for another and more vigorous campaign in the ensuing spring. He had succeeded, also, in detaching from

[53] Lettre de remercimens, &c., Hist. de Bourgogne, tom iv. preuves, p. cccvi.—Edward addressed also a letter of thanks to his "dear and especial friends" the magistrates of Bruges (Dupont, Mem. de Commines, tom. iii. preuves, p. 202), who, seeing that the continued prosperity of their city was greatly dependent on his success, doubtless considered any donatives made to him a sound mercantile investment.

[54] He does not appear to have sent an embassy to the English court until late in 1472, when he appropriately selected for this mission the lord of Gruthuse, whom Edward, in gratitude for the civilities he had received from that nobleman, created a peer of England. About the same time Charles received from his brother-in-law a reënforcement of two thousand archers, and there were intimations of an armament to be sent to the coast of Brittany. But in the mean time the campaign was over. See a letter from the Burgundian camp, without signature, in Lenglet, tom. iii. p. 227.

the royal cause one who had been of late among its chief and most active adherents. The duke of Lorraine, the affianced husband of the king's daughter, now dissolved the engagement, as if Louis had become bankrupt, and came to join the throng of suitors for the hand of the rich Burgundian heiress.[55] The king's sister, too, the duchess Yolande of Savoy, who had hitherto maintained her position as regent by means of her brother's support, suddenly veered about, and solicited the protection of his rival.[56] Foreign powers, without a single exception, had apparently ceased to set any value on an alliance with the monarch of France. The king of Aragon seized the opportunity afforded by the withdrawal of French garrisons from Roussillon and Cerdagne to reassert his right to those territories; while the nobles of Castile, rallying around the rightful heiress to the throne and her husband the heir of Aragon, frustrated any chance which the French king might have had of creating a diversion through his alliance with the Castilian monarch. The belief was universal that Louis stood upon the brink of ruin. The confederates in the west, exulting in the prosperity of their schemes, looked forward to nothing less than the entire dismemberment of the monarchy. "The fox," they said, "was exhausted: there were so many hounds upon his track that he had no chance of escape." Their agents at the court of Burgundy pressed the duke to hasten his preparations and strike the decisive blow without waiting for

[55] De Troyes, p. 93.

[56] Guichenon, Hist. de Savoie tom. ii. p. 128 et seq.

the expiration of the truce. Still adopting the hypocritical pretence employed on a former occasion, they represented that the "welfare of the kingdom" depended on his invading it. Charles himself was more candid. "Do you think," he inquired of his chamberlain, the Sire de Commines, "that if I lead my army into France, it will be for the *welfare* of the kingdom?" And receiving a smiling negative in reply, he sarcastically added, "I love France better than these people imagine — so well that I would fain see it ruled over by six kings, instead of one.[57]

The month of May, 1472, had now arrived, and the truce was on the point of expiring. Charles had assembled an immense army on the borders of Picardy. He himself arrived at Arras about the middle of the month, prepared apparently to take the field. But almost at the same moment he suddenly withdrew his objections to the treaty, and consented to ratify it without waiting for the restitution of the towns.

In the presence of the royal envoys he swore to observe the conditions to which he had affixed his seal. The representatives of Louis took a similar oath; but it was still necessary for the completion of the formalities to obtain the ratification of the treaty from the king in person. The ambassadors were, therefore, accompanied on their return by an envoy from the duke, Simon de Quingey, who was directed, after he should have accomplished his mission, to pro-

[57] Commines, tom. i. p. 271.

ceed to the west and give notice to the dukes of Brittany and Guienne of the peace privately concluded between Charles and Louis. Such were the ostensible instructions given at the request of the king, who had good reason for doubting whether a communication of so astounding a nature, if made by himself, might not be received with disbelief and derision. But a sealed letter of a very different tenor was intrusted to an equerry of the duke with orders that it should be delivered to, and opened by, De Quingey after he should have taken leave of the French court. The real message he was to carry to the confederates was an assurance that they had nothing to fear from the engagements which Charles had entered into with the king. These engagements he had made with the full intention of breaking them. His object was to recover the territory that rightfully belonged to him. When this object was gained, he would send a warning to Louis to abstain from any act of aggression against his allies, and, if it were disregarded, he would come at once to their support. He attempted to justify this second and glaring breach of faith in his relations with his sovereign by arguments that show how the commission of the first had weakened his natural sentiments of honor, and rendered it easy to overcome such scruples as on a former occasion it had cost him so violent a struggle to subdue. He had to deal with an enemy who gained all his advantages by dissimulation and fraud, and against whom, therefore, the same arts might properly be employed. The seizure of the towns, in time of peace, without any lawful pretext and by insidious means, had itself been a flagrant violation of treaties solemnly sworn to and repeatedly confirmed. To violate a new treaty, or rather to give a pretended assent to such a treaty, was a fair method of recovering what had been thus feloniously taken. This would restore the parties to their original footing; for as to the other stipulations in his favor, it was not Charles's intention to avail himself of them. Much as he detested the counts of Nevers and Saint-Pol, he would offer them no harm during the continuance of the peace, but would extend to them the same immunity as he intended to claim for his own allies.[58]

On his arrival at Plessis, where the king was then residing, De Quingey met with a gracious reception, but with less facility for the prompt despatch of his business than from its simple nature he had reason to expect. Under various pretences Louis deferred giving his final assent to an arrangement, with the terms of which he was fully acquainted, which he had himself proposed, and for the speedy conclusion of which he had been so urgent but a short time before. At length, after having been detained for more than a week, the envoy was again summoned to the royal presence. But he found, to his surprise, a total alteration in the royal language and demeanor. Louis declined to sign the treaty, and dismissed the

[58] Commines, tom. i. pp. 280–282.

envoy with a curt and somewhat uncivil speech, that afforded no explanation of this singular conduct.[59]

The explanation, however, was not long delayed. The game had been a deeper one than some of the players had supposed. There had been duplicity on both sides; but on that of Louis, if the voice of rumor and the denunciations of his enemies might be believed, there had been something far worse than duplicity.

For several months past the young duke of Guienne, always of a delicate constitution, had been reported to be seriously ill of a quartan fever. Notwithstanding the interruption of their intercourse, the king, as appears from letters of his own, was furnished with frequent and minute accounts of his brother's condition. These accounts were the more trustworthy that they came from a person high in Charles's confidence, a monk who sat daily by his bedside and assisted him in his devotions.[60] While the prince himself was sending to the Burgundian court assurances of his improving health and capacity for fulfilling his engagements, warlike and matrimonial,[61] his spiritual attendant was privately furnishing the French court with more accurate information. On the 8th of May, Louis had written to his generals on the frontier of Guienne not to commence

[59] "Renvoya le Roy ledict Symon avec tres maigres parolles sans riens vouloir jurer." Commines, tom. i. p. 278.

[60] Lettres secrètes du Roi au Grand-Maître, Cabinet de Louis XI., Lenglet, tom. ii. pp. 242–244. Other letters to Dammartin, Duclos, tom. iii. preuves, pp. 320, 324.

[61] Instructions, &c., Hist. de Bourgogne, tom. iv. p. cccxi., and Lenglet, tom. iii. pp. 164, 165.

hostilities or attempt to make themselves masters of any towns or fortresses in that province; since he should be obliged, if his negotiations with the duke of Burgundy led only to the continuance of the truce, to restore such places as might have been captured in the interval.[62] But a week later we find him writing again, in a different strain, ordering that the war should be at once opened and carried forward with the utmost vigor.[63] In a letter to Dammartin of nearly the same date, he says that he has received intelligence by express that his brother cannot survive many days. "I am astounded at this news," he adds, "and have crossed myself from head to foot."[64]

[62] Lenglet, tom. iii. p. 186.

This letter, though short, is amusing, and shows the management which Louis was obliged to exercise in controlling his numerous agents, subordinating their operations to his own intricate policy, and preventing the zeal which he had himself kindled from outstripping his intentions and thus deranging his combinations. "Keep cool for the present, I beg of you," he writes. "If the duke of Burgundy declares war against me, I will set out at once for that quarter [Guienne and Brittany], and in eight days we shall despatch the matter. On the other hand, if peace is made, we shall have every thing without striking a blow or running the risk of being obliged to give any thing back. However, if you can get hold of any thing by negotiation and manœuvring, take it! As to the artillery [for which you have applied] it is close by you [though I do not choose at present to tell you exactly where]; and when it is time and I shall have heard from my ambassadors, you shall have it incontinently."

[63] Letters of May 14 and 15, in Duclos, tom. iii. preuves, p. 326, and Lenglet, tom. iii. p. 187.—In the former of these two letters he tells where the artillery may be found, adding, "Envoyez en querir tant que vous voudrez."

[64] "Depuis les dernières lettres que je vous ay escriptes, j'ay eu nouvelles que Monsieur de Guyenne se meurt, et qu'il n'y a point de remede en son fait, et me l'a fait sçavoir un des plus privez qu'il ait avec luy, et par homme exprès, et ne croit pas, ainsi qu'il dit, qu'il soit vif à quinze jours d'icy au plus. . . . Celuy qui m'a fait sçavoir les nouvelles, c'est le Moyne qui dit ses heures avec Monsieur de Guyenne, dont je me suis fort esbahy, et m'en suis signé depuis la teste jusqu'aux pieds, et

Charles of France expired, in fact, on the 28th of the month, somewhat less than a year after he had deserted the royal cause and renewed his alliance with its enemies. Louis, who, several years before, when told of the death of the Castilian Prince Alfonso, the brother and rival of Henry the Fourth, had dryly remarked that "the king of Castile was a fortunate prince," discerned in the present event a more potent and mysterious agency than that of fortune. The True Cross of Saint-Laud had by this awful example vindicated its miraculous power.[65]

The death of the duke of Guienne, occurring at such a crisis, could not fail to have important results. By his will, signed shortly before his decease, he had bequeathed his possessions to his brother.[66] But apart from this bequest Louis had the twofold claim of inheritance and reversion. The nobles of the province, and the magistracy of the towns, from whom Charles had recently exacted an oath of fidelity even against the sovereign himself, had now no other resource, whatever might be their real inclination, than to return to their allegiance. Guienne was thus again annexed to the royal domain. Brittany was once more separated from all its confederates. The Foix and the Armagnacs must again take to flight or again sue for pardon. The main knot of the conspiracy

adieu. Escrit au Montils-les-Tours, le 18 May." Cabinet de Louis XI. Lenglet, tom. ii. p. 243; also in Duclos, but with a wrong date. The king had received this news on the 14th. See De Troyes, p. 94.

[65] See Letter of Louis to Tanneguy du Châtel Duclos, tom. iii. preuves, p. 319.

[66] Testament, &c., Lenglet, tom. ii. p. 244 et seq.

was unloosened;[67] and it was no longer worth while for Louis to purchase the duke of Burgundy's permission to cut that knot asunder at so enormous a price as the surrender of his conquests in Picardy. This sacrifice he had been willing to make, if the end could be attained by no other means, and if assured that by this means it would be attained.[68] As long as one solution alone of his difficulties presented itself, he had resolutely closed his eyes to the dubious character of that solution. But, when thus suddenly and miraculously extricated, he perceived that he had been treading on unsafe ground; and in the letter to his generals already cited, he expresses his newly-formed conviction that the negotiation on the part of his rival had been a piece of mere dissimulation from the first.[69]

The return of his envoy with the treaty unratified, and even contemptuously rejected, followed by the intelligence of the death of the duke of Guienne and the consequent rupture of the league, had the

[67] "Croy bien que si ledict duc de Guyenne ne fust point mort, que le Roy eust eu beaucoup d'affaires; car les Bretons estoient prestz, et avoient dedans le royaulme des intelligences plus que jamais n'avoient eu, lesquelles faillirent toutes à cause de ceste mort." Commines, tom. i. p. 275.

The change of position consequent on this event is neatly and pithily indicated in an epigram of the time: —

"Berry est mort,
Bretaigne dort,
Bourgogne hongne,
Le Roy besogne."

Leroux de Lincy, Chants historiques et populaires du Temps de Louis XI.

[68] "Cuyde l'intention du Roy telle que s'il eust achevé son enterprinse aupres de là, ou que son frere vinst à mourir, qu'il ne jureroit point ceste paix: mais aussi que s'il trouvoit forte partie, il la jureroit et executeroit ses promesses pour se oster de peril." Commines, tom. i. p. 280.

[69] "En effet, ce ne sont que toutes dissimulations." Lenglet, tom. iii. p. 187.

effect of rousing the darkest and most violent passions of Charles's nature. The consciousness of his own meditated treason [70] served only to sharpen his indignation at the successful perfidy of his rival. The graver accusation pointed against Louis by the Sire de Lescun, who now fled to Brittany, taking with him the monk already mentioned and a person suspected as his accomplice, found eager acceptance at the Burgundian court, and was hurled forth in public letters and manifestoes, with a vehemence and fury that indicated the spirit in which hostilities were to be carried on. The king was charged with having conspired against his brother's life, and with having effected his cruel and horrible intent by means of "poisons, malpractices, sorceries, and diabolical invocations," as had been confessed by his suborned agents, the immediate perpetrators of the crime. The virtues of the murdered prince, not any fault or misdemeanor of his, were declared to have been the sole motives of this "execrable fratricide." All the princes and noble persons of the realm were adjured to unite in punishing the author of his death — a death so piteous and inhuman that the like had never before been heard of in France or elsewhere. The duke of Burgundy himself, laying aside for the present his original purpose in taking up arms, — that of seeking redress for his own wrongs and regaining the territory of which he had been despoiled, — was

[70] The statements of Commines in regard to Charles's conduct on this occasion have been denied. Those who care to see the question discussed may turn to the note appended to the close of this chapter.

about to march into France, to unite his forces with those of the duke of Brittany, and to exact such vengeance as God the Creator should permit on the king and all who sought to favor and protect him in his cruel and detestable course.[71] This announcement was speedily followed by corresponding acts. Though the truce, having been again renewed, was not to expire till the 15th of June, Charles, who considered it as already broken by the king, set his army in motion, and took his departure from Arras on the 4th. The troops, as presently appeared, were fully imbued with the stern spirit and furious passions of their prince. It was no War of the Public Weal they were now about to wage on the territory of France, but a war such as they had more recently waged against Liége — the war of "fire and blood," of waste, plunder, and extermination.

The first and most terrible outburst of their ferocity fell on the small town of Nesle in Vermandois, on a

[71] The manifesto in Haynin (tom. ii. pp. 202–205), and Lenglet (tom. iii. pp. 298–301), bears the date of July 16; but similar declarations had been issued in June. See Hist. de Bourgogne, tom. iv. preuves, p. cccxix.

That Louis had in fact caused his brother to be poisoned, is what Basin, who gives the particulars, knows for a certainty, and what Commines — who makes only a very delicate allusion to the subject — does not venture expressly to deny. Had Louis been tried before a modern jury, with a Phillips or a Choate for his advocate, he would doubtless have been acquitted. As he was not to be tried, he seems to have troubled himself very little about the accusation, taking probably the same philosophical view as Commines, who says that nothing was gained by making the charge, for no popular rebellion followed. Yet, not being able with certainty to foresee this result, the king, on hearing that his brother was at the point of death, had made provisions, though without effect, for preventing the Bretons from getting possession of the monk. (See his letter to Dammartin before cited.)

tributary of the Somme. There were no tenable defences with the exception of a castle, and the garrison numbered only five hundred archers, drawn from the militia of the province. When, therefore, the place was summoned (10th of June), the commandant, having, of course, no choice but to surrender, endeavored to obtain terms of capitulation. Possibly his efforts might have proved successful; but in the interval of the parley, some dissension seems to have arisen between the citizens and the garrison; the herald who had brought the summons was put to death; missiles were discharged from the walls, and two of the Burgundian soldiers killed. Then the troops, their fierce temper inflamed to the utmost by these provocations, burst into the town, which at once became the scene of an indiscriminate massacre. In the streets, in the houses, but especially in the churches, whither, as usual, the greater number of the inhabitants had fled for refuge, the slaughter raged for several hours. Such as evaded the sword in the first fury of the pursuit, were subsequently dragged from their hiding-places and hanged; while the archers, or most of them, were suffered to go free — after each man's right hand had been lopped off at the wrist. When the duke made his entrance into the town, after the carnage was over, but while the frightful evidences of it were still fresh and unconcealed, his demeanor and language seem to have betokened a stern though sombre satisfaction. "Such is the fruit," he is said to have exclaimed, "that grows upon the tree of war!" He entered the principal church without dismounting from his horse, whose hoofs plashed through a stream of blood that ran several inches deep upon the floor. As he gazed at this appalling sight, and at the corpses — already rifled and stripped — of men, women, and children, that lay scattered or in heaps around, he crossed himself repeatedly, muttering, as he drew his breath, "Here is a fine spectacle! Truly I have good butchers with me!"[72]

When the place had been plundered and burned, the army resumed its march, the reports of its numbers and ferocity spreading terror on every side.

The king, however, had made his preparations against the inevitable storm, with the forethought, sagacity, and promptness of decision and of action characteristic of the practised mariner, accustomed to a perilous navigation, to the rapid shifting of the wind and the fury of the rising gale. His first object was to prevent the proposed junction between

[72] De Troyes, Lenglet, tom. ii. pp. 94, 95. — Commines, tom. i. pp. 275–277. — Basin, tom. ii. — Bulletins de la Société de l'Hist. de France, 1833–4.—The last-mentioned work contains the depositions of several old inhabitants of Nesle, taken fifty years after the event, and, as may easily be supposed, filled with evident exaggerations. Every thing is represented as done in cold blood and by the express command of Charles, who orders that so many shall be hung, so many shall lose their hands, &c. On one important point this evidence admits of direct and sufficient contradiction. According to the venerable deponents, the place was captured by surprise and without any previous summons. On the other hand, the king, in a letter to Dammartin of June 19, 1472, asserts that a formal surrender had been made, and a promise given that the lives of the inhabitants should be spared. (Duclos, tom. iii. preuves, p. 327.) Had this been true, the affair would have been still blacker. But both stories are refuted by the unexceptionable testimony of Commines. De Troyes, who makes the same charge as Louis, says the town was summoned on the 11th and captured on the 12th of June.

the Burgundians and the Bretons, which, if effected, must lead to the same disastrous results as on a former occasion, when the sudden and combined influx of his enemies had thrown him wholly on the defensive, while the consequent defection and treachery in his own ranks had soon rendered him defenceless. He could not hope to accomplish his purpose by merely placing himself between the hostile forces to meet and repel their attacks. On one side or the other he must assume the aggressive, and that with a preponderance of strength which would enable him to make quick work, subduing all resistance before he should be in turn assailed from the opposite quarter. No such complete and speedy triumph was to be gained over a foe so formidable as Charles. Louis proposed, therefore, to make his principal demonstration against Brittany; and having stationed the bulk of his army on that frontier, he now went thither to direct the operations in person.

But though the forces he left behind were insufficient to cope with the invaders in the field, they were adequate to the defence of the large and strongly fortified towns, which would thus become places of shelter to the people of the surrounding country. He had given orders that the smaller fortresses should be dismantled and their garrisons recalled. If Charles should undertake the siege of any places capable of a protracted resistance, this loss of time would probably be fatal to the main object of his enterprise. If, on the other hand, he should leave these places unassailed, persisting in the purpose he had announced, he would inflict comparatively little damage in his advance, and foes would be constantly accumulating in his rear. The garrisons might then sally forth, intercept his communications, capture his convoys, and harass his detachments. He would find himself, at last, compelled to a precipitate retreat, or perhaps be left, with diminished numbers and scant supplies, where retreat would be no longer open to him.

Such was the plan devised by Louis; and with the means at his disposal it seems to have been the best that could have been devised.[73] Unhappily his instructions, though clear and reiterated, were neither fully nor promptly carried out. It had devolved upon the Constable to raze the fortifications at Nesle, and to provide for the safety of the inhabitants.[74] But at a crisis so perilous to his particular interests, Saint-Pol had thought first of providing for his own security; and shutting himself up in Saint-Quentin, he remained there, safe but inactive, until the torrent had swept by.

Meanwhile Charles had recovered possession of Roye, one of the towns taken by Dammartin in the previous campaign. The works, originally strong, had been recently put in a state of complete repair

[73] This policy is indicated both by his operations and by his letters to Dammartin, in Duclos, tom. iii. preuves, pp. 328–330, 333, 335, 336, 338.

[74] Louis, in a letter to Dammartin, expresses a just indignation at what had there happened through a neglect of his orders, which he reiterates. "Si ladite place eût été abatue et rasée comme j'avais ordonné, il n'en fût pas ainsi avenu; et pour ce faites que toutes semblables places soient rasées, car qui ne fera, on perdra les gens de dedans, et si me sera accroissement de deshonneur et dommage." Ibid. p. 328.

and provided with all the material for a vigorous defence. But the garrison, though numerous, was seized with a panic at the enemy's approach; and even before the summons was delivered, the archers, scrambling from the walls, came to purchase their lives by a timely surrender. A formal capitulation followed; the soldiers were allowed to depart without arms or baggage, and the inhabitants, professing unbounded loyalty to the house of Burgundy and attachment to the person of their rightful sovereign, were taken under his protection.[75] But if the atrocities committed at Nesle produced in some quarters abject fear and instantaneous submission, they aroused in others a desperate courage and a determination to resist to the last extremity. Having crossed the Somme, the army continued its march, watched on either hand by firm though anxious glances. Dammartin had taken post at Compiègne, a place deemed of great importance by the king.[76] Amiens, a more probable point of attack, was not less vigilantly guarded, Salazar and other able and experienced captains having there united their forces. Neither of these places was assailed or menaced by the duke, who, passing between them, held his course towards the west, intending to penetrate into Normandy, and expecting to be there joined by the forces of his ally.

The ancient town of Beauvais, situated in a low and fruitful valley on the Therain, one of the main branches of the Oise, lay directly in his route. It

[75] Commines; De Troyes; Ancienne Chronique; Basin, &c.

[76] Letters to Dammartin, Duclos, tom. iii. preuves, pp. 329, 337.

was a place of great strength, memorable for the sieges it had sustained and successfully withstood in the wars with the English. The walls were high and massive, the ditch was deep and wide, and flooded by canals that still drain the surrounding valley and intersect the streets. Recently, as will be remembered, the king had made it his head-quarters, as a convenient *point d'appui* in the defence of Amiens. Owing, however, to the sudden outbreak of hostilities and the more imminent danger on the frontier, the town was now left without the protection even of its customary garrison. A handful of archers, part of the affrighted garrison of Roye, had taken refuge at Beauvais; but their presence even in greater number might have been expected to spread the contagion of panic rather than inspire confidence. Yet active preparations were made for resistance, and messengers were sent abroad to spread the alarm, and solicit succors from the neighboring towns. The inhabitants of every rank and of both sexes were filled with that spirit of fierceness and resolution which the same peril that intimidates the bold sometimes develops in those who are ordinarily timid and weak.

Early in the morning of the 27th, some workmen employed in repairing the roof of the cathedral, an ancient but still unfinished structure which forms the chief ornament of Beauvais, discerned in the distance the approaching vanguard of the Burgundian army. It was commanded by Philippe de Crèvecœur, who, informed of the unprotected state of the inhabitants, but not of their courageous determination, hoped to gain immediate entrance, or, if his summons were rejected, to carry the place by a *coup-de-main* before the main body of the army should have come up. He accordingly sent forward a herald, and, a parley being declined, arranged his troops in two divisions and led them forward to the attack. On one point his men succeeded in getting possession of the fauxbourgs, though protected by strong outworks. But the inner defences were still stronger, and were more strenuously maintained. The soldiers were fain to take shelter in the church of Saint Hypolite and the adjacent houses, the walls of which they pierced, thus prolonging the combat with greater safety to themselves, but with little damage to the foe.

The other assault was directed against one of the gates. Two pieces of artillery opened upon it, but the wagons that carried the balls and other ammunition being still far behind, after a few rounds the fire was discontinued. Scaling-ladders were then brought, and, though found to be much too short, enabled a few of the more active and daring assailants to spring upon the parapet. But ere they could secure a lodgment or receive assistance from their comrades, they were overpowered and hurled back into the ditch. An attempt to storm the gate, in which a small breach had been made by the cannon, was equally unsuccessful. A hand-to-hand combat was maintained through the opening; heavy stones and other projectiles were dropped from the walls; a constant discharge of arrows was kept up; and when the attack had been repulsed, lighted fagots were thrown down in front of the gate, fresh combustibles being continually added until the burning pile had assumed such proportions as effectually kept the enemy at bay. To animate the defence, a procession of priests arrived upon the ramparts, bearing the relics of "the glorious virgin Saint Angadresme," the patroness of the town. In former sieges, according to the tradition, the figure of the saint, clad in the garments of the cloister, had often been seen gliding along the battlements and lending a superhuman aid to the valorous efforts of her townsmen. But a more real and not less glorious sight was beheld on the present occasion. Among the women who, not content with furnishing supplies of arrows and other missiles as they were needed, took a personal and active part in the combat, a girl of humble birth, named Jeanne Laisne, was conspicuous by the calm fearlessness of her bearing. Without weapon of any kind she stood at the post of greatest danger, and carried off the chief honor of the day by wresting the Burgundian standard from the hands of a soldier who had succeeded in raising it on the wall. Amidst the applause of her companions she carried this trophy to the church of the Jacobins, from which it was afterwards removed to the *hôtel de ville*, where its tattered silk and tarnished gold, emblazoned with the proud ducal arms, still commemorate an exploit not often surpassed in the annals of female heroism.

Though his own attempt had been thus foiled, Crèvecœur was still confident that the town might be carried by a larger force without the preliminaries of a regular siege; he therefore sent a message to the duke, acquainting him with the state of affairs, and begging him to hasten his advance. It was late in the afternoon when Charles came up; but after surveying the defences, he ordered the assault to be immediately renewed. The resistance, however, was as firm and as effectual as before. At a critical moment, the besieged were reënforced by the arrival of two hundred men-at-arms, who having marched from Noyon, a distance of fourteen leagues, in the course of a sultry day, entered Beauvais while the summer twilight was still shedding a clear though subdued radiance on the scene of combat. Without halting for a moment, they disencumbered themselves of their baggage as they passed through the streets, and pressing forward to the ramparts, brought timely relief to the weary and hard-pressed citizens, and compelled the foe again to retire baffled and discomfited from the attack.[77]

Had Charles, on the following day, completed the investment and opened the siege in regular form, the place, however valorously defended, must shortly have fallen into his hands. But owing either to an error of judgment, as Commines asserts, or perhaps to his reluctance to be drawn aside from the declared object of his expedition, the duke neglected until too late to close the approaches to one of the principal avenues, called the Gate of Paris, on the further side of

[77] Discours veritable du Siége de Beauvais, tiré d'un viel manuscrit, in Lenglet, tom. iii. p. 205 et seq. — Commines. — De Troyes.

the river. Troops meanwhile poured in from every quarter to the succor of the beleaguered town. Dammartin arrived from Compiègne, Salazar from Amiens, the Marshals Lohéac and Rouhault from still more distant points. Carpenters and other artisans, needed for repairing and strengthening the works, were despatched from Paris and Rouen. In the course of two days a force amounting to fifteen thousand men was assembled at Beauvais; and so great was the quantity of supplies received, that the price of bread and other necessaries, instead of advancing, fell below the ordinary rates. The besiegers now formed their camp, extending over several leagues of ground, constructed batteries, and opened a fire, which was kept up without intermission for more than a week. Sluices were cut to carry off the water from the fosse, and attempts were also made to undermine the walls; but the soil being every where porous and wet, this project had to be abandoned. The loss of life from the cannonade was unusually small. A stone ball of great size fell in the choir of the cathedral while the priests were celebrating mass, but without injury to any one — a circumstance piously attributed to the powerful protection of "Madame Saint Angadresme." Many buildings, however, including several churches, were destroyed or irreparably damaged; and the breaches being considered practicable, the assault was ordered for the 9th of July.

On the night before the attack, Charles, as he lay dressed upon his camp-bed, discussing with his attendants the probabilities of success, declared his own belief that the enemy would be found to have abandoned the defences; and he even treated with derision the contrary anticipations expressed by all who were present.[78] His confidence was doubtless derived from his uniform experience in similar affairs, and especially in the capture of Dinant and of Liége. But his career of victory was now to meet with a mortifying check. In the face of a heavy fire from the ramparts, the Burgundians succeeded in crossing the ditch, and commenced their assault not only at the breaches, but against the whole extent of the curtain between two of the gates. More than once they mounted to the summit, and planted their standards; but these were speedily torn down; and the numbers as well as the courage of the besieged being adequate to the emergency, no point was found unguarded, no sign of weakness or of wavering appeared, no such chance advantage presented itself as forms, when promptly and boldly seized, the turning-point in a hard-contested but successful assault. While the archers and men-at-arms, in close array, made good use of their accustomed weapons, the towns-people had recourse to huge stones, caldrons of scalding oil, burning fagots besmeared with pitch, and similar means of annoyance. After a combat of three hours' duration, the assailants were beaten off, with a loss of twelve hundred or more in killed and wounded; and

[78] "Demanda à aulcuns s'il leur sembloit qu'ilz attendissent l'assault: il luy fut repondu que ouy, veu le grant nombre de gens qu'ilz estoient, et n'eussent ilz devant eulx que une haye. Il le print en mocquerie, et dict: 'Vous n'y trouverez demain personne.'" Commines, tom. i. p. 288.

the repulse was too complete, the failure too discouraging, to allow of a fresh attack by the reserves which had been held in readiness for that purpose.[79]

The strength of the place and the ability and resolution of its defenders had now been sufficiently tested. If the siege was to be carried on, Charles must abandon the schemes with which he had set out, and devote all his energies and all his resources to this single object. For such a conclusion he was not prepared; yet, loath to acknowledge himself balked and defeated, he remained some time longer in the vicinity of Beauvais, forming fruitless plans for its reduction. In this interval the troops were twice compelled by heavy rains, that inundated the whole valley, to shift their encampment; and they were not less annoyed by the frequent and vigorous sorties of the besieged, emboldened by their late success, though it sometimes happened that the sallying parties were cut off in their retreat and made to pay dearly for their temerity. At length, after having wasted three weeks in an abortive undertaking, and lost more than three thousand men in the different assaults and skirmishes, the duke broke up his camp on the 22d of July, and pursued his march into Normandy.

He attempted to cover up the disgrace that had befallen his arms by a vaunting proclamation, reiterating his opprobrious charges and menaces against

[79] The chief authorities for the siege of Beauvais are the contemporary "Discours veritable du Siége, in Lenglet, tom. iii. pp. 205–216; Commines, tom. i. pp. 283–289; and De Troyes, Lenglet, tom. ii. pp. 95–97.

the king, and boasting that he had devised such expedients as must speedily have enabled him to make himself master of Beauvais but for the necessity of fulfilling his engagements with the duke of Brittany. In truth, however, his failure at this point had lost him the opportunity of obtaining the coöperation of his ally and of carrying out the main design of the campaign — that of again plunging the kingdom into anarchy and civil war, and again reducing the king to helplessness and despair. Louis had already besieged and taken several of the strong places on his enemy's frontier, and was now pushing forward, at a brisk though cautious pace,[80] upon Nantes, the capital of the province. Francis found himself enveloped in a net, that was gradually tightening around him, and from which he had no means of escape except by some powerful diversion in his favor, some great and decisive advantage gained by his allies. The fall of Beauvais would have brought him immediate relief. Had a town so strong, defended by the best troops and the ablest captains in

[80] Ludwig von Diesbach, in his autobiography, gives, with his usual *naïveté*, some amusing exemplifications of the difficulty experienced by the king, during these operations, in restraining the ardor which he knew so well how to excite. On one occasion, the royal pages having taken part in an assault which had been discountenanced by Louis, and got nothing but a sousing in a wet ditch for their pains, were greeted on their return with ironical congratulations and a hope that they had enjoyed their bath. At another time, when they had succeeded in a similar exploit, and expected something handsome by way of guerdon, they were told by their master that he had a mind to hang them for making the attempt both against his orders and without a proper force. Schweizerischer Geschichtforscher, B. VIII. ss. 178, 181.

France, yielded to the attacks of the invaders, the main bulk of the resistance would have been shattered, all obstacles to their further advance would have vanished, the king would have been compelled to drop the prey already within his grasp, and hasten back to the protection of the capital. There he would again have been environed by foes, and must again have become impotent and desperate. But the struggle having ended so differently, he was now at liberty to follow up his own successes, leaving to his generals, whom, however, he continued to ply with letters filled with admonitions and suggestions[81] the prosecution of his original plan of defence. His satisfaction and gratitude were, as usual, exuberant and loud. To his heavenly benefactress, whose special interpositions in his favor he never failed to recognize, he promised a "town of Beauvais" in silver, of the value of two hundred marks, to be deposited on her shrine at Celles; and he vowed to abstain from meat until his promise should have been

[81] "I commend my affairs in that quarter to your zealous attention. If you do not put your hand to the work, the duke of Burgundy will do us great damage and dishonor. . . . I know the trouble you have on my behalf, and will reward it well. Let but God and Our Lady save Dieppe and Arques, and we shall get the better of our embarrassments. Reënforce those places. Keep your cavalry between the Burgundians and their own frontiers. . . . Sally upon them in a body and inflict all the damage you can. . . . Since they move so slowly and have advanced so far into my land, you ought to be able to break their communications and cut off their supplies. . . . Be before the enemy wherever he moves. . . . Send a force into his territory to burn and plunder, as he has done in mine. . . . Blondin will tell you how finely we treat the Bretons; do you give the Burgundians as good treatment on your side." Letters of August and September, in Duclos, tom. iii. preuves, pp. 333–338.

redeemed.[82] To the inhabitants of Beauvais, whose loyalty and courage had been so signally displayed, he granted an enlargement of their privileges and a reduction of imposts, instituting at the same time an annual procession, in which the women, in commemoration of their gallantry during the siege, were to take precedence of the men.[83] Jeanne Laisné received a husband selected by the king, with a dowry from the royal purse, and an exemption for the worthy couple and their descendants from the payment of taxes of every description — no small boon to subjects of Louis the Eleventh and of *his* descendants.[84]

Meanwhile the duke of Burgundy, after raising the siege, advanced by slow marches to the right bank of the Seine, and waited with vain though commendable patience for the arrival of his ally. There

[82] In his letter on this subject to the Sire Duplessis he shows an extreme anxiety that the commission may be promptly executed, but also that no money may be wasted. "Send a sure agent to have it done, and see that there is no loss. Let Briçonnet give you the first sum he can lay hands on. If necessary let him take it from the war fund, though you know how much I need that. But let there be no difficulties, and do not send back to me for fresh orders. Being so near the Bretons, I am afraid if my vow be not soon accomplished, I may meet with some mishap." Ibid. p. 330.

[83] Documents in Lenglet, tom. iii. pp. 216–225. — The procession, interrupted at the Revolution, was subsequently resumed, and is continued, we believe, at the present day.

[84] Letters-patent, in the Ordonnances des Rois de France. — In the Discours veritable du Siége this heroine is wrongly called Jeanne Fourquet, and an erroneous tradition has spoiled the charm of her exploit by representing her as armed with a hatchet and killing the soldier from whom she snatched the standard. Hence the *sobriquet* given to her of "La Hachette." The artist employed to commemorate her fame by a monument has had the bad taste to adopt this notion.

was, in fact, no concert possible between them, and neither had any certain information as to the movements or situation of the other. Charles's course through the plains of Normandy was marked by all the barbarities of that mode of warfare in which his troops had become eminently skilful. The Pays de Caux, the most fertile and populous region in all France, was devastated from the walls of Rouen to those of Dieppe. Many small fortresses were captured and demolished, every village and farm-house burned, the standing crops destroyed, and the country reduced to the condition of a desert. But neither Dieppe nor Rouen opened its gates. The former place, where an attack might have been supported by a fleet which had moved along the coast to coöperate with the army, was judged to be impregnable by land and sea;[85] and Rouen, though menaced and summoned, received such reënforcements as would have enabled it to defy any attempt of the invaders. Their failure at Beauvais had robbed them of that *prestige* of Terror on which they had inconsiderately counted as a means of conquest. Now, too, they began to perceive that their position was one of considerable peril. Dammartin and his associates, carrying out the tactics enjoined by the king, hovered about them in whatever direction they moved, speeding before them into the strong places whenever these were in danger, declining combat in the open country, but inflicting constant annoyance, especially by the capture of

[85] Letter from the Burgundian camp, in Lenglet, tom. iii. pp. 225–227.

supplies and convoys. For several days a dearth prevailed in the camp, and the spirits of the troops were much affected by this calamity, as well as by a suspicion they began to entertain, that their leader intended to cross the Seine with the purpose of going to the aid of his ally.[86] The duke himself, though he had formed and was loath to relinquish this design, grew solicitous, and with good reason, respecting the unguarded state of his own frontiers. The Constable having assured himself by a visit to Beauvais, that the Burgundians had there met with a repulse, had now got up a campaign on his own account, and was ravaging the borders of Hainault and Flanders. The duchy of Burgundy suffered similar inroads from the feudal levies of Dauphiné and Champagne. Under these circumstances Charles found it necessary to abandon the hope with which he had entered on his expedition. Early in September he turned his face homewards, having first despatched a letter, which would seem to have been intercepted on the way, to acquaint the duke of Brittany with the reasons for his return, and with such of his proceedings as he supposed to have reflected credit on his arms.

In his return through Picardy he followed the same remorseless policy, spreading havoc and waste from the sea-coast up to the walls of Amiens. Having again reached the banks of the Somme, he resolved,

[86] "Doutoient fort que mondit Seigneur deust passer la riviere de Seine et tirer en Bretagne, qui leur a esté chose griefve, car desja par l'espace de six ou sept jours on n'avoit peu recouvrer pain en l'ost." Ibid. p. 226.

before closing the campaign, to ravage the territory of Saint-Pol. When this operation had been thoroughly performed, he paid off his forces, disbanding, as was usual at the approach of winter, that portion of them which consisted of feudal levies and civic militia.[87]

What had the duke accomplished by this campaign? He had razed or burned, as appeared from the record kept by his provost marshal, two thousand and seventy-two towns, villages, and castles.[88] He had, as he boasted to his ally, so treated the territory he had traversed that for a long time to come it would contribute nothing to the resources of the enemy.[89] By his slaughters and devastations he had gained for himself the designation of "Charles the Terrible." Nor can it be denied that in spite of his failure at Beauvais, he had added something to his military reputation. The distance to which he had penetrated, the comparative immunity with which he had moved his army in all directions in the midst of strong fortresses and of vigilant and enterprising foes, his leisurely retreat unmarked by disaster or by any appearance of flight, seemed a striking evidence of his superior power or skill, and enabled the Burgundian chroniclers to add another page to the list of their master's "glories."

[87] Ibid., ubi supra. — Basin, tom. ii. pp. 298–300. — Haynin, tom. ii. p. 208 et al. — Ancienne Chrònique, and Discours veritable, in Lenglet.

[88] Haynin, tom. ii. p. 209.

[89] "J'ay ards et brûlé tout le pays de Caux, par maniere qu'il ne nuira de long-temps, ny à vous ny à autre." Lenglet, tom. ii. p. 258.

The exploits of Louis in the mean while had been of a less pretentious but more solid description. He had put a steady and increasing pressure on the duke of Brittany, until that prince, finding himself uncomfortably squeezed, had begged for permission to breathe. The king, with his accustomed humanity, had lent a ready ear to this appeal. In opposition to the remonstrances of his generals he granted an armistice, confident from the information which had reached him that the Breton levies would take advantage of the pretext afforded by a suspension of hostilities to retire to their homes, and hoping to derive from this circumstance a double profit, as it left him at liberty to send off a large reënforcement to Dammartin.[90] His expectations that the latter would thus be enabled to strike a telling blow at the duke of Burgundy were doomed to disappointment. The general showed himself for once more cautious than his master, overawed by the fearless attitude of the enemy, or made uneasy by the dubious demeanor of his coadjutor Saint-Pol.[91] In other respects the king's anticipations proved correct. The duke of Brittany was reduced to the necessity of again abandoning the confederacy and accepting such terms as the lenient Louis thought fit to impose. Again the Armagnacs and the Foix were exposed to the vengeance of their sovereign, which descended with a

[90] Letter to Dammartin of Aug. 11, in Duclos, tom. iii. preuves, p. 334.

[91] See the remarks of Basin, tom. ii. p. 299.

weight that put a final stop to his troubles from that source.[92]

The game of intrigue and conspiracy was played out; and the first to perceive and appreciate this fact was the master-spirit of the whole movement, who accordingly, like a worn-out *roué* turned preacher and saint, lost no time in assuming a new character and preparing for a change of life. The envoy sent to negotiate on behalf of the duke of Brittany was instructed by the Sire de Lescun to inquire on what terms he might expect to be received into the royal favor. Louis, trusting and generous as ever, returned a *carte blanche,* which was filled up with the government of Guienne and a long list of inferior posts and emoluments. The matter was speedily concluded, and under the new title of "count of Comminges," Odet d'Aydie, so long the disturber of his sovereign's peace, became thenceforth the ablest and most devoted of his servants.[93]

A similar accession — one less important at the moment, but far more interesting to the student of French history and literature — had been made by

[92] The count of Armagnac, hunted from post to post, was slain at Lectoure, in March, 1473, after he had surrendered himself to his pursuers. His brother the duke of Nemours perished on the scaffold some years afterwards.

[93] Before visiting the king in person, Lescun took the precaution of exacting an oath for his safety on the True Cross of Saint-Laud. Louis would not incur the risk of this solemn engagement until he had sent notice to his generals, lest they might have thought of doing him a signal service by posting an ambuscade for the veteran conspirator. "Je ne voudrois point," he writes, "être en dangier de ce serment-là, vu l'exemple que j'en ai vu cette année de Monsieur de Guyenne." Duclos, tom. iii. preuves, p. 319.

Louis at a somewhat earlier stage of the campaign. On the night between the 7th and 8th of August, 1472, while the duke of Burgundy with his army lay in the neighborhood of Eu, his favorite chamberlain, Philippe de Commines, vanished from the camp.[94] From the time of their meeting at Péronne, Louis and Commines had felt the influence of that attraction which acts upon kindred intellects with a force proportioned to their vigor and depth. A great service had then been rendered on the one side, and the desire to make a corresponding return had ever since been acutely felt on the other side. In the summer of 1471, Commines had gone on a private mission to the king, then at Orleans.[95] Without doubt a personal engagement was then formed between the astute king and the skilful diplomatist. By way of provision for his intended flight the latter deposited a large sum of money with a banker at Tours. Yet after his return he would seem to have fallen into a state of hesitation, from which his impatient friend took a summary method of relieving him. On the outbreak of hostilities the money left at Tours was confiscated and seized as the property of a notorious

[94] M. Gachard, who has established the date of this event, says he has searched in vain for some document that would show where the duke of Burgundy was then encamped. It is strange he should not have thought of looking into the Journal or Itinerary (Ancienne Chronique) printed by Lenglet, where all Charles's movements are noted with great precision.

[95] Mademoiselle Dupont says, "We shall not attempt to discover the avowed or secret object of this journey." (Notice sur Philippe de Commines, p. xxxiii.) The subject of the mission is, however, apparent from the documents she has herself produced, read in connection with others relating to the same matter. See the "remarks" appended to this chapter.

adherent of the king's rebellious vassal.[96] This was a happy and decisive stroke, and the earliest opportunity was seized for escape. At the French court Commines was greeted with open arms. A wealthy marriage,[97] great estates, lucrative employments, and the title of prince, formed the reward of his desertion, and enabled him to remember without regret the master by whom he had been reared and protected in his orphanage, promoted with an unexampled rapidity, and treated with a singular confidence and kindness.[98] He has told us nothing of his own feelings on the occasion of his change of service.[99] Those of Charles are indicated by a single fact. The estates of the runaway were of course confiscated, and they were bestowed upon the duke's former enemy, the lord of Quiévrain. The instrument by which this transfer was accomplished bears the date of "*six o'clock in the morning* of the 8th of August."[100]

Having arrived at a satisfactory settlement with the duke of Brittany, the king was ready for a fresh

[96] Dupont, Notice. pp. xxxiv. xxxv. and preuves, p. 7.

[97] Among the descendants of the great historian may be counted several European sovereigns and princes, including Victor-Amadæus II. of Savoy, Louis XVI. and Charles X. of France, and the present legitimist pretender to the French throne.

[98] This conduct of Commines has been by some writers too rigorously, by others too leniently, judged. Mademoiselle Dupont renders an impartial and discriminating verdict. It is, however, a mistake to suppose, with some of the authorities whom she has quoted, that Commines had been intrusted with all Charles's most secret affairs. It is plain, from his own statements, that he knew little or nothing of the important negotiations with the imperial court, on which we shall enter in the next chapter.

[99] He says, shortly and characteristically, "About this time I came into the service of the king."

[100] Gachard, Particularités et Doc. Inéd. sur Commines, &c. pp. 3, 4.

negotiation with the duke of Burgundy. An arrangement of some kind was rendered necessary by the cessation of hostilities, which neither party had any present desire to renew. Again Charles was invited to conclude a treaty without mention of the ally who, on this as on former occasions, had shown himself alike faithless and weak; and again he refused, on the ground that, whatever promises had been extorted from Francis, his position and his sympathies must still bind him to his old associate.[101] This, however, under the circumstances, had ceased to be any thing more than a point of etiquette; and Louis yielded the more readily that, on another point, one of vital importance, he and Charles were perfectly united. The stream of their confluent hatred — as full and impetuous as the nature of the one, as dark and treacherous as that of the other — was directed against Saint-Pol, the false friend, the presumptuous servant, of both. At first insensible to his danger, the Constable, by a display of overbearing insolence towards the Burgundian diplomatists, — the Chancellor Hugonet and the lord of Humbercourt, — helped to pave the way intended for his own descent. Then, alarmed, he sought by offers and promises to gain pardon and protection from the king. Louis, amused with his terror, was well content to grant him a respite, lying quietly in wait till the victim should recover heart,

[101] Commines, tom. i. p. 295. — In his letter, before quoted, to the duke of Brittany, Charles had said, "Ne me departiray des armes sans vous, ainsi que certain suis que ne le ferez sans moy." Lenglet, tom. ii. p. 258.

when a spring and a single shake might put an end to his gambols.[102]

Although the negotiations resulted only in a truce terminable at the expiration of a year,[103] yet this agreement, renewed from time to time, was virtually the conclusion of the wars waged between the French king and the duke of Burgundy. Occasional hostilities broke out along the frontier; petty acts of encroachment or aggression were not unfrequent; but Louis never afterwards assembled his forces with the purpose, or asserted purpose, of reducing his stubborn vassal to obedience, and Charles never afterwards led an army into France. The recent passage of arms, short, vehement, and apparently indecisive, had been of service to the combatants chiefly as affording an exact measure of their relative strength. It had shown far more plainly than mere observation could have done the changes which had taken place since the War of the Public Weal. It was not so much that the feudal power had grown weaker in the interval, as that a new power had arisen in the realm of France. In the former struggle the towns had looked on with complete indifference, had traf-

[102] The particulars of the negotiation in regard to Saint-Pol will be noticed hereafter. In a letter to his envoys, — Dammartin and Craon, — written on the 29th of December, Louis expresses himself as well satisfied that the Constable can hope for no reconciliation with Charles; so that, whatever may be the terms of the treaty, or even if no treaty be concluded, "I shall have *Monsieur Saint-Quentin* where he will not be able to deceive me again about capturing places." "I have had an offer from another quarter," he says, "to put me in possession of the town. As for the troops, I can get them back whenever I want them." Duclos, tom. iii. preuves, p. 340.

[103] Lenglet, tom. iii. pp. 247–255.

ficked and maintained amicable relations with the assailants of the monarchy, and had given no assistance to the king. On the late occasion they had received the invaders as enemies, offered them a determined and successful resistance, rendered their passage perilous and their retreat unavoidable. The experiment was not likely to be repeated; and at all events the sovereign, secure of the support of the nation, might henceforth contemplate without the fear of ruin the possible necessity for a war of defence upon his own soil.[104]

The sword had been returned to its scabbard. Was then the ancient hostility laid to sleep? Far otherwise. As we have before said, it was never more deadly than when carried on under the show of peace. The sword had been returned to the scabbard — that the stiletto might be clutched. The ground of rivalry and of enmity was as strong as ever. Events had shown that the feudal vassals were no longer able to cope with regal authority; but they had shown also that the duke of Burgundy was emancipated from the condition of a feudal vassal.

The career of Charles the Bold divides itself naturally into two periods. During the first he was chiefly engaged in attempts to undermine the French monarchy. The second period was occupied with

[104] "Il m'a maintefois dict que, . . . quant le duc de Bourgogne entroit, il ne faisoit que fort bien garnir ses places, au devant de luy; et ainsy en peu de temps l'armee du duc de Bourgogne se deffaisoit d'elle mesmes, sans ce que le Roy mist son estat en nul peril." Commines, tom. i. p. 316.

efforts to establish a power which should rise beside and overtop that monarchy. To this latter and far more complex portion of our subject we now turn.

Remarks on the Account given by Commines of a Treaty projected between Louis and Charles in May, 1471.

COMMINES says. "I was present when the treaty was sworn to by the duke" — an averment which, in our opinion, ought to place the fact beyond suspicion. It has, however, been called in question by a learned and distinguished Belgian historian, Kervyn de Letterhove, who, in an article on Commines, written throughout in an exceedingly depreciatory strain (Bulletins de l'Acad. de Bruxelles, 1859), impugns his good faith and discredits the whole transaction. After citing the statements of Commines that on the 15th of May, the day following the arrival of the duke of Lorraine and Calabria at Arras, letters announcing the death of the duke of Guienne were there received from De Quingey, whose stay at the French court lasted about eight days, M. Kervyn remarks, "La chronologie se prête mal à ces assertions. Charles le Hardi arriva le 16 mai à Arras. Le traité secret ne put être conclu, au plustôt, que le 17. Simon de Quingey (même en supposant qu'il soit parti dès le lendemain avec les ambassadeurs français) eut-il le temps de se rendre au Plessis et d'y passer huit jours avant d'écrire des lettres qui arrivèrent à Arras, non pas le 15 mai, comme le porte les textes imprimés (le duc n'était pas alors à Arras), mais le 25 mai, c'est-a-dire, le lendemain du traité d'alliance conclu entre le duc de Calabre et le duc de Bourgogne? Cette lettre pouvait d'ailleurs annoncer tout au plus l'aggravation de la maladie du duc de Guienne, car il ne mourut que le 28 mai."

In regard to the date, there is an obvious mistake, either of Commines himself or of the copyist—more probably of the former; for, as if mistrusting his memory on this point, he adds, "as I believe" (*il me semble*). Charles, as M. Kervyn correctly states, did not reach Arras until the 16th; and the duke of Lorraine did not arrive till the 20th. (See the journal in Lenglet, tom. ii. p. 201.) Nevertheless the difficulties with which the matter is encumbered are not so great or so many as M. Kervyn supposes. Commines does not say that the ratification of the treaty took place at Arras. If it took place in May, but before the 16th of the month, it was probably at Bruges, where Charles was staying from the 29th of April to the 5th of May, and where he is known to have given audience to the French ambassadors. (Lenglet, ubi supra.) Now there are reasons for believing that an arrangement of some kind was concluded early in May. The truce was to expire on the 4th, and it was necessary, unless hostilities were to be immediately opened, that some new agreement should be made. It is said that the truce was then extended to the 15th of June. (De Troyes, p. 93.) This may have been so; but on the 8th of May the king had received no notice to that effect, and no hostile indications having appeared, he drew the inference that a treaty of peace had been concluded. ("Se la Paix est faite, ce que je croy que ainsi soit; car les gens de Mons. de Bourgogne, nonobstant que la Treve soit failie, n'ont point courru en mes pays, et n'en font nul semblant." Letter to Tanneguy du Châtel, May 8, Lenglet, tom. iii. p. 186.) Of course the truce may have been extended and the treaty sworn to by Charles at the same time; for the latter would not be binding until ratified by Louis. Again, Commines does not say that the letters of De Quingey were simultaneous with his dismissal by the king; and the opposite might perhaps be inferred, since, after his departure from Plessis, he would probably have made his report to the duke in person. But it may be asked, How could his letters announcing the death of the duke of Guienne have been received at Arras on the 15th, 16th, 17th, or even on the 25th, when the death did not occur until the 28th? We reply, that De Quingey might well have written a letter at Plessis on the 14th announcing that event; for, although the announcement would have been premature, it would have been stating what was fully believed at the French court in regard to the contents of the despatches which the king had on that day received from Guienne. ("Ce jour — Jeudy 14. May — le Roy eut *certaines nouvelles* que luy fist assavoir Mgr. de Malicorne, serviteur et bien fort aimé de mondit Sgr. de Guyenne, que son dit Sgr. et Maistre estoit alé de vie à trespas." De Troyes, p. 94.) And it was the conduct of Louis himself which, without doubt, gave rise to that belief, since, as we have before seen, he considered the intelligence he had then received as tantamount to that of his brother's death, and acted upon it accordingly.

The only error, therefore, that can be clearly proved against Commines by a comparison of dates, lies in his statement that the dukes of Burgundy and Lorraine were at Arras on the 15th of May. Such a mistake — a mistake which being rectified leaves no inconsistencies in the account, a mistake, too, where the assertion, far from being positive, was left, as it would seem, designedly open to correction — will not authorize an impeachment of the general credibility of the narration. Yet M. Kervyn goes on to say, "*Personne n'a jamais vu le traité secret* dont parle Commines en témoin oculaire, et je ne sais s'il ne faut pas reconnoître dans cette assertion *une apologie peu sincère des enterprises de Louis XI. contre son frère.* Reprenons les faits d'après les sources ies plus dignes de foi." And, after reciting a few of the facts already noticed in our text, he concludes by asking, "Ne résulte-il pas évidement de tout ceci qu'aucun traité secret relatif à l'abandon du duc de Guienne, ne put se conclure à Arras peu après le 16 mai?" The question, however, which he has really raised is, not simply whether such a treaty was concluded at Arras, or elsewhere, either shortly after or shortly before the 16th of May,—certainty as to the exact time and place being of course immaterial,—but whether such a treaty was ever concluded at all, or even negotiated. It is a question involving the characters of two persons, one of them the most conspicuous actor in scenes of which the other is the most accomplished delineator. Was Charles the Bold guilty of the perfidy attributed to him by Commines? Or has Commines blackened the memory of Charles by a falsehood put forth as an apology for the conduct of his rival? We should be glad to see Charles's reputation cleared from this stain; but we cannot consent to the wanton sacrifice of a more precious reputation.

We say, then, with M. Kervyn, "Let the facts be produced from the most trustworthy sources." But let *all* the attainable facts be produced, from *all* the trustworthy sources. M. Kervyn, as appears from his discussion of the circumstances, as well as from the authorities whom he cites, had read some of the published documents relating to the negotiation. But he had not read them all. Those which he had failed to read are the most important. He had not, so far as appears, consulted the collection made by Plancher and Salazar, in which are to be found the copious instructions given by the French king, under date of November 17, 1471, to the Sire de Craon and Pierre d'Oriole, the envoys whom he was about to send to the duke of Burgundy. In these instructions, with no conceivable motive for any misstatement on such a matter, Louis says that the duke of Burgundy, through his ambassador, Ferry de Cluny (an ecclesiastic of high rank), has already agreed with him upon the terms of a definitive treaty of peace ("traité de la paix finale"), which treaty he refers to as being already in a complete shape; that in addition to the said treaty of peace, the parties have further agreed to enter into a "confederation and alliance," to be called "the treaty of especial friendship and confederation," containing among other provisions a mutual promise of "service, aid, and succor against all others," and particularly, on the part of the duke of Burgundy, against the dukes of Guienne and Brittany, and on the part of the king against two persons to be afterwards named (Nevers and Saint-Pol); that the terms of this special treaty are to be embodied in a separate instrument, of which the duplicates are to be signed and exchanged; that, as a condition of both these treaties, the king is to restore all the places which he has taken from the duke; that the duke has required, and the king has assented, that the special treaty shall bear a somewhat later date—ten or twelve days—than the treaty of peace; that the duke has also demanded that the town should be given up before the delivery of the "letters" containing the special treaty; that on this point the king has refused to concur, but that the difficulty which has hence arisen may be obviated by any one of various expedients which the envoys are directed to present to the duke of Burgundy for his choice and confirmation; and lastly, that, although the treaty of peace provides for certain heavy penalties attaching to the infraction of it, the king is content, in the case of the treaty of confederation, to accept simply the duke's word and oath. (Hist. de Bourgogne, tom. iv. preuves, pp. cccviii.–cccxi.)

In subsequent instructions relating exclusively to the mode of settling certain points connected with the "treaty of peace," the king, while agreeing to a renewal of the truce during the continuance of the negotiations, tells the envoys not to permit Charles, if he should so propose, to include the dukes of Guienne and Brittany, inasmuch as it has been understood from the first that they were not to be mentioned in any prolongation of the truce. (Ibid. p. cccxiv.) And it would seem probable that rumors of what was going on had reached those two princes, and raised some apprehensions in their minds; for by an embassy despatched on the 10th of April, 1472, after urging the duke of Burgundy to take up arms and assuring him of their assistance in recovering the towns in Picardy, they beg that if the truce is renewed they may be included, and they wish to be informed of Charles's object in consenting to the renewal — whether it is merely to gain time or with a view to the conclusion of a *final peace*. (Ibid. pp. cccxvi.–cccxviii.)

But there are also extant, in good legible print, letters addressed by Louis to his envoys during the negotiation, and referring to the special treaty. In one of these, he alludes with some asperity to the suspicions which had been intimated in regard to the duke's sincerity. "To remove all doubt," he writes, "if he is willing to make me those promises, either in writing or otherwise, which *we agreed upon at Orleans*, I wish you to accept, and to conclude the arrangement, for I am resolved to confide in him. And as to the question you raise about *his wishing to put the* PRINCIPAL PROMISES *in separate letters, without inserting them in the treaty of peace*, you know that I have already agreed to this." (Letter of Dec. 11, 1471, Duclos, tom. iii. preuves.) We have seen also that in a letter written on the 8th of May, 1472, to his general on the frontier of Guienne, he forbade any hostile movement until he had seen the issue of his negotiation with Charles. "Peradventure," he wrote, "the duke of Burgundy would not wish me to make any attack upon the duke of Guienne *until* the towns have been restored to him." "Besides, if the peace is made, we shall get all without striking a blow." How could this be, unless the duke of Guienne was to be excluded?

There were, therefore, two distinct treaties pending between the French king and the duke of Burgundy — one a treaty of peace, the other of alliance; the latter complementary of the former, filling up, so to speak, a space there left vacant. An examination of the former treaty would therefore throw some light on the intentions of the parties. But does this treaty exist? Has any one ever seen it? It does exist. Some one has seen it. It has been printed. It may be found in the collection of Lenglet-Dufresnoy (tom. iii. pp. 171–176), as well as in Dumont's and other collections. It bears the date of October 3, 1471 — more than a month earlier than the date of the paper in which Louis alludes to such a treaty as having been already framed. It is the duplicate intended to be ratified and delivered by the duke. It bears the ducal seal, and is signed by the duke's secretary. It answers in all respects to the description given by Louis. It speaks in the same terms of a "final peace;" it specifies penalties; it stipulates for the rendition of the towns. It contains, indeed, the usual clause providing that the allies of either party may, on signifying their desire within a certain time, be included in it; but the contracting parties do not, as was also usual, name the princes and powers whom they consider as their allies. There is no mention in it of the dukes of Guienne and Brittany. Nay, they are impliedly excluded; for former treaties, those of Conflans and Péronne in particular, are confirmed — so far, and only so far, as the king and the duke of Burgundy are concerned. With what purpose could such a treaty as this have been drawn up, unless Charles intended either to abandon his allies or to deceive Louis?

We say that this treaty bearing the date of October 3, 1471, contains an evident gap, that a supplementary treaty is written "between the lines;" and hence the mention by Commines of only one treaty. For looking at the position of the parties at the time, it is inconceivable that a treaty intended to be final should have been projected between the king and the duke of Burgundy without some agreement in reference to the dukes of Guienne and Brittany. There is another case in the present history exactly parallel in this respect. Commines tells us that a treaty was concluded at Péronne, in 1468, by which it was agreed that the province of Champagne should be granted to Charles of France. With equal force, in that case, might M. Kervyn have denied the fact and contradicted the witness. "No one," to use his own words, "has ever seen the treaty of which Commines speaks." The treaty of Péronne, as printed in different collections, contains no clause of the kind. Yet no one has ever doubted that such an agreement was made. The very absence in the treaty of any provision for the king's brother was itself, under the circumstances, a proof that there had been a secret and supplementary article on the subject, and the course subsequently pursued placed the matter beyond a doubt.

But further, there is extant in regard to the negotiation, and more especially in regard to the duke of Burgundy's intentions, or professed intentions, evidence not of a mere inferential kind, or based upon statements of the French king, but direct, positive, emanating from the Burgundian court, and consisting in part of declarations in the handwriting of Charles himself. From this evidence, anterior in date to any that has been already adduced, it appears that the first steps had been taken as early as the beginning of August, 1471, if not previously. A royal equerry had conveyed to Charles a communication from Louis. Having carried back the answer and received further instructions, this person despatched a messenger with a memorandum in writing to be presented to the duke, who returned it to the bearer with marginal annotations of his own. We subjoin, in a condensed form, some extracts from this paper :—

"On my arrival I found my master in the best disposition I have ever seen, and resolved to do all for you that is possible, [i. e. to agree to your conditions as far as he possibly can.]

"Without the" previous "restitution of the towns, which they tell us we must not expect, the matter cannot be settled.

"ITEM. I have assured my master that he may feel confident that you would prefer his friendship to that of *those who have deceived you* [i. e. the dukes of Guienne and Brittany. See ante, pp. 65, 73, et al.], at which my master was more joyful than I ever before saw him; and he said in reply that he knew well that you might be depended upon, and that in what you promised you would not fail. [The old flattery—'You are a man of your word, my brother, and it is with such men that I desire to have dealings!'] And on his part he desires nothing else" than to conclude this affair; "for he knows well that there is no other secure way either for you or for him, and thinks both would have acted more wisely by beginning it long ago [At Péronne, for example, as the king had wished ?], for then neither would have had the trouble that has since befallen.

"You have assured your master of what is the truth. As to him, the result will demonstrate whether he is joyful. He who is wisest will have the least trouble.

"ITEM. Soupplainville [an agent of the duke of Brittany] has been with my master. The duke and Lescun have let him know that they are sending an envoy to you to treat of the marriage of Monseigneur" of Guienne with your daughter, "and to offer to join you in making war" upon the king; but they have also told him "that he need not feel any distrust on this account, as the experience of the present year has shown; that it

"This has nothing to do with the subject. The effect will show what we are to believe. [We are not to be talked over in this way !]

is only done to deceive you, as in former instances. [With more to the same purport — an attempt to make Charles believe that his allies are still playing a double game, and that he need have no scruples in deserting them.]

"*Commines* [for he is the seigneur de Revescure, or more properly Renescure, having inherited that title with — not an estate, but — the debts attached to the estate] was met with at *Orleans;* therefore he *must* have been with you." [Very true; and it was because he *was* with the king at Orleans, and there concluded, not merely an agreement between Louis and Charles, but another between Louis and himself, that Commines has passed over in silence his personal part in the negotiation.

"ITEM. The seigneur de Revescure has gone to Saint-Jacques, by the way of Brittany, and has not been with my master; which is contrary to what I had told him" would be the case. [This Revescure, therefore, was one of the agents employed in the transaction, and would no doubt know all the particulars. Who was he? The note in the margin will show.]

This paper exhibits, to our thinking, not only the nature of the proposed arrangement, but the purpose of Charles to violate it. He was a clumsy hand at deception; and, had Louis not been blinded by his own eagerness, the tone of the marginal remarks would have shown him at the outset that he had nothing but "dissimulation" to expect. It was apparently to obviate this probable effect of Charles's indiscreet sharpness and irony that a letter was at the same time addressed to the equerry by a person in the duke's confidence and an active party in the whole transaction. "I have presented your man to Monseigneur," he writes, "who has himself made a reply on each article; but as he has done it with his own hand, the answers are shorter than they might have been, for you know that he writes badly and reluctantly. [Charles, though accomplished in many points, was, it would seem, 'no clerk.' However, he had not the contempt entertained by many princes and nobles of his time for a knowledge of penmanship.] He has therefore directed me to write to you that you may say confidently that *he is ready to take the engagement with the king as soon as the towns shall have been given up; and that the lowest officer in the king's service will not then be more prompt to serve him and to accomplish his will.* [Alas, that a proud and honorable nature should stoop to such baseness! This is a very different tone from that of the duke's own reply. Had the writer and others about him led him into this vile business?] And in regard to sending some one to the king, as you have desired, he says he can well do so; but he has not yet determined, and he will think it over." As accordingly he did, and sent Ferry de Cluny, who concluded the treaty of peace, leaving the treaty of alliance suspended on the single point by which Charles was endeavoring to save himself from the commission of absolute perjury. This letter bears the date of Aug. 9 (1471), *and the signature of Simon de Quingey.* (Dupont, Mém. de Commines, tom. iii. preuves, pp. 2–7.)

M. Kervyn has not made the slightest allusion to any one of the documents we have cited, although the facts, surely, are relevant and the sources authentic. He must therefore have overlooked them. He has, however, perceived the improbability that the story should have been utterly destitute of foundation; and he seeks to guard himself by observing that if Charles lent an ear to such proposals, it must have been merely with a view of gaining time while he assembled his army. But it is certain, on the evidence we have adduced, that Charles had done much more than merely listen to the proposals; he had declared his intention to close with them, provided one difficulty were removed. It is certain, also, on the same evidence, that his object was, not to gain time for warlike measures, but to recover the towns without having recourse to warlike measures.

The discussion is therefore narrowed down to this single inquiry, whether Charles, after vainly endeavoring to recover possession of the towns, without first swearing to engagements which he had formed without the least intention of keeping them, did at last — as Commines, declaring himself to have been an eye-witness, asserts — take the oath while preparing to violate it. Which is the more likely — that Commines, whose statements, as far as the evidence goes, are fully substantiated, sent forth to the world, without any apparent inducement, a wilful and absolute lie; or that Charles, whose dissimulation up to the final moment is not less clearly established and is fully accounted for, took the step to which his course from the first had naturally tended?

In regard to Commines, he wrote his account long after both Louis and Charles were in their graves. He is the admirer of Louis, but not in any proper sense his apologist. He does not condemn the duplicity practised by the king. It did not seem to him deserving of condemnation. For this reason he never conceals it. In the present instance he is the apologist, not of Louis, but of Charles. He relates the story, as he himself says, in order to explain the cruelties practised by the duke in the subsequent campaign. Commines deserted Charles; but he never speaks of him with hatred or scorn. He thought, and with good reason, much more highly of his character and intellect than the world has been willing to think of them. He denies that Charles was cruel, asserts that he had a noble nature, and considers that the combination of his better qualities with those of Louis would have made a perfect prince. He is sometimes unjust in his criticisms; but it is because no real sympathy was possible between men so unlike. He ceases to be an authority when he comes to the latter part of Charles's career; but it is because he was obliged to gather his information at second hand. It is evident from numerous passages of his Memoirs, as well as from their general tone, that, necessary as he considered deception to be in the practice of state-craft, he understood and felt better than many others the responsibilities of the historical writer.

With regard to Charles of Burgundy, he was not, like the king of France, a liar and an oath-breaker by nature and habit. In few men has the instinct of veracity been more deeply implanted; few have developed and preserved it in the same degree amid similar seductions and examples. His conduct at Péronne and on the present occasion was, as the baron de Reiffenberg has justly observed, altogether exceptional. And in both these cases it is Commines who, by depicting the struggle and the excuse, helps us to perceive that it was exceptional. In the present instance, with the documents that have been cited before us, but without the account of Commines, we might have suspected that Charles intended to betray, not his enemy, but his allies. This was what the king, who fully appreciated his rival's honesty, and who sought to use that honesty as a snare for its possessor, but who, on the other hand, would have considered such an act a mere trifle, expected him to do. But it was an act of which Charles was in truth incapable. In general scrupulously upright and honorable in his dealings both with foes and friends, he was guilty but in two cases of a direct and proved violation of faith, the victim, or intended victim, being in both cases the same — not an ally or a fair enemy, but the most unfair of enemies, the greatest master of falsehood and treachery that ever existed, who had repeatedly broken faith with Charles himself, and against whom it seemed all but impossible to find protection without resorting to his own arts.

BOOK IV.

CHAPTER I.

POLITICAL TENDENCIES OF THE AGE.—CONQUEST OF GUELDRES.—NEGOTIATIONS BETWEEN CHARLES AND THE EMPEROR.—THEIR MEETING AT TRÈVES.

1473.

WE seize upon this moment, when about to enter upon new fields of action, to notice the particulars which, apart from—or rather in connection with—its biographical details, give to our subject its distinctive character.

Its rapid and continual growth from a mere provincial or even family history — the earlier scenes being laid in the household of Philip the Good, and the disputes and intrigues of that household forming the constituent incidents — until it embraces within its scope all the chief political movements of the time, will have been already perceived or will become apparent as the narrative proceeds. That this is not a mere shifting of scenes, or transition from one ground to another, but an actual development of the theme by the gradual unfolding of its meanings and effects, will perhaps be rendered more evident, if we glance at some of the peculiar features and tendencies of the age.

The close of the 15th century is universally recognized as a remarkable epoch, the starting-point, in fact, of Modern, in distinction from Mediæval, history. The 16th century was emphatically a great century — an era of great changes, of great men, and of great deeds. Mankind seemed then to have raised itself suddenly to a higher level, and to have grown proportionally taller. The principal states of Europe are then seen consolidated in the forms and within the limits which, for the most part, they have since retained. Government is seen resting on a new basis, having become at once authoritative and dependent — in a word, representative. Four great powers — France, England, Spain, and Austria — hold up the balance of empire. Rapid and astonishing revolutions are witnessed in science and art. The New World has been discovered, and is in process of conquest and colonization. Printing, invented somewhat earlier, now first begins to reveal its enormous energies and influence. Poetry, painting, and others of the fine arts, bloom all together, with a fulness and richness never before and never since equalled. The Catholicism of the Church is shattered, and Faith, set free from a long imprisonment, follows through all its devious explorations the guidance of Reason.

Looking back but a few years from the period at

which *all* these revolutions were accomplished, we find that *none* of them had been accomplished, or *apparently* commenced. In the year 1470, Spain is still a mere collection of independent, petty sovereignties; France is also a mere name, though the name for an idea that has obviously not long to wait for its realization: the throne of England is still the shuttlecock of faction or of fortune; the house of Austria, though it wears the sole imperial dignity, has not yet laid the broad foundations of its territorial dominion. Columbus, whether boy or man is uncertain, has already put to sea, but not with his vessel's prow pointed to unknown shores. Neither Luther, nor Cortés, nor Michael Angelo, is yet born. The few books that have been printed on movable types are valued as curiosities, and as such find their way into a few princely libraries — into that most especially of the duke of Burgundy, where they are diligently examined by William Caxton, who has been several years resident at the court.

It is with reason, therefore, that the intermediate epoch is fixed upon as a line of demarcation between two different eras. But this line has been, perhaps, too sharply drawn, and too rapidly crossed. Seizing eagerly upon that point where the Past becomes openly connected with the Present, historians have often failed to trace with sufficient care the connection, less open but not less intimate, with a remoter Past. It will, however, be readily acknowledged that the suddenness and simultaneousness with which great changes are effected, far from indicating a previous inertness and sterility, afford the strongest proof of a general and long-continued state of active preparation. What are called the Dark Ages — perhaps properly so called, not because they have been so little understood by succeeding ages, nor because themselves so little acquainted with the classical antiquity that had preceded them, but because so unconscious of their own purpose and destiny — present, it may be, a spectacle of chaotic confusion, but not of slumber, imbecility, or positive retrogression, such as have been sometimes ascribed to them. The evidences are abundant of the subtlety, the energy, the inventive and constructive power, displayed by the human intellect throughout that period. Those two great agents in the embodiment and diffusion of ideas, the Imaginative and the Logical faculties — one providing the framework of system and dogma, and ever insatiable in the discovery of fresh deductions and consequences, the necessary complements of its scheme, the other investing its material with beauty, visual or intellectual, rooting it in myths, informing it with ceremonies and with symbols — were never, surely, more busily or grandly employed than in the blending, taming, ordering, and christianizing, of the Celtic, Gothic, and Scandinavian races. The Catholic Church, with its hierarchy and its rites, its legends and its liturgies, its beautiful temples and its cloistered fraternities — the feudal system, with its consecration of the soil, its minute, stringent, personal obligations, its orders of chivalry, its vows of fealty and protection — the civic communities, with their chartered jurisdiction and self-government, their organization of labor and of trade, their leagues and confederacies, commercial and political, — all had their share in the work, and were themselves, not mere growths of time and circumstance, much less devices of ignorance, stupidity, tyranny, or knowledge purposely clouding itself in error, but products of the shaping intellect, of fine intuitions, of sincere and noble endeavors.

If, therefore, the time came when these things were to fall, it was not because they were radically vicious and false, because their dominion had been wrongful or usurped, because they had been tried and found wanting. Nor would it even be correct or sufficient to speak of them as temporary expedients originating in the confined views and suited to the necessities of a crude civilization, and finally displaced, when their purpose had been fulfilled, to make room for more perfect or adequate contrivances. We cannot say that their overthrow was a greater intellectual feat than their creation had been. They were, indeed, self-destroyed. They crowned their work, gave their last proof of vigor, exhausted their vitality, in stimulating men to escape into simpler and broader forms of opinion and of life. They were shattered, not by assaults from without, not through any process of corruption and decay, — for this was only a result and a sign of the internal change that was going on, — but by the matured strength and the irrepressible struggle for a wider diffusion and freer play of the great principles which they had themselves embodied, and which they had nurtured to proportions beyond their capacity to contain. The general extension of popular freedom and commercial rights was the cause, not the consequence, of the decline of the communes, by which those rights had so long been fostered and enshrined. Feudalism, though endued with a centrifugal force ever fruitful of alarming phenomena, and though engaged — at what seemed the period of its rampant strength, but what was in truth the period of its feebleness and decline — in a desperate contest with monarchical power, was nevertheless the chief source from which that power derived its nutriment and growth, weaving the countless threads that when grasped by a skilful hand drew together all the revolving particles and atoms, and distilling the copious fountains of loyalty that were at length to overflow and mingle in a common reservoir. The unity of the Church — besides arming Christianity for its triumphs over Paganism, shielding it against the inroads of Mahometanism, and saving it in the early crises of its existence from infinite divisions or absolute extinction — developed those sentiments of fraternal sympathy and concord, those perceptions of a boundary line however fluctuating or uncertain to the domain of religious thought, those mistrusts of self and of the capacity of the private judgment, and those longings for harmony in faith and worship, which, under all the conflicts of opinion, the distinctions of sect, and the rancor of polemics, still constitute the strongest bond between the civilized nations of the earth, restrain the excesses of fanaticism and superstition, blend tolerance with zeal, and give a convergent direction to all the lines of human progress.[1] In short, the ideas and institutions of the Middle Ages, far from having been obstacles and impediments to the advance of civilization, futile experiments abandoned as soon as their inefficacy had been demonstrated, or mere props and scaffoldings broken up and swept away when more solid supports had been erected, were the broad and enduring foundations for the superstructures of all succeeding ages; and the great revolutions which marked the termination of mediæval history were not so much a sudden inburst of new and before unheard-of truths, or a return to primitive usages, to earlier and purer concep-

[1] It may be thought paradoxical to derive the diffusion of a sentiment of tolerance from the teachings or influence of the Church of Rome. Let us be permitted to explain our notion on this point. We are not speaking of that toleration which, seeing the impossibility and inutility of restraining the aberrations of human opinion, suffers men to go wrong on their own responsibility. This is a conclusion of experience and of common sense for the establishment of which the world is no doubt indebted to Protestantism, for, if not always proclaimed or practised by the Reformers, it was a necessary deduction from their principles. But the same word is also applied to a deeper sentiment — that sentiment of sympathy and appreciation which, recognizing unity underneath diversity, does not even *desire* that all men should travel by the same road towards the common goal. This is a principle not proclaimed by any sect, yet acted upon, consciously or unconsciously, by thousands of all sects. But where did it originate? Not, certainly, in the division and clash of the 16th century. We believe it to have been developed by that long unity of creed, which drew together the nations of Europe and separated them so broadly from the rest of the world. It was because men had been disciplined to regard each other with a peculiar feeling as fellow-Catholics that they were able, in spite of subsequent divisions, to regard each other with a peculiar feeling as fellow-Christians.

tions and beliefs,[2] as the full development and open triumph of principles which had all along been moulding the destinies of mankind, a taking possession of the inheritance that had accumulated through a long minority, the accomplishment of a design to which all that had gone before had tended and conduced.

Society — we sometimes hear it said — is always in a state of revolution. So the river is always in motion; but with what a difference of velocity when it meanders calmly through the plain, with imperceptible though continual change of level, and when, rending the rocky barriers that have risen to obstruct its passage, it hurls its tumultuous waters into the abysm below! But long before it makes this sudden plunge, there is an acceleration of its flow, and the current sweeps along with ever-increasing strength. In like manner does the stream of history, when great changes are at hand, grow rapid and resistless; and this is the distinctive character of the period of which

[2] Few Protestant churches are willing to admit that they owe any thing to that of Rome, much less that they are products of its internal activity and fiery elements, shot forth at a red heat when the huge sphere burst and caved in, and since cooled in a very perceptible degree. Each endeavors by getting rid of whatever it judges to be extraneous, and by adhering tenaciously to some particular doctrine or practice, to assert its full possession of the primitive and undefiled truth. There is one small but amiable and respectable sect whose members make good this claim by calling themselves simply "Christians," and clinch the argument by pronouncing the *i* long. Meanwhile it seems to be forgotten that the Primitive Church was distinguished, not alone by the purity of its dogmas, but by its gifts, its miracles, and the living voice of infallible oracles. The only faithful attempt at a literal reproduction of the Apostolic Church was that of Edward Irving, which, notwithstanding his possession of the Apostolic spirit in a greater degree than any other modern, ended in a pathetic and tragical failure.

we write. Confining our attention to political matters, we may remark that the "struggle for power," already spoken of as having "become in the 15th century vehement and universal," indicates the transitional character of the age. Disconnected from its causes and results, it seems only a general outburst of fierce and unscrupulous ambition, with its attendant violence and anarchy. In every kingdom and state a parricidal, suicidal conflict is going on. Feudalism is in flaming rebellion against the suzerain — that is to say, against its own essential principle. Every crown has its disputed claim or disputed succession. In every realm, in every princely family, there are bitter feuds and dark tragedies. The heir cannot wait till his father's death shall put him in possession of his inheritance. The brother, the uncle, clutches at the inheritance of the unborn or infant heir. The aspiring favorite seeks to dethrone his master. The haughty noble hopes to disinthral himself from the double, rival claims on his allegiance, and place himself on an equality with princes. Every one is eager to seize and appropriate the power that, Proteus-like, eludes the grasp by passing into a new shape, assuming new attributes, and becoming as it were intangible.

For the result was not what might well have been apprehended at the time, — the dismemberment of states, a minuter division of territory, and the consequent dissolution of political society — but the exact reverse of this, the fusion of elements that had before been separate and antagonistic; the union and incorporation in a single state of provinces hitherto independent or connected only by feudal or federative bonds; the rise of nations breathing a common life and stirred by a common sentiment — of monarchies the different parts of which were no longer seamed but welded together, too strongly to be henceforth rent asunder either by domestic treason or the hands of a foreign invader — of governments, arbitrary, indeed, in form and tyrannical in practice, but so far enfranchising the many as they curtailed or destroyed the privileges and monopolies of the few, and rested on the principle that political society is composed, not of classes, but of individuals. Since these changes were so general, we are fain to believe, not that they were worked out in spite of the previous conflict and confusion, but that this was the very process of their accomplishment.[3] Thus in Spain, the rivalry between the little kingdoms of Castile and Aragon, and the internal feuds in each of the royal houses in regard to the succession, led directly to the union of the two crowns, the consequent overthrow of the Moslem power both in the Peninsula and on the Mediterranean, and that portentous display of energy in the Spanish monarchy and people during the 16th century which seems, when we now look back upon it, like the bursting forth of a new volcano that has spent itself in a

[3] Even Guizot sees in the institutions of the Middle Ages merely a series of experiments. One system supplants another; barbarism, the violent conflicts of society, retard civilization; progress is the result, not of a collision of forces, but of certain elements that survive such collision.

single and fierce eruption. In France and in England, a long series of divisions and convulsions terminated in a similar manner. In the former country the principle of national unity, after a long struggle for existence, was firmly secured and became the lodestar of statesmanship and the rallying point of popular sentiment. In the latter country a want long felt was supplied in the establishment of a stronger government, and that not by the mere solution of a dynastic problem, but by the recognition, open or implied, of those two grand ideas of representation and responsibility[4] which permeate and are the life-blood of the constitution.

It may be thought that, since the plans and enterprises of the duke of Burgundy ended in failure, defeat, and ruin, his history is ill chosen to illustrate the prevailing tendency of the times, exemplifying rather the resistance which that tendency had to overcome and the obstacles which it swept away. What we are here concerned with, however, is not the result, but the struggle itself, every phase of which is vividly reflected in the ambitious and warlike career of Charles the Bold; while the position which he occupied, forcing or tempting him into active interference in the internal affairs of many foreign states, offers a vantage-ground for a wider survey than is to be obtained from any other point. That eagerness to possess and exercise authority and rule which he

[4] Of course we are not speaking of mere parliamentary representation or ministerial responsibility. The distinctive features of the English government will be noticed in another chapter.

had exhibited during the lifetime of his father was not the mere ordinary impatience of expectant heirship acting on a mind peculiarly vehement in its desires and unscrupulous in its aims. It was an epidemic that seized on all his contemporaries who were exposed to its influence, on the timid as well as on the resolute, on those who would naturally have shrunk alike from peril and from guilt, as well as on those who had no fear either of God or man. Louis the Eleventh while dauphin, his brother Charles of France, the duke of Clarence and the duke of Gloucester, Alfonso and Isabella of Castile, Carlos of Navarre, Albert of Austria, Philip of Savoy, Adolphus of Gueldres, — persons in whom there was the widest diversity, the strongest contrast of character, — are among the instances that might be cited. As in common revolutions power unsettled from its old foundations seems to offer itself as a prize and becomes an object of contention, so at this period of general change and reorganization every hand was stretched out to secure its right or to profit by its opportunity.

His fierce struggle with his father's ministers brought Charles into direct collision with the French king. The contest now opens between the two men on whom the master passion of the age has taken the strongest hold, and whose superior energies find nourishment and scope in their superior resources. Each looks around him for adherents and instruments, which readily present themselves when similar impulses and similar divisions are every where at work. Louis gives encouragement to the rebellion of Liége, to the pretensions of Nevers, to the ambition and cupidity of Saint-Pol. Charles allies himself with the aggrieved vassals of the crown, and becomes the soul of a reactionary movement, which threatens to undo all that Philip Augustus, Philip the Fair, and the ablest of their successors had been able to accomplish.

Again the theatre expands. The two rivals, suspending their direct attacks, turn their eyes upon a third power, each hoping to effect such a combination as shall cause the too equal balance to incline decisively on his own side. England is the natural ally of the Burgundian states, the natural enemy of France. But there, too, an internal feud, suppressed but not extinguished, offers Louis an opportunity of which he skilfully avails himself. Through his connection with Warwick, through the connection which he forms between Warwick and the Lancastrians, the French king is able to unsettle an ancient policy and to set up in England a government friendly to France, hostile to Burgundy. His triumph, however, is of brief duration. The government thus set up is undermined and overthrown. Louis, deprived of all support abroad, is once more exposed to the combined attacks of his enemies at home. Yet again there is a reaction, a sudden recoil. Though the king achieves no victory over his enemies, their stratagems are eluded, their plans for his destruction are baffled, the equilibrium is once more restored.

It might seem, therefore, since the combatants are

again equal and their attacks again suspended, that no advance has been made towards a final solution of the questions at issue. But a moment's reflection will enable us to perceive that the situation is in fact greatly changed, that the successes on both sides, though balanced by failures, have not been unproductive of results, and that a stage has now been reached from which a glimpse is to be obtained at the ultimate and destined conclusion. We have seen how, in England, the house of York, by means of the very efforts made for its overthrow, has gained a position from which no further plottings between a hostile faction and a foreign enemy — nothing, in short, but its own crimes and incapacity and a consequent change of sentiment throughout the nation — will be able to dislodge it. So also in France, the throne has been more firmly established, the coalition formed against it has been broken up, a national feeling has been roused to its support. The duke of Burgundy has recovered the alliance of England, and its continuance is guarantied by the evident stability of the government which he has helped to restore. But he has lost his allies in France, and those fountains of discontent and treason which formerly played at his command are now in a great measure dried up. His perception of this fact serves, however, only to stimulate his ambition and to widen its sphere. Since the same principle is every where at work,— since the time has come when the weak are to fall before the strong, when petty states are to be absorbed by the greater, when monarchical authority is to become absolute, and all lesser titles to command, losing their original force, are to be valid only by its decree, — who is there that with better right may expect to profit by this revolution, to maintain his independence, exalt his position, and extend his sway, than a prince already superior to most others in the extent of his resources and in conscious ability to wield them? The dreams of his boyhood are now to inspire the energies of his manhood. The tapestried glories with which he has loved to surround himself, the exploits and achievements which have been his favorite studies, are now to be emulated or excelled. He aspires to a place among the Conquerors, the founders of realms or of empires.

Such aspirations, such efforts, never fail to arrest the attention of mankind; and even when, in other respects unfruitful, they give an impetus to the current of events, and by their sudden and disturbing influence awaken society to the consciousness of its own changes. The "Napoleon of the Middle Ages," as Charles has been sometimes called, — a designation suggested not merely by certain outward resemblances of fortune, but by certain similar exhibitions of temperament and will, concentrated upon himself the observation of Christendom. For the short remainder of its duration, his reign becomes the main stream of European history. His relations with foreign governments were those either of strict alliance or of determined hostility. The troops of many different nations are found serving under his banner or under the banners of his enemies. Whoever was not for him was against him. His constant aggressions, the fears and suspicions they excited, and the banded opposition which he at length encountered, had a powerful effect in rousing the states of Europe to a perception of their analogous condition and mutual influence, to a closer study and more vigilant observation of one another's policy and aims. It is to this period and to these circumstances that the rise of modern diplomacy, or, more properly speaking, its introduction from Italy and general adoption by Cisalpine governments, is to be traced. It is at the Burgundian court that foreign envoys are first found permanently resident; and the correspondence recently discovered of certain Milanese ambassadors, who accompanied the duke in many of his expeditions, is probably the earliest specimen of a long and consecutive series of despatches not confined to the mere formal business of a particular negotiation, but furnishing personal details and general information in regard to the court to which the writers were accredited.

It was not, then, a mere wilful or insane ambition plunging recklessly into collision with the spirit and tendencies of the age, but the exigencies of the time and of his own position conspiring with the native impulses of his character, — what, accordingly, may be termed his Destiny, — that drew Charles into a career in which war was to be his occupation, conquest henceforth his settled aim.[5] But what was to be the scheme, what the precise object, of his endeav-

[5] Von Rodt is one of the very few writers that have treated this subject impartially and philosophically. "So abentheuerlich," he remarks, "und auschweifend Karls Plane uns erscheinen mögen, so fehlte es ihnen doch weder an rechtlicher noch historischer Begründung." Feldzüge Karls des Kühnen (Schaffhausen, 1843), B. I. s. 149.

ors? His was not a mind to feed on unsubstantial dreams, or to follow the beck of shadows. Yet it was a peculiarity of his situation that it offered on every side prospects as vague as they were alluring — temptations surrounded not merely by obstacles and dangers, but by mists that bewildered speculation and obscured the gradations between the feasible and the impossible. The case was different with the French king; it was easy to foresee the ultimate aim and assign the limits of his ambition. Wherever the French race existed, wherever the French language was spoken, wherever mountain or river offered a bulwark to the integrity of the French soil, there the French monarchy must seek to fix its sway and establish its supremacy. France, in distinction from all other nations or countries, aspires to uniformity and completeness. Her foreign wars, her foreign conquests, for the most part, have had for their object the attainment or recovery of her "natural boundaries." Again and again the tide has swollen to those limits, often with a force that carried it beyond them. Again and again it has receded, leaving a margin still to be reclaimed but bearing still the traces of a former flood. To England has belonged the grander mission of spreading whatever is English over every continent. This is at once the glory and the foible of her people.[6] France seeks rather to draw within herself

[6] When it is sometimes said — apropos of an Irish riot, an Indian mutiny, or a colonial disturbance — that the English character is ill suited to the government of foreign races and dependent states, it seems to be forgotten that England is the only modern nation which has ever

whatever is French, to transform, to Gallicize, whatever comes to her from abroad.

The duke of Burgundy, on the other hand, had no such determinate field for his operations, no such chart to direct his course. His position, as before remarked, was already an anomalous one: would the anomalies disappear as the range expanded? He ruled already over a discordant aggregate of states; would the discordancy diminish as other states were added? Even in his present dominions he held his power only by a deputed title, and if not by a doubtful, at least by a new, and in some instances — in Holland for example — by an ill-gained and odious tenure; *beyond* the boundaries of his actual possessions there was not a foot of territory to which he could assert the faintest shadow of a right.

And yet — it must be again asserted — to follow up that course of aggrandizement which had marked the whole history of his house was now not merely a natural instinct; it had become a necessity. In such an age, in such a position, to remain stationary was to perish, not to conquer was to be conquered, not to absorb was to be absorbed. The defects of the structure already raised, the weakness of its foundations, the incongruity of its parts, could be remedied

succeeded in this task. Is it Spain, long since stripped of her European provinces and her great colonial empire — is it France, always incapable of striking root upon a foreign soil — is it Austria, with her unassimilated populations perpetually revolting — that can prefer a superior claim? The mistake of England has been, not in her treatment of subject nations, but in her occasional forgetfulness that there are nations which she has not subjected.

or concealed only by fresh additions and supports. Unless these were obtained, it must speedily fall to pieces. If Burgundy and Flanders continued mere provinces of France, their fate was already foreshadowed, and the hour of their absorption was fast approaching. If Franche Comté and Holland continued mere fiefs of the empire, they must shortly be ingulfed in the ever-widening vortex of imperial anarchy. It was only by the acquisition of a higher title, of loftier prerogatives, that the present ruler of these states could establish an indefeasible right of sovereignty. It was only by the acquisition of new territory that he could bind together and secure the old. The states which he could not help coveting — as connected by affinity or intermingled with his own — would not, in any event, long preserve their independence. Their union with the Burgundian dominions would give not merely enlargement of boundaries, but what was of far more importance, continuity, compactness, strength. Separated from the Burgundian rule, they offered to its enemies and rivals channels of invasion, vantage-grounds for assault, all the facilities for conquest and disruption. On the eastern frontier of the Netherlands, Gueldres and Friesland, sister provinces of Holland, must either follow the same law of attraction, accept the same destiny, acknowledge the same master, or be drawn within the grasp of a king of Denmark, a margrave of Brandenburg, or some other rising potentate of Northern Europe. Between Luxembourg and Burgundy lay the duchy of Lorraine, a fief of the

Germanic empire, but geographically and historically a province of France; ruled over by a French prince, and inhabited, for the most part, by a people of French descent. The dukes had been by turns the allies of Charles and of Louis; but the alliance, had it been more constant, was not sufficient for either, and each was waiting for the opportunity, even now at hand, of obtaining in this quarter a more efficient and continuous support. In Alsace and the territory of the Upper Rhine, Charles, as before mentioned, had already acquired a foothold; and this acquisition, important to the maintenance of his present dominion, still more important in reference to his prospective dominion, he was the less likely to relinquish, since by no other hands could it be preserved intact from the encroachments of the Swiss Confederacy.

When separate considerations, each based on a distinct group of facts and circumstances, are found on review, to have a mutual relation and a common tendency, they naturally suggest a comprehensive scheme or idea, which includes, however, besides these leading features, others that have no such original and independent claim to adoption, but which are taken in as requisite to fill up the outline and complete the details. The annexation of Gueldres and Friesland was to be regarded only as a next and necessary step in the extension of the Burgundian dominion eastward along the marshy border of the Northern Seas — an extension that could only receive its final check when some not less vigorous rival was encountered whose star of empire led towards the west. Imperative exigencies, political and military, demanded the acquisition of Lorraine, as the only means of linking together provinces now dissevered and remote, closing a perilous breach, and opposing a solid curtain, strongly flanked, to the hostile aggressions of France; while the possession of Alsace offered a cover to this line of defence, besides securing to some extent communication by the Rhine and affording that protection to commerce which was so essential to the prosperity of the Netherlands. But the combination of these various ends pointed to a further result, so natural, so desirable, that we can hardly wonder that the hopes of Charles himself, the expectations of his friends, and the apprehensions of his enemies should have concurred in anticipating it. At all events, the evident aim of his undertakings, their inevitable consequence if crowned with complete and durable success, was the formation of a Kingdom of the Rhine — of a realm, that is to say, commanding the whole navigable course of that river, comprising the territory between its left bank and the actual French frontier, and, while composed both of Celtic and Teutonic elements, constituting a longitudinal and massive barrier between Germany and Gaul.

The grandeur of this idea might serve to recommend it to a mind which, whatever its defects, had a natural bias towards lofty conceptions and great attempts. Such a realm, too, would form the counterpart to that earlier Burgundian kingdom which, leaning on the Vosges, the Jura, and the Alps, had guarded the waters of the Rhone to their junction with the sea. But would the Rhine, the proud and capricious Rhine, — ever sporting with the schemes of conquerors and the longings of nations, parcelling out its domain among petty princes and republics, but jealous and resentful of the encroachments of any single power, — consent to wear this gilded chain, accepting regal state in exchange for freedom? Nowhere in Europe had the different elements of mediæval society struck deeper root than in the Rhineland. What, however, was peculiar to this region was the tenacity with which each separate germ maintained its own isolated life, refusing to be grafted from other stocks, or to endanger is primitive hardiness for the sake of greater symmetry and productiveness. The towns, though neither populous nor rich, rejoiced in the titles of "imperial" and "free," seldom acknowledging any lord but the emperor, the source and the nominal guardian of their immunities. Among the fruitful valleys and vine-encumbered hills numerous ecclesiastical powers, abbots and bishops, ruled in serene and pompous state, guarded by well-fed and well-armed vassals and by the potent thunders of the Church. The "castled crags" that rose precipitously from the river's brink, the forest-clad ranges that overhung the narrow plains, were the abodes of a race of nobles, who adhered with a laudable conservatism to the customs of their ancestors, maintaining the right of private warfare, waging inherited quarrels among themselves or with the neighboring prelates and towns, and making the passage of the trader, whether by land or water, a hazardous emprise. Lastly, the Swiss Confederacy, a nation of warrior freemen, the sworn foe of tyranny, the pledged protector of free communities, looked down like a battery from the Alpine sources of the Rhine, and watched with a sleepless distrust every movement along its shores.

But enough has been said to intimate the steep and rugged character of the path on which Charles was about to enter. On the other hand, Opportunity, which, whether in the guise of fiend or angel, never fails to greet the adventurous spirit as it surveys its intended enterprise, stood ready to unlock the gates before him, and to direct him onward — where his Fate awaited him.

The circumstances which opened to the Burgundian sovereign an easy road to the conquest of Gueldres are strongly illustrative of what has been already described as a characteristic feature of the times. For many years the duchy of Gueldres, including the county of Zutphen, had been governed by Arnold of Egmont, a prince connected by marriage as well as by a long and intimate alliance with Philip the Good, whose affability, lavish generosity, and fondness for luxury and ease were qualities congenial with his own. Like Philip, too, he had an only son; and Adolphus of Gueldres, who had wedded Catharine of Bourbon, a sister of the countess of Charolais, displayed the same early impatience of restraint and inordinate appetite for power as his brother-in-law, unmodified in him by any scruple of conscience, any touch of filial affection, or any sentiment of humanity. In his efforts to gain premature possession of his birthright he was stimulated and assisted by his mother, Catharine of Cleves; and their intrigues having been defeated, the duchess withdrew from her husband's court, and Adolphus in like manner abandoned his home, and sought consolation for his disappointment — or fresh inspirations to villany—in a pilgrimage to the Holy Sepulchre.

Returning, after an absence of several years, part of which had been passed at the court of Burgundy, he found no difficulty in obtaining his father's forgiveness. The recovery of the prodigal in a supposed state of penitence was celebrated by a sumptuous festival in the ducal palace at Nimeguen. At midnight, while the revelry was at its height, Arnold, who had begun to feel the infirmities of age, retired silently, and without interruption to the gayety of the guests, to his bed in another quarter of the palace. He was awakened from his first slumber by the bursting open of his chamber door, through which the blended sounds of distant mirth and music stole like a perfume of sweet essences into the room. Beguiled by these festal tones, the duke imagined that his friends were come to complain of his abrupt departure and to press his return to the company. He began therefore some gentle apologies. But when his curtains were thrust aside and the glare of lights fell on the steel casques and drawn swords of a throng of men surrounding his bed, a sudden alarm — yet not for his own safety — took possession of him. Starting up, he demanded whether any accident had befallen his son. "Rise quickly! resistance will be useless," was the stern reply, in the voice of Adolphus himself, who, like Louis of France when contemplating a similar attempt, had deemed it prudent to be present in person, lest the confederates of his guilty purpose should be surprised at the moment of its accomplishment by a weakness to which he knew his own superiority. It was the depth of winter: some scanty covering was thrown over the old man's body, but his feet and legs were left bare; and in this state he was placed on horseback, dragged several leagues across the frozen waters of the Waal to the castle of Buren, and there thrust into a subterranean dungeon, lighted by a single window, small and closely barred.[7]

In this terrible captivity the dethroned duke languished for more than five years.[8] The peasants of the neighborhood shuddered as they passed the spot, hearing, either in reality or in imagination, the plaints and groans of the aged prisoner. It was even reported that the parricide came at times and stood beneath the window, cursing his victim and taunting him with the tenacious love of life that enabled him to linger amid such miseries.[9] Horrible and incredible as the whole

[7] Pontanus, Hist. Gueldr. lib. ix. pp. 524 et seq.—Sligtenhorst, B. IX. bl. 255-260.—Commines.—Basin.—Pontus Heuterus, Rerum Burgund. lib. v.

[8] Commines, from an apparent slip of the pen, says five *months.* The Bohemian travellers Tetzel and Schassek mention Arnold's imprisonment in the account of their passage through Gueldres in 1467. The time of his release is settled by documentary evidence.

[9] Rembrandt found in this tradi-

story may appear, it is attested in its main particulars by writers whose veracity and knowledge of the facts are beyond question or suspicion. When similar tragedies are depicted by the genius of the dramatist, we are convinced of their possibility without being called upon to believe in their actual occurrence. History gives us assurance on this latter point; but it presents too often only the naked facts, without those accessaries and that vivid characterization of the personages and the scene by which the poet is able to make us not merely believe, but feel and understand.

One circumstance, not before mentioned, helps in part to explain the transaction. The inhabitants of the capital and other principal towns, disgusted with the lax discipline, neglect of justice, and general incapacity which had characterized the father's administration, connived at the son's usurpation, if they had not instigated his revolt. What is called the "public conscience" is not like the conscience of the individual, an introspective faculty, the source of self-approval or self-condemnation, and is therefore never awakened by crimes from which the public itself expects to reap some advantage. The people of Gueldres, or the more influential portion of them, accepted the benefits of a more vigorous rule, and asked no questions. But as the story spread, gaining fresh horrors in the repetition, the scandal became greater than Christendom even in that age was prepared to endure. The duke of Cleves, the neighbor

tion a subject admirably suited to his pencil; and we can hardly doubt that it suggested to Schiller his famous scene in "The Robbers."

and kinsman of Arnold, interposed in his behalf, but with resources ill proportioned to the goodness of the cause. The emperor was then appealed to, and, after the usual forms of justice intermixed with more than the ordinary amount of legal fiction — since the means of enforcing them were altogether dubious — had been exhausted without effect, the duke of Burgundy, who had already attempted a peaceful mediation, received the mandates both of the emperor and the pope to exert his superior power and take the adjustment of the matter into his own hands.

This was at the close of 1470, when Charles saw himself suddenly menaced on different sides by a host of enemies, when his allies in France had declared against him, and Picardy had been overrun by a French army. Yet he lost no time in executing the imperial decree. His methods of compelling the submission of his weaker neighbors had furnished frequent warnings that were not to be disregarded. Arnold was released from prison by a body of Burgundian troops;[10] and Adolphus received a summons, which he did not venture to disobey, to appear before his accuser and his judge and plead his defence in person. Philippe de Commines was present when the father and his unnatural offspring were confronted with each other, and when the gray-haired prince, bowed down by age and his unparalleled sufferings, but stung into a fit of passionate vigor by the sense of his wrongs and the brazen presence of the culprit, cast down his glove before the assembled

[10] Ancienne Chronique, Lenglet, tom. ii. p. 197.

court and defied his enemy — his son — to mortal combat.[11]

The arrangement proposed by Charles seems to have been suggested exclusively by the political expediencies of the case. He decided that Arnold should retain the nominal sovereignty of Gueldres, with possession of a single town and an income adequate to his wants, while the government should continue to be administered by Adolphus. Yet it was the latter — not the former — who rejected this proposal, in coarse and fiery words, that, like his acts, reveal the savage nature which degrades ambition, the noble instinct of manly hearts, to a brutal and sensual lust. "I had rather," he said, "see my father thrown head foremost into a well and follow him myself, than submit to such terms. *He* has been duke four and forty years; it is time that *I* should begin to reign."[12] Confident in the support of the people, and not less in the chances, which then seemed imminent, of some fatal turn in the fortunes of the Burgundian prince, he seized the opportunity afforded by Charles's departure for France amid the bustle of military preparation to make his escape. Pursuit, however, was ordered, and at Namur, when about to cross the Meuse disguised as a Franciscan monk, he was recognized and apprehended. Subsequently a process was instituted against him in a chapter of the

[11] "Je les veiz tous deux en la chambre dudict duc par plusieurs fois, et en grant assemblee de conseil, où ils plaidoient leurs causes; et veiz le bon homme vieil presenter le gaige de bataille à son filz." Commines, tom. i. p. 307.

[12] Ibid. p. 308.

Golden Fleece, of which illustrious order he had formerly been elected a member, and after degradation he was condemned to perpetual imprisonment in the castle of Courtrai.[13]

In 1473, on the final cessation of hostilities with France, the affairs of Gueldres were the first to engage Charles's attention. The question presented a dilemma. The restoration of the rightful prince, unpopular, imbecile, and now standing on the verge of the grave, was obviously impracticable. On the other hand, to replace Adolphus in the government, or even to concede his right to the succession, after his name, by the sentence of his brother knights, had been stamped with infamy, would blemish the dignity and be prejudicial to the authority of the Burgundian duke. Concurrent, therefore, with a change of view which had brought before him bolder visions of the future, an opportunity was here presented to Charles of gaining an accession of territory by a course which might seem justified by responsibilities that had been thrown upon him, not courted by him or usurped. A pension and residence were assigned to Arnold, who readily consented to sign a renunciation of his sovereignty in favor of the duke of Burgundy, and who, by his will, made three months before his decease, formally disinherited his own posterity, bequeathing to his protector his titles and estates. In order to facilitate as far as possible peaceable enjoyment of the rights thus acquired, eighty thousand gold florins

[13] Ibid. ubi supra. — Extrait d'un ancien manuscrit, Lenglet, tom. iii. p. 295 et seq. — Basin. — Meyer. — Reiffenberg, Hist. de la Toison d'Or.

were promised to the duke of Juliers in compensation for an old claim which that prince had recently revived to the possession of Gueldres, and which the emperor had been induced to recognize.

Yet it had been necessary, in effecting this arrangement, to set aside one fact, which would not be overlooked by the world, and which must throw an undesirable light on the character of the transaction, and a permanent suspicion on its validity. Though Adolphus might justly be held to have forfeited his birthright, his children — and, besides two daughters, he had a son, Charles of Egmont, a boy of eight years — could scarcely be considered as involved in his crimes or as lawfully sharing in his exclusion. Thus a grasping and arbitrary hand might be detected in this pretended act of righteous retribution.[14] The citizens of Nimeguen, where the family of Adolphus had continued to reside, were enthusiastic in their devotion to the cause of the rightful heir, and prepared to maintain it with the sword. In August, 1473, the duke entered Gueldres at the head of an army. The greater part of the province consented without demur to accept him as its lawful prince.

[14] It must, however, be acknowledged that in that age the rights of an infant heir were not unfrequently set aside, his own inability to uphold them being equivalent to a tacit surrender of them. Had the duke of Burgundy recognized Charles of Egmont, it would still have been incumbent upon him to establish a military protectorate over Gueldres, and he would have met with the same resistance as he did in enforcing his own pretensions. So obvious was this, that we find a secret agent of the French King suggesting that the claims of the boy had been put forward merely as a means of obtaining the liberation of Adolphus. See the letter published by M. Quicherat in his edition of Basin, tom. iv.

Venlo and other fortified places offered only a momentary resistance. The capital alone still rejected his authority, and bade defiance to his arms. A siege was opened and carried on with vigor. The defence, while it lasted, was not less valorous. But after the walls had been breached, and one assault bravely repulsed, the inhabitants, finding themselves unsupported from without and doomed to destruction in the certain prospect of their defeat, retrieved their safety by a seasonable surrender, sending a deputation, in the ignominious plight usual on such occasions, to make acknowledgment of their contumacy, and agreeing to assume, by way of fine, the payment of the sum which the duke of Juliers was to receive in exchange for the abandonment of his pretensions. Thus a fifth duchy, comprising a large extent of territory, had been added to the Burgundian dominion at no greater cost than such a display of his power as Charles was not perhaps ill pleased to have an occasion for exhibiting before the eyes of his new subjects.[15]

He would willingly have followed up this stroke by the conquest of Friesland — an enterprise attempted at an earlier period by the counts of Holland, and, though difficult of achievement, regarded as

[15] Dewez, in his comparison of the career of Charles the Bold with that of Napoleon, draws an analogy between the affair of Gueldres and the attempted change of dynasty in Spain. To carry out this analogy as far as possible, it would be necessary to go beyond the limits of the present history. Charles of Burgundy had no further trouble from this source. But Gueldres was a thorn in the side of the Emperor Charles V. during many years of his reign.

an heirloom by the greater and more powerful line which had succeeded those princes. Several years before, when the overthrow of Liége, in 1468, had extorted for the victor a general tribute of respect and awe, the tempest-tost republic of Friesland, beating about amid the waves of faction, had well-nigh drifted, not without the connivance of a portion of the crew, into the secure haven which the Burgundian rule in the Netherlands offered to all such distressed mariners. A party among the nobles, friendly to the duke's designs, had laid a plot for handing over to him the sovereignty of the state. But before the scheme could be carried out, Charles's attention and resources were fully absorbed by dangers of his own, the old indomitable spirit of Frisian independence took the alarm, and the opportunity of effecting any thing by underhand management or treasonable complicity was entirely lost. An open and direct attack was not, indeed, a project to have daunted such a temper as that of the Burgundian prince; and his acquisition of Gueldres, besides being a spur to the attempt, added materially to the chances of success. But no sufficient preparations had yet been made, and one essential requisite was the previous outfit of a fleet to coöperate with the army in a region where the land and the water were strangely intermingled and not always distinguishable.[16]

[16] Basin, &c. — Steenstra, Geschiedenis van Friesland, — an excellent work, for the use of which the writer is indebted to his friend the Rev. P. H. Steenstra, son of its author.

The characteristic pertinacity with which Charles adhered to this

Moreover, Charles's glance was now diverted from this as well as from other projects that had begun to unveil their attractions, by what seemed the approaching realization of the most magnificent of his hopes. He had reached, in fact, the critical point in his career. The efforts, the struggles, the successes of the past had been productive of remoter but not less remarkable consequences than those which have already been mentioned. Other agencies had been operating, other combinations had been forming, around him, with what influence upon his fortunes was now to be seen. At this stage, therefore, of our narrative, — which hitherto has seldom halted in its course or wandered from a direct and even road, it will be necessary to pause at every step and examine the track, to explore the ground on either side, to pursue a winding route, and to double on our former footsteps. If many important matters have been left for retrospective notice, this has not been from the mere desire to preserve a continuity and smoothness in the relation, but because the circumstances and events thus passed over lay hidden and ineffective, waiting for the contingencies to occur that were to summon them to the light and put them successively in motion.

There is still another reason for the windings and eddies which for a time at least must retard the current

project while apparently absorbed in more momentous affairs is evidenced by a treaty which he formed in November, 1474, with the count of Oldenburg, brother of the king of Denmark. See Hamelmann, Chron. der Grafen von Oldenburg, s. 274.

of our story. Hitherto it has been busy with incidents and scenes having, indeed, internal affinities with those which are recognized as elements in the existing order of things, but belonging in their outward aspect almost wholly to the past, and therefore seldom dwelt upon by writers who have traced the progress of modern civilization from its apparent dawn. But the negotiations and intrigues, the alliances and the wars, with which we are henceforth to be engaged, have a more obvious bearing on the history of later times; we come into immediate contact with at least the more distant links in a familiar sequence of events; and the phenomena of a departing age assume the characteristics of a new era, as the midnight sun of arctic summers begins to shed a different light at the moment when it passes from its setting to its rising.

No political transaction of the 15th century has had so marked an influence on the subsequent course of history, as the matrimonial alliance formed between the houses of Burgundy and Austria with the effect of uniting their dominions under a common sceptre. From that alliance sprang the great rivalries and the dreams of universal sway which guided the policy and inflamed the ambition of powerful sovereigns from Charles the Fifth to Louis the Fourteenth. The great religious wars of the 16th century, the rally and reconquests made by the Church of Rome, and the efforts by which the Ottoman power was crippled and made impotent, derived their chief material and support from the same source. How this memorable union was projected and brought about —

from what motives and through what discussions — has never been told with fulness or precision.

The idea had been first conceived — not without prophetic intimations as to the destined results — during the childhood of the persons in whom it was to find its accomplishment. It had been one of the schemes of Æneas Sylvius Piccolomini for restoring the grandeur of the Church and the strength of the empire, and uniting the resources of both against the common foe of Christendom. The establishment of a vast temporal power acting in harmony with Rome and imposing laws upon Europe, was already contemplated as the instrument for suppressing anarchy and discord, resuscitating the spirit of the Crusades, and protecting the Papacy in the enjoyment of its spiritual dominion.[17] That the means were not ill calculated for the end was shown by the subsequent success — one of countless proofs that individual activity is not so inoperative, nor human skill and foresight so superfluous, in the conduct of the world's affairs, as those who see in history only a science of statistics would have us believe.[18]

[17] See the extract from a letter addressed by Pius II. (Piccolomini) to Philip of Burgundy in 1463, in Müller, Reichstags Theatrum unter Keyser Friedrichs V. Regierung (Jena, 1713), s. 590.

[18] That human actions and events are subject to controlling laws is what no one, we imagine, has ever thought of denying. To investigate those laws as far as they can be supposed to admit of being comprehended by finite beings is the highest office of reason; for each man, whatever his peculiar fardels, is doomed, Atlas-like, to carry the weight of the universe. One objection to the statistical system is, that it merely promises great results, when it shall have collected its materials and prepared its instruments. Another is, that it practically denies two principles without which the subject ceases to deserve any attention — human responsibility, and the divine government of the world.

The suggestion, however, fell unheeded at the time, and when revived several years later, it was with more contracted views, or at least with a larger mixture of mere personal considerations. Sigismund of Austria, a cousin german of the reigning emperor and the representative of the Tyrolean branch of his family, after having passed some weeks at Bruges in the spring of 1469, with results which have been in part narrated, returned to Innspruck, not with the depressed spirits natural in one who has been forced to part with his patrimony, but in the state of exaltation produced by a new-found treasure. He had been dazzled by the magnificence of the Burgundian court, astonished at the wealth and commerce of the Netherlands, and deeply impressed by the fact that, in case of Charles's death without male children, — a contingency even then regarded as highly probable, — this greatness would devolve upon an only daughter, now approaching a marriageable age. Though far from having a wide repute for prudence in the management of his own concerns, Sigismund was not deficient in that vigilant outlook for the interests of the house of Habsburg which has generally characterized its princes. He lost no time in despatching his agents to the imperial court, to report the discoveries he had made and propose that steps should be immediately taken to secure the hand of the Princess Mary for the Archduke Maximilian, the emperor's only son. If the matter could be brought to pass, it would turn out, with Heaven's blessing, — which is always counted upon on such occasions, — " the greatest piece of luck that had befallen the house of Austria for a long period."[19] Formerly this same project had been opposed by Sigismund himself. He had proffered his services in finding a more suitable bride for Maximilian in the royal family of France. But he now declared that there could be no comparison between the inducements offered by the two alliances; and with the perversity of a new convert, and a knowledge of the less versatile disposition of his imperial cousin, he intimated that, if a treaty with the French king were still preferred, he must be excused from taking any part in effecting it.[20]

The answer, though delayed by the long process of deliberation requisite for enabling Frederick to make any change in his views, was such as Sigismund had hoped for. His plan was approved, and the initiatory proceedings were committed to his own direction. Early therefore in the next year his ambassadors arrived at Bruges, to open the negotiation.

The policy pursued by Charles with reference to his daughter's marriage has been before explained.

[19] This is all stated by Sigismund with a business-like simplicity: "Die weil wir aber nw her ein zeit in seinem hof gewesen sein vnd ein erlich furstlich wesen gesehen gemerkt und erkannt auch seine land einstails erkundet vnd dabey betracht haben das er nwr allair elichs manns namens von Burgundj lebt vnd nwr ain tochter hat darauf alle seine lannd erben vnd gefallen mechten . . . so wollt vns vast gut bedunken vnd gefellig sein ob ain heyrat zwischen seiner maiestat sun vnserm vettern, vnd desselben von Burgundj tochter gemacht werden möchte, dann es durch schickung Gottes wol dartzu komen möchte, das ain so merklicher fal widererumb an das haus Österreich käme vnd fyel, als in langer zeit ye gescheen were."

[20] Instruction Herzog Sigmund's für s. Abgesandten zu K. Friedrich IV.; Chmel, Actenstücke and Briefe zur Geschichte des Hauses Habsburg (Wien, 1854–5), B. II. s. 131–135.

None of the offers tendered to her had yet been accepted, but none had been met with a direct and absolute refusal. The present proposal was one which must be listened to with peculiar attention, which must form a subject of real deliberation, which must receive an intelligible, if not a conclusive, reply. In itself, indeed, the match offered no such advantages as might alone be expected to win the duke's consent. It would not necessarily bring him an accession of strength or weaken the ranks of his enemies. No active assistance could be looked for from such an ally as Frederick — by whom, on the other hand, much would no doubt be demanded from such an ally as Charles. Even as a means of elevating Mary to a higher title and a greater dignity — the light in which the project would naturally be presented by its promoters, a light which might well have blinded an ambitious mother or a doting grandfather, but not the only light in which it must be viewed by a father still in the prime of life, whose wishes were neither centred in another nor to be satisfied by a reflected glory — it presented a twofold aspect. It was altogether doubtful whether Maximilian would be suffered to succeed to the imperial crown, and without the imperial crown he would be no fit husband for the duchess of Burgundy. That he would be elected king of the Romans if before his father's death he should have acquired for himself a great dominion, or the certain prospect of a great dominion, placing him at a height above all conceivable competitors, was, indeed, more than probable.

There could be no more feasible mode of achieving such a position than by marriage with a great heiress. But it would then be the husband that would owe to his wife, over and above the dower she had brought to him, his elevation to the empire. Standing alone, the scheme had the single merit which had recommended it to Sigismund and to Frederick. There could be no doubt that, if carried into effect, and followed by Heaven's blessing, it would prove the greatest piece of luck that had long befallen the house of Austria.

That it had no other merit than this was, however, its chief recommendation to Charles. Had it offered any of the ordinary equivalents, it would have been treated like others of the same nature: it would have been civilly, perhaps evasively, answered, and it would never have been taken into serious consideration. But it was naked of all such pretensions. It was wholly and avowedly one-sided. It was a simple proposition to the duke of Burgundy to assist in the aggrandizement of the house of Austria. The proposers must, therefore, anticipate a counter-proposition; they must be prepared to see their own scheme balanced by another, equally one-sided; *they* must be willing to assist in the aggrandizement of the house of Burgundy. Destitute as Frederick was of the more common means of supporting an ally, he had that to bestow which no one else could give, and which had long been the highest object of Charles's desires. But those desires now rose with the chances of their being gratified. Vain notions and hopes, evaporated by the heat of a brain so incessantly at work, were suddenly condensed, or at least made luminous and enchanting. What personal sacrifices the emperor might be induced to make for the benefit of his family, as well as of the world at large, was a subject on which those who had not the honor of an intimate acquaintance with him might speculate without restraint. Unchecked in its flight, Charles's ambition soared upwards to a pinnacle which hitherto had seemed unattainable, or even unapproachable. He could resign himself to the thought that his possessions and his glory were to pass to another line than his, if that line should have become his by adoption, if its interests were identified with his own, if he was hereafter to be remembered, not as the mere stepping-stone, but as the real founder of its greatness.

His answer was given, not to the envoys of Sigismund, but through a counter embassy sent to that prince in May, 1470. He was ready to give his consent to the marriage on condition of his own election as King of the Romans, — "so that coming to the empire, either at the death or *by the good pleasure* of Frederick, he might in his turn procure the election of his son-in-law as his successor, and thus secure the transmission of the imperial crown to Maximilian and his descendants in perpetuity." Intimations had recently reached him of the feasibility of such a scheme. If he himself desired its accomplishment, it was only that he might devote the prime and vigor of his life to the defence of the Christian faith, and to the renovation of the empire. Should the idea be favorably received, a day might at once be named for the representatives of the parties to meet and arrange a treaty.[21]

It was characteristic, surely, of the man, that a question of this kind seemed to him so simple and so tractable — one that might be approached without circumlocution and discussed without reticence or embarrassment. Had it been a matter involving military enterprise, his own exertions would have been called forth, preparing him for the obstacles to be

[21] Instruction de Charles, Duc de Bourgogne, à ceux qu'il devoit envoyer vers le Duc Sigismond d'Autriche; Lenglet, tom. iii. pp. 238–245.

This document — to be hereafter cited in connection with another subject — is without date. Lenglet assigns it to the close of the year 1472. Zellweger and Rodt place it in 1471. As an earlier and more precise date has been given in the text, it is proper that our reasons should be stated: 1st. There is an allusion to Sigismund's visit to the Burgundian court, which is known to have been in 1469, as having taken place "last year." 2d. It is mentioned that Sigismund's envoys had recently had an interview with Charles at Bruges, and that he had promised an immediate reply, but had been obliged to postpone it till the beginning of May. Now Charles spent several weeks at Bruges in February, 1470, and except for a single day, which was in June, 1470, he was not there again until after 1471. (See the Ancienne Chronique.) 3d. The allusions to the affairs of Brittany and of England — allusions wholly misconceived by Zellweger — are inapplicable to any other period than the spring of 1470. For instance, it is said that Edward's enemies had just been endeavoring to get possession of Calais. This must have been Warwick's attempt to land there about the 1st of May, 1470. 4th. Among the documents published by Chmel is one, to be presently noticed in the text, which is evidently Sigismund's answer to this message from the duke of Burgundy. That document bears the date of September, 1470. From three to four months formed the usual interval between the different stages of the negotiation.

Many of the documents in Chmel's collection are undated; and it is rarely that we are able to accept the conjectural dates given to them by the learned editor. We cannot stop to discuss the question in each particular case; but in every case we have examined and been guided by the internal evidence.

overcome, and the faculties brought into play would have been such as he himself possessed or could at least appreciate. The attempt would then have seemed to him arduous, but would in truth have been proportionably more easy. The present project was no doubt feasible, demanding only infinite tact, a long series of delicate manœuvres, the setting in motion of a thousand springs, and the employment of a thousand arts. For Charles of Burgundy it would have been a less impracticable idea to place himself on the throne of Germany by force of arms.

Charged with this surprising mission, Sigismund now betook himself in person to the imperial court. The task he had undertaken was to imbue the mind of Frederick with a correct sense of its own imbecility, — a revelation for which his long experience might possibly have prepared him, — and to suggest that he should either exercise his "good pleasure" by an absolute abdication in favor of the duke of Burgundy, or at least relieve himself of all the weightier cares of sovereignty by receiving a coadjutor, whose zealous and indefatigable spirit would find the burden light. He must also be led to admit that his influence with the electors would be vainly exerted in favor of his son, but would prove all-potent in promoting the ambition of a stranger. It would seem that these two points must have been happily settled, since the difficulty — for a difficulty there was — arose from another and remoter source. After looking deeply and earnestly into the matter and holding many consultations upon it, his imperial majesty found that there was no precedent for such a course, and that his duties and obligations to the empire and to the electoral and other princes were of such a nature as made it impossible that the proposed scheme could by any method whatever be carried into execution.[22] He, however, expressed his strong sense of the advantages to be derived from the alliance, and his hope that some different mode might be devised in which he could contribute to the elevation of the house of Burgundy. Being pressed to declare himself more plainly, he sagaciously hinted at the erection of the Burgundian states into a kingdom, stipulating, however, that the crown thus granted should be held as an imperial fief, and that its wearer should pledge himself to the support and defence of the house of Austria against all its enemies, both within and without the empire. The especial service demanded was the reduction of the Swiss cantons to their former state of vassalage; but the expulsion of the Turks from Germany, to be followed perhaps by the recapture of Constantinople, was also among the contemplated results.[23]

It cannot be denied that of the two proposals that of Charles was the more reasonable. If it were carried out — and followed by Heaven's blessing —

[22] "Sein k. g. hat in die sachen gesehen mit fleiss darynn rat gehallten und meniger ursach funden, damit sein k. gnad dem heiligen Reich und den Kurfürsten und fürsten des Reichs also verpunden gewanndt und verpflicht dadurch solichs . . . nicht muglich noch in ainicherlay wegen zu bescheen sey." Chmel, B. I. s. 11.

[23] Letter and memoranda (more closely connected than the editor seems to understand) in Chmel, B. I. s. 10–13, 20–23, 25–29.

the empire would pass for a time from the house of Austria, but would return to it reinvested with its ancient lustre and supremacy. To expect that from his own resources alone, and with the bribe of an empty title, the duke of Burgundy was to attempt the same or even greater feats, betrayed perhaps a miscalculation of his abilities, certainly a misconception of his character. He did not, as he wrote, desire a crown, unless some general advantage — meaning of course some solid personal benefit — were attached to it.[24]

His rejoinder, however, is to be found, not in a brief note with his own signature, — in which this remark is made and the emperor's proposition coldly declined, — but in a letter ostentatiously professing to proceed from the sole hand and head of its writer, a German vassal of the Burgundian house, in which the propriety and feasibility of Charles's plan are argued warmly and at length.[25]

The diplomatic campaign thus opened was carried on throughout the years 1471 and 1472. Embassies went to and fro; conferences were held; private influences were set at work; money was distributed, or at least promised; the usual amount of manœuvring was practised; more than the usual degree of secrecy seems to have been preserved. Yet no real progress was made so long as Charles adhered to his original demand, modified only by the withdrawal of his

[24] "Non affectamus dominia nostra in regnum erigi neque alio pacto coronari quam si id in Rem publicam et communem salutem fiat." Ibid. s. 13, 14.

[25] Ibid. s. 28–30.

unfortunate innuendo as to the mode in which the emperor might exercise his "good pleasure." The merits of the scheme were elaborately set forth, the imperial scruples learnedly combated, the objections to the marriage on any other terms plainly stated and vigorously urged. The house of Austria was now in a state of evident decline. The reënforcement it had gained by its connection with the house of Luxembourg was wholly spent. It had been weakened by foreign attacks, by its own internal divisions, and by the increasing pressure of a charge which it had no longer the strength to sustain. It had lost Switzerland, it had lost Bohemia, it had lost Hungary. It was incapable of defending its dominions on the Rhine; it was incapable of retaining its position at the head of the empire; it was incapable of saving the empire from impending overthrow and dissolution. By an alliance with the house of Burgundy, its energies might be recruited, its losses more than made good, its supremacy established on a new and solid basis. It would in all probability become the greatest and the wealthiest house in the whole world, able to defy its enemies at home and abroad, able to recover all its former possessions, able to dispel the fears and to secure the safety of Christendom.[26] These advantages would not be risked, on the contrary they would be guarantied, by admitting the claim

[26] "Que mon dit seigneur Maximilien au moyen dudit mariage sera en aparence de auoir les plus grandes et belles seignouries de la crestiennete . . . et seroit la maison Dotriche la plus tresgrande, et trespuissante que toutes les maisons du monde." Instruction à messire Pierre de Haguembac, Chmel, B. I. s. 33.

of Charles of Burgundy to gather and transmit them with his own hand. If they were left to be reaped by other hands and at a future time, the opportunity for improving them might in the mean while have escaped, or might then be wasted. By the method proposed, present evils would be cured and prospective good made greater and more certain. All the elements of the alliance would be blended and transfused; the interests of both parties would become identical; the two families would be made one. Frederick was old and infirm; Maximilian was still a boy. Charles was at an age when experience and vigor are combined. He was to stand in the relation of a father to Maximilian; he wished also to stand in the relation of a son to Frederick. He was ready to become the guardian of the one — watching over his interests and preparing him for the part he was to play — if he were allowed to become also the stay and support of the other, releasing him from anxieties and labor, sharing his responsibilities and authority.[27]

There was no want of logical consistency in the plan, no lack of force in the arguments by which it was supported. Why, then, was not Frederick convinced? It is not at all certain that he was not convinced, or in a fair way to be convinced. His slowness in forming a resolution, still more in acting on a resolution, was proverbial. He sent the friendliest messages to the Burgundian court, though he instructed his agents that it would be well not to take

[27] Ibid. ubi supra.

any step which might interfere with the renewal of the French negotiation in case the present one should prove abortive.[28]

Charles, on his part, was not more open, while he seems to have been much less deliberative, in his proceedings. The bait at which the emperor thus cautiously nibbled was placed before a less wary but also less desirable gudgeon, and eagerly swallowed. In June, 1472, a formal contract of betrothal was actually exchanged between Mary of Burgundy and Nicholas duke of Lorraine, and that prince, tempted by the brilliant prospect thus held out to him into an unchivalrous abandonment of his similar engagement with the French king, accompanied Charles in his last hostile expedition into France. At the close, however, of the campaign, he was induced — in what manner or by what representations does not appear — to renounce the claim which he had acquired with a sacrifice both of interest and of honor, and to sign a paper absolving Mary from the obligations contracted in her name. Yet, strangely enough, we find that, a few months later, hints were thrown out with a view of inciting him to renew his proposals. Naturally, he was desirous, before making a second attempt, to assure himself that it was indeed the substance, and not again the mere shadow, that was offered to his grasp. But before this interesting question could be solved, the negotiation was cut short by his sudden death — an event productive of consequences to be

[28] Ibid. s. 24.

hereafter related, and attributed by rumor, in accordance with what had become a strict article of the popular faith, to poison administered by the agents of Louis.[29]

The more important negotiation with the emperor, to which that with the duke of Lorraine had been a mere interlude, made at length a decided advance. The differences admitted of compromise, and from an early period there had been on both sides, if not a positive intention, at least an idea of compromise. Some share of real power must be granted to Charles, while Frederick's supremacy must remain untouched. Though loath to make the least abatement in his pretensions, the duke had instructed his envoys, in the last resort, to fall back upon a proposition which though it differed rather in form than in substance from his earlier demand, seems to have been regarded by himself as a great concession, and may possibly have been so regarded by the emperor. It was accordingly proposed that, in addition to the regal title, Charles should receive the appointment, "irrevocably and for life," of "Vicar-General of the whole Empire," with a pledge from the electors of his elevation to the throne when vacated by Frederick's death.[30]

That this proposal, either in whole or in part, was accepted as at least the basis of a settlement, may be inferred from the fact that a personal conference between the parties was now arranged. The invita-

[29] Lenglet, tom. iii. pp. 192–195, 255–257.

[30] Instruction, &c. Chmel, B. I. s. 30–37. — This plan had formed part of the original scheme as devised by Æneas Sylvius.

tion was given by the emperor in letters written with his own hand, and filled with the strongest assurances of his good will. A special embassy followed, in July, 1473, to congratulate Charles on the late success of his arms, and to promise investiture, in the usual form, of the two fiefs, Gueldres and Zutphen, which he had just added to his dominions.[31] The propriety of his obtaining this ratification of his conquest, in a public ceremony, afforded an ostensible motive for the interview about to be held, while the real or principal design was left to be conjectured from the preparations, or announced by the result.

Instead, therefore, of returning from Nimeguen to Brussels, the duke now set out in the direction of Metz, where the conference was appointed to be held — a free imperial town situated within the borders of Lorraine, but not subject to the same rule. He was about, for the first time, to traverse foreign territory without the declaration of a hostile purpose. But it was territory which he already looked upon as a future field of hostilities and the destined prize of his victorious arms. He intended also, before his return to the Netherlands, to visit his possessions on the Rhine, and receive the homage of the people; and thence to continue his progress through Franche Comté and Burgundy, where he had not yet been since his accession, and where his subjects were impatient to receive from his lips the usual confirmation of their privileges and assurance of protection.

[31] Chmel, B. I. s. 37, 38.—Ancienne Chronique.

These important objects, and especially that which was the chief, though unavowed, object of the journey, made it a fit occasion for exhibiting all the wealth and pomp of the Burgundian court. The rich tapestries, the costly plate, the heaps of jewelry and precious stones to which Philip the Good had "given his heart," were forwarded from Antwerp by the duke's directions. A general hunt had been ordered in the forests of Luxembourg to provide a profusion of the rarest game for the entertainments he proposed to give. His retinue was unusually brilliant, including, besides the functionaries of his household and the chief members of the nobility, several neighboring princes, who, though nominally independent, were yet the clients and pensionaries of the Burgundian sovereign. He had dismissed a portion of his troops, but retained under his command not less than fourteen thousand men, the *élite* of his army, distinguished by their superior discipline and the splendor and completeness of their equipments. Four hundred pieces of artillery gave a still more warlike aspect to his march. It seemed as if he were prepared to seize by force, if his claim were resisted and his solicitations denied, the crown which he aspired to wear.

On the 22d of August, he arrived in the neighborhood of Aix-la-Chapelle. The magistrates presented to him the keys of the town and a vase of silver gilt adorned with gems and filled with gold pieces. Charles, however, was not satisfied with these tokens of submission and respect. The place had formerly incurred his displeasure by affording a harbor to the fugitives from Liége, and more recently by betraying its sympathy with the besieged inhabitants of Nimeguen. The blame of these offences was thrown upon certain of the citizens, who appeared before him barefoot and in their shirts, and knelt to solicit his forgiveness.[32] In his passage through Luxembourg, he was met by a deputation from Metz, bringing, as a gift from the city, a hundred vessels of choice wine, and an assurance of its desire to welcome, in a suitable manner, so illustrious a guest. A gracious reply was given, and the deputies were sumptuously entertained at the duke's table.[33]

But this interchange of civilities was presently followed by an exhibition of mistrust on the one side and resentment on the other. Charles, by an embassy, requested that the whole, or the greater portion, of his forces should be lodged in the town, and that, for his greater convenience, the keys of one of the gates should remain in his possession during his stay. Such a proposal was well calculated to excite apprehension. The free cities of the Middle Ages were generally surrounded by hostile territory, and perpetually menaced by powerful neighbors. Their chronicles, like the annals of nations, are filled with details of battles and sieges and all the incidents of war. The citizens were ready to don their armor and repair to the walls at a moment's notice. The

[32] Pontus Heuterus. — Ancienne Chronique. — Gollut. — Rodt.

[33] These and other details are taken from the Memoirs of Philippe de Vigneulles — an interesting work, printed by the Literary Society of Stuttgardt. Vigneulles, a native of Metz, was one of the envoys on this occasion.

burgomasters were constantly employed in strengthening the defences, maintaining a vigilant watch, and otherwise providing against the hazards of a sudden attack. Few places had had a longer experience of this kind than Metz. The inhabitants were almost always engaged in hostilities with the subjects of the duke of Lorraine, and only a few months had passed since they had repelled an attempt of Nicholas to make himself master of the town. Rumors were already rife that Lorraine was about to pass under the dominion of a prince whose hostility was more to be dreaded than that of its former sovereigns. It was even doubtful whether Charles were now approaching in the guise of a friend or of an enemy.[34] The magistrates, therefore, confident in the strength of the fortifications, which were unsurpassed by those of any city in Christendom, rejected his demand on the plea of want of room occasioned by the previous arrival of the emperor with a numerous suite. They offered to furnish accommodation for five hundred men-at-arms, and provided wine and other refreshments, without the walls, for the remainder of the army. The duke, however, disdained to accept what he regarded as a churlish hospitality. He intimated his ability to force an entrance if he were so disposed. As for the keys, he said, they were already in his possession — referring, doubtless, to the ordnance which he had brought with him.[35]

[34] "Cives reputantes et armato, et potentiori, et inter hostem amicumque dubio credere periculosum." Letter of Arnold de Lalain, in Lenglet, tom. iii. p. 258.

[35] Ibid. ubi supra. — Vigneulles. — Meyer.

Frederick now consented to change the place of meeting, and the venerable city of Trèves, beautifully situated on the right bank of the Moselle, sixty miles from its junction with the Rhine, was designated as the spot. Thither accordingly he proceeded, and was followed two days later (Friday, September 30) by Charles. On his approach, the duke was met and welcomed by the emperor and his son, accompanied by several of the electors and a numerous escort, as well as by the authorities and principal inhabitants of the town. The greetings between the two princes were marked by that deference on the one side, that condescension on the other, and that mutual cordiality, which the scrupulous etiquette both of the German and Burgundian courts had the faculty of eliciting on such occasions. Charles uncovered, dismounted, and made an inclination as if to kneel, when he was raised and affectionately embraced by his imperial lord. A debate then ensued as to the order of procession, the duke, with proper humility, declining to ride side by side with the head of the Holy Roman Empire, and yielding to the entreaties of the monarch only when the allotted period of resistance — "more than a long half hour" — had expired.[36]

The avenues and streets were densely crowded with spectators, curious to behold the far-famed splendors of the Burgundian court, and to scan the

[36] Extrait d'une lettre contenant une relation des premières entrevues de Charles-le-Téméraire et de l'empereur Frédéric à Trèves; Gachard, Doc. Inéd. tom. i. p. 233.

features of a prince whose character and actions had produced so deep an impression on the minds of his contemporaries. Charles, who was now in his fortieth year, had that in his countenance and bearing which could not fail to fix attention and command respect.[37] His robust and vigorous frame seasoned by temperance and exercise, his mien indicative of authority and self-reliance, his glance full of sternness and of fire, the general expression of his features, betokening the concentration of the mind upon a single and lofty purpose, seemed to proclaim his right to occupy the foremost place among the princes of the time.[38] Over his armor of polished steel he wore a short mantle, so thickly sprinkled with diamonds, rubies, and other gems, that its cost was estimated at not less than two hundred thousand gold crowns. He carried in his hand a velvet hat, on the front of which blazed a diamond of inestimable price, while his jewelled helmet was borne behind him by a page. His horse, a famous black steed of incomparable strength and beauty, was equipped in warlike harness, but covered with caparisons of violet and gold that descended to the ground.

[37] "Dux autem circiter quadraginta natus annos, in ipso ætatis robore medio rerum gloriæque cursu conspicuus." Letter of Arnold de Lalain, Lenglet, tom. iii. p. 259.

[38] Trausch, one of the contemporary chroniclers of Strasburg, whose peculiar hostility to Charles will be hereafter noticed, was far from being prepossessed in favor of the Burgundian prince by the glimpse he obtained of him on this occasion. He was particularly disgusted by Charles's "large black eyes" with their "haughty and bold expression," his "broad shoulders," "limbs *excessively* robust," and "legs slightly bowed from his being so constantly in the saddle." De Bussierre, Ligue formée contre Charles le Téméraire (Paris, 1846), p. 65.

The emperor, arrayed with sufficient magnificence in a long robe of cloth of gold bordered with pearls, and worn "in the Turkish fashion," presented, in other respects, a striking contrast to his proud and powerful vassal. His reign, the longest and the feeblest in the annals of the empire, had already lasted thirty-three years. Age had somewhat bent his form, but added nothing to the dulness of an eye always expressive of indolence, irresolution, timidity, and incapacity, — of a character, in short, ludicrously ill adapted to his position at the head of Christendom, the immense interests that demanded his care, and the anarchical elements he was expected to control. The purple, though it concealed his distorted foot — the result of a disease said to have been contracted by his inveterate and lazy habit of kicking open every door through which he wished to pass — could not hide the vulgar features, vulgar manners, and slothful intellect, of the German boor. From his Polish mother, Cimburga the "pouch-mouthed," he had inherited the large, protruding under jaw which, transmitted to his descendants, is still designated as "the Austrian lip." When the all-important and ever-recurring question of the defence of the empire against the Moslems came under discussion in the diet, Frederick, lulled by the frequent iterations familiar as a nursery song, dropped fast asleep. He was not altogether deficient in a certain homely shrewdness, relished proverbs, and could point the application of some old German fable learned in childhood. He also took considerable pains, like other princes of the time, to discover the philosopher's stone, having strong acquisitive tendencies, and some skill in keeping money — when it could be obtained. Unfortunately, the management of the German empire, at that period, was one of the last businesses to insure profitable returns; and if Frederick failed to merit the title bestowed upon his successor, of "the Penniless," it was only because he *did* "take care of the *pennies*," while "the *pounds*," in reality, "took care of themselves." [39]

The Archduke Maximilian, a youth of eighteen, of agreeable and intelligent countenance, and clad in crimson and silver, came next in order, having for his companion an Ottoman prince, a brother of Mahomet the Second, who, having been captured in war, and converted by the pope, was now attached to the imperial court. His swarthy complexion, his Eastern dress, and especially his long hair twisted and knotted "in the Sarmatian mode," so as to form a peak above his head, gave him, in the eyes of a people to whom "the Turk" was still a name suggestive of all that was fearful and detestable, a wild and ferocious ap-

[39] These details in regard to the character and habits of the emperor have been gathered from a variety of sources, both descriptive and anecdotical. Perhaps no monarch was ever the object of a more complete and universal contempt. The following impatient summary of his moral and intellectual characteristics, by two French envoys who endeavored to transact some important business with him in 1458, is, we may hope, slightly overcharged: "C'est un homme endormi, lâche, morne, pesant, pensif, mérencolieux, avaricieux, chiche, craintif, qui se laisse plumer la barbe à chacun sans revanger, variable, hypocrite, dissimulant, *et à qui tout mauvais adjectif appartient*, et vraiement indigne de l'honneur qu'il a." Duclos, tom. iii. preuves.

pearance. Amongst the immense throng of nobles that followed, the Germans intermingled with the Burgundians, whom they had vainly attempted to rival in the gorgeousness of their apparel and the number and splendor of their retinues, were the archbishops of Mayence and Trèves, the prince-bishop of Liége, the dukes of Bavaria and Cleves, the margrave of Baden, Count Engelbert of Nassau, surnamed "the Rich," — the head of that branch of his illustrious race which had established itself in the Netherlands, — and the count of Chateau-Guion, the representative of the house of Orange-Chalons, whose princely possessions in France and in Franche Comté were one day to be united with those of Engelbert's descendants, and to be ungrudgingly sacrificed by them on the altar of their country's freedom.

Never — say the describers of the scene, not unfamiliar with the pomps and pageants of the age — had there ever been witnessed such a blazing of gold, such a sparkling of gems, such a flaunting of damasks and velvets of the richest hues and costliest texture, such a prancing of steeds and waving of banners — until the eye was dazzled and strained by the continuous stream of confused magnificence. Even the troopers wore habits of cloth of gold and silver over their steel harness, while their embroidered saddle-cloths were fringed with silver bells. The archers of the ducal body-guard surpassed, as usual, all the rest in the sumptuousness of their equipments. The heralds-at-arms of the fourteen different states which acknowledged the Burgundian sway rode immediately in front of the duke, clothed in their armorial coats; a band of trumpeters in a gay silken uniform of white and blue, with silver instruments, were somewhat further in advance; and foremost of all went a troop of one hundred beautiful boys in garments of the most delicate texture, their long yellow hair flowing over their shoulders, — exceeding, it was thought, the feminine grace and loveliness of a bridal cortége. In such a display of his grandeur, wealth, and power, strangers as well as vassals might be expected to discern the propriety of Charles's claim to a title already worn by princes far inferior to him in all the essential attributes of royalty.

When the procession had reached the market-place, a new point of ceremony was raised — whether the duke, as was the duty of the vassal, should conduct the emperor to his lodgings, or the latter, waiving the privileges of his superior rank, should pay that honor to Charles. After the requisite degree of courtesy had been exhibited by both parties, the conclusion was adopted, in accordance doubtless with the prearranged programme, that they should now take leave and repair to their separate quarters, each with his own escort. The Burgundian army occupied a portion of the town and the villages around. The emperor took up his abode at the archiepiscopal palace, and Charles at a great conventual house, where the honorary office of its "protector," conferred upon him some years previously, entitled him to hospitality.[40]

[40] The authorities for all the external accompaniments of the meeting at Trèves are very numerous, and the descriptions of the pageant-

During the next eight weeks a series of shows and entertainments gave to the ancient town — already more noted for the many relics of its former importance than for any existing signs of wealth or animation — the aspect of a gay and splendid capital. Jousts, banquets, ceremonial visits, and public formalities, occupied the two courts, exciting the amazement of the citizens, besides keeping their curiosity on the stretch. The Abbey of Saint Maximin had been fitted up with the furniture and decorations brought from the palaces of the Netherlands. In the refectory, piles of gold and silver plate were displayed on a buffet of ten stages, twenty feet broad, which rose from the floor to the ceiling. The shrines and altars of the church gleamed with the images, the candlesticks, the crucifixes, and the reliquaries, of pure gold embossed with precious stones, which had inspired the *devotion* of Philip the Good. The great hall was hung with tapestry of the rarest and costliest materials depicting the conquests of Alexander, the story of whose achievements was commonly thought to have first inspired the ambition of Philip's son. The floor, the seats, the dais, the canopy, were resplendent with embroidered cloths of crimson and gold, exhibiting the arms of Burgundy, the pictured legend of the

ry very minute. See, in particular, the letters printed by Lenglet, Gachard, and Chmel; the Diary of Knebel with the extracts in the appendix from Gerung, Libellus de magnificencia ducis Burg. in Treveris visa; Fugger, Ehrenspiegel des Hauses Œsterreichs; Trithemius Chronicon Hirsaugiense; Müller, Reichstags Theatrum; Gesta Trevirorum (ed. Wyttenbach); Diebold Schilling, Die Burgundischen Kriegen; Basin; Meyer.

Toison, and other heraldic emblazonments and decorations. Here, on a chair of state raised several feet above the dais, the emperor took his seat, on Sunday, the 2d of October, not without much ceremonial coyness — probably not without some real disinclination. On his right were the electoral princes and other great nobles of the empire. On his left was placed the duke's chair, not less elevated than his own, but somewhat further in the background. The principal persons of the Burgundian court were stationed near their sovereign; the rest occupied their accustomed places in the hall. Hugonet, chancellor of Burgundy, delivered a long oration in Latin, setting forth the reasons why his master was unable at present to comply with the imperial request that he should employ his vast resources, and turn his arms, victorious on all former occasions, against the encroachments of the Moslems. The blame of his inability was laid, of course, upon the French king, whose boundless ambition, incessant aggressions, and treacherous manœuvres, had disturbed the harmony of Christendom and prevented it from putting forth its united energies in defence of its common interests. The whole career of Louis formed the subject of a furious diatribe, his ingratitude to the house of Burgundy and the dark transaction of his brother's death being dwelt upon with especial emphasis. Had the king been present he would have found it necessary to appease the excited indignation of the audience by one of his mildest and most pathetic harangues. The orator concluded by assuring the assembly of the settled intention of the Burgundian prince, when the safety and tranquillity of his own dominions were no longer endangered, to undertake that crusade against the infidel which had ever been the great and ultimate object of his aspirations.[41] After the usual service of wines, spices, and conserves, Frederick was conducted back to his lodgings by the members of both courts, amid a display of martial pomp rendered more effective by the blazing of countless flambeaus.[42]

The festal entertainments given by Charles, who, though he might more properly have been considered as the guest, chose throughout to play the part of host, were of the same sumptuous description as those which have been perhaps too frequently noticed in previous parts of our narrative. A more public but less pretentious display was the ceremony of his investiture by the emperor with the sovereignty of Gueldres, which took place in the principal square. Frederick was seated in state on a lofty scaffold, around which the duke, alone and bareheaded, but clad in complete armor, made three circuits on horseback. Having then assumed the mantle of a prince of the empire, he ascended the steps, preceded by an officer of arms bearing an escutcheon, on which the

[41] Lamarche affirms in the most positive manner, as a thing within his own knowledge, that Charles always looked forward to a crusade against the infidel as the crowning achievement of his career. "Et, si Dieu luy eust donné vie et prospérité, il eust monstré par effect, que mon recit, en ceste partie, est véritable, car je le sçay par luy-mesme, et non pas par ouir dire à autruy." Mémoires, tom. i. p. 199.

[42] Gachard, Doc. Inéd. tom. i. pp. 234–236. — Lenglet, tom. iii. pp. 260–262. — Gerung, De magnificencia ducis Burg. in Treveris visa, ap. Knebel, s. 194. — Müller, Reichstags Theatrum, s. 564, 568, 569.

heraldic insignia of the newly-acquired fiefs were quartered, for the first time, with those of Burgundy. Kneeling at the emperor's feet, he laid two fingers on the crossed hilt of a sword held up before him by Frederick, and pronounced the oath of fealty and service in low but distinct tones. The usual formalities of investiture followed, ending with the proclamation of his new title.[43]

Meanwhile many private conferences were held, the Chancellor Hugonet, who acted as interpreter between the two sovereigns, being apparently the only person who was taken into their confidence. Conjectures, however, served to supply in some measure the void felt by those who were eager to fathom the mystery. Besides the host of strangers drawn to Trèves by the mere external attractions of the occasion, the secret agents of many states and cities, interested in the probable result, were present to watch the proceedings and transmit whatever hints or items of intelligence they might be able to collect. The extraordinary length and pompous accompaniments of the visit, — so disproportioned to the cause assigned for it,—above all, the secret interviews, from which even the electors and the great officers of the imperial chamber were excluded, made it certain that a business of no ordinary kind was in process of negotiation. The whole town, indeed the whole of Western Germany, was in a fever of speculation and inquiry. Rumors were sent abroad in the shape of authentic informa-

[43] Basin, tom. ii. pp. 323, 324.—Müller, Reichstags Theatrum, s. 587.

tion, detailing all the particulars of the contemplated arrangement, and even forestalling the announcement of its actual consummation.[44] The council of Berne, which had shown from the first an extreme anxiety in regard to the affair,—sending a special embassy to the French king to warn him of the necessity for vigilant observation,[45]—communicated to its confederates, in a circular dated November 29, the receipt of despatches from Metz, with the startling news that, five days before (the date, as we shall presently see, of a very different occurrence), Charles had been solemnly crowned at Trèves, the territorial limits assigned for his kingdom embracing not only his actual possessions held of the empire, but Savoy, Milan, and other imperial fiefs, and whatever states and cities south and east of the Jura had been comprised in the earlier Burgundian monarchy. It was added that the Venetian government, informed of this event by its own agents, had hastened to pay the most distinguished honors to the representatives of the new king resident at Venice, and to intimate its desire of entering into a more strict alliance with him.[46]

At Trèves itself, meanwhile, other reports had circulated, of a more authentic character, and facts within every one's knowledge dispelled all doubt as to the intentions of the princes. The various artificers of the town were busily employed in making

[44] Knebel, s. 13.—Müller, Reichstags Theatrum, s. 597.

[45] Rodt, B. I. s. 178.

[46] Zellweger, Versuch die wahren Gründe des burgundischen Krieges aus den Quellen darzustellen; Archiv für Schweiz. Geschichte, B. V. s. 27.

the necessary preparations for the ceremony which was to place Charles in a more exalted position, set a seal upon his past triumphs, and open before him a new vista of glory. The diadem, sceptre, and other regalia, the banners, the new dresses and equipments which were to throw into the shade all the previous displays of his magnificence, were no longer mere air-drawn visions, but had taken tangible shapes under the hands of skilful workmen. By the imperial orders, the interior of the spacious cathedral had received the suitable decorations and arrangements. The scaffoldings had been laid. The thrones were raised, and the altitude and collocation of the different seats with due regard to the rank of the personages who were to occupy them were determined, under the superintending eye of Frederick himself. The bishop of Metz, designated as the prelate who was to officiate on the occasion, — to celebrate the mass and administer the unction, — had his mitre and robes and other paraphernalia in readiness. The day — November 25th — was set.[47]

It was, however, hardly possible that an affair of such importance, snugly and dexterously as it had been managed, should proceed with perfect smoothness, or be hurried to its completion without encountering obstacles. The correctness of the general surmise being now established, — if not by an open and explicit avowal, by the evidence of facts that admitted of no misconstruction, plausible explanation,

[47] Basin (then a resident at Trèves), tom. ii. lib. 4, cap. 9. — Diebold Schilling; Müller, Reichstags Theatrum; Chmel, B. I. s. 4 et al., &c.

or denial,—it was natural that a counter-movement should begin, that intrigues should be set on foot by those who viewed the project with jealous or hostile eyes, but who had waited till their suspicions were confirmed, till the cup was already at the lip, before they dashed it away. The right of the emperor to confer the regal title on an imperial vassal could hardly be questioned. The case of Bohemia, erected into a kingdom in the 12th century, afforded a sufficient precedent. Nor could it be denied that of all the imperial vassals the sovereign of the Netherlands had by far the strongest claims to such an elevation. Apart from his superior power, his superior energies, and the historical prestige which invested his pretensions,—the inducements offered had the natural effect of making the avaricious Frederick the more eager party of the two in a transaction of which the benefits were to accrue to his own posterity and to aggrandize the house, not of Valois, but of Habsburg. For the closeness and cunning with which the affair had been so nearly brought to a successful conclusion, the credit, doubtless, was mainly due to the commercial instincts and aptitudes of the imperial brain.[48]

On the other hand, the electors had at least a right to be consulted, or at all events to be heard, before the bargain was carried into effect. They were the chief members of a body, every part of which must

[48] "Der Keyser," wrote Albert of Brandenburg to his friend the duke of Saxony, "hat das alles aus Vollkommenheit Keyserliches Gewalts gethan, und meint, es soll nymantz davon disputiren; doch hätt der Herzog die Verwilligung der Kurfürsten gern, und ist hart darnach gestanden." Müller, Reichstags Theatrum, s. 598.

be affected directly or indirectly by the proposed changes. Some of them were present in person; others had their representatives at Trèves. But while they had been expected to swell the pageant, no share had been assigned them in the action. Even in the subordinate parts of silent but ornamental figures, they had been excelled and outshone by their inferiors in rank; and they had repaid the ill-disguised contempt of the haughty Burgundian nobles by expressions of scorn, real or affected, for a luxury and ostentation with which they were unable to compete.[49] Their discontent was stimulated by the agents of France, and more especially by the free cities of the Rhineland, where the matter had produced an extraordinary ferment, and where preparations were even made for resisting by force of arms the projected extension of the Burgundian power.[50]

Charles had, it is true, friends and well-wishers among the German princes and people. His audience chamber was daily thronged by those who came, not only to pay their respects or to gratify their curiosity, but to petition him for favors or to proffer their support. Matthias Corvinus, who had successfully disputed the possession of the crown of Hungary with

[49] Letter of Arnold de Lalain, Lenglet, tom. iii. p. 262. — "Les Allemans mesprisoient la pompe et parolle dudict duc, l'attribuant à orgueil. Les Bourguignons mesprisoient la petite compagnie de l'Empereur, et les pauvres habillemens." Commines, tom. i. p. 167.

[50] "An alle Landsassen in Elsass, Sundgau und am Rhein ringsum gelangte der Befehl, sie sollten sich Waffen verschaffen: Alles berietet sich zum Kriege. Was soll daraus werden! Gott möge uns bewahren nach seiner Barmherzigkeit!" Knebel, s. 12, and more to the same effect, s. 14.

the Austrian house, and the elector-palatine, a Bavarian prince, — called by his admirers "Frederick the Victorious," but by his enemies, "Fritz the Bad" — who had resisted not less successfully the efforts of that house to regain its supremacy in Suabia and the Rhine provinces, — sought the alliance of the Burgundian duke, and hoped through his mediation to obtain from the emperor a formal recognition of their rights. There was also a very general belief that the active participation of so powerful and redoubtable a prince in the affairs of the empire would remedy the evils which had arisen from a long course of weakness and mismanagement, and overcome the paralysis which had left the heart and head of Christendom insensible to the sufferings of its crushed and bleeding extremities.[51] His position and achievements, his warlike disposition, indefatigable industry, and zeal for justice, encouraged the hope that the spirit of Henry the Saxon or of Frederick Barbarossa might again shine forth in a time of darkness and trouble. These favorable impressions were confirmed by the stern discipline of the Burgundian camp, where the frequent spectacle of a convicted thief dangling from the branch of a tree gave great satisfaction to the inhabitants of the surrounding region.[52]

[51] The probable benefits of the scheme were not overlooked even by those among the electors who had reasons for opposing it. "Es würdt dadurch gemeyner Fried im Reich, und gewinnt der Keyser in seinen Landen auch Friede, ob Gott will, damit man dem Türcken desterbass wiederstehen mag." Letter of the Margrave Albert of Brandenburg to Duke William of Saxony, in Müller, Reichstags Theatrum, s. 598.

[52] "Si quis ei furtum, aut rapinam fecisse delatus fuisset, etiam in re minima, sine misericordia mox

But whatever contributes to any end raises obstacles to its attainment. Every effort provokes opposition, every alliance creates an enemy. Charles's connection with the king of Hungary and with the elector-palatine — between whom and the emperor he was laboring to effect a reconciliation — placed him in an attitude of hostility to the king of Bohemia, the successor of Podiebrad and the implacable foe of Corvinus, and to the house of Baden, the rival of that of Bavaria. His high expectations, founded on his unquestionable merits, could not fail to excite in the breast of the margrave of Brandenburg, the famous Albert Achilles, those feelings with which one aspiring mind is prone to regard the successes of another. The elector and the duke of Saxony had no peculiar motives of interest or of jealousy for abandoning the neutrality they had at first assumed and throwing their weight into the adverse scale. But besides their close relations with the Margrave Albert, with whom they generally acted, they were influenced by an apprehension which was common to the whole body of the nobility, and which was no doubt the most potent element in the sudden frustration of the plan when apparently on the eve of its accomplishment. Let the duke of Burgundy, it was said, unite his power with that of the emperor, and such of the

eum fecit suspendi. . . . Unde et suis metum incussit, et *laudem sibi Justitiæ apud omnes Mosellanos acquisivit.*" Trithemius, Chronicon Hirsaugiense, p. 481. — What deepened the impression was the punctilious honesty with which the duke paid for the use of a tree near his quarters which his provost-marshal had appropriated to this purpose.

imperial vassals as wish to have a will of their own will have cause to look to themselves.[53] Thus the strongest reason for assenting to the scheme was the strongest reason for resisting it. Then, as ever, the Anarchy of Germany rose against the attempt to extinguish it.

Serviceable arguments for shaking the imperial purpose were easily found. The duke of Burgundy was by birth a foreigner, a member of a reigning house whose interests were often hostile to those of the empire. He had no love for the German nation, no sympathies with the German character. The air with which he now trod the German soil was that, not of a vassal or a friend, but rather of an enemy and a conqueror. His insufferable pride and insatiable ambition had been evinced in every act of his career. Was it politic to give new wings to that ambition, new supports and new additions to a power which already exceeded that of other princes? Was it certain, or even probable, that Frederick would himself derive from the arrangement the advantages he anticipated? Charles was still young. Nothing was more likely than that, either by his present wife, or in case of her death by a third wife, he might have male offspring to inherit his dominions. In that contingency Maximilian, instead of making a

[53] "Wann der Keyser das Land zu Schwaben ganz einnimbt, das Hertzog Sigmund kein nuz is und die Lantvogtey darzu hat, und den Herzogen von Burgundy an der Seyten, warten all Unterthanen des Reichs, was sie zuthon haben, die mit dem Keyser und Im nicht eins wollen sein." Letter of the Margrave Albert, in Müller, Reichstags Theatrum, s. 598.

wealthy marriage, would have gained not a single rood of territory — nothing but the inconsiderable dower in money and personal effects which the duke had consented to pay down. But there was another and still more difficult calculation to be solved before the venture could be safely made. Was Charles sincere in his promise to bestow his daughter's hand on the archduke? Would he, after he had received the equivalent, hold to his engagement, if strong temptations to break it presented themselves? His repugnance to accepting of any son-in-law was notorious. He thought himself fortunate among the princes of the time in having no expectant successor to interfere with or oppose his authority, and was reported to have said that sooner than incur the vexations that might be expected to follow from his daughter's marriage, he would assume the cowl and bury himself in a convent. One unexceptionable suitor he had rejected, at the cost of incurring the enmity of his oldest allies when he stood most in need of their support. Another had been insnared by delusive promises, cheated by vows made only to be broken. If the duke intended a faithful adherence to the obligations he had now contracted, why had he not brought with him his wife, his daughter, and the ladies of their court, instead of coming attended by an armed host and consuming the time with mere empty parade and idle festivities? Why had not the same occasion been fixed upon for the celebration of the nuptials and the bestowment of the crown? Finally, it was contended that, if a new realm was to be created, or an extinct title revived, the whole body of the electors ought previously to be summoned, their advice asked, and their consent obtained.[54]

Such are the representations said to have been addressed to the emperor by the archbishop of Trèves, a brother of the margrave of Baden, and the person third in rank in the electoral college. They were supported by the agents of Brandenburg and Saxony, and it may be presumed of other courts. They were the more effectual that they coincided with the secret alarms of a dull and phlegmatic but obstinate nature, in danger of falling under the turbulent dominion of an active and fiery will. Yet the same timidity and lack of resoluteness which made Frederick incapable of adhering to his plans when firmly opposed, raised impediments in the present instance to his changing them. On what plea could he retract his plighted word? How was he, at this late hour, to confess that he had promised more than he was able to perform? How was he to face the brunt of that anger which disappointed hopes, mortified pride, broken faith, and apparent duplicity must excite in a passionate and haughty mind? Was it still *possible* to draw back? Might not compliance be enforced? With so large a body of troops at his disposal, Charles was virtually

[54] Conf. Calmet, Hist. de Lorraine, tom. ii. p. 925, tom. iv. p. 50, tom. vii. preuves, p. lxix. et al. (a terribly confused account); Pauli, Preussische Staatsgeschichte, B. II. s. 300 et seq.; Gesta Trevirorum, p. 341, and additamenta, p. 34; Chmel, B. I. s. 53, &c. — All the details on this subject are evidently mere rumors and conjectures.

master of the town; and it was doubtful whether even the sacredness of the emperor's person would in such circumstances shield him against constraint.[55] The treatment which the king of France had experienced at Péronne was a terrible warning to those who, with a double purpose in their breasts, placed themselves in the power of the duke of Burgundy.

A mode was suggested of evading the difficulty — one which, though ill suited to the dignity of the emperor, was exactly suited to his character. On the evening of the 24th of November, surrounded by his whole court, he gave audience to the chancellor of Burgundy, and other members of Charles's council. Some unsettled questions of minor importance afforded a pretext for adjourning the negotiation to the 1st of February, when another meeting, it was intimated, might be held, at Besançon or at Basel. It is doubtful whether this announcement was altogether unexpected; but the remonstrances of the Burgundian ministers were not the less earnest, and the conference, which had begun at six o'clock, did not break up till twelve.[56]

Several hours later, but while the old imperial town, once a summer residence of the Byzantine Cæsars, still lay buried in slumber, the imperial majesty, accompanied only by his son and some half dozen attendants, stole through the silent streets to the river's side, and without waiting for any custom-

[55] "Man hat gesagt ob sy nicht vberains komen, so sull es vasst kumerlich werdn der k. maiestat aus seinem Reich mit frid ze komen." Letter in Chmel, B. I. s. 53. Conf. Knebel, s. 22.

[56] Chmel, B. I. s. 50.

ary flourish or formality, without bidding adieu to the host by whom he had been so magnificently entertained, without even, we are told, discharging the private debts he had incurred, — not an uncharacteristic trait, — embarked in a pinnace which had been moored in readiness, and which was speedily set floating with the stream.[57]

Daylight had scarcely dawned when his flight became known, and swift horsemen, it is said, were sent along the shore to communicate with him, and persuade him if possible to defer his voyage at least for a few hours.[58] But the shouts and signals of the messengers received no response; and the vessel which carried Cæsar and his *mis*fortunes held its course down the charming waters of the Moselle and thence into the broader current of the Rhine, until its illustrious freight was landed safely at Cologne.[59]

The inquisitive spirit that had been so strongly perplexed in the early stages of the affair found itself altogether baffled by the strange and abrupt

[57] See Basin, Knebel, Schilling, Wursteisen, and in fact all the chroniclers and journalists of the time — most of them jubilant over the occurrence.

[58] Basin, tom. ii. pp. 326, 327.

[59] Chmel (B. I. s. lxxvii.) considers the emperor's secret flight as one of the "nachträglich erfundenen bei allen derlei unvorhergesehenen Ereignissen gewöhnlichen Mährchen." He bases this remark on a document we have just cited from his collection, establishing the fact that Charles had been made acquainted, some hours before, with Frederick's determination to adjourn the negotiation. But there is not the slightest inconsistency in the facts — as Herr Chmel might have seen by a comparison of the documents he has himself edited. See Actenstücke, &c. B. I. s. 51, where it is stated that Charles had expected the emperor to take formal leave of him, but was not ill pleased at finding that he had gone off in the night.

termination.[59] A letter from the French king, the offensive warmth with which Charles had advocated the interests of his allies the king of Hungary and the elector-palatine, disagreements respecting the details of the arrangement, the limits of the proposed monarchy and of the prerogatives to be connected with it, were among the causes assigned for the rupture. The wiser heads, little satisfied with partial and superficial explanations of this kind, came to the conclusion that the event was just what they had anticipated from the first: the fault lay in the sluggish and vacillating temperament of Frederick, who was incapable of bringing any important business to a final and practical result, and whose conduct on the present occasion was of a piece with that by which he had rendered so many high designs and great deliberations impotent and null.[60]

In the course of the morning of the 25th, Charles was waited upon by an imperial chamberlain, Count Ulrich von Montfort, authorized to make the excuses of his master for his abrupt departure,—on the plea of important and urgent affairs that demanded his presence elsewhere,—and to assure the duke that the arrangement which had been discussed between them was not broken off, but merely postponed till a more convenient occasion should occur for putting it in execution.[61] Nothing remained, therefore, but to

[59] "Eramus tunc in civitate Treverensi; . . . sed nec tunc, nec postmodum, licet satis sollicite de causa illius subitæ discessionis perquisierimus, ad verum et certum eam noscere potuimus." Basin, tom. i. p. 326. And see Lamarche, Commines, &c.

[60] Chmel, B. I. s. 51–54.

[61] Pauli, Preussische Staatsgeschichte, B. I. s. 331.

According to the veracious and

pack up the crown and sceptre, to await the arrival of that occasion. But when Charles quitted Trèves, which he did on the evening of the same day, — the day that was to have seen the fulfilment of his loftiest desires, — the vision that had beguiled him had already vanished, and other projects, other illusions, again engrossed his thoughts.

well-informed chroniclers of Strasburg, Charles was in a towering passion during this eventful forenoon. He clinched his fists, ground his teeth, and shutting himself up in his apartment, employed himself in kicking about the furniture (Bussierre, p. 83). The truth is, his time was wholly taken up in giving audiences. A discussion which he held with the envoys of Sigismund will be noticed in the next chapter.

CHAPTER II.

INFLUENCE OF MONARCHICAL RULE ON THE FORMATION OF STATES. — LORRAINE. — ALSACE. — THE SWISS CONFEDERACY. — CHARLES AT DIJON.

1473.

THE most conspicuous fact in modern history — one which is indeed the staple of that history, all other facts having been subordinate and subservient thereto — is the rise and establishment of a commonwealth of nations separately but similarly organized; divided from each other, and still more from the rest of the world, by differences of language and blood, of customs and laws, by independent coequal sovereignties, and by geographical boundaries marked in general with a distinctness that had previously given to the countries thus limited their respective designations; yet bound together by community of origin, by internal resemblances or a real identity in all points of outward or apparent diversity, and by a long course of mutual influence, of action and reaction, of conflicts and alliances, of temporary combinations and permanent ever-extending interrelations.

The state of things thus described is peculiar to modern Europe. If something of the same kind was exhibited in ancient Greece, this might almost seem to have been by way of model or experiment, so small was the scale on which it was presented — so rapid, so transitory, so theoretical, were the successive developments — so radical was the destruction, leaving no material for wider foundations, no germs of further progress.

The political institutions of ancient Greece were formed in a great degree by the spirit of speculation and empiricism, being artificially adapted to the supposed necessities of each state. The political institutions of modern Europe arose from a chaos occasioned by the most violent concussion, followed by the completest amalgamation, of races which the world has ever witnessed, and received their consistency and shape through many and gradual processes of growth and assimilation. In ancient Greece, various forms of government — despotisms and republics, oligarchies and democracies — existed side by side, or followed each other as the advocates of the different systems triumphed or fell. In modern Europe a single form of government, having once become predominant, has maintained itself almost every where without dispute or interruption: royalty and nationality have been considered as inseparable, and their coexistence still testifies to their common origin.

That origin was a conquest — the subversion of a world-empire, the displacement of a refined but corrupt polity, the subjugation of countries where a civilization that had long before attained the maximum of its development was in a state of rapid decay — by races still barbarous but endowed with a primitive vigor and with a boundless capacity for improvement. The conquest of an uncivilized by a civilized people is simple in its results: it either exterminates the vanquished, effaces their external characteristics, or leaves a line of demarcation which is never crossed. When the case is reversed the results are more complex and more equitable. The Teutonic invaders of Western Europe adopted, to a great extent, the language, the manners, and the religion of the people whom they had subdued. But, until the distinctions of blood had been obliterated they kept in their own hands the dominion which they had acquired by their superior strength. They applied their own rudely shaped but effective implements to restore in a new form the edifice they had overthrown. They parcelled much of the conquered territory among themselves. They established that landed and military aristocracy which, even where shorn of its power, is still an exclusive caste. Above all they established thrones around which society slowly reorganized itself; which became the centres of political life and activity; which, though shaken, were yet in the end rendered more stable, by successive revolutions; and which for the most part are still occupied, if not by the lineal descendants of the original possessors, at least by those who boast affinity with, and assert a title derived from, them.

Regal government is the skeleton of every living European nation.

It is not to be wondered at that those who have professed to anatomize bodies thus formed should have devoted more attention to the bony framework than to the muscles that adhere to it. The chronicles of states are often a mere collection of family records. History runs into a series of royal biographies. It studies with a courtier-like assiduity the actions and characters of princes; and the geographical map or chronological table is less indispensable as its accompaniment than the genealogical tree. It tells us little of the soil in which the tree has grown; but it numbers the branches and the grafts, and, as far as such industry is possible, it lays bare the roots. Deep down in the Dark Ages it traces the Teutonic ancestry of some royal or imperial stock—of the Capets, the Habsburgs, or the Hohenzollerns.

If a glance be cast at the catalogues of the different European dynasties, it will be perceived that, as a general rule, each list closes with a female name. The explanation of this fact is sufficiently obvious. It can seldom happen that any family having extraordinary inducements to perpetuate itself will become extinct in all its collateral branches. But in almost every kingdom the regulations by which the crown is transmitted make it probable that after a few generations the succession will devolve upon a female; and whenever this occurs there is the further probability that by her marriage a union will be formed with another house, and that a new dynasty will commence with her husband or her posterity.

The crown of France offers the most important and best known exception to this rule. By a custom of the French monarchy females were not, as in other countries, simply postponed to males standing in the same degree of affinity to a deceased sovereign or to the original founder, but were absolutely excluded from the right to succeed, or even to transmit the succession. This fact was not an unimportant ingredient in the glory and greatness of the monarchy.[1] It contributed to that extraordinary prestige which attended the royalty of France through a long course of ages. There was an unbroken line of kings inheriting through males from a common ancestor. The houses of Valois and Bourbon, with their respective branches, were all male offshoots of the Capetian race. No foreigner ever legally came, or could by any possibility legally come, to the throne. It contributed to the preservation of the integrity and independence of the kingdom, which was never in danger, through the intermarriages of its princes with foreign royal families, of becoming annexed and subordinate to other realms. It contributed to save the country from wars arising from a disputed succession — the only species of wars which it has never had to endure, and one from

[1] "Sia certa la serenità vostra," says the Venetian minister Marino Cavalli, "che niuna causa ha operato più alla grandezza del regno di Francia, che questo non dividere la corona, ne lasciare ereditare le donne nè i secondi genti." Relaz. Venet. tom. i. p. 232.

which scarcely any other kingdom has been exempt.

But in some other parts of Europe, had the same custom prevailed, it would have operated as a bar to national unity and national greatness. Though a country of great extent, and for a long time virtually divided into many states, France, as we have more than once remarked, had from the first revealed its homogeneous tendencies, had conceived the plan and laid the foundations of its political system. There were in the Middle Ages many sovereignties in France; but there soon ceased to be more than one royalty. The possessor of that royalty always claimed, if he did not always receive, the homage and allegiance of all inferior princes. Even while the feudal vassals were setting at nought their feudal obligations, the rules of feudal tenure were enforced in cases where they had no original application. Provinces which had never been bestowed by the crown were held, on the failure of direct heirs, to have reverted to the crown. The annexation of territory which had never before belonged to France was technically termed a *re*-annexation. Apart from special efforts and special agencies, and in spite of occasional reactions, a deeply-seated principle, based on physical as well as moral causes, was steadily working towards the enhancement of a single power and the depression of all conflicting powers. From the moment at which the practice was discontinued of creating new fiefs, the ultimate incorporation of all the fractional sovereignties of France in an indivisible whole might be looked upon as a certainty.[2]

But the case was otherwise with regions where one or more of the predisposing causes of national unity, that so happily coexisted in France, were wanting — regions where the extent and bounds of empire had been less clearly traced by Nature; regions in which there had been either no conflux or no commixture of races; regions never enriched by the fertilizing deposits of Roman civilization, or never completely inundated by the subsequent tide of Teutonic invasion; regions where Christianity had been slow to penetrate, or where the moral influence of the Church had passed at once into temporal dominion. Every where but in France the process of coagulation was, not merely imperfect, but locally confined. Petty kingdoms continued to rival each other on the same soil. Petty states maintained an autonomy repugnant to the scheme of national existence. Petty ecclesiastical principalities strove to realize the idea of a theocracy; and petty republics proudly reared their heads like relics of the ancient world. These impediments to the general tendency of modern civilization were overcome by methods which had scarcely any share in the consolidation of the French monarchy. Local independence was extinguished, not as in France through the operation of an organic law, but through

[2] "Da ottanta anni in quà si à andato tanto dietro a questa strada di unir alla corona, e non alienar mai. . . . Il che, oltre al tener sempre ricca la corona, unita, e in riputazione estrema, fa che ella sia sicura dalle guerre civile." Ibid. pp. 234, 235.

direct and personal action. The barriers between cognate states were either swept away by conquest, or—as more commonly happened—were surmounted by a dynastic union which led in most cases to their gentle and gradual removal. Conquest, indeed, was so difficult, so seldom permanent, and even where easy and permanent so slow in producing the desired fruit, that we may regard it as an exception to the general rule. Had what is popularly termed the Salic Law been adopted throughout Europe, Scotland would never have been united with England, nor Aragon with Castile; the Belgian provinces would never have been brought under one rule; the whole of Germany would have remained a mere aggregate of discordant communities, vainly seeking in a visionary and pedantic scheme of headship the means not of coalescence, but only of coalition; no great power would have risen up as a bulwark against France at the moment when confluent streams had filled the fountain of her energies to the brim; and the 16th century would have witnessed the spectacle—beheld both at an earlier and at a subsequent period—of the temporary establishment on the French soil of a gigantic empire, spreading out its arms over the European Continent.[3]

[3] In the long struggle for supremacy between Charles V. and Francis I., the former is commonly regarded as the more ambitious and aggressive of the two, and as aiming more directly at the establishment of a universal monarchy. But this was not at the time the view of intelligent and impartial observers, who looked less at the characters of the parties than at the nature of the resources which they commanded and the tendencies by which they were impelled. "Questa legge salica," remarks Marino Cavalli, "sebben non ha fatto Francia pa-

Hence it is that we find in no other nation the same symmetry of features, the same cohesion of parts, the same harmony of action, the same accordance between the spirit and the body, as in France; that none has preserved through all changes the same unchanged identity; that none has exhibited so many of the advantages with so few of the evils arising from the centralization of all administrative functions. Every where in Europe national life has developed itself, or has perpetually struggled to develop itself; and nowhere has that development been effected except through the agency of monarchical government. But in one country alone do we find, through a long period, a complete correspondence between the two principles, a perfect unison in their operations, and an equal ratio of progress. This at once suggests — what few perhaps would require to have demonstrated — that the connection, however uniform, is not essential or inseparable. Monarchy is no more a necessary condition of national life than national life is an invariable adjunct of monarchy. The nation which has owed the most to monarchical government, which has maintained the longest and most intimate association with it, which has embodied its loftiest qualities and displayed them

drone di tutta cristianità, almeno gli abbia mostrata la via sicurissima di farlo, e l'abbia portata tanto innanzi, che se il presente re Francesco non si abateva aver per incontro un così potente principe e tanto conoscitore di questa via francese, come è Carlo V. imperatore, certissimo alli giorni nostri non solo quasi tutt' Italia ma parte di Spagna (per occasion di Nivarra), tutti li Paesi Bassi, e qualche stato dell' Impero obbediva alla fiordiligi; e saria ritornata la corona imperiale, certissimo, nel regno di Francia."

in the strongest light, is of all nations the one which is the best able to dispense with it, which has made the most persistent efforts to discard it, and which is now the least imbued with that sentiment of loyalty and that idea of legitimacy which were first aroused by itself as the chief defences of kingly rule. We know that in some instances regal government arose not so much from indigenous causes as by the reflex action of those events which led to the formation of the French monarchy. We know that in other instances admiration of France and fear of France were powerful stimulants to the growth and extension of the monarchical system. We know that in recent times a counter-movement from the same quarter has more than once unsettled every royal seat in Europe. If, on the one hand, we are forced to acknowledge that the national spirit has never yet found its complete expression in a republican government, we can assert, on the other hand, that it has not in general been adequately represented by monarchical government. While there have been points of sympathy between the two principles and a frequent coöperation resulting from the peculiar circumstances of their simultaneous origin, there have been also points of repulsion between them and a mutual resistance resulting from an inherent difference in their aims. The aggrandizement of monarchies has been the work of personal ambition and personal energy, effected by conquest or by family compacts, with little regard for any natural laws of expansion or of limitation: the efforts of every people to become a political unit have sprung from an original and universal instinct, and have not unfrequently led to the dismemberment of monarchies. Kings have sometimes found their safety, not in arousing, but in stifling, the sentiment of nationality; and nations, from the like impulse of self-preservation, have risen to overturn the thrones of kings.

The different monarchies of Europe exhibit, therefore, various degrees of congruity and coherence, according as circumstances originally favored the growth of a homogeneous people and the maintenance of territorial integrity, and according, also, as the national principle and the monarchical principle coincided with or controlled each other. At one end of the scale is France — so entire in herself; embracing within her borders nearly every population of French extraction, excluding from her borders nearly every population not of French extraction; never permanently losing any territory by conquest or intermarriage; never permanently gaining any foreign territory by conquest or intermarriage; subject throughout to the same code, animated throughout by an undivided patriotism. At the other end of the scale are the Austrian dominions — a vast conglomeration of states all differently constituted, and of populations having no near affinity with one another; held together by the single chain of a dynastic union, and ready to fly asunder whenever that chain shall break. Yet the Austrian dominions as at present constituted are far less extensive and far less incongruous than they once were, and infinitely less extensive and incongruous than they once appeared destined to become. The genius of no conqueror has ever conceived, the plan of no empire has ever approached, such an accumulation of possessions and of power as the dexterity and good fortune of its matrimonial speculations promised in the first half of the 16th century to bestow upon the house of Habsburg. It then seemed as if nearly all the reigning houses of Europe were about to merge in this single house, as if the march of discovery and colonization were heralding its rule in the four quarters of the globe — as if that Providence, which had made of one blood all the nations of the earth, were intending to make of one family all the rulers of the earth. There was, however, a counteracting impulse continually in operation. Royalty and nationality, which almost every where else have been more or less in harmony, are in the Austrian empire utterly antagonistic. In proportion as the house of Habsburg added to its acquisitions did it weaken the true foundations of its power. In the earlier stages of its greatness, its luck was that of the gambler or the speculative trader — alternate gains and losses — a hazardous and fluctuating situation, from which it was rescued, at the moment when its decadence seemed inevitable, by the Burgundian alliance. But after that event, and when it had reached the acme of its prosperity, when there was no longer any external check to arrest its career of aggrandizement, the incompatibility of its position with the natural laws of progress and of national development — an incompatibility which the talents and the versatile, or, as we might rather call it, the composite character of the greatest sovereign of the line did but partially conceal — was suddenly made apparent. In the middle of the 16th century, the house of Habsburg was compelled to divide itself into two great branches; and each of these branches had still to struggle with the same inherent difficulties. No sooner had the ill-assorted union of the German dominions with Spain been dissolved, than the continuance of the ill-assorted union of the Netherlands with Spain was found to be impracticable;[4] while the possessions of the German branch were only saved from a like disintegration by the same causes which had originally frustrated every attempt to incorporate them in a genuine whole — namely, the diversity, the conflicting claims, and the artfully balanced strength of the elements composing them.

Thus, while the French monarchs owed the steady increase of their power and the enlargement of their dominions chiefly to natural or constitutional causes — to the same process by which the French nation was acquiring fulness and solidity — the Austrian monarchs, on the contrary, owed their temporary preponderance in Europe almost wholly to special and fortuitous advantages. But wherein lay the peculiarity of their adventitious successes? In what did the

[4] The dissolution of that union had been generally foreseen long before the accession of Philip II. or the outbreak of the revolution. The Regent Mary of Hungary had observed the gathering signs, and in England it was believed that Charles V. would be unable to leave the Netherlands to his natural successor.

proverbial felicity of the Austrian marriages consist? This is a point on which some misapprehension seems to prevail. Matrimonial alliances have been the almost universal means of family aggrandizement. With one great exception, every royal house in Europe acquired a large proportion of its territories and fortified its power by those means. But as each of these families had, in turn, become great by the absorption of other families, so each in turn was destined to be itself absorbed into other families. The rights which had been acquired by its male heirs were alienated by its female heirs. Against this contingency the house of Capet was permanently secured by express provisions of the French law. The Capetian line might become extinct; it could never be merged in another line. The throne might become vacant; the crown might necessarily resume its ancient elective character; they could never be transferred by a marriage. The house of Habsburg was, of course, in a different position. The greater number of its dominions, having been bequeathed through females, must continue to be inheritable through females. Accidentally, however, its position was not less exceptional than that of the house of Capet. For a far longer than the ordinary period it enjoyed an exemption from the ordinary lot. During several centuries there was always a male heir to inherit its increasing possessions — a prince of the house of Austria to espouse the heiress of a foreign house. Daughters of the imperial house of Luxembourg, of the ducal house of Burgundy, of reigning houses in Spain, Portugal, and England, — families which had all been enriched or established by marriages, and whose rights, after a short succession of males, had already devolved, or were about to devolve, upon females, — were successively wedded to sovereigns or prospective sovereigns of the house of Habsburg. In the case of England alone, the marriage, being barren, brought no accession of dominion.

The proverbial felicity of Austria was therefore the "accident of an accident." While it continued, the house of Habsburg held a position in reference to many other sovereign houses analogous to the position which the French monarchs held in reference to their feudal vassals, analogous to the position which the destined survivor of a tontine partnership holds in reference to his less fortunate associates. There was, however, this intrinsic difference: the unity of France did not depend upon the perpetuity of a race, while this was a condition essential to the integrity of the Austrian dominions. On the total extinction of the house of Habsburg, the union of its numerous possessions would be *ipso facto* dissolved: each state must return to its original independence or become the prey of its aggressive neighbors. The mere failure of male heirs would not necessarily have the same result; but the danger at any early period would have been almost as great. That this event, had it happened a century sooner, would have led, not to the transference to another family of the inheritance so diligently amassed, but to the partition of that inheritance among many claimants, will hardly admit of doubt when it is recollected that in the 18th century Europe was twice convulsed by a general war consequent on the successive extinction of the male line in the two great branches of the house of Austria.

Occurring, however, at so late a period, when the oscillations of power were tending to an equilibrium, the termination of the Habsburg dynasty both in Germany and in Spain was comparatively unproductive of change. The greater part of the possessions of the Spanish branch passed to the house of Bourbon. The greater part of the possessions of the German branch passed to the house of Lorraine. The connection through which this latter transfer was brought about marks an epoch in the history of royal marriages as affecting the organization of states. Genealogists have found, or invented, a common ancestry for the families of Habsburg and Lorraine; and it is at least certain that both had started from the same soil — the prolific Rhineland, the cradle of illustrious races and the debatable ground of rival empires. But their characteristics and their fortunes, down to the period of their union, had been strongly contrasted. Among the princely houses of Europe, all struggling for regal rank and dominion, none had been more ambitious, more adventurous, more unfortunate than that of Lorraine. In spite of its splendid alliances, its alluring opportunities, and that combination of softness and fire, of personal beauty, romantic ardor, graceful accomplishments, and varied talents, by which it was eminently distinguished,[5] it had never attained the state of full-blown royalty, it had never, like so many of its rivals, thriven in the foreign soils to which it had been transplanted, and its original domain, far from becoming the nucleus of wider possessions, had been the disputed prize of all its neighbors, invaded and rifled in every war and by every belligerent. It finally surrendered this property, from which it had derived its status and its name, and received in lieu thereof the Austrian inheritance and the imperial title. Not until he had been thus despoiled of his patrimony could the last duke of Lorraine be considered as a suitable consort for the last of the Habsburgs, the descendant of so many Cæsars, the heiress of so many kingdoms.[6] The jealousy of nations and of governments would no longer suffer a matrimonial alliance to be the

[5] It was a remark of the maréchale de Retz that the princes of the house of Lorraine were as much distinguished among other princes as these were among ordinary people. Michelet thinks that the more ardent qualities belonged originally to the house of Lorraine, and that the grace and sensibility were acquired through its intermarriage with the house of Anjou. But we believe the reverse to have been the case. René of Anjou was an exception in his own family. For centuries before that union the dukes of Lorraine had been noted less for a spirit of warlike enterprise than for their *gentillesse*, their refinement, and their devotion to the sex. They were always faithful, not to their wives indeed, but to their mistresses; and both wives and mistresses were celebrated, not only for their beauty, but for their tenderness, disinterestedness, and amiability. There is a whole romance — such as has never yet been composed — in three charming letters of Alix de Champy to her lover, the Duke Raoul (1329).

[6] This statement may not seem to be borne out by the exact details. It must be remembered, however, that when such a union was first contemplated, half a century before it actually took place the surrender of Lorraine to France was looked upon as a necessary condition even by William III. of England.

means of consolidation or of aggrandizement. Royal blood would still mingle with royal blood, but not with the same views and motives as heretofore. States might still grow by the annexation of other states, but from a different principle and through a different process. The system of "family compacts" had run its course. It had largely aided in combining the various elements of distinct nationalities, by giving political unity to mixed or cognate races and securing to different countries their geographical integrity. Then, for a time, it had threatened to undo its own work, by overleaping all boundaries, effacing all distinctions, crushing all independence. But this had been only the exuberant demonstration of strength by which every triumphant principle proclaims the accomplishment of its purpose, and which is sure to be followed by a reaction. A new system, that of "the balance of power," — adverse to the former system, yet founded upon and recognizing its legitimate results, — was called into play, and still remains the cardinal maxim of European statesmanship.

It has been necessary, at the risk of exhausting the reader's patience, to direct his attention to some of the phenomena belonging to what may be termed the geological formation of the European monarchies, because, as we have before intimated, the period of our history was that in which the long process of solidification was hastening to its completion, and nations with fixed and well-defined forms began to appear above the ebbing waters of the deluge;—because the events with which we are concerned all bore upon that consummation, with reference to one monarchy more especially, but to others not indirectly or remotely;—because the career and the fate of Charles the Bold had a decisive influence on the fortunes of many states and ruling families. It was written in their several horoscopes that the conjuncture would be a critical one when their stars were crossed by that of Burgundy.

Having reëntered the duchy of Luxembourg, Charles ascended the Moselle as far as Thionville, where he remained a week transacting business, and receiving embassies and deputations. Resuming his journey by land, he arrived on the 16th of December at Nancy, the capital of Lorraine, where he was greeted by the prince and by all classes of the inhabitants with cordial demonstrations of respect.[7]

Somewhat more than forty years before, the then youthful René of Anjou had inherited the duchy of Lorraine in right of his wife and by virtue of her father's will.

The house of Anjou, it will be remembered, derived its origin from the second son of John of Valois, king of France. The numerous descendants of that monarch were the princes whose ambition and contentions gave so turbulent a flow—without, however, changing its direction—to the current of French history in the 15th century. Their inter-

[7] Ancienne Chronique, Lenglet, tom. ii.—Calmet, tom. vii. preuves, p. lxviii.

nal quarrels divided and distracted the monarchy; but their separate achievements contributed to its ultimate union, stability, and grandeur. The rivalry between the eldest and the youngest branch forms the groundwork of our narrative, and the subordinate part played by the intermediate branch has been occasionally noticed.[8] This family augmented its possessions and acquired its importance by somewhat different means from those to which either of the others was indebted for the elevation of its power and the extension of its dominions. The house of Anjou owed its short-lived greatness to a series of adoptions and bequests.

René had already been declared the heir of the cardinal-duke of Bar, when he was selected as the son-in-law and successor of Charles the Second, duke of Lorraine. But at the moment when the settlement thus made was about to take effect, its validity was contested by another claimant, Antony, count of Vaudémont, the representative of a collateral male branch of the earlier line, whose pretensions would have been easily overborne had they not received the powerful support of Philip the Good of Burgundy, then at war with his rightful sovereign and hostile in his feelings towards all the princes of his family. Like other minor questions of the time, the disputed succession in Lorraine was drawn into the vortex occasioned by the anarchy in France.[9] The army raised by the

[8] There was another intermediate branch, the house of Berry, but it soon became extinct.

[9] Hence the fact that a peasant girl of Lorraine, which was not a French fief, was inspired with a patriotic "pity for the realm of France."

count of Vaudémont consisted chiefly of English archers and Burgundian men-at-arms. That of René consisted chiefly of German mercenaries and a body of the French chivalry under the redoubtable Barbazan. The nobles of Lorraine were mingled with the ranks of each. A single but decisive battle was fought. René, defeated and taken, became the prisoner of his kinsman of Burgundy, and spent several years in strict though not harsh confinement in the "Tower of Bar," a keep attached to the ducal palace at Dijon.

[Battle of Bulgnéville, July 2, 1431.]

He solaced himself, during this long separation from his family, by the cultivation of tastes which have often softened the captivity of princes less refined or less frivolous. He passed his time in painting miniatures, illuminating manuscripts, writing sonnets and rondeaux, and composing musical airs. In such occupations lay the natural harmonies of his life. But Fate was meanwhile equipping it with other strings, on which a hand like his could strike nothing but discords. He had entered his prison a duke without a duchy: he came out of it a king without a kingdom.

The legacy bequeathed to the house of Anjou by two successive queens of Naples proved fatal, indeed, to all the princes of that house, and even continued to exercise its fascinations and transmit its curse long after that house had become extinct. The grandfather, the father, and the elder brother of René had each in turn entered Italy in pomp and anticipative triumph, had each in turn seen the gorgeous phantom which had beckoned him to the enterprise fade into a colorless shadow, had each in turn been the victim of a disappointment that embittered and shortened his existence. The sole dependency of the Neapolitan crown which they were enabled to retain was the county of Provence, which was certain to be ere long transformed into a dependency of the French crown.

The rights and the hopes of the house of Anjou were now centred in René. His liberation was effected through a treaty which left him burdened with a ransom better proportioned to his rank than to his means, but which established the claim he had failed in attempting to make good with his sword. His daughter Yolande became the wife of the Count Ferry of Vaudémont, his rival's son; and on them and their issue, failing his own male posterity, was entailed the succession to Lorraine — thus affording a prospect, afterwards realized, to the original line of recovering through a marriage the inheritance which had been diverted from it by a marriage.

Impelled by the fatality of his race, rather than by any ambition of his own, René now plunged into that conflict which had its sources in the internal divisions and anarchy of the Neapolitan states — or, to speak more correctly, in those deeper and more general causes which rendered Italy, though as cunning as she was fair, so helpless in her abasement. His enterprise was attended with a greater show of success than fortune had bestowed upon those of his predecessors. For four years his standard floated from the Castle of Saint-Elmo. Pomp if not power, possession of the capital if not of the country, the acclamations of a populace if not the obedience of a people, were the signs and assurances of his sovereignty. But the dream, though more vivid and more brilliant than before, was not less transitory. Could any dominion established on the Italian soil be substantial and permanent? The revolutions of Italy were volcanic in their origin; the fires of antiquity still burned beneath the crust of centuries; the ghosts in Hades still wailed and threatened when they remembered the triumph of the barbarian, the fall and dishonor of the world's mistress.

The latter half of his life, though the least eventful portion of it, is that by which René of Anjou — called by his contemporaries king of Sicily and Jerusalem — is best remembered. Having ceded to his son the sovereignty of Lorraine, he fixed his residence in regions where the climate, the scenery, and the associations were well adapted to the requirements of a mind too flexile to be broken, too spiritless to be soured, by reverses. His subjects, if little benefited by his active care, were neither oppressed with taxes nor harassed by levies or conscriptions. His mimic court — for such it might be called — was neither divided by factions nor burdened with business or with ceremony. It was frequented, not by warlike barons, adventurous knights, or crafty politicians, but by the wandering rhymester, the troubadour, the dilettante, the trader in articles of virtu, the possessor of some rare bird of plumage or some exotic plant or fruit. The solemnities were such as formed the pastimes of other courts, if at any court indeed such pastimes were still in vogue. Debates were held in the "Parliament of Love;" the distinctions most coveted were those awarded in the "Floral Games." Nowhere were the laws of chivalry so minutely studied or its exercises so little practised. If a tournament were ever held, the feats of knight-errantry were burlesqued rather than imitated,—the demoiselles being mounted behind their cavaliers, the combatants and officers fantastically appareled, and the prize to the victor a bouquet from the whitest hand or a kiss from the rosiest lips. The common routine of life with the sovereign and his courtiers partook of the extravagance of a masquerade or the insipidity of an idyl. Fêtes and processions were instituted, combining all that was whimsical and revolting in the mediæval Carnival. But more often the "Good King René" and his queen — not the faithful Isabella of Lorraine, who had shared but had not long survived the storms of his earlier career, but the fair young Jeanne de Laval, the more juvenile and more suitable partner of his maturer follies — disguised as shepherds and attended by a pastoral train, roved over the enamelled meadows of Anjou or through the olive groves of Provence, piping to their flocks or rehearsing amorous plaints, mingling in the dances and the rural sports of the villagers, discovering Perditas in the country nymphs and Florizels in their swains. Some of these traits, it is true, are traditionary rather than historical;[10] and the miniatures and manuscripts of René, the fruits of a lasting passion and an unwearied industry, are still commended by the connoisseur as exhibiting the proofs of much patience and of some talent. His sacred anthems are still chanted in the churches of Aix; the remains of his terraces and aqueducts still attest his love of agriculture; and the foreign roses and carnations, the white peacocks and the red partridges, which he introduced into France, are still propagated in its gardens and aviaries. What was more singular than the eccentricities of his existence was its placidity — so strikingly contrasted with the turbulence of the times, with scenes and events in which, however he might abstract himself from them, his interests and his affections (and his affections were at least as keen as his regard for his interests) were alike involved. He labored, or idled, amidst wars and revolutions, unexcited and unruffled by their din, unsuspicious that he was indebted, but might not be indebted always, to the absorbing fury of the strife or to the mutual jealousy of the combatants for his own security and ease. While his children were battling for lost thrones, while his provinces were attracting a rapacious gaze or were actually overrun, René preserved an equanimity of soul that enabled him to give the finishing touches to a painted panel or a stained

[10] Chastellain, however, alludes to these freaks in his "Recollection des Merveilles advenues en nostre Temps:" —

"J'ay un roi de Cecille
Veu devenir berger,
Et sa femme gentille
De ce propre mestier,
Portant la pannetière,
La houlette et chapeau,
Logeant sur la bruyère
Auprès de leur troppeau."

window. When tidings of family disasters reached him,—the death of the gallant John, the final overthrow of the proud and passionate Margaret,—the bereaved father shed a profusion of tears, wrote touching letters of condolence, and abandoned himself to the composition of a didactic treatise or an allegorical romance, for which his afflictions supplied a moral or an incident.[11]

It will not be thought surprising that René should have outlived nearly all the members of his house, his descendants as well as his contemporaries. A few months before the bloody occurrences which made his youngest daughter a childless widow, his only son, who had met with the hereditary failure in his Italian expeditions, fulfilled in another quarter the destiny of his race. Offered the crown of Aragon by a people disaffected to the rule of a usurper, he perished at Barcelona, in December, 1470, in the midst of a triumph, and on the eve, as it seemed, of a complete success. His actual possessions were inherited by his son, Nicholas of Anjou, who, as we have seen, after a brief enjoyment of them, died unmarried in July, 1473. Old King René had now become the heir of his own grandchild, and was invited by the nobles of Lorraine to resume the sovereignty he had abdicated nearly thirty years before. His wise refusal left the succession to his daughter Yolande, the

[11] For the materials of this sketch we have been chiefly indebted to the interesting life of René by the count of Villeneuve-Bargemont. A few particulars have been gleaned from the chroniclers and from modern works of travel.

widow of the count of Vaudémont, who in turn resigned her rights in favor of her son, named after his maternal grandfather, and the more welcome to the people of Lorraine, that he united the claims which, on a former occasion, had divided their sympathies and allegiance.

But if that quarrel was now extinguished, the greater rivalry on which its issue had depended was still alive, transmitted to a new generation, and burning with a fiercer heat, if with less destructive effect, than at an earlier period. There seemed reason to apprehend that the accession of the second René would prove the signal for a more prolonged and sanguinary conflict than that which had followed the accession of the first. We have seen the importance of Lorraine, from its geographical position and the policy of its dukes, in reference to the struggle between the French king and the duke of Burgundy. The advent of a new and youthful prince, at a moment when these two sovereigns, from the very circumstance of a suspension in their active hostilities, had leisure to revolve and means to execute any project with that end, offered a temptation to interference or aggression; and each was the more likely to adopt such a course from his fear of being anticipated by his rival. Across the neutral but open territory, Charles and Louis glared upon each other; each, however, waiting for the first movement from the opposite side before pouncing on the prey.

It is said, indeed,—but on no good authority,—that in the interval between the death of Nicholas and the election of René, the latter was abducted from the castle of Joinville, where he was residing with his mother, by a German officer in the Burgundian pay, but released on the seizure, as a hostage, of a nephew of the Emperor Frederick, then pursuing his studies at the University of Paris. A story so improbable in itself should be supported by documentary — or at least by circumstantial — proof; and corroborative facts can as little be adduced as any declarations emanating from the supposed parties. It was, however, a rumor of the time, and, like most rumors, betrayed the sensitiveness of the public mind to approaching events.[12]

[12] It would have been unnecessary to allude to this story, had it not been repeated, without the slightest intimation of its doubtful character, by every modern writer who has treated of these events. (See Barante, Sismondi, Michelet, Rodt, Huguenin the Younger, Bussierre, &c.) Yet it is mentioned by only one contemporary writer, De Troyes, who could have no personal knowledge of the facts, and who himself notices it merely as a report. (Lenglet, tom. ii. p. 104.) Had there been any truth in it, we should have found all the details in the two works from which a knowledge of the affairs of Lorraine at this period must be chiefly derived, namely, the chronicle written by Jean Chrétien, secretary of René (Dialogue entre Joannes Lud et Chrétien, publié pour la première fois par J. Crayon, Nancy, 1844), and the anonymous chronicle inserted among the "proofs" of Calmet (Hist. de Lorraine, tom. vii.). The improbability is heightened by an examination of the dates, — which seem to leave no space for the occurrence of such an incident, — and still more by the very friendly relations then subsisting between Charles and René. But we are not confined to purely negative testimony. There was, as we have said, a rumor of the kind floating about, not indeed in Lorraine, but at Paris and other distant points; and rumors, while they take their various shapes from the notions of those by whom they are propagated, are commonly built on some foundation, however unsubstantial. In the present instance we have no difficulty in detecting the foundation. René arrived at Nancy, to take possession of his new dignity, about the 15th of August. After staying there for a

The real proceedings were more in keeping with the characters of the actors and with the course which has been commonly pursued in similar cases. A diplomatic trial of strength preceded the resort to violence. Louis, with his accustomed promptitude, despatched a brace of envoys, at the instant when the occasion had arisen, to establish his own influence in Lorraine, by methods which, from his natural inclinations, he preferred as the least disturbing, while his experience had taught him to consider them the most efficacious. So swiftly and judiciously were they applied, that, on the 27th of August, a week after René had assumed the government, a satisfactory treaty was obtained, and the nucleus of a French party had been formed among the nobles.

Charles moved with a slower but more assured step. He had, indeed, less reason as well as less aptitude for haste. The great families of Lorraine shared the common sympathies of their class with the defender of feudal privileges and feudal independence, were connected by marriages or friendship with those of Burgundy and Franche Comté, and had repeat-

few days, he returned with his mother to Joinville. Some hours after his departure an alarm was raised. A report that he had been waylaid and carried off, no one knew where or by whom, spread through the town. Parties were sent out in all directions — some towards Metz, whose inhabitants, always hostile to the dukes of Lorraine, might have placed an ambuscade; some to Joinville, where, as it soon appeared, René had arrived safely and without interruption. "Le lendemain tous ceulx du Pays se trouverent tous esbahis de ce qu'ils virent bien qu'on les avoit abusez." (Chron de Lorraine, Calmet, preuves, tom. vii. p. lxviii.) In truth every one perceived, from the moment of his accession, that René stood in a highly perilous position.

edly sent their sons to fight under the Burgundian standard against the innovating monarch of France. Throughout the summer and autumn, communications were kept up, and reciprocal engagements were framed and adopted, if not formally ratified. During his sojourn at Trèves, and his shorter stay at Thionville, Charles was constantly attended by the ambassadors of Lorraine; and his subsequent presence at Nancy, at the head of a powerful force, but with no inimical purpose,—on his passage by a convenient or even necessary route to the capital of his own dominions,—annihilated the plots so newly and hurriedly laid by his adversary.[13] In renouncing the alliance of France for that of Burgundy, René, while he conformed to the necessities of his situation, was also obeying the impulses of his character. It was natural that one who, at the age of twenty-two, had been suddenly and unexpectedly removed from a life of seclusion and submission, in the sole society of a devoted mother, to a position of elevated independence; who had been trained in the admiration of

[13] The slight basis and flimsy material of the French alliance is indicated in the following passage from the Dialogue entre Lud et Chrétien (pp. 16, 17): "Quel besoing avoit-il esté à nostre Seigneur," asks one of the interlocutors, "de prendre ce party, . . . veu que son pays n'estoit en rien subject de France . . . ? LUD. Je croy que à traicter cestre alliance . . . il n'y eust guerre de Lorrains, car à mon aduis, Messire Charles de Beauveau et Me Nicolas Melin de Bar conduisirent ceste matière principalement auec les François, comme affectez avec leur nation avec le bon desire que nostre dict seigneur, jeune prince et non experimenté de telle chose auoit au roy, cuidant qu'il seroit grandement remuneré et plus volontiers veu en France. JOAN. Et quel ayde trouva-il en France . . . ? LUD. Certes nulle."

martial and chivalrous exploits; in whom the finer qualities of two illustrious and well-matched races had met and mingled; whose open brow, clear blue eye, regular features, and graceful, modest bearing, were no fallacious indications of an artless and amiable as well as of a courageous and enthusiastic soul, should see the hero of his fancies, his proper friend and protector, in the most powerful and enterprising of princes; in the man of firm purpose, dauntless temper, bodily prowess, self-reliant mien, and lofty ideas; in the representative of a cause hallowed by external associations which appealed to the youthful imagination, similiar associations to those which in a subsequent age were to cluster around the very different ideas of monarchical legitimacy and absolutism. The aspect of Charles, surrounded by the evidences of a supremacy which was likewise betokened by his personal appearance and demeanor, had just produced a similar impression on the Archduke Maximilian [14] — an impression such as often predominates in the short season of adolescence, before deeper influences and stronger enthralments have asserted their empire. A treaty, which had already received the approval of the principal nobles, was now, therefore, carried into execution. Mutual aid in resisting the designs of the French king was its avowed object. Lorraine was placed under the protection of the duke of Burgundy. It was to be occupied and traversed by his armies at his discretion; and four of

[14] Chmel, B. I. s. lxvii.

the frontier towns were to be permanently garrisoned by his troops, under officers selected by himself from among the vassals of his ally.[15]

Thus dislodged from a position which he had seized without any provision for holding it, Louis, like an experienced campaigner, immediately assumed a more formidable front, guarding against the possible results of the mishap, and waiting for an opportunity to strike with better effect. He had no scruple, since his rival had occupied Lorraine, in sending his own troops into the adjoining duchy of Bar; and as Charles pursued his journey to the south, a French army of observation spread its lines along the frontier of Burgundy, and watched his communications with Switzerland, Provence, and Northern Italy.[16]

Although the year was now drawing to its close, winter had not yet set in. The whole season had been distinguished by an extraordinary dryness and warmth, and was long remembered in many parts of Germany and France as "the hot summer." The streams and fountains had dried up; the forests had been all on fire. The harvest had been abundant, but the mills being stopped for lack of water, bread, instead of declining, had risen in price. The vintage had commenced in August, and the yield had been prodigious; but the wine, rendered fiery by a tropical sun, had soured as soon as made, or had been

[15] Traité entre le duc Charles et René II., ap. Huguenin jeune, Guerre de Lorraine, pp. 343–351. And see Barante, ed. Gachard, tom. ii. appendice, pp. 708, 709.

[16] De Troyes, p. 105 et al.

wasted for want of purchasers or of sufficient vessels to contain it. Light showers in September had prepared the earth for a second spring, and throughout the autumn months the air had been as soft, the herbage and the foliage as green, as in May. The gardens, the meadows, and the hedgerows had decked themselves anew with violets and roses. The trees had put forth fresh blossoms; ripe cherries had been gathered in November; the vines, the apple-trees and the pear-trees had exhausted their juices in the effort to mature a second crop. The mild weather still continued, the flowers had not all faded or the leaves all fallen, snow had not yet whitened the rounded tops of the Vosges or the wilder summits of the Suabian Alps, when Charles descended into the deep and extensive basin which is enclosed between these opposite ranges, and intersected longitudinally by the Rhine.[17]

The western and wider section of this basin is itself intersected by the tributary Ill (or Ell), which descends into the valley by an opposite curve from that of the Rhine, but creeps along it in nearly the same direction for sixty or seventy miles before mak-

[17] Knebel, s. 10–12, 26, 44, et al. — Boyve, Annales Historiques du Comté de Neuchatel et Valangin, tom. ii. p. 77. — De Troyes, p. 105. Code historique et diplomatique de Strasbourg, première partie, Chroniques d'Alsace, tom. i. pp. 90, 205. — Wurstisen, Baszler Chronick, s. 433.

In a much slighter degree these phenomena are not unusual at the present day. In 1473 there would seem to have been an extraordinary drought followed by a very prolonged "été de Saint Martin." There was no frost at Paris until Candlemas, and in the vicinity of Basel the snow did not lie on the mountains till late in the spring, when the cold became extremely rigorous and blasted the newly-sown crops.

ing the final bend by which it pours its waters into those of the greater stream. Hence the name of "Der Elsass" (in the French form, Alsace),—*Ell settlement* or *seat,*— borne for more than twelve hundred years by a district which is both fertile and populous, but which owes its historical importance chiefly to its situation. Inhabited by a people of almost purely Teutonic descent, but lying within the ancient limits of Gaul, though beyond the mountain heights where the true boundary might seem to have been marked, it was of all the border lands that of which the possession was the longest contested, and of which the ultimate destination appeared the most doubtful. Deserted by the Romans at the beginning of the 5th century, it was invaded and devastated by every successive horde that crossed the Rhine to prey upon the crumbling empire. When these irruptions had begun to cease, the Alemanni and the Franks contended for the permanent occupation of it. On the dissolution of the Carlovingian empire, its place was midway in the fissure between the Frankish and Germanic nations, to the latter of which it finally adhered, but not till after inclining from side to side and sharing in more than one attempt to establish an intermediate and composite monarchy.

Thus torn from France, where the work of organization was at least commencing, Alsace, under the German emperors, remained for centuries in a distracted and unconsolidated state. For a time, indeed, it was constituted as a duchy, and, being soon after joined to Suabia, formed with it a species of domain for the sovereigns of the Hohenstaufen line. But neither at this nor at a later period does it seem to have experienced the operations of any regular machinery of government. Divided and subdivided, with no general representative or administrative system, no common principle of subordination except to a distant, inefficient, and for the most part merely nominal authority, it cannot be said to have had any proper and distinct existence as a province or state down to its incorporation with the French dominion, two centuries ago. Its history can be traced only in the fractional annals of separate communities and classes. The emperors derived an uncertain revenue from tolls and imposts, and in return granted charters to the towns and bestowed investiture on the nobles. These relations were occasional and special. Within the towns there was some degree of order and considerable industrial development. Strasburg, Colmar, Mühlhausen, and other places, had their magistracies and codes, their crafts and guilds, their spacious cathedrals and civic halls — the productions and still surviving memorials of that earnest and laborious but silent, reflective, and self-absorbed spirit which penetrated the inner life of mediæval Europe, a life so strangely contrasted, yet so naturally blended, with its outward din and confusion. And nowhere was this contrast more strongly marked than in Alsace. Beyond the limits of the towns the land was distributed among a large number of proprietors, allodial as well as feudal, whose mode of life was that of the territorial aristocracy in its primitive and rudest form.

With no court in which to congregate, no public duties to perform, none of the incitements to a peaceful emulation or a lawful ambition, the Alsatian nobles were strangers to the amenities and the splendors which in a greater or less degree already dignified the existence of the same class in other countries. Their poverty and their pride contributed to this result. Not recognizing any right of primogeniture, they were unable to accumulate or to mount above a common level; and their properties, besides being small, were heavily encumbered. So much the more did they pique themselves on the purity of their blood, scrupulously abstaining from alliances with the wealthier burgher families — an intermixture by which they might have bettered their fortunes while sullying their pedigrees. Needy, high-born, and independent, they sought occupation and a career in a life of adventure or of robbery. As soldiers of fortune they earned distinction in the service of foreign princes. At home they were the foes of industry and a terror to commerce. In common, and often in concert, with their brother knights of the Black Forest, they waged perpetual war upon the towns, lay in ambush for the vessels and the caravans on the rivers and the highways, and carried off the traders and the freight to their fastnesses among the hills, appropriating the booty and exacting ransom from the prisoners. The towns, however, in spite of these drawbacks, were constantly growing in importance and strength. The nobility, notwithstanding its predatory successes, was constantly decaying. The combinations it had once formed became in time impracticable. Its enterprises, though not discontinued, were confined to petty and isolated attempts, which were commonly revenged, if not upon the guilty parties, on their kinsmen or allies. The feud, nevertheless, remained unextinguished; the hatred felt by those who were commonly the assailants had become more intense as their powers of mischief had diminished. While in most parts of Europe the two great classes of society were gradually drawing nearer, establishing mutual relations and recognizing a reciprocity of interests, in the Rhineland the division had widened, the intercourse had grown less frequent, and the differences of sentiment and manners were more sharply drawn and more rigidly fixed.[18]

One noble family had proved in all respects an exception to the general rule, had outstripped and overtopped the rest, had leagued itself with cities and drawn the sword in their behalf, had amassed possessions, and had reached an exaltation that might have been expected to exercise an important influence on the destinies of the country. Long before its accession to the imperial dignity and its settlement in Austria,

[18] The materials for this sketch of the history and condition of Alsace have been gathered from the native chroniclers, Herzogen (Edelsasles Chronick, Strassburg, 1592); Königshoven (Elsassische und Strassburgische Chronicke, mit Historischen Anmerkungen von Schiltern, Strassburg, 1698); the authors of the works inserted in the Code historique et diplomatique de Strasbourg; the well-known works of Schöpflin, Alsatia illustrata and Alsatia diplomatica; and Strobel, Vaterländische Geschichte des Elsasses (Strassburg, 1841–1849) — a valuable work, but in its arrangement, or lack of arrangement, reflective of the chaotic nature of its subject.

the house of Habsburg had acquired a large amount of territory and certain rights of seigneury in the southern portion of Alsace — commonly called "the Sundgau" — as well as in the adjacent districts on both sides of the Rhine — the Thurgau and the Aargau in Helvetia, the Breisgau and other parts of the Black Forest region in Suabia. Since the 11th century the landgraviate of Upper Alsace had been hereditary in the counts of Habsburg. Their predominance had reached that stage of inchoate sovereignty which by a bold and skilful management had so often been transformed into a complete dominion. But all their efforts in this direction had been paralyzed or thwarted. Their elevation to the empire and the subsequent enlargement of their field of operations — their establishment in Southern and Eastern Germany — had unloosened the roots of their earlier and partially developed power. The *emperors* of this line were content with the specious authority which their predecessors had possessed in the Rhineland, while the *dukes* of Austria, forgetful of the earlier traditions of their race, sought in conquest alone the means of territorial aggrandizement. In this quarter they experienced only defeats; for the house of Habsburg had here to encounter a resistance far more stubborn, an enmity far more formidable, than that of the rival princes or the insubordinate barons with whom it was elsewhere contending.

The Swiss Confederacy, as it existed in the middle of the 15th century, had a peculiar and portentous character. It was no longer that miniature republic —

an inspiration from the glaciers and the avalanches, from the resistless torrents and the inaccessible crags — which early in the 14th century had enshrined itself in the heart of Helvetia, behind her northern barrier of rivers, lakes, and hills, in the wilds of her subalpine forests, and beneath the awful shelter of her ice-crowned peaks. Much less was it the Switzerland of the 19th century — more ample in its dimensions, more symmetrical in its form, but relatively weak and insignificant, propped up and held in place by external pressure and support. Numbering only eight cantons, — linked rather than bound together by the single obligation of mutual protection and defence, but retaining their individuality, their separate and diverse systems of internal government, and connected by a similar though subordinate alliance with thirteen neighboring towns, or diminutive states, — it constituted, not indeed a nation, but a unique and terrible power, exultant in its indomitable strength, and defiant of the storms that were sweeping around it, convulsing and dislocating all the adjoining lands. The time had gone by when, attacked upon its own soil, it had put forth what seemed a supernatural force in a desperate resistance to oppression. The triumphs of its arms and the magnetism of its example had awakened its unconscious energies, and given a new impulse to its bold and adventurous spirit. It had now entered upon a course of retaliation and foreign enterprise. Its former assailants, stripped of their possessions in Helvetia, and unable to arrest the flood which their own temerity had set in motion, were treated with a retributive and scornful insolence, saw their provinces exposed to perpetual incursions, and their towns, if not in open mutiny, inviting the friendship of the invaders and seeking admission into the league.

The Swiss character, with all its homeliness, its hardness, and its pettiness,—the ineffaceable marks of a peasant origin and of peasant life,—was ennobled by a sustained fervor, a daring and obstinate valor, a fidelity and self-devotion in the maintenance of the common interests, to which modern history at least will be searched in vain for any parallel display. These qualities, it will be admitted, were the natural fruit of an intense patriotism, of glorious examples and traditions, and of a hardihood, an indifference to danger, a self-possession in confronting obstacles and a skill in surmounting them, engendered and confirmed by the habits of a daily life of peril and endurance, a familiarity with the sternest scenes and wildest strifes of nature, with the terrors of the dizzy precipice and the treacherous crevasse. But it must also be conceded that such a unity of spirit and steadiness of action are impossible—or, if possible, are far more wonderful—where lofty aspirations entail corresponding sacrifices, where the penalties of progress and refinement are constantly exacted in financial revulsions, the consequent prostration of industry, gross inequalities of fortune and of privileges, the distractions, the anxieties, the mental tortures, which flow from unattainable conceptions and illimitable desires, unnerve the physical system, and render bodily suffering infinitely more poignant. Switzerland was not more isolated from the general plan of national organization than it was exempt from the burdens and excluded from the benefits of a progressive civilization. There were no sites for either palaces or populous cities on those tremendous and snow-clad heights, in those narrow and sinuous valleys. There were no strongholds for tyranny, no avenues to luxury, no incentives to rivalry. There could be no inordinate wealth with a soil which, if not unproductive, was scanty, limited, and difficult of cultivation, and with scarcely any facilities for commerce: there could be no destitution where industry and frugality were absolute conditions of existence. While there was little room for ambition, little opportunity for enlightenment, little capacity for culture, there was no excuse for indolence, no means of enervation, no motive for envy. If in the smaller cantons a pure democracy prevailed, every male inhabitant of eighteen and upwards having a right to speak and vote, this was the mere spontaneous product of a simple and equal life, not the forced growth of fermenting corruptions and heated opinions. If, on the other hand, in the larger cantons there were certain distinctions of caste, and a decided oligarchical tendency in the government, such distinctions were far less obvious and jarring than in other countries, that tendency had not yet hardened into a fixed system, an oppressive usurpation. It was still in the incipient stage of an authority resting on popular consideration and gratitude.

The burgher patriciate, and a small and decreasing race of nobles who, retaining the relics of their ancient manorial properties, had early acknowledged their allegiance to the state and wisely availed themselves of the legitimate methods for obtaining a share in its administration, wielded an influence strong in proportion to the moderation with which it was displayed. Above all, there was a uniformity, or at least a similarity, of sentiment and habits such as had no existence elsewhere. The condition and ideas of the noble or the burgher were essentially those of a superior class of peasantry. If life had not been levelled to the Spartan standard, there are many indications that a puritanical precision and rigidity were stamped upon the Swiss communities even in the old Catholic times when religion appealed to the senses rather than to the intellect, when penance gave a secret stimulus to indulgence, and a riotous festivity was tolerated if not licensed by the Church. Art was overawed by the grandeur of Nature; desire was stifled by the constant demand for exertion. In a word, the social condition of Switzerland was the antipodes of that of Flanders.

These various circumstances may account for the accomplishment, in such a region and by such a people, of a work which neither the fair and stately cities of Italy — each clinging to the forms and ideas of an extinct past, aspiring only to municipal independence, and sacrificing to a dream all the practical securities and solid benefits of freedom — nor the rich and populous towns of the Netherlands — absorbed in a commercial competition, envious of each other's natural advantages, jealous of each other's power and activity — had ever had the sagacity to conceive or the boldness to attempt. The federal republic of which the Forest Cantons, Uri, Schweiz, and Unterwalden, formed the core, Berne, Lucerne, and Zurich the most important members, was no achievement of statesmanship or a refined policy, had been formed without study, contrivance, or discussion, was neither poised upon artfully balanced principles nor guarded by artfully constructed checks. Yet it was destined to grow and to endure. It was a loose and slender thread that yet united all hearts and strengthened all hands. It seemed to have scarcely any of the elements of nationality; yet nowhere have national pride, national sensitiveness, national sympathy and coöperation, been more strongly developed. Internal divisions, untinged by acrimony, were harmonized by mutual concessions. Against the foreign enemy the Confederacy was at all times a unit. Provocations such as in any other land would have passed unnoticed by the people, unheard of by the government, — a word of contempt applied to the Swiss authorities, a refusal to accept the coarse copper coin of the Swiss cantons, or the seizure *in transitu* of a boat-load of Swiss cheeses by the "robber knights" of the Rhineland, — were sufficient to create a stir that extended from the town hall of Berne to the remotest châlet of the Alpine pastures.

Such insults were tolerably certain to be followed

by punishment or reparation. There could be no more joyful proclamation to the inhabitants of the Swiss territory than the call to arms. The mountain herdsmen had arrogated to themselves what had been deemed the distinguishing traits of a martial aristocracy. War had become the passion, heroism the instinct, of the Swiss people. Their military organization was simple in the extreme, but within the bounds of its natural sphere of action, was not less efficient. When a member of the Confederacy had been menaced or assailed, notice was given to its allies, a diet called, the plan of operations concerted, the means prepared. Each district furnished its quota of able-bodied men, or in cases of emergency and dire need — when the signal-fires crimsoned the snow upon the hill-tops, or the breathless messengers hurried from vale to vale — sent into the field the whole of its population capable of bearing arms. Each of these contingents formed a complete and separate troop, with officers appointed by the civil authorities of the town or canton. A council composed of the principal leaders was intrusted with the chief command. If a general were elected, he was merely the organ by which the decisions of this body were announced and carried out. Such a method of conducting war may seem little favorable to strategical combinations, to rapid and continuous movements, or to any of the purposes and necessities of a long campaign. But though, in the 15th century, a natural military genius — as in the case of Edward the Fourth of England — might intuitively seize upon the leading ideas of strategical art, its scientific principles were in general but little practised or comprehended; while the defects in the management and formation of the Swiss armies were in some degree remedied or counterbalanced by the enthusiasm and single-minded zeal which pervaded all ranks, by the absence of any personal ambition in the chiefs and of any cause of disaffection among the men, and, as will be hereafter seen, by the superiority of their tactics.

The campaigns were shortened by the most natural of all methods — a swift and decisive action. The armies were rendered invincible by that which will render any army invincible — a unanimous and firm resolve to conquer or to die. Overwhelmed by numbers, the Swiss might be destroyed: to rout them was impossible. Arrived upon the battle-ground, they were formed in phalanxes or in solid squares. Their spears, eighteen feet long, were firmly grasped with both hands widely extended, whereas the knightly lance or the common pike was held near the butt and wielded by the right hand alone. The defensive armor, when complete, consisted of two narrow plates of iron for the breast and back, buckled together at the shoulders, arm-pieces of the same material, a tunic woven of iron rings, and a head-piece of iron or tin. A sword, or a long knife, was carried at the side, to be plunged, if the square were broken by an onslaught of cavalry, into the bowels of the horses. Among the Swiss themselves cavalry constituted no regular branch of the militia; but the nobles and principal citizens of Berne and other towns were expected to appear equipped in the harness of knights, and were stationed on the flanks or in the rear, prepared, not to make or sustain a charge, but to cover the manœuvres of the infantry and to lead in the pursuit. A few crossbowmen and other light troops hovered between the cohorts or were sheltered in the enclosure of spears. A short prayer preceded the combat, the soldiers all dropping on their knees. Then the final dispositions were made. The officers fell into their places; the banners were unfurled. The men of each district had their separate standard — the Bear being the well-known emblem of Berne, while the White Cross had been adopted as that of the whole Confederacy. Drums and fifes gave the signal of advance and marked the time. But harsher sounds — sounds so wild and strange as often to appall the embattled foe — were emitted by the rude horns of the Forest Cantons, that of Uri, of enormous length and great antiquity, having an especial fame.

The troops moved forward with a strictly measured tramp, with a steady but intrepid front. No shouts were heard except the battle-cry, uttered from time to time with a quick and simultaneous roar. There was no counter-marching, no falling back, no hurried or impulsive advance, until the opposing array was shattered and put to flight. If victory were unattainable, death with an honored place in the remembrance of a country loved as no other country has ever been, was the welcome alternative. To fly was contrary to the soldier's oath. Even the wounded were forbidden to retire. The craven who betrayed his fear was hewn down by his comrades. They who returned unscathed from a lost field hid themselves from the sight of their fellow-citizens, of their wives and relatives, of the grandsires who had conquered at Sempach, of the children who had been taught to lisp the incidents of that immortal day. But the annals of Swiss warfare were seldom stained with a defeat, and never with a disgrace. The chief drawback to the military power of the Confederacy lay in the thinness of the population, the paucity of its resources, the impossibility of keeping any large forces on foot, the difficulty of engaging in distant expeditions, or of following up a success by the conquest or occupation of a hostile territory. The victory achieved, the spoils collected and fairly distributed, an irrepressible longing for home took possession of every breast. The return was marked by a series of sober but hearty ovations. In every town and village, tables loaded with rustic fare were spread in the open streets. Warm greetings were exchanged between those who had hitherto been strangers. The magistrates assembled to speak words of praise and to send messages expressive of their persistent zeal in the common cause to their allies. Every such event cemented a league which had little need of parchment treaties or formal pledges, which had nothing to fear from conspiracies or factions. Even the consciousness of their separate interests, the egotism excited by local independence, served on such occasions to strengthen the attachment between the different cantons. Each felt as if the peril had been all its own; each experienced a particular sense of relief and a corresponding emotion of gratitude. The tie between them was less that of compatriotism than of brotherhood. When the moment of separation came, those rude warriors, who would meet no more until a new summons brought with it a new community of dangers and of triumphs, parted with embraces and tears.[19]

"God fights on the side of the Swiss," became a saying in the Rhineland. Their exploits unemblazoned by the pomp, uncommemorated by the pride, which shed a factitious lustre on the achievements of feudal war, failed not to receive their due estimate from those who witnessed the deeds and participated in the effects. The Swiss might be placed under the ban of the empire; but the bolt was sure to fall innocuous and unheeded. Austria might continue to announce in diplomatic whispers her intention of subduing the Swiss "rebels" and "upstarts;" her nobles might mutter — not too loudly — their disdainful curses on the Alpine "cowherds" and "dairymen;" but never without betraying latent sensations of astonishment and dread. Nor in more distant regions was there any lack of consideration and re-

[19] See the works of Rodt, Tillier, Müller, Boyve, &c.; the chronicles of Etterlin, Diebold Schilling, Edlibach, and Stumpfen; and Macchiavelli, Arte di Guerra; passim. Some particulars for the foregoing description have been taken from passages in the Venetian Relations, Brantôme, and other works of the 16th century. It can hardly be necessary to give more exact references to the authorities consulted.

spect for the government recognized under the dignified title of "The Old Alliances of Upper Germany." A government so constituted had little reason to expect sympathy; but there was an instinctive disposition to keep clear of any embroilments with it, and to cultivate its good will. Small honor and less profit would result from victories gained over such a people and territory; the loss and dishonor of being vanquished in the contest might well be left to the house of Habsburg.

These are facts that require to be borne in mind, for the misrepresentations that pervade the portion of our subject which we are now approaching, have their root in the fallacious notion that the Swiss power was at this period still shrouded in obscurity; that the weakness of its proper lords was commonly believed to have alone prevented the suppression of its insolent revolt; that whoever sought its friendship evinced an extraordinary sagacity; that whoever incurred its enmity was led away by prejudice, ignorance, and a blind presumption.[20] How little such representations are warranted by facts will appear from the negotiations and intrigues of which we are presently to give an account. The effect of those proceedings was to complicate and in the end entirely reverse the relations which the Confederacy had before maintained with the other states concerned.

[20] It must be allowed that these notions have derived a certain weight from the authority of Commines; but if that great writer was left by both his masters, the duke of Burgundy and the French king, in complete ignorance of their relations with the Teutonic world, we cannot help it, however much we must regret it.

Its attitude in reference to foreign governments, and their attitude in reference to it, should therefore be clearly understood.

It was a fixed maxim with the Swiss Confederacy to enter into no entangling alliances with other powers. Herein it differed widely from the Burgundian government, which was ever enlisting support, lending its aid, and assuming a prominent part in the combinations or dissensions among its neighbors. There was also a striking contrast in the outward aspect of these two powers, in the principles on which they rested, and in the nature of their resources. And yet there were analogies and resemblances between them, which might be expected to have at least an equal influence whenever they should come in contact. Both were of recent origin; both had the alacrity and audacity of youth; both were violent and aggressive, with little aptitude for craft or circuitous courses, and with still less inclination to mildness or forbearance. Each was on terms of amity with all governments save one; each waged a perpetual contest with the dominion which it had thrown off. In the Swiss cantons, as in the Burgundian provinces, the opposite races of Germany and Gaul were found united and yet distinct; their place was on the same boundary line where those two races have always pushed against and struggled with each other; their growth would have the same tendency to establish an intervening barrier. The Confederacy was invited by opportunities and urged by an internal impulse to extend its operations downwards along the Rhine, as the house of Burgundy was invited and urged to extend its operations upwards along the Rhine. One had its natural allies in the free towns, in all the chartered communities of the Rhineland; the other had its partisans, and even its vassals, among the princes and nobles of the Rhineland.

Yet with no other ruling house had the Confederacy been so early and so cordially connected as with the house of Burgundy. The Swiss nobles, and especially those of Berne,—the most important and the most numerous,—often visited the Burgundian court, where their chivalrous tastes and recollections were gratified and kept alive. There was also a commercial intercourse, dating from ancient times and provided for by treaties. The Swiss drew their supplies of corn, wine, and salt from Franche Comté and Burgundy, and sent thither in return the surplus product of their dairies. Philip the Good had earned the particular thanks of the Confederacy by rejecting the emperor's solicitations for assistance when a feud between Zurich and the other cantons had offered the single opportunity of that kind for reëstablishing the Austrian sway. Some years later he had been hospitably entertained at Berne, where the graciousness of his manners and the splendor of his escort had produced their wonted effect. One of the last acts of this prince, in conjunction with his son, had been to propose to the Swiss a strict alliance, offensive and defensive; and although such a compact had been declined, as incompatible with a settled policy, the republic had availed itself of the occasion for renewing former agreements, with an additional stipulation that neither party should render aid or allow a passage through its territory to the enemies of the other.[21]

Had the motive for making these overtures existed at an earlier period, or had the temptations to accept them continued to a later period, a strong bond of union would undoubtedly have been formed between the Burgundian and Swiss governments. From the moment when Charles the Bold began to control the resources of his house, all its efforts, as we have seen, were concentrated against France. As long as Austria remained formidable or unappeased, the policy of the Confederates was distinguished by a like singleness of aim. Now, between France and Austria there had been an old friendship cemented by a long series of mutual courtesies and good offices. At one time this alliance had assumed a most threatening shape towards the Swiss league. The assistance refused by Philip the Good was granted to the house of Habsburg by Charles the Seventh. In 1444, peace having been concluded with the English, it was necessary to find some employment for a refractory and rapacious army and a not less troublesome heir to the crown. Louis accordingly marched against the Confederates at the head of thirty thousand troops. A handful of Swiss — amounting, it is supposed, to

[21] Zellweger, Versuch, &c. s. 11, and Beilage, No. 2. — Duvernoy, note to Gollut, col. 1884. — Tillier, Geschichte des eidgenössichen Freistaates Bern, B. II. s. 141. — Rodt, B. I. s. 26.

two thousand at the most — threw themselves, with the effrontery of their race, in the way of the invaders, and far from choosing an advantageous post and awaiting the attack, crossed a river in face of the enemy, pressed forward until surrounded, and fought until slain.[22]

[Battle of St. Jacob's, Aug. 26, 1444.]

A marvellous piece of stupidity — which saved the republic in the greatest of its perils. Instead of following up his success over a people so unskilful in the art of self-defence, the victorious general penetrated only far enough into their land to observe its nakedness and its strength, and then, with that readiness to reverse his plans which the reader has so often had occasion to admire, withdrew his forces into Alsace, the rich and fertile territory of his allies, which was forthwith given up to pillage and devastation. It was not until the Armagnacs, as they were called, gorged with plunder and mad with riot, were in danger of being cut off in detached parties by the people of the towns or hemmed in by the armed bands of Burgundy, Lorraine, and the neighboring states, — outraged by their occasional inroads, — that

22 "Ad extremum non victi Suitenses, sed vincendo fatigati inter ingentes hostium catervas ceciderunt." (Letter of Æneas Sylvius, ap. Chmel, Geschichte Kaiser Friedrichs IV. B. II. s. 285, note — a work of immense labor and of great merit, but unfortunately, after an interval of twenty years since the publication of the 2d volume, still unfinished.) "Fut me dit sur cette matière, par aucuns nobles hommes qui avoient esté autrefois ès guerres de France, . . . tant contre les Anglois comme autres, qu'en leurs temps ils n'avoient vu ne trouvé aucunes gens de si grand' défense, ne tant outrageux et téméraires pour abandonner leurs vies." De Coussy, tom. i. p. 18.

The Swiss were prouder of this defeat than of any of their victories. Their chroniclers claim for it the right to a greater renown than that of Thermopylæ.

the Rhineland was released from the plague to which it had unwittingly exposed itself.[23]

Before his departure Louis concluded a treaty with the Swiss cantons — the first they ever formed with his house. Nine years later, being apprehensive of another hostile combination, they sent for the first time an embassy to the French court. At this period the house of Habsburg — in general so little subject to domestic divisions — had found an addition to its ordinary troubles in the enterprising and undocile disposition of the emperor's younger brother, the Archduke Albert. The mediation of Charles the Seventh had been invoked — whence the perturbation in Switzerland, speedily quieted, however, by friendly assurances and the ratification of the existing treaty. In 1459 the French monarch condescended even to negotiate a truce between the Confederates and Duke Sigismund, to whom, by an arrangement made under the auspices of France, the Sundgau and other Austrian possessions in this quarter had in the mean time been transferred.[24]

[23] These events occupy a conspicuous place in the annals of Alsace — annals filled with the records of similar though less extensive calamities. The horrors of this period are vividly depicted in the chronicles. (See Code hist. et diplomatique de Strassbourg, tom. i. deuxième partie, pp. 57–64, 157–171). And in a spirited contemporary ballad the emperor is keenly reproached with having brought so terrible a pest upon the soil which he was bound to protect: —

"**Bistu ein Konig von Osterich,
Des romischen Reychs ein herre?
Du soltest meren das Romysch rich,
So wiltu es zerstoeren;
Du hast die morder har geladen
Allen stetten uff yren schaden:
Scham dich der grossen uneren!**"

Ibid. pp. 62–64.

[24] Zellweger, s. 6, 7. — Rodt, B. I. s. 28, 29. — Urkundenbuch der Stadt Freiburg im Breisgau, B. II. 2te Abth. s. 459. — Duclos, tom. iii. preuves. — The German writers seem to be unacquainted with the part taken by the French court in

But this truce, hollow and futile because guarantied by no renunciation of old claims or pledges against future conquests, was quickly violated. The Swiss, tempted by the weakness of their enemy and impatient to free the Helvetian soil from the last vestige of his rule, recommenced hostilities in 1460, and overran the Thurgau, which they continued to hold in common as a subject territory. A new armistice was concluded, to last for fifteen years. Before half that period had expired, war again broke out; the occasion being presented by one of those broils which, springing from some trivial cause, revealed by their rapid spread the constant inflammation arising from an unhealed sore.[25] Alsace and the Schwarzwald were invaded and ravaged, the allied places supplied with garrisons, and Waldshut, a town of some strength on the Upper Rhine, closely invested. This last event, however, proved favorable to a negotiation undertaken by several prelates and princes in the neighboring region. It was in siege operations that the military strength of the Confederates was especially defective, both from their want of practice and the inadequacy of their means. On the other hand their poverty, their contracted notions, — to speak plainly, the mercenary meanness which has ever been

mediating between the hostile princes of the house of Habsburg, who, according to the statements of the French envoy, had been so highly inflamed against each other that they could hardly be restrained from drawing their knives.

[25] This was known as "the Miller's War," having grown out of a dispute respecting wages between a miller and his apprentice at Mühlhausen — a dispute that involved in its consequences the fate of Charles the Bold of Burgundy and other grand and important issues!

a conspicuous feature in the character of the Swiss,—rendered them susceptible to pecuniary offers. On the promise of ten thousand guilders, to be paid within a year, they consented to a suspension of hostilities,—Waldshut, and indeed the whole of the Black Forest, remaining pledged for this inconsiderable sum.[26]

Inconsiderable as it was, Sigismund found himself unable to raise it. The gold accumulated by the careful savings of his father[27] had been swallowed up, the debt incurred by his cousin Albert and others of his predecessors had been raised to mountainous dimensions, by the expenses of a court which for a brief season had attempted to vie with that of Burgundy, and of a seraglio not much surpassed by that of the Grand Turk. His coffers were drained and his revenues sequestrated. He was losing by piecemeal the dominion which his ancestors had acquired by piecemeal. But the very extremity of his present need, making palpable the total extinction of his resources and the total ruin impending over him, suggested the hope that, by an arrangement with some foreign power, he might be restored to solvency, or at least be secured in the undisturbed possession of a remnant of his states. His first appeal was naturally addressed to the emperor, from whom he received an approval of his plans, with the excellent advice to carry his proposals to another quarter. He set out, accordingly, to make an application in

[26] Diebold Schilling, s. 1–34.—Tillier, B. II. s. 152 et seq.

[27] Lichnowsky, Geschichte des Hauses Habsburg, B. VII.

person at the court of France. Sigismund had married Eleanor of Scotland, sister of the unhappy Margaret, the first wife of Louis the Eleventh; and he may have supposed that their not very dissimilar treatment of women so nearly related constituted a bond of sympathy between that monarch and himself.[28] But Louis, if he appreciated the force of this consideration, did not permit himself to be influenced by it. He refused even to listen to any overtures of such a nature. He begged that the intended visit might be given up. The Austrian prince, who had come as far as Troyes, saw himself obliged to beat a sudden retreat.[29]

The scruples of the French king had arisen from his fear of giving offence to those who regarded Sigismund as their natural foe. The duke of Burgundy, to whom the application was now transferred,[30] had the same motive for rejecting it. But he had stronger motives for embracing it—motives which did not exist with Louis, who, though he regarded Alsace as included within the natural limits of the monarchy,[31] knew the impossibility of gaining any present foothold in a

[28] It is interesting to find that Eleanor, like her unfortunate sister, was an ardent lover of poetry and art. Her amiable character made her much beloved by the subjects of her good-for-nothing husband.

[29] See Sigismund's instructions to the envoys whom he sent to the imperial court in 1469 (not, as the editor conjectures, in 1470), Chmel B. II. s. 131 et seq.

[30] Not, however, at the suggestion of Louis—as stated by historians generally. See Sigismund's own account, ubi supra.

[31] The propriety of attempting by open force or by a ruse to make himself master of Alsace, as within "the natural limits" of France, had been suggested to Louis while dauphin by the French envoys, at the imperial court. See Duclos, tom. iii. preuves.

territory still separated from his own by that of his formidable rival. It was not, however, in forgetfulness of his earlier engagements, or with the slightest inclination to depart from them, that Charles became a party to an agreement, the precise terms of which must here be stated.

By an instrument executed at Saint-Omer on the 9th of May, 1469, the duke of Austria, moved, as he himself confesses in the preamble, by his indigent and necessitous situation, which had rendered him incapable of defending his states and subjects against the invasions of his hereditary enemies, conveyed to the duke of Burgundy, from whom he was to receive as an equivalent fifty thousand florins, — forty thousand to be paid to Sigismund himself, and the remainder to the Swiss in acquittal of their claim, — the chief hereditary possessions of the house of Habsburg on both sides of the Rhine, comprehending the landgraviate of Alsace, the county of Ferette, Breisach, and the four "Forest Towns" — Rheinfelden, Seckingen, Lauffenburg, and Waldshut, — with full and peaceable enjoyment of all established rights of lordship and sovereignty, and with the privilege of discharging the whole or any part of the mortgages already existing, and amounting in the aggregate to a hundred and eighty thousand florins. Liberty of redeeming the property thus transferred was reserved, a compliance with the conditions hereafter enumerated being required as preliminary to a claim for restoration. In addition to the purchase-money and whatever other sums might appear to have been defrayed in the liquidation of former claims, Charles was to be reimbursed for any necessary or useful outlay in the construction and repair of fortifications, in regard to which the attestations of his officers were to be accepted as sufficient vouchers. These various payments were to be made at one time, in one sum, and at one place, namely, at Besançon in Franche Comté; and the commissioners appointed for that purpose were to receive, on application, a safe-conduct from the duke of Burgundy, who, when all this had been done, would be bound to make a full and formal surrender of the territory in question to the original possessor, his heirs or successors.[32]

Other documents, of the same date with the foregoing, specify the nature of a personal bond between the two princes. Sigismund, by a separate act, acknowledged himself the servant of the duke of Burgundy, engaging to render him aid and secure him from harm to the extent of his ability and whenever required, and received in return letters of protection, the tenor of which will presently appear.

It might have seemed — it did undoubtedly seem to Charles — that this arrangement, far from leading to a new and deadly strife, would have the effect of putting an end to that which had so long been raging. Sigismund was removed from a vicinity where his danger had been great, where his presence had been a constant source of irritation and

[32] The documents relating to this transaction may be found in the Schweizerisches Museum, B. II. s. 299–322; and in the Œsterreichische Geschichts-Quellen, B. II. s. 223–241.

mutual rancor. Instead of an enemy, powerless against their assaults but arrogant in his pretensions and implacable in his hatred, the Swiss would have for their neighbor a friend, too strong to be attacked with impunity, too faithful and too much occupied to offer any wanton injury. By legitimate means the duke of Burgundy had acquired certain possessions of the house of Habsburg on the borders of Helvetia. Had he therefore adopted the enmity of that house towards the Swiss Confederacy? Not in his own estimation — so much is certain; not, so far as we have been able to discover, in that of the Confederates.

But Austria, as it soon appeared, had very different impressions. The relief purchased by its loss of territory was a mere negative gain, creating a vacuum to be filled with new views and expectations. Hardly had the money been paid, receipts given, possession taken, when Sigismund called upon his ally to furnish the protection he had promised by sending "a great and good army" against the Swiss, whose "tyrannies and cruelties" had drawn upon them the repeated censure of emperors and popes. What assurances had Charles given to warrant this demand? He had taken Sigismund under his safeguard, engaging to give notice thereof to the Swiss, to require them to abstain from any acts of aggression, and to exhort them to submit their differences to the head of the empire, the common sovereign of both parties. If this invitation were rejected, and Charles's intervention were requested, he was to make all possible exertions to bring about an amicable settlement of all the subjects in dispute. Finally, if the Swiss, in defiance of all warnings and in contempt of all proposals for an accommodation, should commence hostilities against the Austrian prince and invade his territories, the duke of Burgundy was to furnish assistance, so far as his honor and his convenience would permit, in repelling such attacks.[33]

Sigismund was now reminded of the restrictions under which protection had been promised and the contingencies in which it was to be afforded. He had been informed at the time of the good relations subsisting between the duke of Burgundy and the Swiss.[34] These relations could be changed only through some provocation on their part. Charles had already addressed letters to them, acquainting them with the purport of his alliance with Austria, and proposing to mediate between them and the latter.[35] It did not appear that any fresh injury had been sustained. There were, therefore, no grounds for the appeal: the necessity for assistance had not yet arisen. The Swiss had, in fact, no longer any motive or pretext for violence.[36] Even if an attack were threatened, it would not be consonant with

[33] Chmel, B. I. s. 96, 97.

[34] "Laquelle intelligence fut considéré et pesée, quant lesdites Lectres de garde furent despechées." Instruction de Charles, Duc de Bourgogne, à ceux qu'il devoit envoyer vers le Duc Sigismond d'Autriche, Lenglet, tom. iii. p. 242.

[35] Chmel, B. I. s. 8.

[36] "Attendu que lesdits Zwitsois n'ont encore commencé ladite guerre, et qu'ils n'ont procedé à aucune voie de fait depuis lesdites alliances. . . . Aussi ils n'ont occasion ne matiere de la mouvoir." Lenglet, tom. iii. p. 241.

Charles's reputation for probity and good faith to declare war against a people with whom he had been so long allied, without first calling upon them to submit to the arbitration of the pope, the emperor, or some other impartial umpire. Nor would the situation of his affairs allow of such a course. To issue any hostile proclamation while his forces were fully employed would be only to invite attacks which he had no means of repelling, and expose his southern provinces, ill prepared for such a danger, to the depredations of a new enemy.[37] Sigismund was, however, requested, in the possible event of war, to furnish information as to the mode in which it might best be carried on, the places to be occupied, and the quarters from which supplies could be drawn. But it was Charles's hope and design, by the methods he had mentioned, to avert any risk of war. His honor was pledged to the maintenance of his good understanding with the Confederates — a circumstance fully explained and taken into account when the letters of protection had been given.[38]

Intimations have been found in this reply of an ulterior and covert purpose little accordant with its general tone.[39] But Sigismund himself deduced from

[37] It is worth while to notice the very different estimate which Charles here and elsewhere puts upon his own ability to deal with the Swiss and that which was put upon it by Sigismund. Modern writers attribute to the former notions which belonged only to the latter.

[38] Lenglet, tom. iii. pp. 238–242.

[39] See Zellweger, s. 20, where the conclusion is deduced that Charles had already formed a plan for the conquest of Switzerland. The facts brought forward in support of this notion go to prove that Austria entertained the project, which, however, is a very different matter. Mallet, in his continuation

it no such comforting conclusions. He believed, however, that his end might be attained through a more elaborate diplomacy. This was his private aim in laboring to bring about the marriage of Maximilian and Mary. He endeavored to make it a provision of that alliance, that the Burgundian power should be employed for the subjugation of the Swiss. But on this question the attitude of Charles remained unchanged. His answer, in the summer of 1472, to the repeated solicitations of Sigismund — who insisted that the Confederates, if they had committed no actual aggressions, still preserved a menacing air, and who declared that he had placed his confidence in Charles as a "lover of justice and a famed suppressor of sedition"[40] — was the same in substance as that which he had given in the spring of 1470. He would do all, and more than all, that he had promised in writing or by word of mouth. He acknowledged the claim of his cousin of Austria to be secured against any future peril or offence. If war were necessary for this end, his power and his person should be devoted to it. But he trusted to effect an honorable arrange-

of Müller, expresses the same opinion, and cites in confirmation of it the paper of which we have just given an abstract. But Mallet had obtained his knowledge of this document at second hand, and the only passage which he cites is that in which Charles requests information as to the mode in which war might be carried on. There cannot, however, be the slightest doubt that these inquiries were made for the mere purpose of keeping Sigismund in good humor during the negotiations for the marriage, that being the chief business which the Burgundian envoys were to transact.

[40] "Omnem spem nostram in dilectionem vestram tamquam cultorem iustitie, temeritatis et rebellium subditorum prout omnis fama canit correctorem continuo gerimus." Chmel, B. I. s. 25 (with a wrong date).

ment, — to execute his engagements, not by embarking in a war, but by establishing a firm peace. At all events, other methods were to be exhausted before resorting to arms.[41]

His proceedings were in strict conformity with these declarations. The envoys sent to the imperial court to negotiate the marriage had orders, both in going and returning, to repair to Zurich, where deputies from the different cantons assembled to meet them. The Confederates were admonished to abstain from any belligerent demonstrations against the Austrian prince. Grievances of which they had complained should be redressed. It was the desire of the duke of Burgundy to mediate between the two parties and bring them to consent to a perpetual agreement. His own dispositions towards the Swiss, whatever they might have suspected to the contrary, were altogether amicable. If the present treaties were considered insufficient, he would enter into a closer union with them. He would gladly, indeed, coöperate with them against Milan — the friend of the French king and an old enemy to several of the cantons. Venice, from motives of her own, would become a party to such a league. Offers of money were made. Such

[41] Ibid. s. 14–16. — In this message Charles again leaves it to Sigismund to devise a plan for carrying on the war in case war should be commenced by the Swiss. But he resolutely refuses to become himself the assailant, and persists in declaring his intention to meet any difficulty that may arise by other methods. "Omnia prius experiri quam armis decertare decet sapientem," he remarks — a somewhat curious saying, it may be thought, in the mouth of Charles the Bold.

results were predicted that "children in the womb would leap for joy." [42]

These, as well as many similar endeavors, failed in accomplishing the object. Why? Primarily, because neither of the two parties — Austria still less than the Swiss — had any real desire for a reconciliation. Partly also, no doubt, because Charles was ill fitted for the office of mediator in a case so complicated and embarrassing. Moreover, his acquisition of Alsace had opened new and unforeseen sources of trouble. The chief administration of that province had been vested in Peter von Hagenbach, who bore the title of *landvogt* (steward or bailiff). This man's character as depicted by his enemies — and no portrait has been left of him by a friendly hand — was that of a demon, a compound of diabolical sensuality and untamable ferocity. Without pausing at present to discuss the fidelity of the picture, we shall notice such points as may be supposed to bear upon the subject under consideration, — the circumstances, namely, which contributed to imperil the friendly relations between the Burgundian and Swiss governments.

Hagenbach was himself a native of the Sundgau, of noble though obscure parentage, and deeply imbued with the prejudices of his order. But while he shared in its contempt for the burghers and its hatred of the free communities, he seems to have cared as little for the sympathies of his own class. A

[42] Zellweger, s. 20, 24. — Rodt, B. I. s. 25, 127, 161–167. — Zellweger regards these offers as mere hypocritical pretences. Sigismund, as we shall see, viewed them in a very different light.

mastiff in his fierceness and fidelity, he knew but one object of respect and attachment, the master to whose service he had chained himself. He had been found useful in many capacities. He had given blunt but sagacious advice at the council-board of Philip the Good. He had docked the hair of the young Flemish nobles at the time of Philip's illness. He had detected plots formed against Charles's life. He had directed with signal ability the bombardment of Dinant. He was one of the principal agents by whom the duke communicated with the court of Vienna and with the German princes and nobility. His devotion, his talents, his knowledge of the country — above all, his readiness to assume responsibilities, and to brave odium — were his qualifications for a post where daintier hands, a less ardent zeal, or a more refined intelligence might have attempted no solution of the embarrassments.[43]

The first duty incumbent on him — one for which he would be held to a strict account — was to provide for the security of travel. Attended by a bodyguard in a livery of dusky gray, on which was embroidered the significant motto, "I spy!" he perambulated the various routes, clearing them of thieves and vagabonds of all kinds, until, as we are told, gold or silver might be carried openly from place to place, and journeys made with perfect safety by night as well as day.[44]

[43] Rodt; Lamarche; Duclercq; Chmel; &c.

[44] Schreiber, Taschenbuch für Geschichte und Alterthum in Süddeutschland, 2ter Jahrgang, s. 10. — Rodt, B. I. s. 213.

Other difficulties were not of a nature to be grappled with in this fashion. A new rule was to be instituted among a people scarcely accustomed to any rule. Power was to be exercised where only immunities were known. A revenue was to be raised where all the ordinary sources were exhausted. Creditors were to be paid — or put off. Debtors were to be constrained — or the claimants left to choose their own irregular methods of compulsion. All was to be done under the eye of those to whom no responsibility was due, from whom no support was to be obtained, but who were deeply interested in the event, who had established a prescriptive right to intermeddle, and who might feel themselves aggrieved by any attempt at innovation.

A tax on commodities being the common resource in such cases, Hagenbach laid an impost, popularly known as the "Bad Penny," on wine — an article of domestic production, of universal consumption, and yet not of absolute necessity. Thann, the chief town in the county of Ferette, rose in revolt, and was punished by the loss of its privileges and the execution of four of the ringleaders. The landvogt seems to have relied, as another source of income, on gifts such as the towns throughout Europe were in the habit of making on special occasions to the sovereign or his representative. He expected also to reap some profit from the pecuniary transactions in which he was an intermediary agent. But few douceurs or percentages found their way into his purse, unless forcibly exacted or withheld. Every penny was counted, every florin was weighed. Hence a multitude of petty squabbles, a violent outcry, followed by loud and abusive retorts. Basel, a free imperial city on the northern borders of Helvetia, but not yet included in the Swiss league, held a mortgage on Rheinfelden, one of the four "Forest Towns" now subject to the duke of Burgundy. The debt, amounting to some twenty thousand florins, was paid in two or more instalments; but three hundred florins of the interest were retained by the landvogt, who pretended—truly or not—that he had been promised this commission. A violent altercation ensued. Hagenbach raged and threatened, in the civic hall, in the market-place, on the streets and bridges, and allowed his soldiers outside the gates to intercept and carry off a wagon-load of chattels belonging to the burgomaster. The council of Basel—not the celebrated ecumenical body of that name, but the worthy body of burghers who transacted the business of the town—caused its clerk to insert in the register a minute record of the Herr Landvogt's violent acts and unseemly language.[45]

On the other hand neither principal nor interest was forthcoming of certain sums due from Mühlhausen to subjects of the duke of Burgundy. Milder measures failing, and the creditors being with difficulty restrained from seeking satisfaction by the common mode of private warfare, Hagenbach attempted to cut off the trade of the place, with the effect of rais-

[45] Ochs, Geschichte von Basel, B. IV. s. 241–246.—Knebel, 1ste Abth. s. 5, et al.

ing the prices of the chief necessaries of life. He forbade also the payment of rents and other dues by the population of the surrounding region. But Mühlhausen was an imperial town, and what was much more to the purpose, had lately been received into an alliance with the Swiss. The agents of Berne interfered, and drew upon themselves the coarse, though not groundless, reproaches of the landvogt. "It was the Swiss who encouraged the delinquents. But for them the money would long since have been paid. If the Bear of Berne were stripped of its hide, a serviceable fur might be made from it."[46]

Complaints on these and the like matters were sent to the court of Burgundy. What direct response was given we are not informed. Privately the duke was reported to have said — and the expression will perhaps be thought sufficiently characteristic — that he had appointed a governor to please himself, not his subjects or his neighbors.[47]

In glaring contrast, however, with the speeches ordinarily attributed to Hagenbach, was his declaration, on another occasion, that he had it in strict charge from his master to suffer no injury or insult to be offered to the Confederates. A party of Swiss merchants, on their passage by the Rhine to the annual fair at Frankfort, had been captured near Breisach by a Suabian noble, a vassal of Sigismund, notorious for his hatred of their nation. The Confederates flew to arms; and although in the mean

[46] Knebel, s. 6, 11, 13, et al. — Rodt, B. I. s. 177.

[47] Ochs, B. IV. s. 196.

time the prisoners had been released by an expedition sent from Strasburg,—a friendly city,—an immediate renewal of the war with Austria would have ensued, had it not been for the interposition of the duke of Burgundy. Hagenbach, suspected of connivance in the affair, protested his innocence. He would not, he averred, for a thousand florins, that such a thing had happened in territory subject to the Burgundian rule. The duke would see that reparation was made. The same assurance was given by Charles himself in the embassy already mentioned.[48]

Such events as these, if we may accept the common statements of history, had an important influence, were indeed the primary agents, in disturbing the friendly relations between the duke of Burgundy and the Swiss. And we are far from asserting that their trivial character deprives them of significance. Nay, possibly, the more trivial they appear, the greater their significance. They perhaps betray the existence of a state of things which demanded the most prudent and careful handling. Hagenbach's harsh and unpopular rule, his vituperations, his scornful menaces, his arbitrary methods of procedure,—apparently countenanced, or at least unrebuked, by a sovereign whose own temper and conduct were too open to censure in the same particulars,—formed an element in the crash beneath which both were to be overwhelmed. The clamor may seem disproportioned

[48] Schilling; Müller; Zellweger; Rodt; &c.—This was the affair of Pilgeri von Heudorf, which fills a monstrous space in the chronicles and diplomatic papers of the time.

to the cause. But in such a region and atmosphere every sound was perilous. When the avalanche had gathered, a mere echo might suffice to set it in motion.

There was, however, a far greater agency at work — that which thaws the under surface of the torpid mass and prepares it for its descent. The process, though noiseless and slow, will not baffle our observation. With the active power we are already well acquainted.

Louis of France had gained his first knowledge of the Swiss in the character of a foe. He had improved the opportunities afforded by his subsequent residence in Dauphiné to cultivate an intimacy with several of the leading citizens of Berne.[49] The proximity of that canton and the familiarity of its inhabitants with the French tongue were not the only motives for this intercourse. Peculiar relations had long existed between Berne and Savoy; and in the affairs of the latter state Louis, before as well as after he became king, took a deep concern.

It was to the solicitations of Berne that Philip of Bresse was indebted for his liberation — a boon which the king had denied to his uncle of Burgundy, and for which he was thanked by a special embassy. At the head of that embassy was Nicholas von Diesbach, a member of the richest family in Berne — a family which, having prospered by industry, had recently been ennobled by the emperor. Diesbach, born in

[49] Duclos, tom, i. pp. 66, 89.

1430, had in his influential dealings with his fellow-townsmen, already acquired experience and address — qualities united with a plausible staidness or even dignity of manners,[50] and soon to be ripened by an acquaintance with courts as well as by extensive travel. He had just been elected *schulteiss*, or chief magistrate, of his native city, and was personally known to Louis, who hailed the occasion for a closer acquaintance, having recognized in Diesbach — as a kinsman of the latter somewhat naïvely boasts — "a man who could be used." [51]

It followed as a natural sequel, that when, in 1468,

[50] Knebel records an altercation between Diesbach and Hagenbach, in which an "austere regard of control" on the side of the former is amusingly contrasted with the violence of the latter.

[51] "Nun bekannt ihn der Küng wol, denn er ihn meh gesechen hatt, und wusst, das es ein Mann zu bruchen was." Ludwigs von Diesbach Selbstbiographie, Schweiz. Geschichtforscher, B. VIII. s. 167.

There are a good many details in this little work illustrative of the social state of Switzerland, as well as of its political relations, at this period. The author, a posthumous son of the good knight Ludwig von Diesbach, was born at a castle in the neighborhood of Cologne, whither his parents had removed, in consequence of some unpleasant disputes and lawsuits at Berne. His cousin Nicholas, then twenty-two years of age, became the guardian of the orphan children, and removed the elder ones to Berne, leaving little Ludwig under the charge of a shoemaker at Cologne. There he remained till his eighth year, when he was taken into his cousin's family and educated in a manner becoming his birth. When fourteen or fifteen years old he accompanied Nicholas on the embassy mentioned in the text. They journeyed in the suite of Philip of Bresse, who was attended by a Burgundian noble; and many were the good-humored discussions carried on relative to the respective virtues and rights of the French king and the duke of Burgundy. On their arrival at the French court, Nicholas found no difficulty in providing for his young kinsman, whom Louis placed among his pages, and for whom he seems to have conceived a great liking — so that the way of advancement was open, had not Ludwig, as he confesses, been inexpert in the proper methods of pursuing it.

the Confederates, learning that Sigismund of Austria was on his way to the French court for the purpose already stated, determined on sending an embassy to guard against any ill effect to themselves, the management of the affair was committed to Berne; and the envoys selected were Nicholas von Diesbach and his cousin William, his companion in a recent journey through Egypt and Palestine[52] — "as those," said their letter of credence, "who, we are aware, will be the most agreeable to your grace."[53] The object of the mission had been forestalled by the acuteness and benevolence of the king; but it was not the less instrumental in drawing tighter the personal bond which had been previously formed. Louis, as was his wont in such cases, took the whole family of the Diesbachs under his wing. Liberal pensions were granted to the older members; a youthful relative and his comrade were admitted as pages into the royal household. It was not till the end of 1469 that the cousins returned home, singing the praises of the French monarch, and loudly proclaiming his affection for the Confederacy and his benefactions to themselves. Far from rebuking its servants for having accepted the wages of a foreign government, the council of Berne acknowledged these and other favors in a cordial letter of thanks to the king.[54]

From this moment Berne became the focus of an

[52] Ibid. s. 169.

[53] Rodt, B. I. s. 105. — Zellweger, s. 13.

[54] Rodt, ubi supra. — Stettler, Gründliche Beschreibung Nüchtländicher Geschichten, B. I. s. 196–199. Tillier, B. II. s. 164.

"A proof," says Zellweger, "that a Swiss was not believed capable of being seduced by presents into intrigue, which was carried on and gradually extended with an industry, but also with a discretion, that justify the early prepossessions of Louis in favor of its conductors. In his desire to ally himself with the Swiss he was not at all singular, nor did he display a greater earnestness than others; but in his choice of agents and his mode of proceeding his superiority is incontestable. In May, 1470, he had the satisfaction — not unexpected, we may presume — of receiving a fresh message (William von Diesbach being the bearer), inviting him to send commissioners to Berne, to negotiate, under the auspices of that state, a new treaty with the several cantons. This was accordingly done, and on the 13th of August, a treaty was signed, by which the parties bound themselves, in addition to the observance of former agreements, to render no aid to the duke of Burgundy in case a war should arise between that prince and either of the contracting powers.

This, of course, was only a preliminary move — the first in a long series of manœuvres. It was, however, an important one, and had not been accomplished without much difficulty. The proposition, conceived in a spirit hostile to a prince whom the Swiss had not yet learned to regard as an enemy, seems to have been received with a general coldness.

doing any thing that might be injurious to his Fatherland." Indubitably! And a proof also, by parity of reasoning, that Louis XI. was the most open-handed of monarchs, and delighted especially in showing marks of his esteem to men of incorruptible purity. It is, however, pleasant to know that his generosity in the present instance were not requited with ingratitude.

Zug and Glarus positively refused to concur. From the deputies of the other cantons nothing more than a verbal assent could be obtained. The instrument bears the seal of Berne alone, which, empowered by five other members at the most, had thus pledged the faith of the whole Confederacy.[55]

At Berne itself there was a division of sentiment. The old nobility — headed by Adrian von Bubenberg, who in his youth had spent several years at the court of Philip the Good[56] — adhered to its traditional sympathies, and showed its aversion to the novel line of policy now pressed upon the state. But the number of those who thus felt was probably small. Their influence, too, was waning before that of the new families, enriched by trade, and brought by their pursuits, as well as by kinship, into a more constant and active intercourse with the town population, in whose hands political power had been wholly concentrated.[57] There was a third class, strongly democratic in its proclivities, which had at this period acquired a momentary ascendency, having just succeeded in electing a *schultheiss* from among the lower orders. But that moderation, founded on a deep and fervent patriotism, which has been noticed as charac-

[55] Lenglet, tom. iii. pp. 139, 140. — Rodt, B. I. s. 110, 111. — Zellweger, s. 15, 16.

Zellweger thinks this treaty was a consequence of the report just received of Charles's remark that he had not appointed a governor to please his neighbors. If so, it must have been from a sagacious anticipation of this report that Berne had sent for the French envoys.

[56] Tillier, B. II. s. 146. — Rodt, B. I. s. 264.

[57] See the remarks on this subject of the contemporary Bernese chronicler Valerius Anshelm, ap. Rodt, B. I. s. 266.

terizing the internal disputes of the Swiss, gave a peculiar advantage to men like the Diesbachs, who, with aspiring dispositions and with a particular aim in view, an aim unconnected with the special interests of any party, knew how to avail themselves of the accommodating temper common to all parties. Instead, therefore, of finding an impediment in the dissensions which had arisen from another source, they were enabled by their dexterous use of those dissensions to secure the triumph of their own plans, with a consequent increase of their popularity and influence.[58] The first effect of that triumph was a mandate issued by the council, forbidding the subjects of Berne to enlist in the military service of any for-

[58] See, for accounts of the "Twingherrenstreit,"—a peculiar and interesting passage of Swiss history with which our readers may possibly not be as familiar as with Tell's apple and other bits of Swiss fable,—Diebold Schilling, s. 36–55; Tillier, B. II. s. 169–196; Rodt, B. I. s. 110–112.

The statement in the text in regard to the connection between this affair and the triumph of the French party at Berne is matter of inference. It is altogether opposed to the views of Von Rodt and other Swiss writers, who assume that the party contest then raging threw obstacles in the way of Diesbach, since he seemed, by his adherence to his own order, to be divided from the mass of his fellow-citizens. But Diesbach was not an ordinary demagogue. It was not necessary for his purposes that he should stand forward as the advocate of popular measures, or openly assume the guidance of public opinion. There is nothing which throws a stronger light upon those serviceable talents that rendered him the fit coadjutor of Louis XI. than the fact that, whichever party carried the elections at Berne, his personal ascendency remained undiminished. Thus Kistler, the radical *schulteiss* chosen on the present occasion, was speedily brought under the influence of Diesbach, himself a defeated candidate, and was made to carry out the foreign policy suggested by the latter. (See Tillier's remark, B. II. s. 196.) When the conservatives, to whom that policy was far from agreeable, again came into power, it was too firmly established to be opposed by them, and Diesbach still continued, openly or privately, to direct the action of the state. See Rodt, B. I. s. 266.

eign state. This was a blow aimed directly at the duke of Burgundy. Their martial qualities, combined with other national traits, had already begun to inspire the Swiss youth with that eagerness to fight under any standard and to touch the pay of any prince which was afterwards to lead to memorable results; and the count of Romont, under a commission from the Burgundian sovereign, had established a camp in the territory of Geneva, where he was daily receiving recruits from the neighboring Oberland.[59]

From the point we have now reached we may obtain a view of the objects and motives of the different parties, preparing us for the evolutions that are to follow. Austria had conceived the hope, by means of its alliance with Burgundy, — an alliance to be rendered intimate and indissoluble by a family compact, — of regaining the territory it had lost, and of revenging itself for a long series of humiliations and defeats. The duke of Burgundy was to be a tool in its hands: he was to fight out its old quarrels, redress its past injuries, renew the attempt which had been so often repeated and so signally foiled. But Charles had no purpose or thought of lending himself to this design. He had no motive for embarking in such a war. He had engagements which were incompatible with it. He had projects which were utterly repugnant to it. It was his fixed intention to continue on terms of amity with the Swiss.

[59] Rodt, B. I. s. 111, 112.

It was his strong desire to win them to a concordance with his own views, and even, if possible, to a coöperation in his own enterprises. The nature of his relations with the Italian states, with the Rhenish princes, above all with France, made this a matter of essential importance. True, he had entered into an agreement with Austria, and meant to execute that agreement to the letter. But he had taken care, in framing it, to commit himself to nothing which, in his own opinion, could drive him from his original ground. He had given his word — not indeed without limitations, but without any wish to lay such a stress upon those limitations as might have rendered the promise nugatory or deceptive — that Sigismund should hereafter suffer no harm from the aggressions of the Swiss, or that, if wrong were done, reparation should be obtained. But he had reserved to himself to decide in what manner and by what means his promise should be redeemed. He had expressly stated that his endeavor would be to accomplish the object by pacific methods. He had given the reasons — founded both on honor and necessity — which impelled him to this course. He entertained the fullest confidence that such methods would prove successful. By insisting that the whole frontier should pass from Sigismund's possession into his own, he had averted almost every possibility of chance collisions such as had kept alive the ancient animosity, frustrating every attempt to arrange a lasting peace, and subjecting every truce to hazards of hourly occurrence. He stood ready, if in spite of his precautions any new cause of trouble should arise, to step in and arbitrate or invoke arbitration — one side being expressly bound to accept this solution, while the other would have no good excuse for rejecting it. Finally, he made repeated and strenuous efforts to have all the questions that lay at the foundation of the mischief investigated and set at rest; and there are grounds for believing that, despite the coldness with which his overtures were received by the Confederates, the desired result would in the end have been attained had it not been for the open reluctance or secret antagonism of the Austrian prince.

Let it be admitted that Charles had placed himself in a position of much delicacy, requiring a greater tact than he possessed, exposed to greater risks than he had foreseen, calculated to arouse a jealousy which others had more skill to foment than he to allay. Yet he had not assumed that position thoughtlessly, without any comprehension of its responsibilities, much less with any mad project of barren victories or impossible conquests. He wished and intended, not to revive but to extinguish, not to take upon himself but to remove altogether, a quarrel which, far from coinciding with what had been the policy of his whole career, must embarrass or defeat it. He may have set too high a value on the Austrian alliance, on the acquisition of Alsace; but a rupture with the Swiss Confederacy, which he is commonly supposed to have accepted as an equivalent for these advantages, or even to have intentionally provoked, seeking in it a new opening to his ambition, was a price not contemplated in the bargain, and one which he steadily refused to pay.

On the other hand, the French king had conceived the scheme — a scheme suggested by the circumstances which had arisen — of having *his* cause upheld, *his* battles fought, *his* ancient grudge satisfied, by the strong arms and invincible courage of the Swiss. Similar arts to those which, exerted upon Liége, had brought ruin upon his instruments, misfortune and indelible disgrace upon himself, were now to be employed with very different results. There were, however, far greater difficulties to be encountered. The Swiss were not an excitable people. They had a well-grounded confidence in their own prowess, bearing no resemblance to the rashness that springs from conscious weakness and despair. Unlike the people of Liegé, they had no original impulse urging them to the contest and requiring only to be stimulated and fed. They had no hostile feeling towards the house of Burgundy. On the contrary, they had an old friendship with it, which, like Charles himself, they purposed to maintain. But among a free people unanimity of sentiment is felt to be the chief desideratum, and is seldom called forth except in the presence or under the alarm of external danger. When such an alarm is once aroused, the dissentients, even if a majority, make but a faint resistance, and soon subside into silence or suffer themselves to be borne along by the current. What was required in the present case was, to give a new direction to that hostility with which one foreign power had ever been regarded by the Confederates. Yet the very depth and violence of that feeling rendered its diversion into a new channel a work of immense labor. How it was ultimately accomplished will be seen hereafter. For the present we must still confine ourselves to an examination of the concurrent circumstances that tended, or are supposed to have tended, to the same result — circumstances believed, indeed, to have been all-powerful, and to have made the execution of the plan a facile or even superfluous undertaking.

We have shown — and the evidence will become clearer and more positive as we proceed — that the duke of Burgundy harbored no such purposes or ideas as have been commonly ascribed to him. On the other hand, his real design — a design to which his own antecedents as well as the general course of mediæval history plainly point — has been strangely overlooked. In the persuasion that his occupation of Alsace was to be permanent — a belief founded not only on the necessities which had compelled Sigismund to part with it and the uselessness of his attempting to hold it against the inroads of the Confederates, but also upon his verbal promise that in the lifetime of his ally no steps should be taken to transfer the possession and the mortgage to other hands[60] — Charles looked forward to raising up a firmer and loftier dominion in this quarter than that

[60] Such was the statement of the duke himself to the envoys of Sigismund, and it was not contradicted by them. Chmel, B. I. s. 51.

which the house of Habsburg had been able to establish. The house of Habsburg, as we have before said, had acquired only an imperfect authority in the Rhineland — an authority invested with few of the attributes of princely sway. Over the larger towns it exercised, and claimed to exercise, no sovereignty whatever. Within their respective limits these places enjoyed equal rights and immunities with the numerous princes of the empire. Similar *enclaves* were to be found in the German possessions of the house of Burgundy. But in those cases a protectorate or some other abnormal connection gave to a line of sovereigns so potent and so intrusive sufficient means of making their own influence paramount. Neighboring princes or states had submitted in a greater or less degree to the same ascendency. The solidity and splendor of the Burgundian rule, the prosperity and comparative tranquillity enjoyed by its subjects, the even-handed justice for which it had become renowned, rendered it the centre of a natural gravitation of power amidst weak and isolated communities, torn by continual feuds and exposed to continual perils. Charles could not fail to perceive this tendency, and could not forego any chance of promoting or of meeting it. Determined not to run against, but to shun, the rock on which the efforts of Austria had been wasted and its strength shattered, — a conflict namely with the Swiss cantons, too united among themselves, too secure in their impregnable location, too resolute in their independence, to invite or to suffer any foreign interference, — he saw his proper field of enterprise in all the intermediate territory, hoping to gather up and twine together the loose threads of empire that seemed to await, if not to court, his grasp.

Traces of this design, so far as Alsace was concerned, are to be found in the reported conduct and language of Hagenbach, as well as in some obscurer proceedings of the duke himself. Direct invitations were given to Mühlhausen in particular to make a willing acknowledgment of allegiance — accompanied with magnificent descriptions of the benefits to follow, as well as with significant hints of the dangers that might flow from a persistent refusal. The order and security established by the Burgundian lieutenant were triumphantly contrasted with the feebleness and discord that prevailed under a different system. "The rule of tailors and shoemakers" was sneeringly contrasted with that of the greatest and wealthiest of princes. Noble vassals of the house of Austria were encouraged to enter the service of Burgundy. Negotiations were opened with certain prelates of the Rhineland, with the view, as was suspected, of inducing them to place themselves under the Burgundian protection.[61]

These, it must be confessed, are facts which, even if better authenticated than some of them appear to be, would constitute no strong evidence. The real evidence must be derived from those general facts of Charles's career which indicate the nature and the

[61] Ochs, B. IV. s. 227 et seq. — Schilling, s. 82. — Stettler, B. I. s. 210. — Chmel, B. I. s. 86. — Knebel; Hertzogen; &c.

objects of his ambition. But at all events the towns of the Rhineland were seized with an alarm, and a movement was organized, quite distinct from that which we have seen started at Berne, but convergent in its course and auxiliary in its effects. Basel, Colmar, Schlettstadt, and Strasburg consulted on the feasibility of unseating, before it should have become too firmly placed, a dominion so menacing to their own independence. They proposed to redeem the mortgaged territory, with the purpose of either holding it themselves or transferring it to the margrave of Baden. But neither they nor any foreign prince had the right to reclaim it. The only practicable step was to furnish the means of doing so to the original possessor and lawful proprietor, by whom, in default of other security, a new mortgage might be given, and to whom an offer was accordingly made.[62]

The reply was not considered favorable. Was Sigismund, then, so well satisfied with the course of affairs as to shrink from any proceeding that would deprive him of the advantages he had reaped, or still expected to reap, from the Burgundian alliance? Far otherwise. Disgusted with continual proffers of mediation in reply to his demands for an armed intervention, he had already begun to think of new means of bettering his prospects. In the spring of 1473 he made a second trial in the quarter where he had before met with so unceremonious a rebuff. He

[62] Ochs, B. IV. s. 210–214. — Neither Zellweger nor Von Rodt alludes to these negotiations, the importance of which will appear from the results at a subsequent stage of the affair.

offered, through a secret embassy, to abandon the service of Burgundy for that of France. Louis was on the point of returning the same curt denial as before, when he reflected that a connection with Sigismund would have its advantages, were it purified from the taint of his present ill relations with the Swiss. The Austrian prince was therefore informed that an appointment and a pension commensurate with his rank would be granted to him, provided he should first conclude a peace with the Confederates on terms which had recently been proposed. Fearful that he might have been too hasty in giving even this qualified assent, or that the qualification itself might be little palatable to those whose sentiments he must study in order that he might ultimately guide them, the king at once communicated to his friends at Berne the steps which had been taken, offering to follow up the negotiation if it were agreeable to them: otherwise he would proceed in it no further.[63]

But what were the terms of agreement with the Swiss, which Sigismund, it would thus seem, had shown an aversion or had even positively refused to accept? At the request of the Burgundian agents the bishop of Constance had joined his efforts with theirs and had drafted a treaty of amity and commerce, confirming the rights of the respective parties to the territory at present occupied by each, and referring to the arbitration of the bishop himself all casual

[63] Zellweger, s. 25. — Sigismund had previously made an application of a similar kind to the duke of Milan. See Schilling, s. 86, 87.

subjects of complaint.[64] Thus the French king and the duke of Burgundy were apparently playing into each other's hands. In reality the former had seized upon his adversary's combinations, and was turning them against him. Charles was laboring with all his might to effect a reconciliation between Austria and the Swiss, ignorant that he himself was the destined victim, with whose sacrifice the peace was to be ratified.

The Diesbachs, who since our last mention of them had spent several months at the French court, where they had accepted posts in the household and had even served in the war against the duke of Burgundy,[65] were now at home again, ready to promote the interests and to carry out any suggestion of their master. Acting at their instigation and assuming to act on behalf of the whole Confederacy, Berne made approaches to the house of Austria — a suitable occasion being found in the arrival at Basel of the Emperor Frederick on his way to Trèves.[66] But Sigismund could not yet bring himself to swallow the bitter mixture presented to him by every hand. He had returned to his earlier schemes, for the success of which the moment seemed propitious. His ambassadors followed in the wake of the imperial cortége, prepared to take a leading part in the negotiation, or even to hold the reins of the discussion. But it was in vain that they proffered their services to the Bur-

[64] Zellweger, s. 21, and Beilage, No. 8.

[65] Tillier, B. II. s. 201, 202.

[66] Chmel, B. I. s. 43 et al. — Conf. Zellweger, s. 20.

gundian prince. Their advice was not asked; no confidence was given to them. The door of the penetralia was kept studiously closed. It was with some difficulty that they obtained a hearing on their master's own affairs — the greater matter now in progress being pleaded as a reason for delay. They sent in their papers by the officer who collected the memorials in the crowded antechamber. When they were admitted to an audience, it was in order that they might make as well as receive explanations.

Charles had heard something of the recent overtures to Louis, which he construed as a design to put the latter in possession of Alsace. To the denial of the Austrian envoys he listened with an air of incredulity. He was in no doubt, he said, that there had been some underhand practices. But he had no wish to engage in unseemly recriminations. He would rely on the loyalty of Sigismund's intentions. For himself, he meant to adhere faithfully to his pledges. He would never desert his ally, whose interests should receive from him the same attention as his own. He had made propositions to the Swiss, on which they had promised to deliberate. To establish a peace between them and his cousin of Austria would continue to be the object of his care. He was going to Alsace and to Burgundy, where he should remain for several months, and would take pains to inform himself by personal observation of the state of affairs. To renewed complaints of the inimical demeanor of the Confederates, a declaration that Sigismund could no longer endure it, and an urgent request that troops might be sent to his assistance, no reply was given.[67]

Another interview took place at noon on the 25th of November. Frederick had left Trèves; Charles was on the point of leaving. It was matter of notoriety that the treaty had been broken off. Yet the envoys affected ignorance. They regretted that they had not been called upon to assist in the negotiation, but trusted that a satisfactory conclusion had been arrived at. Without deigning any answer on this point, the duke reverted, in a sterner tone than he had before used, to the clandestine dealings with France. He insisted on the fulfilment of the promise that had been made to him. He had incurred great expenses, he had exposed himself to the hostility of a friendly people, while he had derived no compensatory advantages from the possession of the mortgaged lands, which should never, with his consent, pass into the hands of another.[68] This was plain speaking; and the silence and dissimulation on the other side were not less significant. This, assuredly, was not the intercourse of conspirators — of men united in the pursuit of a common object, in a hostile design against a third party. In fact the utter divergence of their aims, the disagreement of their interests, the miscalculations on which the alliance had been founded, were now apparent. From this moment Sigismund ceased to indulge the notion of launching the Burgundian thunderbolt

[67] Chmel, B. I. s. 44–48.

[68] Ibid. s. 49–51.

against the rebel Swiss; while Charles abandoned the attempt to bridge a chasm which was already tending to close over his own head.

Meanwhile the proceedings at Trèves had, as we have before seen, created a ferment, which the council of Berne, under the guidance of the Diesbachs, had done its best to spread and keep alive. Reports were disseminated that the coronation had taken place, that the new kingdom of Burgundy was to embrace the limits of the old, — which had included all the western portion of Helvetia, — that Besançon had been fixed upon as the capital, that Venice and other Italian powers had hailed the announcement with satisfaction, and that certain alarming combinations might be expected as a result. The Confederates were exhorted to consider what these events might portend, and to prepare themselves for following in the footsteps of their fathers.[69] The same reports were echoed from Milan, which had previously sent an agent to Basel to suggest the formation of a defensive league against the duke of Burgundy.[70] It was proposed that the towns of the Rhineland should be admitted into an alliance with the Swiss.[71] At Berne the same precautions were taken as were usual in time of war. Spies were sent out, the passes watched, signals and places of rendezvous appointed.[72]

Where and why this excitement died away without

[69] Zellweger, s. 27, 28.

[70] Ochs, B. IV. s. 215. — Schilling, s. 86.

[71] Rodt, B. I. s. 169. — Ochs, B. IV. s. 229.

[72] Rodt, B. I. s. 168, 169.

producing the intended effect, we shall hereafter see. In Alsace, the news of Charles's approach awakened more real, though vague apprehensions. The free towns called in the population of their subject territory, caused all the movable property to be brought within the walls, examined their defences, and maintained a vigilant guard.[73] Deputies from the different places assembled at Basel, and were joined by the commissioners of Berne, Milan, and France.[74] At Mühlhausen, where better grounds of alarm existed in the consciousness of default and the menacing intimations still received, the consternation rose to a panic. The fate of Dinant and of Liége was remembered. Women rushed wildly through the streets. Relics were carried in procession. The intercession of the Blessed Virgin and of all the saints in the calendar was continually invoked. The churches were thronged to suffocation, and the modulated chantings from the choir mingled, like the wailing of departed spirits, with the sobs and screams of the agonized crowd. When the frantic uproar had subsided, arrangements were made for enduring a siege.[75]

Before his departure from Luxembourg, Charles had dismissed the larger portion of his army. Another portion had been left to garrison the towns in Lorraine. He arrived in Alsace with a number not much exceeding that of his ordinary body-guard, and

[73] Ochs, B. IV. s. 228. — Knebel, s. 22. — Schilling, s. 90. — Wurstisen; Strobel, &c.

[74] Knebel, s. 22, 23. — Ochs. — Strobel.

[75] Schreiber, s. 24. — Mieg, Geschichte de Stadt Mühlhausen, B. I. s. 102 et seq.

amounting, with the addition of fifteen hundred men hastily levied by Hagenbach, who had come to meet him on the frontier, to less than five thousand in all.[76] He had brought no artillery, warlike munitions, or stores of any kind. With this force and in this state, he who had never been willing to undertake any military enterprise without extensive preparations was apparently suspected of meditating some vast project — the overthrow of the free institutions in the Rhineland, or an attempt to force his way across the Alps![77]

The refusal of Colmar to admit any considerable body of his followers within the walls was viewed as an insult by the Burgundian prince, who thereupon declined the hospitalities tendered to himself.[78] Nor does it seem to have been a quite judicious measure on the part of the authorities. It necessitated the scattering of the troops in quest of forage and supplies, with a consequent relaxation of the stringent discipline which had been enforced while Charles was personally in command, and which he had shown both in word and in act his earnest desire to maintain. The injunctions he had issued were the less effectual that this small residue of his army was composed in great part of Italian mercenaries, reputed more skilful in the manœuvres of the field, but also more dissolute and brutal in their habits, than other

[76] Rodt, B. I. s. 185. — Knebel. — Ochs.

[77] The diary of Knebel fairly throbs with pulsations of terror and wonderment. "Gott möge uns mit dem Arm seiner Macht beschützen! . . . Möge uns Gott vor seinen bösen Ueberfällen bewahren!" &c.

[78] Ochs, B. IV. s. 230, 231.

soldiers of that period, and conducted by chiefs who were merely hired agents, not subjects, of the duke, little interested in his safety or his fame, and as unsuited to administer as their men were unused to obey any regular code of military law. The march resembled that of disorganized bands returning from a successful campaign. The cottages of the peasantry were forcibly invaded, provisions consumed without payment, and similar acts of petty plunder committed. Violence was also offered to women;[79] but no instance of bloodshed is mentioned. Charles is not accused of having given any license for these excesses. When complaint was made to him, he strongly expressed his displeasure, and ordered off Hagenbach, at the head of a sufficient corps, to quell the disorders.[80]

At Breisach he received a letter written by the council of Berne, with the approval of the Confederates. In a diet recently held at Lucerne it had been agreed that the visit of the duke of Burgundy to his dominions on the Rhine would present a proper occasion for sending him a complimentary message, and for making certain representations touching the affair of Mühlhausen and other matters. The choice of envoys and the business of preparing the instructions were left with Berne[81] — a proof how little its allies felt themselves concerned in the negotiation.

[79] Knebel, however, after stating this last fact, adds, as if in some doubt as to its correctness, "So ist erzhält worden." s. 26.

[80] Knebel; Ochs; Strobel; Barante; &c.

[81] Rodt, B. I. s. 190.

A safe-conduct for the embassy was accordingly requested; and the letter contained also a reminder of the long friendship between the house of Burgundy and the Swiss, with the expression of a desire that the same feeling might continue and might increase in strength.[82] These wishes were cordially reciprocated by Charles. He could say with truth, he wrote, that nothing had been left undone by him to confirm and perpetuate the good understanding which his ancestors — and they alone among neighboring rulers — had uniformly preserved with the Confederates.[83] He had seen with surprise their intercourse with the French king, of whose perfidious disposition, known to all the world, they themselves had had early experience. He had already, out of consideration for them, shown greater lenity to Mühlhausen than was perhaps right. It was a fundamental principle of friendship, that nothing should be asked by one party which the other might not honorably grant.[84] The people of Mühlhausen were debtors in respect

[82] See this letter in Schilling, s. 93, 94.

[83] "Euer Gemeinwesen haben wir von Jugend auf lieb gehabt, also den Fusstapfen Unsrer Vordern nachfolgend, die Eure Stadt allerzeit begünstigt haben. Darum wann Wir der verflossenen Zeitalter Achtung haben, so ist kein Land in Eurer Nachbarschaft, das Eurem Nutzen nicht etwan schon widerwärtig gewesen sei, ausgenommen Burgund allein. Und damit Wir die Worte Eures Briefes wiedermelden: wenn Ihr begehret, die uralte Gnade, die zwischen Unseren Vordern und Euch festiglich bestanden, night allein zu bewahren, sondern in der Bewahrung noch beharrlich zu befestigen; — so umfassen Wir Euch mit nicht minderer Wohlgewogenheit und halten in Warheit dafür, es sei nichts in dem von Uns unterlassen worden, das zur Fortdauer dieser gemeinsamen Freundschaft gehören könnte."

[84] "Denn es heisst: der Freundschaft erstes Gesetz ist, dass man von Freunden nur Ehrbares begehre."

to money; but he was a debtor to justice,[85] and was constantly appealed to by the creditors to enforce the payment of their lawful dues. If, however, any other town or state were willing to assume the debt, it would be easy for him on this point to gratify the Confederates, — as in all matters, indeed, he was desirous of doing. He would gladly confer with their representatives, for whom no other safe-conduct would be necessary than the present letter. As the time of their arrival was uncertain, and his own affairs were pressing, he could fix no definite day or place for receiving them. He acquainted them, however, with his intended movements in order that they might meet him at their own convenience.[86]

That Charles was still endeavoring, through a mixture of persuasion and intimidation, to extort from Mühlhausen the surrender of its independence, seems sufficiently certain.[87] That he actually meditated an assault, with the means at his command, — putting out of view the immediate and inevitable consequences to which he cannot have been blind, and which he was totally unprepared to face, — is more than

[85] "Die Mühlhauser sind des Geldes Schuldner, Wir aber der Gerechtigkeit."

[86] See the whole letter (modern German translation) in Knebel, s. 29, 30. — Schilling, a devoted partisan of the Diesbachs and the writer from whom the ordinary versions of the transactions between Charles and the Swiss have been mainly derived, makes not the slightest allusion to this letter, with which nevertheless he must have been perfectly well acquainted. Knebel, a resident of Basel, is not less hostile to the Burgundian prince; but he is an artless diarist, not an instructed advocate, and when he blunders, is merely the victim of false reports.

[87] See the letter of Antonius Hanneron in Knebel, s. 27, 28. Schreiber; Rodt; &c.

doubtful. At all events no such attempt was made.[88] He pursued the exact route of which he had given notice to the Swiss. At Ensisheim, where he remained from the 2d to the 8th of January, he was overtaken by their envoys, who arrived on the 6th, and who followed him two days later to Thann.[89] They had no reason to complain of the manner of their reception. An audience was instantly granted to them, they were welcomed with every mark of friendship and consideration, and, the purport of their instructions having been stated, a courteous answer was returned, with renewed assurances that the duke cherished the same feelings towards the Confederacy which had always been evinced by his predecessors. They were requested to discuss their business with the members of his council, who waited upon them at their lodgings. The most flattering attentions were shown to them during their stay. They were escorted through the streets by heralds and pursuivants. Their table was furnished with a service of silver, with choice wines, and with meats and delicacies of all kinds; and the musicians of the household played beneath their windows at every meal.[90]

[88] Mieg, the historian of Mühlhausen, asserts that the Burgundian army marched towards the town with the purpose of assaulting it; but that the long-deferred autumnal rains having set in, the country was flooded, and an attack rendered impracticable. No doubt the people of Mühlhausen imagined that they saw troops approaching; but it is certain from the authentic records we possess of Charles's movements, that they were mistaken.

[89] Ancienne Chronique, Lenglet, tom. ii. p. 211. Rodt, B. I. s. 194, 196.

[90] Rodt, B. I. s. 195.

This is the official report of the envoys themselves. Knebel also, writing at Basel, through which

The principal question — that which concerned Mühlhausen — was promptly and satisfactorily settled, in the mode suggested by Charles. The time of payment was further postponed, with an understanding that the money would be advanced by Basel and other places; and it was agreed that the retaliatory measures which had been put in execution should forthwith cease. What answer was given to a complaint preferred against Hagenbach for his offensive speeches on various occasions, we are not informed. That it was of a conciliatory tenor may be inferred from the landvogt's own demeanor towards the envoys. Such were his polite attentions, that in a report which they sent off soon after their arrival, he is somewhat emphatically designated as "a good man" [91] — a phraseology which amusingly contrasts with the epithets ordinarily bestowed upon him.

they passed both in going and returning, says they were received in the most friendly manner ("auf's Freundlichste"). See also the extracts from the register of Mühlhausen, in Ochs, B. IV. s. 239. In fact there is no instance of a foreign embassy being treated with equal distinction at the Burgundian court. These facts must have been well known to Schilling, whose official position gave him access to all the documents connected with the matter, and who has published the instructions given to the envoys. Yet, instead of publishing also their report, he has given a totally different account, one which has been copied and amplified by successive writers, and which has perhaps done more than any other falsehood of the time to darken the history of these transactions. He represents the envoys as approaching Charles in a friendly and submissive manner, "hoping to find him a good and gracious lord," but as treated by him with the greatest coldness and haughtiness, left kneeling for a long time at his feet, and at last receiving, as the only reply to their overtures, an abrupt command to follow him to Dijon. Die Burgundischen Kriege, s. 95, 100. Zellweger is so disingenuous as to repeat this story, with the proofs before him of its entire falsity.

[91] Rodt, B. I. s. 194. — Yet Schilling (ubi supra) tells us that Hagenbach, "the raging swine," stood at Charles's elbow, prompting him to insult the Swiss envoys!

The object of the mission having been attained, the envoys took leave of the duke, by whom they were graciously dismissed.[92] On the next day, the 11th of January, he himself set out in the direction of Besançon. He had previously restored to Thann the franchises of which it had been deprived. Ostensibly this was done at the intercession of Hagenbach, who appeared as a petitioner on behalf of the inhabitants, and promised future good behavior in their name.[93] They acknowledged this service by a present of money — a form of displaying their gratitude which was no doubt the most agreeable to him, but which was far from betokening a change in their sentiments, such as Charles had apparently sought to produce.

The hasty departure of the latter was ascribed by his enemies to a fear lest the jealousy and aversion excited by his presence in Alsace might suddenly break out in open hostility.[94] This is not a probable surmise. But it may well have been that the frigid

[92] Ochs, B. IV. s. 239. — Rodt, still apparently under the influence of a story which he has himself helped to refute, says the envoys returned without being able to obtain a settlement of any point except that relating to Mühlhausen. But what else was there that required a settlement? The complaints respecting Hagenbach were merely a subject for civil disclaimers, which were no doubt made. It is evident, both from the instructions given to the envoys and from the report sent off by them after their first audience, that there was no desire on the side of the Confederates to enter into any general negotiations. It seems to have been feared that Charles would avail himself of this opportunity to renew his proposals for a closer alliance and his offers to mediate between Austria and the Swiss. The envoys express their satisfaction at having learned from some of the members of the court, that these matters would not be brought forward.

[93] Knebel, s. 35. — Strobel, B. III. s. 301. — Here we have another contradiction, from trustworthy sources, of the common accounts.

[94] Knebel, s. 34. — Schilling, s. 92.

and distrustful looks with which he had been greeted had inflicted a wound upon his pride, and cast a momentary chill upon his sanguine ambition. If so, there was a speedy reaction. Never had his heart beat higher, never had his eye beamed brighter, than when, after crossing Franche Comté, he entered his native province and was received by the inhabitants with all the tokens of a loyal and affectionate attachment. Here perhaps alone in his dominions he was the object of a sympathizing admiration. At his entrance into Dijon on the 23d of January, with all the state and pomp that befitted the scene, every emblem and device that adorned the route was a tribute to his past exploits or a presage of future glory. On the 26th he presided at a banquet, where the prelates, the nobles, and the deputies of both the Burgundies surrounded the board. At the conclusion of the festivities he addressed the company in a fervid speech, well suited to kindle a respondent glow in the bosoms of his auditors. He talked to them of "that ancient kingdom of Burgundy which the kings of France had usurped and converted into a duchy" — a matter, he added, which his subjects had no less reason to ponder than himself. But suddenly pausing — he had thoughts, he said, which it behooved him to lock up in his own breast and to communicate to no other.[95]

[95] Hist. de Bourgogne, tom. iv. preuves, pp. cccxxvii. — cccxxxi.

Michelet and Hallam have both misconceived this allusion. "Charles," remarks the latter, "had a vague notion of history, and confounded the province or duchy of Burgundy, which had always appertained to the French crown, with Franche Comté and other countries which belonged to the kingdom of Burgundy." (Middle Ages,

Two days later there was another entrance into Dijon, another procession, another appeal to the sympathies and recollections of the people. Before his departure from the Netherlands, Charles had directed that the bodies of his father and mother — the latter of whom had died in 1471 — should be removed from the places of their temporary interment, and conveyed under a proper escort across Lorraine to Burgundy, there to await his own arrival. The cortége was met, at some distance from the city, by the clergy and religious orders, the dignitaries of the two provinces, the municipalities of Dijon, Besançon, and many other towns, and by the duke himself, attended by his household and the nobles of the country. All were attired in deep mourning. The way was lighted by torches. The remains of the illustrious pair were carried to the Sainte-Chapelle, where vigils were held throughout the night. On the following day they were transferred to the Chartreuse, and deposited, beside those of other members of the same house, in marble sarcophagi, which still rank among the choicest specimens of monumental sculpture.

Three years more of storm and strife, and Charles himself was to be laid at rest. But not there, not thus — not in that ancestral tomb, not with that ancestral pomp.

Supplemental Notes.) Whatever Charles's notions on other points of history may have been, he was acquainted with the fact, which seems to have escaped Mr. Hallam's recollection, that the territory subsequently formed into the duchy of Burgundy had formed part of the *first* kingdom of Burgundy, which in the 6th century was overthrown and dismembered by the kings of France.

CHAPTER III.

CHARLES'S CHARACTER AND POSITION. — RELATIONS WITH AUSTRIA AND THE SWISS. — DOMESTIC GOVERNMENT IN THE NETHERLANDS. — ORGANIZATION OF A STANDING ARMY. — AFFAIRS OF COLOGNE.

1474.

That success should be taken as the common and most convenient criterion for judging of men's capacities and merits, is both natural and right. True success — the performance of what a man has undertaken to do, his attainment of the end which he has sought to reach — is not an accidental result; and failure affords an irrefragable proof that, however great the talent and the energy exerted, they have fallen short of the amount required. More was attempted than it was possible to achieve; resources have been wasted, efforts misapplied; and there must therefore have been a lack of prevision, of ability, or of diligence.

But no doubt there is a general proneness to overrate the powers that have accomplished the object proposed, and in a much greater degree to underrate those that have been baffled or unduly tasked. In the latter case not only is there less inducement to examine closely, but the means of forming a correct estimate have been lost through the frustration of the attempt, through the collapse of the project. The building has been left unfinished and surrounded with scaffoldings, and we pronounce upon the "effect;" it has been overthrown and lies before us a mountain of rubbish, and we criticise the design. The climber has fallen from the dizzy height, and we pass a brief censure on his temerity and self-confidence. Persistent trials have been in vain, hopes long indulged in have proved groundless, and we can only condemn the obstinacy and wonder at the delusion. We mistake the motives, we overlook the encouragements, we neither perceive the real situation, nor apprehend the real nature, of the obstacles.

The reputation of much abler men than Charles of Burgundy has suffered to a far greater extent than his from the hasty and undiscriminating sentence which the world is accustomed to pass upon a fruitless ambition. And for posterity at least there is ample excuse, if in his case any injustice has been done. His obvious faults, the obscurity and multiplicity of his involvements, his final complete isolation, his abrupt and terrible fall, left a single and deep impression, easily copied and preserved. The agreement of independent witnesses, the concurrent verdict of contemporaries, — rendered without a solitary audible protest, — afforded no room for an appeal, no chance of obtaining a revision. There was, too, in the accounts transmitted and in the conceptions based upon them, a seeming harmony, an entire freedom from any such palpable inconsistencies as might have provoked suspicion and prompted scrutiny. For four centuries Charles has been recognized as the very type of rashness, presumption, and an arrogant wilfulness — of a wrong-headedness impervious to reason, a violence incapable of reflection, inaccessible to truth, indifferent to consequences.[1]

At this long interval, there can be little inducement to raise objections or to open an inquiry. Why discard representations than which none could be better suited to adorn a startling tale as well as to point an unexceptionable moral? Desire for novelty must have of course its weight; but the risk of indulging it is serious, and the penalties are tremendous. The prospect of being powerfully backed is an excellent stimulant to the combative propensities; but nothing can be more discouraging than to be stationed with the forlorn hope or left upon the breach with a few wounded comrades.[2] A reluctance, a painful hesitation, must be felt in presenting even, without gloss or commentary, a recital of facts opposed to the received version and irreconcilable with settled views. One would fain enjoy the confidence of one's readers; and there is no surer way

[1] Perhaps the general though not the least favorable view is most succinctly stated in the following extract: "Ce prince n'eut d'autres vertus que celles d'un soldat; il fut ambitieux, téméraire, sans conduite, sans conseil, ennemi de la paix, et toujours altéré de sang. Il ruina sa maison par ses folles entreprises, fit le malheur de ses sujets et mérita le sien."

[2] Rodt, Zellweger, Gingins, and other recent writers, have not escaped censure for upsetting the popular version of the origin of the war between the duke of Burgundy and the Swiss.

of winning it than by repeating the story which they have always heard and confirming the opinions which they have always entertained.

When, however, — with no fault of ours, but through the importunate industry of certain archivists and official mousers, ignorant or reckless of the mischief they were committing, as well as by the more culpable explorations of here and there a prying and discontented mind, bent upon resolving doubts which ought to have been resolutely stifled,—a mass of documents and relations have been dragged from their hiding-places, cleansed from the dust of ages, and thrust into publicity, what resource have we but to accept the new and more authentic testimony thus adduced, subversive though it should prove to be of an established belief? To pass it over in silence, to adhere in preference to that which it refutes, would be hardly possible; for not only should we find our fluency checked and our fervency dampened, but many gaps, which in the darkness we might have safely skirted unawares, would require to be boldly leaped, or crossed by a bridge of well-constructed fiction. For such a task we confess our incompetence. Truth-telling—however paradoxical the proposition may appear — is more natural and more easy than lying. A true report is the mere echo of the fact, the unstudied response that finds utterance for itself in language or other vehicle to the interrogatories, tacit or express, which always await it. Truth — to the extent of the knowledge possessed — flows from unconscious and innocent lips, drops from the mouth of the indolent, forces a passage through the embarrassment of the stammerer, writes itself on the forehead in contradiction of the spoken denial. Falsehood, or even evasion, demands invention, imposes a labor, and though not uncommon as a habit among any people or tribe at present known to the ethnological student, is the instinct only of a particular class of active and ingenious intellects.

If it were incumbent upon us to express a decided opinion in regard to the common representations of Charles's character, we should be compelled to declare that they are exaggerated and in a great measure false. We should not propose to substitute for that unfaithful portrait one bearing no resemblance to it. That he was not a man of lofty genius or versatile talents, that his conceptions transcended his ability to execute, that he was especially deficient in that faculty of adapting his policy and mode of action to the dispositions and requirements of others, and to the exigencies of the moment, — so necessary in the management of men and in the conduct of affairs,[3] — in which his great adversary eminently excelled, are conclusions which we should happily leave undisturbed. The sensitive pride, the overstrained self-reliance, the fiery temper, not less fierce and consuming than quickly kindled, would remain conspicuous. But we could not, in the face of many direct manifestations and proofs to the contrary, persist in depicting him as a man of mere ordinary intel-

[3] Hence probably the remark of Commines that Charles was wanting in "le bon sens."

ligence, remarkable only for the gigantic absurdity of his ambition and for his reckless self-destruction. We could not repeat the assertions that he was whirled along by the mere turbulence of his passions; that his perceptions were confused and his plans destitute of meaning or solidity; that he plunged without forethought into difficulties which he might easily have avoided; that he defied all obstacles, despised all considerations either of policy or right, and fell a victim to the insane pursuit of an empty fame. So far are we from subscribing to the truth of this description that our impressions are in many respects altogether opposite. It seems to us that his vision, within a limited range, was singularly clear; that while he had neither the profound sagacity nor the exhaustless invention of his rival, his powers of reasoning were rare and admirable, his principles of action consistent and sound;[4] that with all his impetuosity and all his sternness, he was guided in the main by a sense of equity which can be fitly appreciated only by a comparison with the course of his opponents, and with the common practice of his own and of a later age; that his aspirations, if such as a single lifetime was insufficient to realize, had a definite aim, the attainment of which would have shortened and moderated the contests of subsequent times;[5] that, in fine, if disappointment and disaster

[4] Müller, most eloquent of historians, falls into some strange inconsistencies on this point. See his Hist. de la Conféd. Suisse (trad. de Monnard), tom. vii.

[5] See the remarks on this point of Lichnowski, B. VII.

instead of inducing submission and wariness, goaded him to desperation, this was not because he felt them as the mere recoil of his own arrogance, folly, and injustice, but precisely because of their very different origin, proceeding from attacks which he had done nothing to provoke, which he had taken all possible pains to avert, and which were prompted by the lowest motives, and waged under the shallowest pretences. The virtues for which he stood conspicuous among princes — his continence, sobriety, unequalled laboriousness,[6] rigid economy, strict impartiality, inaccessibility to sycophants and parasites,[7] openness to every appeal,[8] and promptness to expedite every affair,[9] have been the more readily acknowledged that these qualities have been found to possess remarkable affinities with a distempered judgment, extravagant fancies, and an inordinate egotism. His harshest critics, his bitterest enemies, have seldom been willing to deny his sincerity — an indubitable

[6] Lamarche remarks that his proper designation would have been "Charles le Travailleur."

[7] Basin, tom. ii. pp. 424, 425.

[8] Ibid. — "Jamais nul plus liberallement ne donna audience à ses serviteurs et subjectz." Commines, tom. ii. p. 66.

[9] Meyer, fol. 345.

"He was a man of a great and lofty mind," remarks Basin, who deplores the fact that the latter part of his reign should have corresponded ill with its promise at the outset. But why the end proved so inglorious was a question on which Basin, personally acquainted with Charles but ignorant of his private affairs, has thrown no light. He imagines that it might have been possible for Charles to stave off the hostility of his rival, whereas nothing can be more evident than that Louis began his career with the purpose and expectation of getting all the Burgundian dominions into his hands, and only desisted when he had experienced the effects of a resolute opposition. Basin, too, as was natural both from the obscurity of the real facts and from his long residence in the Rhineland, lays the fault of the Swiss war entirely upon Charles.

proof of the dulness of his intellect and a foil to the astuteness of his rival. This sincerity, whether a defect or a merit, we should be tempted to fix upon as the central point, the harmonizing element, of his intellectual and moral nature; making it, when seen through no distorted medium, so easy to comprehend; accounting for the peculiar force of his impulses, the directness of his views, and the pertinacity of his struggles; for his fidelity to friends and implacability to foes; for his readiness to accord and his sternness in exacting what was due; for the logical coherence of his ideas as well as for the vehemence and the depth of his emotions. Were we to contrast his conduct with that of contemporary princes, it might be shown as a distinctive feature that his actions were habitually shaped in accordance with certain notions of right. The notion might be narrow, the right might be pushed to an extreme; but the convictions were honest, the avowal was open, the excuse, if insufficient, was at least intelligible; whereas the French king, impelled by a simple instinct of acquisitiveness not always under the control of prudence, pursued continually a devious and trackless route, disowning his acts, disavowing his agents, deserting or outwitting his allies, hiding himself in clouds of sophistry, or taking refuge in a convenient silence.

May we not, at all events, hope to be pardoned if we should be so far carried away by the zeal of the biographer, as occasionally to remember that the man whose life we have undertaken to describe was after all an organized being, endowed with faculties, mental as well as physical;[10] that he had his own mode of viewing the transactions and events in which he was a principal party; and that it might, on the whole, be as interesting to know in what light the world and its proceedings were looked at by him as in what light he and his proceedings were looked at by the world? Such considerations may be thought the more excusable when it is recollected that, for the latter part of his career, we have no consecutive narrative of any value or note written with a personal knowledge of his sentiments and demeanor; that the information concerning him has been almost wholly derived from hostile accounts; that his own declarations and announcements were carefully suppressed; that the motives and conduct of his antagonists were discreetly veiled and admirably draped. The accused having been convicted and condemned, there can now be no harm in noticing what, if a hearing had been granted, might possibly have been urged in the way of defence or palliation.

Looking simply at his position, one might venture to assert that in the long race of mediæval ambition no prospects were brighter, no hopes of extended dominion more justifiable, than those of the duke of Burgundy. The wisest and most valiant of the Eng-

[10] This is not always admitted. A modern French writer tells us epigrammatically that "the contemporaries of the duke of Burgundy called him *the Terrible;* posterity has named him *the Rash;* but in history he will be more rightly denominated *Charles the Idiot.*"

lish monarchs had made themselves famous by a long series of attempts to appropriate the crown of France, to subjugate Scotland, to subdue and tranquillize Ireland. The house of Austria had occupied itself with a variety of disconnected and perplexing enterprises, besides pouring out its treasure and its blood in a hopeless and endless contest with the Swiss. The soil of Italy was whitened with the bones of hosts of adventurers. Spain had been for centuries a battle-ground of contending races and creeds. Throughout Europe there was a clashing of powers, a struggle for superiority in which many were engaged and a few only could win. The growth of the Burgundian dominions had been rapid and unchecked. Province had been added to province at less cost, with less commotion, than had often attended the acquisition of towns; and the possessions thus easily amassed had passed to the present proprietor without diminution or serious dispute. With this natural tendency to expansion was there not combined a natural destiny for greatness? As the foundations widened might not the superstructure be expected to rise? Where should the errant wings of Empire be folded, if not above the seat of commerce, the focus of industry and wealth?

The downfall of Liége, the purchase of Alsace, the annexation of Gueldres, the establishment of a military protectorate over Lorraine, had shown the various modes in which the Burgundian sovereign was able to profit by the weakness and dissensions of neighboring states, the incompetency and embarrassments of neighboring rulers. The rivalries between the German princes, the conflicts between the princes and the towns, the distractions within the empire and its perils from without, showed the room and the necessity that existed for a stable, dominant, and directing power, a centre of influence and a tower of defence. The decline of the house of Habsburg and the contempt into which it had fallen were attributable as much to its lack of an independent, self-sustaining position as to its personal degeneracy. Its attempts to lean upon the house of Burgundy and to draw from it sustenance and new life, revealed its consciousness of the need and its perception of the source from which that need was to be supplied. In other quarters the same convictions had been felt and expressed. Wherever the imperial title might rest, it was to the house of Burgundy that the empire must turn for help and the means of renovation.

True, in all his undertakings Charles would be watched, followed, opposed, and harassed by an enemy who was never so dangerous as in a time of ostensible peace, never so active as when openly unemployed. But this insidious and ceaseless hostility furnished the sharpest spur to exertion, the most powerful of all motives for pressing forward to a secure and commanding eminence. And though Louis had at home become stronger and less assailable, he had failed as yet to acquire an ascendency or any base of operations abroad. With all his skill and success in winning individual support, he had hitherto been unfortunate in his plans for controlling the policy of foreign states. Of the neighboring governments, those of England and Aragon were his undisguised and unrelenting, if also unenterprising, foes. His sister the duchess-regent of Savoy had emancipated herself from his too active and exacting guardianship, and was warm and sincere in her professions of friendship for his rival. Venice, reserved but scrutinizing, leaned strongly to the same side. The duke of Milan, Galeas Sforza, though leaning from sympathy to the opposite side, had received no advantage from his alliance with Louis, and was now about to enter into a treaty with Charles. Several of the more distant powers — Naples, Hungary, Denmark — cultivated close relations with the court of Burgundy, while none had thought it necessary to keep up any frequent communication with that of France.

In one quarter only was there a speck on the horizon — stationary but dim, whether increasing or diminishing was a question which the keenest eye might have been unable to determine. For three years the French king had been trying to inveigle the Swiss Confederacy into an abandonment of its neutrality — to upheave a body which, once loosened from its base, once tilted from its equipoise, would, he might hope, be carried far and fast enough by the force of its own momentum. The calculations were perhaps correct; but were the practical appliances adequate to such a work? The levers had been well selected; but where was the fulcrum? Was it to be found in the alliance between Burgundy and Austria?

This was certainly a point on which, in the modern parlance of diplomacy, explanations might properly have been asked for. But the alliance had been formally notified to the Confederates, and had not been deemed a subject for remonstrance. The notification had been accompanied with professions and assurances which, if credited, must tend to remove all real uneasiness. In its workings — if we except any irritation which Hagenbach's deportment might be supposed to have created — the arrangement had not been productive of any annoyance or disturbance to the Swiss. It had operated in fact, as Charles had intended and declared that it should operate, to their advantage. If Sigismund were secured against causeless aggressions, he had also been restrained from giving any cause for aggression. If a curb had been imposed upon the military enterprises of the Confederates, greater freedom had been afforded to their peaceful and commercial enterprises. Territorial aggrandizement was not with them an object of spontaneous pursuit; and the impulse had subsided with the removal of the circumstances which had given rise to it. Their interests — and the Swiss, at least, have not been accused of any blindness or indifference to their interests — demanded a sedulous maintenance of their present relations with the neighbor whose friendship was of most importance to them, and who had been the first to proffer friendship. They had declined a closer union with the ally to whom they were thus naturally attracted — but in accordance with a general rule which was itself a guaranty against the formation of such a union with a power which had been originally hostile to them, and with which they had made treaties solely with the view of avoiding its future hostility. The very nature of their own league, the character of their institutions, their situation and mode of life, might be thought to render them proof both against the arts by which governments are corrupted and perverted, and against those by which a populace is inflamed and misled. Easily and strongly stirred by whatever appealed to a common and instinctive feeling, they were equally unused to the whispering of the intriguer and the blustering of the demagogue.

It seemed therefore that, in his dealings with the Confederates, Charles had only to pursue the loyal and straightforward course which best comported with his own temper as well as with his real intentions. There was no people whom he could so ill afford to offend, but none so little susceptible of any extraneous influence. It would be idle to expect their active coöperation; but he had apparently good reason for counting upon their continued friendship.

If his purpose in forming the connection with Austria had ever been liable to misconstruction, it was so no longer. Even those who, with any real acquaintance with the facts, have regarded his earlier attitude as at least equivocal, can find nothing to object to in that which he now assumed, save an inconsistency which belongs, in truth, not to him, but to them. He had stood upon the letter of the agreement when Austria was demanding more than it contained, and he took the same stand now when Austria was secretly violating and preparing openly to renounce the agreement. With the design of compelling Sigismund to unmask, he had invited him to Dijon. The invitation had been accepted — but merely with the view of gaining time. An embassy was however sent, about the end of February, 1474, to cover the manœuvres now in active progress. The youthful but unnamed orator of the occasion, whose fluent and florid Latinity suggests the picture of a newly-fledged doctor of laws, — one of a class of diplomatists not uncommon at the German courts, — after a complimentary exordium in which an affected self-mistrust was speedily vanquished by a pert self-sufficiency, made the excuses of his master, whose detention at home had been caused by a threatened incursion of the Turks and other matters involving the welfare of the empire. The friendship of that illustrious prince for his magnificent ally had been greatly augmented by the messages of good will which he had continued to receive. He lamented the painful rumors which had gone abroad, and which were entirely without foundation. No envoys had been sent, no overtures whatever had been made, to the French king. It was, however, true, that the latter had of his own accord, without any prompting or instigation from the court of Innspruck, and after a former communication had met with no response, sent a solemn embassy to proclaim his unaltered attachment for the house of Austria, with which the crown of France had been so long allied, and to proffer his services in negotiating a permanent treaty of peace between that house and its hereditary enemies. The embassy was composed of distinguished men, and their reception had been open, as the speaker, having been present, could himself testify. A civil but most circumspect answer had been returned: the first approaches must be made from the opposite side; but the king might, if he pleased, feel the way by sounding the inclinations in that quarter. The duke of Burgundy, having now been informed of all that had passed, was solicited to favor his ally with such counsel as might be suggested by his usual wise deliberations. Had his own messages to the Swiss elicited any proposals from them?[11]

Charles commenced his reply "somewhat jocosely" — that is to say, in a vein of sarcasm, from which, as was natural with a temperament like his, the transition was abrupt to open indignation and direct invective. The apologies which had been made were altogether superfluous: the absence of Sigismund was amply explained, not indeed by the causes that had been alleged, but by others which were sufficiently obvious — the business arising out of his public and private intercourse with the French monarch, the duty of entertaining the French envoys and of instructing and despatching envoys in return. The answer he professed to have given to offers which had come from Charles's enemy was the reverse of satisfactory. In view of his actual en-

[11] Vortrag eines Gesandten Herzog Sigmund's, Chmel, B. I. s. 82–86.

gagements it behooved him to have replied that he could listen to no suggestion without the knowledge of the duke of Burgundy, that he could take no steps without the advice and concurrence of the duke of Burgundy, that he could enter into no schemes which were obliquely directed against the duke of Burgundy.[12] With what object, from what necessity, had he sought the intervention of Louis? Had Charles failed to comply with his obligations? Had his pledges proved empty, his protection ineffectual? In former times scarcely a year had passed in which the territory of the Austrian prince was not invaded and despoiled; but since he had been sheltered under the alliance of Burgundy, he could not pretend that a single hovel had been burned, or so much as a chicken carried off.[13] No! the duke had not received any definitive answer to his repeated applications to the Swiss. Nor was there wanting an apparent motive for their silence. They were doubtless better pleased with the prospect of obtaining the mediation of the French king, as an umpire less likely than himself to be swayed by any bias towards the house of Austria.[14]

It was now the turn of Sigismund's representative to assume the part of injured innocence, the tone of

[12] "Honestius respondisset regi Francie, quod in his rebus preter ducem Burgundie nichil vellet attemptare, nec quidpiam quærere nisi cum consilio et scitu ducis Burgundie, nec agitare quidquam quod sit contra ducem Burgundie." Chmel, B. I. s. 88.

[13] "Ymo dux Sigismundus non posset dicere quod sub illa proteccione esset sibi minima domuncula incensa, uel minima gallina ablata."

[14] Karl's Antwort, Chmel, B. I. s. 87, 88.

resentment and reproach. The illustrious prince would hear with astonishment, and would find it difficult to endure, the suspicions that had been expressed, and especially the charges, so contrary to the truth, that he had employed his servants on missions to the French court, and that his transactions with that court had been secret and sinister. It was surprising, it was almost inconceivable, that his serenity the duke of Burgundy should have been ready to open his ears to these calumnies against his ally. Did the speaker know who had carried information so false in so high a quarter, he should not hesitate to denounce him openly as one whose object it was to sow the seeds of discord between two exalted personages knit together by reciprocal benevolence.

Before a simulated emotion real passion not unfrequently subsides, ashamed of the spurious imitation it has called forth. To prolong the altercation would have been, indeed, as inexpedient as undignified. Had Sigismund been personally present he might possibly have been put to confusion and forced to a confession. But it was the business of the envoys to lie, and it was their cue to provoke an angry retort. Charles was resolved that the violation of the agreement should not assume even the color of a breach produced by an accidental variance or mutual dissatisfaction. While intimating that his accusations had not been made on so light an authority as common report, he expressed his willingness to accept the denials with which they had been met. Let the Austrian prince act up to these asseverations and the benefits he had hitherto enjoyed would remain undiminished. An inquiry was hereupon put, what assistance might be expected in case war should be actually declared by the Swiss. All the assistance he had promised, was the duke's answer — in the manner and on the conditions of the promise. Their master had been told, the envoys ventured to say, — though he was of course not credulous enough to lend easy faith to such a statement, — that his ally, while pretending to negotiate on his behalf, had in fact been endeavoring to make a treaty with the Swiss without any mention of him. A contemptuous smile, with the head thrown proudly back, was the only reply vouchsafed to an insinuation that announced the kind of subterfuge to which perfidy was about to resort.[15]

In this scene the disdainful haughtiness which we have found Charles exhibiting in former interviews of the like kind, and which has been used by writers of history as well as of romance to embellish fictitious interviews, was conspicuously displayed. But towards whom, and under what circumstances? Not towards a poor and despised people striving to conciliate the powerful and boastful prince who had determined to trample on their liberties; but towards his own equal in rank, towards the enemy of that people, towards the ally whose projects for enslaving them he is supposed to have encouraged, and who had in reality been converted from an ally into an enemy by his failure to receive such encouragement. There could in fact be no stronger contrast than

[15] Ibid. s. 89, 90.

between Charles's bearing towards Austria at this juncture, and that which he adopted towards the Confederates. Precisely that part in the drama which has been popularly but falsely assigned to them was the one assumed by him.[16] The French emissaries, he was aware, had a twofold commission. What success they might meet with in the one quarter was of little consequence; but steps must be taken to obviate the effect of their intrigues in the other. The first intelligence received was sufficiently alarming; and "with great diligence" he despatched "an express" to Berne, inquiring whether a treaty adverse to himself had been formed with the French king.[17] A denial was promptly returned, with an assurance that the existing relations would be maintained, and that towards all parties an equitable line of conduct would be strictly adhered to.[18] The reply, unless regarded as absolutely disingenuous, was reassuring. Yet a crisis was evidently at hand, and no act of vigilance or caution would be superfluous. An attempt to cope with the enemy with those weapons in the use of which he had ever shown himself an adept would only insure a defeat. But were not other arms available, adapted to less expert hands, but better suited to the present field? It was determined that a special embassy should be sent,

[16] The currency given to erroneous statements on this subject is no doubt attributable to their having been put forth by Commines, whose authority seemed to forbid any deeper investigation. But Commines was himself one of the victims of the deception. He received the account, as he tells us, from Swiss agents at the French court—in all probability from the Diesbachs themselves.

[17] Ancienne Chronique, Lenglet, tom. ii. p. 212.

[18] Zellweger, s. 33.

which, instead of either seeking a formal audience in a general diet, communicating privately with the chief magistrates of the leading cantons, or attempting to initiate a counterplot to that which was still hidden or unhatched, should traverse the whole country, visit the seat of government in each district, demand a hearing before the council, or even before the whole body of freemen, and make and receive publicly such explanations and avowals as might re-establish a perfect understanding, and leave no room for future misrepresentations. The selection of the envoys was left to the count of Romont, a servant and vassal of Burgundy, but also — as a prince of Savoy and the sovereign of Vaud — a neighbor, an ally, and in some measure a dependant of Berne, and therefore not only intimately acquainted with the ground, but doubly interested in the result. The instructions were drafted by the duke himself, but remitted to Romont for such alterations or additions, written or verbal, as might be deemed seasonable.

Of the two persons charged with this important mission, one was a native of the Helvetian territory, and both had private connections among the inhabitants, and were residents of a neighboring region. They were authorized to remind the Swiss people of their treaties with the house of Burgundy, the friendly feeling it had always evinced towards them, and the freedom of travel and of traffic which had been reciprocally granted and enjoyed. It was Charles's cordial desire to continue to live with them upon these terms. Malicious reports to the contrary had, however, been disseminated, and particularly in reference to his alliance with Austria. That alliance had not been of his seeking or procurement. He had consented to it, knowing that a connection would otherwise be formed prejudicial to himself, and not only to him, but to the Swiss. He had entered into it in no inimical spirit towards them, but in the belief that it would contribute to their safety and tranquillity. The treaty had been so worded as not to intrench upon his prior obligations. That his protection of Sigismund was intended as a means, not of fomenting, but of appeasing discord, was clear from the manner in which he had exercised it, as well as from his repeated proffers and declarations. So also his occupation of Alsace, far from having been attended with any inconvenience to them, had conferred upon them direct and positive benefits. Formerly, it had been an enemy's country, which they could enter only with safe-conducts, and even then not without danger; whereas now they could pass through it, make sales and purchases, and transport their goods, with the same freedom and security as in the other Burgundian dominions. With respect to what was alleged against Hagenbach, he had never, so far as the duke had been able to learn, been guilty of any aggressions against the Confederacy, or molested any of its people. Such acts would have drawn upon him the severest displeasure of his sovereign. A court of inquiry had, however, been instituted, which would receive all complaints against him or other officials, and no detected abuse should pass unrectified, no delinquent, of whatever rank, would be suffered to go unpunished.[19]

The envoys set out upon their tour early in March. Their first visit was to Freyburg, which, though nominally subject to Savoy, and not yet included in the general league, was regarded, from its situation and its close alliance with Berne, as an integral part of the Confederate territory. Here they were hospitably entertained by the members of the council and other principal persons, who, on learning the purport of their mission, affirmed the resolution of the people of that state to adhere to the Burgundian alliance, and their satisfaction with the manner in which its provisions had always been executed. They cited as an instance the case of a private wrong received from a subject of the duke, when they had obtained redress without undergoing delay or being put to expense. Under the new rule in Alsace, their facilities for intercourse and commerce had been greater than ever before; and they had nothing to complain of in the conduct of the landvogt or his subordinate officers. At Berne, whither the envoys next proceeded, they wisely requested an opportunity of delivering their message in presence of the mass of the citizens, who were accordingly convened by sound of bell. The heads of what was now commonly spoken of as the French party were absent;[20] but its adherents succeeded in

[19] Ce que Messire Henry de Colombier et Jehan Alard diront aux Srs. des Alliances, Lenglet, tom. iii. pp. 347–349.

[20] Employed, as we shall see, in frustrating the object of the present mission.

defeating the wish of the ambassadors that the answer also should be agreed upon in their presence. After they had retired, it was attempted, by some verbal coloring, to change the character of their statements — an artifice detected and rebuked by the general sense of the assembly. The answer brought to them by the magistrates, who were accompanied by Bubenberg and many of the chief inhabitants, contained warm acknowledgments of past good offices, and strong professions of continued good will, but coupled with a remonstrance on the subject of Hagenbach. It was admitted that, under his government, the mortgaged lands had become a different country from what they had formerly been, open to all peaceable travellers, safe by every route, and for all kinds of merchandise.[21] So far as the Swiss were concerned, his sole offence had consisted in certain rude and opprobrious expressions, which he had afterwards turned off as mere jesting. But their allies, the people of Mühlhausen, had suffered more serious vexations, their fairs and markets having been interrupted, some of their number arrested, and their property detained, at the instance of their creditors. On this point it was remarked in reply, that Mühlhausen, by the payment of its debts, might have saved itself from all such annoyances, and that its condition had, at all events, been far less oppressive than under the former state of things, when the town

[21] "Cognoissent que . . . c'est pays ouvert et seur à eux et à tous par là passans, et toute marchandise il passe seurement et sauvement, *ce que par avant ne se faisoit.*"

had been exposed to continual attacks from the surrounding nobles, encouraged by the Austrian sovereigns. The interview closed with a further interchange of civilities, the magistrates of Berne desiring to be cordially commended to the Burgundian prince, and protesting their determination to abide by their repeated promises of amity and an impartial neutrality.

At Lucerne and at Zurich the same friendly reception was met with as at Freyburg, the same disclaimer made of any cause of offence and of any purpose to offend. But it was in the recesses of the country, on the hearthstone of Swiss liberty, that the ambassadors were greeted with the heartiest welcome, and that their appeals awakened the clearest and loudest responses. They were escorted through the mountain passes and across the lakes, from valley to valley, by the peasant magistracy of these primitive commonwealths; and the scattered population, summoned from their Alpine farms and pastures, gathered to the number of a few hundred in the churches along the route, listened with evident pleasure to the message sent them by so great and powerful a prince, and expressed their thanks for marks of honor to which they were so little accustomed. It was here that the rumors and predictions, set afloat in the preceding autumn, of deep-laid schemes and grand coalitions for assailing freedom in her mountain home, had fallen without impression or rebound. Any real cry of distress however distant, any tangible injury however slight, would nowhere have been more quickly heard or acutely felt; but imaginary dangers and unintelligible alarums had failed to excite even curiosity. The men of Uri, Unterwalden, Schweiz, Glarus, and Zug needed no arguments to convince them of the enmity of Austria, and no persuasions to induce them to encounter it. But of inimical designs on the part of the duke of Burgundy they had seen as yet no symptom; and they candidly and cheerfully admitted that the establishment on the frontier of a friendly in place of a hostile government, of a regular and equitable administration where before there had been restrictions without security and oppression without order, was a practical gain of which they had daily experience. It had enabled them, in their own simple and emphatic phraseology, "to live better." They had obtained new and more convenient markets; they sold their cattle and productions at a better profit; they received corn, wine, and other articles in greater abundance and at cheaper rates. The condition of Alsace was such as they had never seen it at any previous period, tranquillity every where prevailing, and justice impartially administered. They could travel without passports, carry their goods without the risk of being plundered, and transact their business without fear of being defrauded. No impediment or insult had ever been offered to them, and the Burgundian officials had always treated them with courtesy, and when necessary had given them aid.[22]

[22] "Oncques ils n'oyrent dire Mrs. de Bourgogne, ne par leur que dommage leur advenist par pays, mais que tout bien et tout

Such was the testimony borne by the people of Switzerland to the friendliness, the integrity, the consistency of act and word, which had marked the conduct of the duke of Burgundy in his relations with themselves;[23] and indirectly to the general character of his rule, its title to the distinction which was claimed for it, its efficiency under the least favorable circumstances and in a case where it had been the object of unmeasured obloquy. The ambassadors remark in their report that in none of the answers they received was any allusion made to the Austrian alliance, although on one occasion they were privately informed of the "great talk" to which it had given rise.[24] The sole grievance which had been alleged, and this in one quarter only, related to the personal offences of Hagenbach, confined, as to the complainants themselves, to speeches uttered in the

honneur, et depuis qu'ils a les comtés de Ferrette et d'Aussoys jamais ne eurent dommage ne desplaisir par lesdits pays, mais que secours, ayde et confort, et que leurs denrées, bœufs, et autres bestes et fruictages se vendent mieux et à leur profit, que par advant, et que bled, vin et tous autres vivres leur viennent en grant abondance, et en vivent mieux et à meilleur marché, et qu'il ne se sçavent plaindre de Mr. ne des Officiers, mais quant les leurs viennent ès pays de Mr. ses Officiers leur presentent tout bien et honneur, et par advant n'osoient aller sans saufconduit, et ne leur en tenoit-on point, et maintenant il ne leur en faut point, et ne le sçaurions plaindre." Response de la Vallée de Oudewal et Oudrewal [Obwalden and Unterwalden]; with similar statements from other cantons. Lenglet, tom. iii. p. 349–356.

[23] These particulars have not been unknown to historians; but in general they have been cited as illustrations, not of Charles's feelings and conduct towards the Swiss, but simply of their feelings towards him. How rash and ungrateful in that prince to attack a people who had thus courted his friendship! Such is the influence of a prepossession.

[24] This was at Soleure [Solothurm], not then a Swiss canton, but a close ally of Berne.

heat of passion; and in this respect a very similar result was elicited by a mission to Basel.[25] That Charles would have been loath, at the dictation of "his neighbors or his subjects," to dismiss a faithful and useful servant, that the reported grossness of Hagenbach's private life scarcely reached his ears, that the frivolousness of some of the charges and the ascertained falsity of others threw discredit on such as were substantial and well-founded, are admissible conjectures. But the assertions of prejudiced, ill-informed, and unscrupulous writers that, with no motive intimated, he was disposed to treat this man with an indulgence he had never shown to any other, that he was wilfully blind and deaf to all the evidences of his misconduct, that he wantonly staked upon the issue thus presented the success of a policy pursued with all the intensity of his nature, — the fulfilment of hopes locked up and brooded over in his own breast, — are surely preposterous. They are supported by no proof; all the information we possess goes to disprove them. Soon after his arrival at Dijon he summoned thither all the magistrates of the mortgaged territory, in order that Hagenbach's report of its condition and resources might be examined and verified. The landvogt, who excused himself from attending in person, was represented by his brother;[26] but of the course or the result of the inves-

[25] Ochs, B. IV. s. 253–255. — The tone, however, in which the intercourse was carried on, was here very different on both sides. We shall see the reason when we come to speak more particularly of the state of feeling in the Rhine towns.

[26] Knebel, s. 42.

tigation nothing is known. On occasion of a fresh dispute with Basel — in which this sensitive neighbor, though the first to complain, seems to have been the original aggressor — we find Charles sending instant orders that satisfaction should be given, with a strict injunction against similar proceedings in future.[27] Towards the close of March, on his way back through Lorraine to Luxembourg, he was met by Hagenbach; and it was observed that the latter, after his return, adopted a milder and more conciliatory address — a change which was, however, ascribed by his enemies to the premonitions of his now impending doom.[28]

That Charles should have had no such prescience of the coming storm, that to his gaze the cloud on the horizon should have been growing smaller and fainter, will hardly, after what has been narrated, be considered as the sign of an inexplicable fatuity. Yet his mistake was the more fatal, that he was wanting in the alertness and agility by which an error may be repaired before its consequences are developed. The very concentration of faculties and efforts which made it impossible to divert him from his aim by enticements or by feints exposed him to surprises and unforeseen attacks. Whatever was to be accomplished by deliberation, by industry, by an untiring perseverance, he might hope to effect. But his were not the sleight of hand and the comprehensive *coup d'œil* that enable their possessor to pluck a swift suc-

[27] Ibid. s. 42, 44. [28] Ibid. s. 48.

cess, to spring upon a stealthy assailant, or to ravish back a lost advantage, — though the defect might have passed unnoticed, had not Destiny, with its usual fondness for duality and contrasts, pitted him against one so remarkably gifted. This opposition and this contrast give, indeed, to both figures an undue prominence, and a sharper distinctness of outline than is altogether favorable to a just appreciation of the character of either. They were essentially men of different eras, and their juxtaposition, which represents the incongruities of the age itself, strikes us as something unnatural. On the great diplomatic battlefield of the 16th century, the qualities of Louis would have been more closely tested, and his real superiority would have been seen to lie, not in a greater depth of dissimulation and duplicity, but in the greater liveliness and fecundity of his intellect; while Charles, at an earlier epoch and in conflict with men of his own stamp, might not have been thought deficient either in sagacity or in promptness; his honesty and his earnestness would have enlisted sympathy, and his harsher characteristics would have appeared less salient and repulsive.

In the matters to which he now applied himself his adherence to beaten paths — to the ideas and customs of the past — is not the less noticeable that his acts were in a certain sense innovations. Not less ardent in the pursuit, or arbitrary in the exercise, of power than Louis, he had neither the same need, the same opportunities, nor the same instinctive tendency to seek the accomplishment of his ends by novel, underhand, or illegitimate methods. The king, having at present no actual or imminent dangers to confront, was securing himself, by a course of mild preventives, against those of the distant and uncertain future. He was effecting a timely though gradual revolution in the communal system of France. The enfranchisement of the towns had been a means of tapping the deep-rooted and wide-branching tree of feudalism; but Louis was not disposed to see the plant he had thus fostered flourish with the same rankness as that which he had labored to extirpate. The luxuriant bloom of Flanders, of which, it will be remembered, he had himself given glowing descriptions, secretly served him as a warning. While, therefore, he watered and dug as assiduously as ever, he had begun the work of pruning and training while the wood was still fresh and flexible. He continued to bestow new charters, to establish new marts and more frequent fairs; but he so modified the privileges which he granted, and so abridged those of an older date, as to insure the entire subserviency of the municipal governments to the crown. His mode of carrying out these changes was such as makes it difficult to trace them, except in the result, and has prevented them from receiving much attention.[29] Decrees, proclamations, voluminous state papers, seldom elucidate the real business transactions of this reign. Verbal orders, or pithy private letters, often burned

[29] See, in his work on the Ancien Régime, the comments of De Tocqueville — whose censure, however, is far too unqualified — on the system practised by Louis XI.

as soon as read,[30] conveyed the instructions, which were executed by trusty subordinates in the spirit in which they were conceived. Schemes thus pursued would meet with no concerted resistance, and in particular instances resistance was courted for the sake of the example to be afforded by its vigorous suppression. In such cases a wholesome severity, being the offspring of policy and not of passion, was unimpeded by scruples or relentings. A few lines in the royal handwriting sketched the clear and simple programme: "Search out the culprits, especially among the wealthy. Punish rigorously; let none escape. Hang up such as deserve death at their own doors; when they have hung a day I am content to have them taken down. Remove the prisoners to a distance, beyond the reach of rescue. Send me a list from which to select a mayor and magistrates. Henceforth I shall make the nominations myself, as I already do elsewhere." [31]

This kind of procedure, had he been ever so well inclined to it, would have been impracticable for the ruler of the Netherlands. But had Louis been that ruler, the same instinct would, doubtless, have suggested other expedients adapted to the circumstances. The simpler intuitions and more formal habits of Charles's mind neither led him to anticipate, nor would have enabled him to prepare for, a

[30] So at least we may infer from the orders we find Louis giving to that effect, and his reproaches whenever he learned that they had not been complied with. See Duclos, tom. iii. preuves, passim.

[31] See letters in Duclos, tom. iii. preuves, pp. 342–344 et al.

contest between principles not yet developed or openly confronted. His impatient spirit, chafing at all opposition or restraint, as little resembled that of the systematic and crafty destroyers of the nascent germs of freedom, as the turbulent disposition so often manifested by the Flemish towns resembled that of the dogmatizing levellers and revolutionists of a later day. The theory of government on which he acted and insisted had not yet been assailed or analyzed. It corresponded with historical facts and existing relations, and differed widely from that of a modern constitutional monarchy. Popular privileges, where they existed, were concessions from the sovereign, and were strictly in the nature of immunities, setting limits to his authority, but conferring no participation in it. His right to declare war and proclaim peace, to choose his allies and conclude whatever treaties he might deem fit, to appoint his own ministers and to make such legislative enactments as did not exceed the recognized measure of legislative power, was inherent and unqualified, exempt from all restrictions, and exposed to no interference. This complete independence, this purely monarchical rule, carried with it as a corollary the obligation to protect the country against foreign enemies, to watch over its welfare and promote its interests, to preserve internal order and to maintain the supremacy of a vigilant and impartial justice. The people, on their part, were bound to aid their prince, to serve him with their persons, and to supply his necessities. Whatever differences and disputes might arise in the practical application of these principles, the nature of the relations between the sovereign and his subjects was neither altered nor called in question. The promises exchanged between them were such as might have suited—were, indeed, derived from—the connection of parent and child. He was to be their *good prince*, and they were to be his *good people*.[32]

While, therefore, the servile maxims of "passive obedience" and of patient submission to tyranny were neither heard nor practised upon in the 15th century, the tone of authority was not the less that of divine right and absolute rule. "Despotism" was a term not applicable to the lawful possession of power however unlimited, or to the lawful exercise of it however stringent, but to the misuse or neglect of the functions annexed to it. Any such imputations would have been received with a scornful surprise by one who, like Charles of Burgundy, piqued himself on his clear sense and punctilious discharge of the duties of his station. Nor could it have been denied that his policy and his labors had contributed to the improved condition and growing prosperity of his states. The important share he had had in the settlement of the English crown had borne fruit in new and more favorable commercial treaties.[33] His acquisitions of territory had given greater security to

[32] Charles's ideas on this subject are to be gathered from his letters and speeches. In the 18th century we find the ministers of Maria Theresa proclaiming precisely the same principles in their debates with the people of the Austrian Netherlands, who assuredly did not consider themselves as living under a despotic rule.

[33] Rymer, Fœdera.

trade, and opened up fresh sources of wealth.[34] His enterprises in France, if they had failed in effecting the objects with which they had been undertaken, had put a stop to those aggressive operations by which they had been originally provoked, — confining to the enemy's soil the chief calamities of a war that must otherwise have been waged at home. Above all, his domestic administration had been distinguished by a scrupulous regularity in the transaction of all ordinary business, by the correction of abuses, and by a vigorous repression of crime. The effacement, in those parts of his dominions where they still lingered, of the last relics of private war, the abolition of the ordeal of battle, — of which, as practised among the lower classes, he had once witnessed with disgust the brutalizing exhibition,[35] — the removal or disregard of every usage and pretension that had impaired the efficiency or weakened the sanctity of the law,[36] might have gained him some credit with critics of a modern school, had these reforms, instead of emanating from himself, been yielded in compliance with a popular demand.[37]

[34] The advantages arising from the annexation of Gueldres are noticed in the Relation of B. Navagero.

[35] Lamarche. — Gollut. — Basin.

[36] It was not merely in criminal cases, but also in civil suits, that he enjoined upon the courts a prompt administration of justice. See Meyer, fol. 345.

[37] On the ordinary details of his government, those matters that occupied by far the greater portion of his laborious hours, our information, as might be supposed, is extremely slight. He seems to have willingly promoted measures of public improvement, such as the construction of new canals, and to have availed himself, to the extent of his power, of occasions for enforcing reforms in ecclesiastical and conventual discipline. Among the *keuren*, or guild statutes, which re-

A series of efforts in this direction was now completed by a measure which had long been in contemplation. By the treaty of Péronne, the jurisdiction of the French crown and the French Parliament over Flanders and other parts of the Netherlands had, as we have seen, been formally renounced. That jurisdiction had of course never extended to Holland and other imperial fiefs, while the similar right, supposed to be lodged in the imperial council, had seldom been enforced, and had long since fallen into total desuetude. Yet there could be no question that in the sovereign power, the fountain of justice, resided the supreme jurisdiction; or that the actual ruler, in whatever capacity he held this right, was entitled to exercise it. Charles was, therefore, neither usurping the prerogatives of his feudal lords paramount, nor infringing upon the provincial privileges,[38] in instituting a court for the trial of appeals from all the local tribunals of the Netherlands. Prac-

ceived his approval was one forbidding any apprentice to be taken at a lower age than fourteen. We may hope that this rule was suggested by humane considerations, though, if so, it was probably ineffectual, since we find Belgian writers in the 16th century making it a matter of boast that children four years old were able to earn their own living in the towns of the Netherlands.

[38] The former was the allegation of Louis XI. in his attainder of Charles's memory in 1483. It was of course necessary for the support of this assertion to declare the treaty of Péronne fraudulent and null *ab initio*. (Hist. de Bourgogne, tom. iv. preuves, p. cclxxxiii.) Yet the treaty, as we have seen, had been ratified by Louis after his release, and registered by the Parliament at his express command. The latter ground is that taken by some modern writers, who seem to suppose that Holland and other provinces were by their charters exempt from a principle of universal application, and that the sovereigns of the Netherlands had stripped themselves of their right of *haute jurisdiction*.

tically, indeed, he was but deputing to other and better qualified hands a task which he already performed in person, while, nominally, the change was merely in the *manner* of its performance. Those who sought mercy or favors might still have access to the prince in his hall of audience; but claimants of right must approach him through the processes of law, in his "Grand Council of Justice." Thus the name and constitution of the new body were similar to those of the other bodies through which he transacted his affairs: he was himself its titular head, and it nominally followed him whenever he transferred his residence from place to place. But these regulations, which have led some writers to conjure up visions of a Star Chamber, with its private, illegal, and arbitrary proceedings, signified only that the judgments thus rendered were final, and issued directly from that source whence all courts derived their authority and all law its binding force.[39] The Council of Justice had its permanent seat at Malines, conveniently situated between the two great provinces of Flanders and Brabant.[40] Hugonet, chancellor

[39] In like manner the Court of King's Bench, from which the Courts of Common Pleas and Exchequer were offshoots, originally followed the sovereign, and he was supposed to preside over it in person.

[40] There were no appeals in criminal cases. Whether this was an advantage or disadvantage to persons wrongly accused we shall not undertake to say; but at least it affords no place for the fanciful descriptions which have been drawn of innocent parties denied a trial by their peers and dragged before a distant or even foreign tribunal. The greater number of the suits brought before the court being such as arose out of commercial transactions, Malines was as appropriately fixed upon for the sittings as it has since been made the centre of railroad communication in Belgium.

of Burgundy, was appointed president, the assistant members being also selected from among the most distinguished jurists in the duke's dominions. The oaths administered were the same as were taken by other judges, binding them to decide all questions conformably to law, without favor or unnecessary delay, and to take care that the suitors were not subjected to exorbitant costs.[41]

Though no objection had been made to its erection, the Parliament of Malines — for so this court, being framed on a similar plan to that of the Parliament of Paris, was commonly called — was abolished at the demand of the people of Flanders and Holland, in the tumultuary reaction that followed Charles's death. Its utility, however, was only made the more apparent by the inconveniences that ensued, and having been reëstablished in 1505, it continued to discharge its functions as it had previously done, without partiality or reproach, as long as any portion of the Netherlands remained subject to the house of Austria. The only grave imputation which rests upon it, is that of having owed its original foundation to Charles the Bold, by whom it is supposed to have been devised as a means of breaking down the barriers between the different provinces, and consolidating the whole into a single homogeneous state. That it had a tendency of this kind cannot be denied; and as little can it be denied that the jealousies

[41] Meyer; Gollut; Lamarche; Haynin; Ancienne Chronique; &c. — A court of exchequer, very similar in its form, had been already instituted. See Hoynck van Papendrecht, Analecta Belgica.

arising from local independence and ancient rivalry, and the lack of a concentrated patriotism accustomed to be stirred by a single appeal and to act with a single impulse, were among the main causes which made it, a century later, difficult to arouse and impossible to unite the people of the Netherlands against their Spanish rulers, compelled the minority struggling for freedom to apply for foreign aid, and rendered such aid when given of little avail, protracted to fifty years a contest that ought to have been of short duration, and robbed even the final success of much of its value, inasmuch as it left the country divided and crippled, thrown out of its natural course, and forever unfitted for the rank and position which it had long been expected and would otherwise have been enabled to reach.[42]

[42] The great revolution in the latter half of the 16th century, however necessary as a remedy for certain evils and however glorious when regarded under certain aspects, brought with it certainly no fulfilment of the views that had previously existed in regard to the future greatness of the Netherlands. Intelligent observers had anticipated, in the words of Niccolò Tiepolo, the creation of "uno stato amplissimo e così forte e potente, si per lo sito, come per la ricchezza di molte buone terre e moltitudine de' popoli attissimi alla guerra, che si potria forse comparare di forze a qualunque altro regno dei christiani." Perhaps no entirely baseless notion has ever been so generally assented to as that which represents the revolt of the Netherlands as the resistance offered by a weak nation to a strong one. That terrible "Spanish power" of the 16th century had its true foundations in the industry, the wealth, and the position of the Netherlands. The elements contributed by Spain were the lofty spirit and force of character that wield resources, not the patience, the assiduity, and the skill that create them. The Netherlands might easily have closed the door against any force which Philip II. could have sent against them. Their weakness proceeded from their want of union — a want which William the Silent had continual occasion to deplore, and which formed the source of all his difficulties. Yet he also had boasted that the

That his organization of a permanent military force — another matter with which Charles was at this time busily occupied — should have been held up and accepted as the demonstration of a dark and tyrannical design, is less to be wondered at; for the opinion is one of those which do not depend for support on the facts of a particular case, and which incur no peril from examination or discovery. It is one, therefore, which we shall not venture to impugn. It may, however, be made a question whether the evidence of history would alone suffice to prove that intimate connection which a received system of political philosophy enables us to trace between the establishment and maintenance of standing armies and the rise and continuance of irresponsible power. We are told upon eminent authority that monarchy, coexistent with parliamentary institutions and limited by the weakness of the sovereign and the martial spirit and habits of the people, passed, on the Continent of Europe, into monarchy unrestricted by constitutional checks and unrestrained by fears of popular discontent and revolt, as the consequence of a change in the military system,

provinces were independent of each other and recognized their sovereign under distinct titles, even while, with an obvious inconsistency, he claimed for the States General and for the Council of State powers which could only have belonged to them as the representatives of a united nation and of a consolidated government. It would be useless to attempt to controvert the opinion that "centralization" is naturally and necessarily opposed to freedom. Yet we might ask whether Scotland lost her liberties by a legislative union with England, whether Ireland has been worse governed by a British Parliament than she was as a separate kingdom, or whether the communal system was the nearest possible approach to the general enjoyment of equal rights.

resulting from projects of conquest or the necessities of defence, and involving the formation of regular armies, which, composed of men trained to a single pursuit, habituated to the action of a common machinery, and hardened by long campaigns, furnished the instrument for silencing representative assemblies, overpowering all resistance to the will of the ruler, and holding nations in entire subjection. England, it is added, protected by her insular situation from the dangers of invasion, found no occasion for keeping on foot any large and organized body of troops till a much later time, when, instructed by the discussions of a more enlightened age and warned by the experience of her neighbors, she took such precautions as they also might and ought to have taken, confined to its legitimate scope what had elsewhere become an engine of oppression, and placed her liberties on new and unassailable foundations.[43]

If these views be correct, the history of the principal European states, with a single exception, during several past centuries and for as long a period in the future as the same state of things shall prevail, will hereafter deserve to be blotted from record, or to be remembered only with horror and dismay, as that of long ages of withering barbarism, destitute of progress or development — a reign of brute force, as exceptional, if aught can be considered as exceptional, to the general plan of human destiny as those brief intervals in Grecian and Italian history when

[43] This is nowhere stated with so much force and precision as in the first chapter of Macaulay's History of England.

tyrants, encompassed by their armed satellites, bade defiance to the hate and exacted obedience from the fears of unwilling subjects — intervals that might be thought to exemplify the evanescent nature of all governments attempting to dispense with the assent of the governed.

When we look at this theory in the light of historical facts, we find that, if it does not absolutely deny, it at least takes no account of, the essential differences, which all fresh investigation confirms and renders more striking, between the English government and every other government from the moment when its features are first discernible. To say merely that it was the best among a class of governments of a common origin and of the same general character,[44] is to lose sight of that remarkable union of flexibility with strength, which enabled it to withstand so many violent shocks, to endure the constant strain arising from the contention of parties and the promulgation of new ideas, and to adapt itself to each successive stage of a progressive civilization. It was not less true of England in the Middle Ages than in any subsequent era, that she stood alone in the possession of a system in which no one of the elements of political society either preserved a separate existence or merged its existence in others, but each drew its

[44] Such is the remark, made in almost the same words, of the two most eminent authorities on the general character of English history — Hallam and Macaulay. The superiority, in their view, of the English constitution consisted in three or four distinctions, which will be noticed in the text.

vitality from the common source and was active and powerful only in combination with the others. Institutions common to all Europe had grown up — elsewhere side by side, acting and reacting on one another, blending and harmonizing more or less perfectly with one another, — nowhere but in England as adjuncts to a preëxisting system, which held them all in coalescence and subordination. In England the crown, the church, the nobility, the boroughs, were all separately less protected and privileged than elsewhere; but together and in unison they wielded a power more ample and complete than was elsewhere wielded by either or by all. It was not only that, in England, the representatives of the Three Estates were regularly assembled to receive propositions, present grievances, and vote supplies; but that this assembly constituted, as the name implied, the Great Council of the sovereign, sharing in his deliberations and giving force and validity to his decrees.[45] It was not only that the king could make no fundamental change in the laws without the consent of the Parliament; but that by and with the consent of the Parliament there was a perennial stream of legisla-

[45] On the Continent the "council" of the sovereign was, as we have before observed, a part of his household; it had no reference whatever to legislature; whereas in England even the Privy Council had from the first a certain connection with the Parliament. We find Commines and several of the Venetian ambassadors proclaiming the great advantages of a body constituted like the English Parliament, not so much because of the bulwark it afforded to popular freedom, as on account of the vast strength which the government derived from an open concurrence in its measures of the representatives of the whole nation.

tion, unobstructed by privileges or charters, unconfined by class immunities or local rights. It was not only that the king could impose no tax at his simple discretion; but that the control of the public purse vested in the Commons, instead of acting as a mere drag upon his wishes and his plans, was a recognized balance to his prerogative, curbing its irregularities and restoring it, after every momentary deviation, to the sphere of its legitimate influence.[46] It was not only that the servants of the crown were held accountable to the nation, but that the wearer of the crown was continually called to account in his own person[47] — in other words, that the forms of the constitution were never suffered to stifle the manifestations or limit the expansion of its animating spirit. On the Continent the body of the nobles played a far less important part in the operations of the general government than in England; but, unlike those of England, they maintained, each over his own domain, a supremacy that conflicted with and crippled the operations of the general government. On the Continent powers such as in England belonged only to the representatives of the whole country were distributed among provincial assemblies. On the Continent the larger municipalities were endowed

[46] In every mediæval state the legislative power of the prince and his right to impose taxes were more or less limited, either by express constitutional provisions or by principles universally recognized.

[47] This was a fashion not adopted on the Continent until the close of the 18th century. On the other hand mere ministerial responsibility, a necessity for consulting the public taste in appointments to the highest offices and in dismissals from them, was tacitly acknowledged by the most despotic French monarchs, from Louis XI. to Louis XIV.

with an ampler measure of self-government than in England; but in England, and in England alone, the smallest municipality had a voice in the affairs of the state.[48] On the Continent, in more than one country, the spirit of national life burned with an intenser heat, or at least with an intenser brilliancy, than in England; but nowhere save in England do we find from an early period the People standing forth, not as a distinct class or as the refuse of any class, but as the sum of all classes, as an aggregate identical with the Nation.

These distinctions may help us to understand the true causes of that aggrandizement of monarchical power in the 15th and 16th centuries which is one of the most striking features of European history,—as well as the reasons why in England it was comparatively unimportant and was speedily rectified. For it is not denied by those who explain the phenomenon in the manner under discussion, that in England, without any change in the military system, there occurred at the same period, though in a far slighter degree and with a far shorter duration, a similar change in the spirit of the government. It is not denied that the Tudors were more arbitrary in their language and their acts than the Plantagenets had been; that they were addressed with a deeper servility and

[48] It seems singular that English freedom should sometimes have been traced to the municipal charters. English history presents no examples of cities endowed with enormous privileges, such as belonged to those of Castile, the Netherlands, and parts of Germany. But on the other hand, what constituted a borough in England was, on the Continent, generally nothing more than a nobleman's estate.

obeyed with a blinder submission; that their courts were more pompous than those of their predecessors, their decrees more highly venerated, their persons held more sacred. It is said, however, that no real breach was thereby made in the constitution; that the increased power, influence, and estimation of the crown were the consequence and the complement of the effects of the recent civil wars in breaking down the ascendency of the great nobles; that however imperious the tone ordinarily used towards their subjects by the Tudor princes, and however submissive the tone ordinarily used towards those princes by their subjects, no sooner was any grave offence offered to the constitution than the people grew bold and menacing, the sovereign alarmed and ready to retract. This is perfectly true; and it illustrates the positions we have laid down. The shaft of Saxon liberty, raised high and solid in a time of the deepest obscurity, — while the Continental races were still undergoing the crushing and rending of a veritable chaos, — had pierced through the supervening layers of the Norman Conquest and of feudalism, incrusting itself with glittering extraneous decorations, but preserving its simple and massive proportions; and now, in like manner, it towered above the too aspiring pretensions of royalty, reared upon other and narrower foundations. But had those foundations, as on the Continent, offered the *only* basis for a superstructure — had the same problems as were there awaiting a solution occasioned not a partial but a universal perplexity — had fractional obligations and fractional immunities been the sole props of society — England also would have had no resource but to commit her destinies to the single direction of the crown. On the other hand, had the nations of the Continent already attained to the possession of a broad and well-defined popular freedom, there would have been no opportunity, for there would have been no necessity, for the establishment of absolute power. England in the 16th century retained, and in the 17th century extended, a freedom which she had always enjoyed and had always known how to defend: the Continental nations could not lose a freedom which they had never enjoyed, and could not have achieved by an unseasonable revolution a freedom of which the elements were not yet collected. There was a preliminary work to be accomplished; there was an order of progression to be observed in the later as there had been in the earlier portion of that grand scheme in which the destinies of modern nations are marked out, and in the gradual fulfilment of which each nation in turn serves in some respects as the model or the pioneer of the others. Except in so far as all effort tends to excess, and thereby in a proportionate degree counteracts itself, absolutism was not a retrograde step, but a step in advance. The revolutions of a later day have not overthrown, but are consummating, what was then effected. Before there could be real liberty, it was necessary that authority should reach its culminating point: in order that there might be a people, the state had to perfect its organization and to fortify its existence.

That the process was destructive as well as constructive, that it was in one instance succeeded by a long apathy amounting almost to a suspension of vitality, may not be denied. Yet, strictly speaking, what regal supremacy crushed or enfeebled was not liberty, but privilege; liberty, in so far as this was merely in the nature of privilege — liberty, in so far as it was isolated, egotistic, and incompatible with the safety, unity, and harmony of the state — liberty, in so far as it was licentious, arrogant, and incompatible with the acknowledgment of a common and supreme authority. Feudal liberty was struck down, municipal liberty languished, when the animating spirit of each sought for itself a wider form and fuller development. The "parliamentary institutions" — if such they can be called — of mediæval France expired, not only from their inherent weakness, but because (as was instinctively perceived when, in a great necessity and for lack of other machinery, they were temporarily revived) they had never been any thing more than the divided and jarring organs of antagonistic class-interests. The Cortes of Castile and of Aragon lost a greater freedom of debate and a stricter censorship over the action of the executive than even the English Parliament had exercised, as a consequence of the restored unity of Spain, which reduced those kingdoms to mere provinces of an empire; and also because of the very exorbitancy of the powers with which the local legislatures and tribunals had been endowed. If in the Netherlands civic monopolies and provincial independence, by allying themselves with the noblest of all causes, the dearest of all rights, maintained themselves in resistance to the consolidating tendencies of the 16th century, this — as we have before remarked — was at the price of internal disruption, as well as with the further penalty of lasting jealousies and dissensions, until the whole system was swept away in the revolutionary tempest of the 18th century.

The aggrandizement of monarchical power, at the period mentioned, was, then, simply a part of that process through which states were receiving a compact and definite form, nations becoming imbued with self-consciousness, and society becoming so thoroughly cemented as to resist the disintegrating influences to which it is constantly exposed. Now, we may readily concede that, in this case as in all similar ones, the course of events was not smooth and equable, but swollen, turbid, and impetuous; that a natural impulse was exaggerated and distorted by artificial stimulants; that the means of propulsion were often such as to level obstructions that might have been spared, to squander resources that should have been husbanded, and to stifle tendencies that ought to have been called in to coöperate. We may concede the occasional employment, as well as a prevailing inclination to the employment, of sheer force, — although this was in truth a method far less common and far less effectual than craft, advantage being taken of the very jealousies and hostilities it was intended to exterminate, so that each of the ingredients in turn might be subjected to the pressure that was to reduce them to a consistent mass. But how slight, comparatively, was the share performed by any special or secondary agent, how powerless all such agencies would have been had not a strong and bountiful current originally set in this direction, — had not the whole mass of ideas, theories, sentiments, and events been moving towards and closing around the same central point, — needs no stronger arguments than will be furnished by the recollection of two facts, one of present and common notoriety, the other demonstrable from the evidence of history: first, that governments when strongest in mere material resources have been overthrown by the persistent attacks of public opinion; secondly, that the despotic governments of the 16th century were among the weakest in material resources. The introduction of standing armies on a scale commensurate with the uses to which they are said to have been turned was not antecedent to or even coeval with the firm establishment of unlimited monarchy. If the relation between them was that of cause and effect, it was in the reverse order to what is commonly maintained. Was it by means of a peace establishment of less than two thousand lances and a few scattered garrisons of infantry, with provision for calling into the field in time of war, chiefly from external sources, an aggregate of scarcely thirty thousand men, that the French monarchs of the 16th century had risen to so exalted an authority that their twelve millions of subjects are described as receiving their commands with the submissiveness of dumb cattle?

that, if inquiry was made as to the amount of their revenues, it was answered that they could have whatever they demanded? that they were objects not so much of love and respect as of adoration and worship, and even when personally deserving of contempt were still held inviolable and entitled to the same veneration? that amidst the fury of a long religious war, the throne remained unshaken and the order of succession unbroken, the Huguenots never conspiring to unseat a Catholic prince, the bulk of the Catholics supporting the rights of a Protestant prince? that amidst the terrible convulsions and utter prostration which attended that struggle, intelligent observers foretold the subsequent recovery and loftier achievements of the country, not only from its extraordinary and often-proved recuperative powers, but from the continuance of an unimpaired loyalty, based upon the fixed conviction that the unity and existence of France were bound up with the greatness of the crown and the preservation of the ancient royalty unshorn and undimmed? that when, on the occasion of a lull in the same frightful commotions, a people, armed and encamped, inured to civil war, accustomed to agitate the deepest questions, filled with hatred against the nobility, and disgusted with the imbecility of the king, discussed through its leaders the means of remedying mischiefs which were clearly seen to have sprung from the defects in the existing system, propositions for overturning or modifying it — for assembling the States General, opening broader channels for the utterance of the public sentiment, and devising more adequate organs for giving effect to the national will — were deemed impracticable and abandoned, not only because of the divisions in the nation forbidding the hope of unanimity in devising reforms, but because of the unanimity in the nation forbidding the revival of past divisions, and proclaiming that the cure of present evils was not to be sought in projects so hazardous to the integrity and perpetuity of the realm?[49] Was it with no stronger support than that of their troops, — numerous in comparison with those of other powers, but inconsiderable in comparison with the population of the numerous dependencies from which they were drawn and among which they were dispersed, — that the Spanish monarchs of the 16th century had risen to so exalted an authority that their edicts were reverenced as having the sanctity of divine decrees? that the proudest and fiercest of all aristocracies, who had claimed and maintained the right of disowning their allegiance and making war upon the sovereign whenever it pleased them so to do, sur-

[49] The various facts noticed throughout this discussion have been chiefly gathered from the Relazioni of Niccolò Tiepolo, Marino and Francesco Giustiniano, Marino Cavalli, Matteo Dandolo, Giovanni Capello, Giovanni Soranzo, Zaccaria Contarini, Michele Soriano, Lorenzo Priuli, &c. The most instructive are perhaps those of Dandolo, Soriano, and Priuli. The Relazioni form a running commentary on the documentary and narrative material of the period. In them we see the age reflected in its own mirror — the judgments on passing events pronounced by the most sagacious contemporary observers. Such judgments, too commonly neglected, should be carefully studied before those of posterity are formed. Among the other works consulted we may particularize the Ritratti di Francia and the Arte di Guerra of Macchiavelli.

rendered these arrogant pretensions without losing a tittle of the arrogance of their nature, found the highest gratification of their pride in the very depth of their self-abasement, and branded the independence of which they had once boasted, the disloyalty which they had once practised, as ineffaceable dishonor? that the proudest and fiercest of all races saw itself stripped of immunities and privileges, narrow in amount but enormous in degree, without any united or rèsolute protestations,[50] and, while retaining its martial vigor and its haughty and fiery patriotism, became of all nations the least refractory or turbulent? that amidst perpetual foreign wars, with their long train of burdens and calamities, — the government bankrupt, armaments overthrown, and subject states torn away, — scarce a murmur of complaint was heard, and internal tranquillity grew ever more profound, until it settled, unhappily, into a death-like torpor? that on the shores of the New World the national lust of conquest and dominion was still attended by the national fidelity and devotion to the crown, the most daring and skilful adven-

[50] Lord Macaulay remarks, "In Spain, where they [the old parliamentary institutions] had been as strong as in any part of Europe, they struggled fiercely for life, but struggled too late. The mechanics of Toledo and Valladolid vainly defended the privileges of the Castilian Cortes against the veteran battalions of Charles V." This would be a strong argument in support of Macaulay's theory respecting standing armies if the facts had been as stated. But at the time referred to, Charles V., having as yet fought no campaigns, possessed no veteran battalions: such regular troops as he had were not then in Spain; the government was powerless and inert, and the contest lay between the commons and the nobles, the latter fighting in self-defence rather than for the prerogative of the sovereign.

turers of whom history has taken notice contenting themselves with adding to the possessions of their masters, when they might easily have founded empires for themselves, and the single recreant to his allegiance falling like Lucifer from the place he had usurped? Are we to believe that if the English monarchs of the 16th century had found the means of raising and controlling a regular army, and had attempted to employ it for the subjugation of the people, English liberty would have fallen and perished,[51] would not rather have put forth latent energies and triumphed all the more completely? that if, prior to the establishment of a regular army in England, fresh constitutional securities had not been obtained, the same spirit which devised those securities would not subsequently and speedily have risen up with the requisite vigor to repair the omission? The cure, it may be said, could only have been applied through a civil war; but was it not through a civil war that the preventive was applied? Standing armies are no doubt able to put down partial revolts;[52] but can they extinguish — will they not, on the contrary, if used as a means of oppression, give an irresistible impetus to — the spirit of revolution? Standing armies contribute to the stability of governments; but have they ever, or any where, been

[51] According to Lord Macaulay such would have been the case. — We trust not to be accused of presumption for assailing the opinions of so great a writer. Those opinions are not peculiar to him. What is peculiar to him is, the admirable manner in which they are expressed.

[52] This is precisely the remark made by L. Priuli in his Relazione di Francia.

the main source of that stability?[53] Were the existing armies of Europe to be disbanded or placed in abeyance, there is perhaps no European government that would not be at once overthrown. But does it follow that this is the aim to which the aspirations and struggles of the nations are directed? Is it certain that this would, in every country, be the achievement of the people, resolved upon its emancipation from thraldom or ripe for its emancipation from tutelage? Should we feel any confidence that when time was given for what is called the expression of the public sentiment, — what, in such a case, might be more properly called the revelation of the popular needs and conscious incapacity, — a reaction would not set in, former governments resume their sway, or new governments equally absolute take their places? The experiment and the results, so far as these are yet developed, have been witnessed by a living generation.

The period, we repeat, at which the principal Continental states assumed the form and character of so-called absolute monarchies was precisely the period at which the military resources of those states were weakest and least efficient. Not that the masses of the population had sunk to a lower level, grown incapable of defending the soil against a foreign foe, and consequently — as might be suggested — incapable of defending their liberties against a domestic

[53] The case of dependencies or of conquered territories is of course not considered here. Whether the resources of one nation may avail for the subjugation of another is a separate question.

oppressor. The weakness lay not in any lack of materials, but in the want of any organization of those materials — a want which proceeded from that very change in the system of government which is alleged to have been the effect of a new and more perfect organization. It was not the people, but the government, which had lost for a time its martial character.[54] With the fall of feudal dominion, the system of feudal warfare had ceased to be practicable; the "ban and arriere-ban" survived only as a cumbrous and inoperative machinery. On the other hand, the far more powerful system of modern times was yet in its infancy, and a century or more was to elapse before it could acquire either the efficiency or the magnitude that would make it possible to depend upon such an instrument or to dispense with the continual use of other instruments. In this interval great and frequent wars were waged, principally between the two rival powers of France and Spain. But those wars were carried on by a method never practised on any similar scale before or since — a method that evinces the utter incompetency of either government to rest the support of its authority on its military resources. For repelling invasions France and Spain were compelled to rely, as England still relied, on a general levy of the people. Nor was the reliance vain; for armies so viciously constituted

[54] Hence the Venetian ministers often speak of the military resources of the larger states of Europe as enormous, but never fail to point out how little available they were for any of the ordinary purposes of government.

and defectively supplied as were those of the 16th century could not advance far into a hostile territory without finding themselves at the mercy of the inhabitants. Operations were, therefore, commonly confined to the extreme frontiers, to provinces in which both parties asserted a right to sovereignty, or to the smaller states of a third party, who entered perforce into the contest with no better choice than between the loss of his possessions and the surrender of his independence. As the chief theatre of the war was seldom either in France or in Spain, so the greater number of the troops employed were seldom raised in those two countries. Each drew the bulk of its forces from abroad — from countries which were able to supply such demands, not because they had themselves acquired new military resources,[55] but because, not having made any change in their political system, they had retained their old military resources unimpaired. Switzerland, Italy, and the minor states of Germany were the reservoirs from which the great battle-stream of the 16th century was fed. Soldiers of the same nation served in the ranks of both belligerents. The same soldiers served alternately in the ranks of each belligerent. Thus the composition of every army was heterogeneous, its material perpetually shifting, and its character perpetually changing. It was held together by no common sentiment of allegiance, it was amenable to no common discipline, it was

[55] In fact, had this been the case, the governments of those countries would themselves have entered upon a career of conquest.

divided by national jealousies, it was pervaded by a spirit of insubordination. It was badly paid and wretchedly victualled by governments ever on the brink of financial ruin and imperfectly acquainted with the economical branches of military science. Hence its activity was frequently paralyzed by excesses which a short-sighted policy had helped to stimulate, or by mutinies which the ablest commander was powerless to quell. Raised for a limited term, for a particular need, it sometimes disbanded before the necessity had ceased, and sometimes refused to disband after the necessity had ceased. It was certain to be demoralized by a defeat, and almost as certain to be demoralized by a victory. In short, it was properly not an army, but merely a substitute for an army — a temporary contrivance, resorted to in that interregnum of the military system of which the causes have been noticed, serviceable in the peculiar field and for the peculiar objects to which its operations were chiefly restricted, but utterly useless for the defence of thrones either against assaults from without or risings from beneath. Neither in France nor in Spain would the government have ventured to call to its support any large body of the foreign mercenaries whom it was accustomed to launch against its rival. Such a step would have been self-destruction. It would at once have produced those effects which the same or similar means are wrongly supposed to have averted. It would have uprooted those feelings of love and reverence which constituted the sure and only protection of royalty, and it would have implanted feelings of aversion and hatred against which royalty had as yet no protection whatever. Or even if the hope could have been entertained of thus crushing the energy of nations, what security would there have been against the fear that the power evoked might consummate its work by the overthrow of governments? The monarchs of Western Europe would gladly have emancipated themselves from their dependence on an engine which performed its task so ill, and which was so little under their control. The impediment lay not merely in the lack of a sound financial system, but also in those vestiges of feudal power and feudal privilege which had survived the overthrow of feudal independence. The establishment of standing armies composed of national troops was accompanied or preceded, not by the sudden depression, but by the gradual elevation, of the people, if not always in the political, at least in the social scale.

The practice, so common in the 16th century, of enlisting armies from among the subjects of different states was first introduced by Charles of Burgundy. His reasons for resorting to it are to be sought for, however, not so much in general causes as in the peculiar circumstances of his own situation. The most warlike of princes, — he ruled over the least warlike of nations. On the other hand, the habits and pursuits which were supposed to have enervated the ancient valor of the Belgian people, inspiring them with a distaste for the dangers and a still stronger aversion to the privations of war,[56] rendered them at the same time more capable than others of supporting its burdens; while the numerous alliances of Charles gave him especial facilities for procuring the services of poorer but hardier races. The course adopted seems, therefore, to have been suggested by necessity rather than preference, and to have resulted from a compromise tacitly agreed to by the sovereign and the people, after the views of each had been strenuously urged and as strenuously opposed. Charles had contended for the full enjoyment of his right to call for the assistance of all his vassals, of the burgher as well as of the noble, in defending his dominions against hostile attacks or securing them against hostile designs. The hazards, he asserted, were at all times such as to require that a force sufficient for repelling any sudden assault should be kept in constant readiness, while the whole militia of the country, civic and feudal, ought, if called for, to be promptly assembled and sent into the field when war had actually broken out. Nor were his positions openly disputed or his claims directly denied by his subjects. But the tendency of a commercial people to make light of risks which martial princes have perhaps an equal propensity to magnify, displayed itself in a series of excuses and evasions, provocative of bitter and angry complaints, and ending in partial and hard-wrung compliances. In the

[56] This is remarked by Basin and other writers of the 15th century, as well as in several of the Venetian Relazioni. Indeed a confession to the same effect was made by the Estates of Flanders in 1475.

years 1470 and 1471, when, as we have seen, the whole military strength of France, hitherto divided and broken, was united and arrayed for the overthrow of the house of Burgundy, when the feudal princes were leagued with the crown against their old ally and leader, and when the government of England had fallen into the hands of his enemies, Charles was engaged in a contest with the people of Flanders, hardly less arduous or perplexing than that in which he had become involved through these changes in his foreign relations. Flanders was of all the provinces the one best able to supply him with aid, the one which itself stood most in need of protection, but the one also which had ever shown the greatest reluctance to make any sacrifices for that object. It had no natural defences and no strong fortifications: if Picardy and Artois were overrun, the wealth from which it so grudgingly contributed for its own security would fall an easy spoil to the invader. Former experience had proved that this was no imaginary danger, and they must be blind indeed who in the present conjuncture did not perceive its imminency. Was it safe to slumber in the neighborhood of a foe so wakeful and so active? Was it right to go unprepared while he could boast of being "always ready"? Yet arguments and appeals on this score were answered only by remonstrances against every precaution taken or proposed, against every fresh levy of troops or demand for money. The duke, while promising modifications on some points, vindicated his proceedings on the grounds of urgent necessity, of his right to claim the support of his vassals, and of their well-known ability to yield it in far more abundant measure. "His intention had been, not to molest or aggrieve, but to guard and preserve them." "From whom," he asked, in an impassioned letter to the Flemish communes, written at the moment when his fears had been justified by the loss of the places on the Somme,—"from whom are we to look for help if not from our own subjects? or how are we to protect them unless they themselves provide the means? If the magistrates of a town may make and enforce such regulations as are needful for its safety, does not this authority still more clearly appertain to us, from whom they receive their commission and their charge? Have we spent what we have obtained for our private use? Have we grudged any expenditure from our private revenues for the general use? Have we avoided in our own person any labor or any peril which we have asked others to undergo? If we be left alone, to be overwhelmed and defeated, what honor or what profit will that bring to Flanders? We cannot believe that it is intended to debar us from the exercise of rights allowed to all princes, or to deprive us of services due from all subjects. We are unconscious of ever having done aught by which we should have deservedly forfeited the love and fealty of our people. Nevertheless, if God, as a punishment for our sins, have ordained that it should be so, we shall not resist, but shall voluntarily submit ourselves to his pleasure. It needs not therefore that our people should menace or oppose us. Though He has endowed us with power to restrain their unlawful purposes, we will not drive them to incur the guilt of disobedience and rebellion. Whensoever they shall send to us declaring that our rule is no longer agreeable to them, and requiring us to lay down the administration of our sovereignty, we shall willingly comply, and resign it accordingly. We shall part from them more gladly than they from us; for we endure greater cares and vexations on their behalf than they have ever sustained through any act of ours."[57]

Such disputes, had their significance been understood, might have furnished an opportunity for the establishment of a far nobler liberty than that which existed in the "Calf-Skin" of Flanders, the "Joyous Entry" of Brabant, or the "Great Privilege" of Holland. Charles's lofty claims and vehement demands were but a confession of his dependence and his necessities. The pride with which he resented the apathy of his subjects proved that he secretly coveted their sympathy. He who wanted so much would have conceded much; and, whatever his defects, he was not one of those weak, dissolute, or perfidious princes on whom confidence is wasted or by whom it is betrayed. He was capable of respecting

[57] This remarkable letter, which bears the date of Dec. 19, 1470, was first printed by M. Kervyn de Letterhove, in his History of Flanders, tom. v. pp. 176–178. M. Gachard had previously found a minute of it, but did not succeed in his efforts to recover the original. That Charles was perfectly sincere in his offer to abdicate we entertain no doubt. It was an idea quite in keeping with his character — a character which that of his great-grandson Charles V., who from similar feelings executed a long-planned project of abdication, was in boyhood at least thought greatly to resemble.

the firmness as well as of requiting the attachment of a high-spirited and generous people. But the communes and Estates of the Netherlands had never been imbued with the feelings or trained to the habits that led the English Parliament and nation to second the enterprising spirit of their monarchs while asserting and enlarging their own constitutional rights.[58] The Fleming and the Hollander felt no interest or pride in the exaltation of the common sovereign, because they had none of the associations connected with the glory and the greatness of a common country. They made no attempt to substitute a system of national liberties for one of mere local privileges, because they had no adequate conception of either liberty or nationality. Charles on his part could see in their indifference to his aims and their passive resistance to his efforts only the sordid and grovelling instinct which shrinks from all exertion and repels all high aspirations.

The result, therefore, of these discussions was not any real unanimity or earnest coöperation. No patri-

[58] We cannot help protesting against what seems to us the most radically false, the most pernicious in the general inferences to be drawn from it, and yet the most characteristic — inasmuch as it even runs through his literary criticisms — of the paradoxes in which Macaulay loved to indulge. Speaking of England under the reign of John, he says, "Her interest was so directly opposed to the interest of her rulers that she had no hope but in their errors and misfortunes. The talents and even the virtues of her six first French kings were a curse to her. *The follies and vices of the seventh were her salvation.*" And so too when he comes to a later period he writes, "Of James the First, as of John, it may be said that if his administration had been able and splendid, it would probably have been fatal to our country, and that *we owe more to his weaknesses and meannesses than to the wisdom and courage of much better sovereigns.*"

otic ardor was kindled on the one side, no bounds were set to the flights of a personal ambition on the other. On the contrary, although the dissension was temporarily allayed, the divergence was made wider than ever. It was a deed of separation, not a contract of marriage, that was framed and executed. What Charles had proposed was a scheme of national defence, national achievement, national aggrandizement; and had it been adopted, all his after-plans must and naturally would have shaped themselves in conformity with this idea. The provinces, insensible to his entreaties, but goaded by his reproaches, or desirous to rid themselves of his importunities, consented to an annual grant for six years of five hundred thousand crowns,—a sum four times greater than they had ever previously granted, yet not disproportioned to their means,—leaving him at full liberty to contract whatever engagements and to pursue whatever enterprises he might be tempted to undertake. Thus, from the very nature and necessity of the case, he was made more independent than he had before been, than he had even pretended or aspired to be. New wings were given to the spirit of conquest; and the executive authority, far from being rendered a complete embodiment of the state, assumed a more entirely personal and proprietary character. The means were provided of raising such a force as would relieve the provinces, in all ordinary contingencies, from the drafts of men to which they had hitherto been liable, and which had of late become so frequent;[59] and they must themselves desire that the troops thus collected, instead of being quartered at home, should be kept engaged abroad. When the precedent thus set had been firmly established in practice, the evils attending it began to be comprehended as well as felt. Under their Spanish rulers the people of the Netherlands, though their burdens had been greatly increased, were still the most lightly taxed community on the Continent of Europe. They could easily, by their own confession, have raised a revenue of twice the amount; and they would gladly have done so on condition of their being suffered to retain in their own hands the control of the expenditure.[60] In other words, they had begun to perceive that true political freedom consists, not in mere immunities, — in a release from obligations, a relinquishment of responsibilities, or even exemption from oppression, — but in that distribution of powers and incorporation of interests by which the policy of the government is made to harmonize with the real tendencies and strivings of the national mind. But this lesson had been learned too slowly, if not too late. That which might once have been effected through a pacific arrangement could afterwards be effected, and then very imperfectly, through a sanguinary revolution. The relative situation of the country and its rulers was very different in the 16th century from

[59] That there was at least a tacit understanding to this effect, may be inferred from the tenor of a ducal ordinance issued in 1475. See Gachard, Doc. Inéd. tom. i. p. 237 et seq.

[60] See the Relazione of B. Navagero.

what it had been in the 15th century. It had been the object of the house of Burgundy to elevate the Netherlands, as the seat of its power, the sole fountain of its resources, the pedestal of its greatness. It was the object of the house of Austria to depress the Netherlands to a condition of inferiority and subordination to others of its dominions, where it wielded a more absolute authority, and whence it surveyed and governed, as from a central eminence, an empire extending over both hemispheres.

The military establishment of Charles, formed by successive steps not necessary to recount, comprised in 1474 about twenty thousand men, three hundred pieces of ordnance of the best that were then constructed, and all such apparatus and accessories as were considered requisite for every kind of operations. The nucleus consisted of certain companies called the *bandes d'ordonnance*, enlisted chiefly from the feudal levies of the two Burgundies and the Netherlands, and embracing such of the nobles, with their tenants and retainers, as belonged to the household of the prince, had the strongest attachment to his person, or were best inclined to a military life. To these were added between two and three thousand English archers, of whom there were five hundred in the body-guard; a larger number of pikemen, halberdiers, *coulevriniers*, or musketeers, and other infantry, recruited in Picardy, Germany, the towns of Brabant and Holland, the principality of Liége, and even the Swiss cantons; and several bodies of Italian soldiers, under the count of Campobasso and other *condottieri*, whose services had been secured with the consent or through the mediation of the Venetian government.[61]

So to mould, equip, and discipline this force as to render it in the highest degree efficient and complete, was a task to which Charles applied himself with his accustomed ardor, regularity, and surpassing energy. Yet in this, more than in any other matter, we have to note, as among the chief causes of his subsequent disasters, the lack of that creative faculty which would alone have corresponded with his lofty aims and the requirements of the time. In a transitional age the common thoroughfares are no longer safe or sufficient; bridges are needed to span the abyss between the Old and the New. Success is not to be won, as in ordinary times, by "patient application," "steady perseverance," or a strict conformity to the precepts and examples of the past. She reserves herself for the far-seeing glance that penetrates the changes of the future, for the far-stretching grasp that borrows from the future some process or implement suited to the emergencies of the present. Necessity had driven Charles into new roads; but Nature had not endowed him with a genius for invention or discovery. His army, in some respects differently composed and constituted from those he had before commanded, was modelled and trained essentially after the same patterns and by the same

[61] Lamarche. — Rodt. — Van Kampen, Geschichte der Niederlande. —Hist. de Bourgogne, tom. iv. preuves (for the negotiations with the Venetian government).

rules. While it was tainted with the vices inherent in that worst of all military systems which was soon to come into general though temporary use, it was destined to exemplify in a yet more remarkable manner the defects of a mode of warfare which was soon to fall into general and permament disuse. The organization of "the lance" was still retained. The brunt of the battle was still to be borne by the men-at-arms, the lighter cavalry — mounted archers, arquebusiers, and *coustilliers* ("cutlers," so called from the long, double-edged knife or dagger carried at the girdle) — acting merely as their followers and assistants; while the infantry performed such subordinate operations as harassing the flanks and impeding the manœuvres of the enemy. Ranged, sometimes in squadrons, but more commonly in a single line, — technically termed "the hedge," — the heavy-armed, strongly-mounted cavaliers, with their attendants behind them, went forward to the attack, presenting, if the field were level, a solid front of steel ("so that an apple thrown towards them must needs have lighted on a helmet or a spear"), plunging, if the defence were weak, into the midst of the opposite ranks, overturning and trampling down all before them; but swerving with every inequality of the ground, reeling from the very violence of their own onslaught, losing their array at the moment of the encounter, and unable without retiring to close, to repeat the charge, or to press forward against continued resistance.

The state of things in which this mode of giving

battle had originated was one of continual and universal, but not of public and organized, war — one in which every man, or at least every landholder, had incessant fighting to do, but did all his fighting on his own proper account. Holding his lands by the right of conquest, he had to make good that right by his individual prowess, not only against those whom he had dispossessed, but against fresh invaders pressing in to acquire by the same process and to occupy by the same tenure as himself. One against many, — one in possession against many seeking possession, — he had to protect and fortify himself, to study the art of defence far more than that of attack. He sheltered his household and movable property behind strong walls, which he girdled with a moat and flanked with high towers. He covered his body from head to foot with mail or iron plates, panoplied his horse in like manner, and thus made his centaur-like person a moving castle, — castle and garrison both, — overlooking his assailants from loop-holes, commanding them from battlements, sallying forth against a swarm, and needing only for his supports his squires and pages, — sons or younger brothers, — less encumbered than the main body, prompt and deft to succor and relieve in case of mischance. At home and abroad he was impregnable, invulnerable; while his lance, axe, or other ponderous weapon, and his horse's hoofs, sufficed for the slaughter or dispersion of his unskilled and naked foes. If in time rivalries arose, and, as a consequence, leagues were formed, if agreements of protection and service took the place of absolute isolation, — feudalism supervening on allodialism, — this was not such a change as could exert much influence on the military system, inasmuch as it effected no revolution in the social system — the mould, in all ages and countries, in which the military system is cast. Feudal society was a combination of landholders. A feudal army consisted of the tenants and sub-tenants owing allegiance to the same suzerain. Each came into the field accoutred and accompanied as his means and the habits of his class prescribed. The "lance" was simply the feudal family — the baron, or knight, with his wonted retinue of kinsmen and dependants.

The towns, it is true, exhibited a different political organization, and consequently a different military organization. Yet here, too, the same state of isolation and constant peril prevailed; and the same object — security against attack — was still more exclusively kept in view. Massive and elaborate fortifications gave to the interior the confined and martial aspect of a courtyard. The burghers were all trained to arms, were familiar with the duties and the necessities of a siege, and were prepared, at a moment's warning, to man the works, foil the devices and strategy of the besiegers, or repulse them on the parapet. But they were little accustomed to service in the open field; they were seldom capable of withstanding the onsets of the feudal cavalry; and hence, in countries where the feudal system was paramount or had merely the municipal system for its rival, the civic militia, which constituted the only infantry, was a subordinate and auxiliary force.

There were, however, countries where neither the feudal nor the municipal system had acquired predominance, where the land had not been monopolized by the aristocracy nor freedom monopolized by the inhabitants of the walled towns, and where, therefore, in case of war, the bulk of the people neither followed the private banners of petty chiefs nor congregated solely for local defence, but might be enrolled or enlisted in the service of the sovereign or the state. The armies thus raised were composed almost wholly of foot-soldiers, armed with a single weapon, arranged in compact masses, and easily disposed and manœuvred so as to seize any advantage of ground, to preserve an unbroken front, to win inch by inch the disputed soil, and to hold whatever had been won. From the close of the 13th century the respective military strength of nations differing from each other in their polities and social systems had been repeatedly tested. At Morgarten and Sempach, at Crécy and Azincourt, in every great battle, in almost every skirmish, between the chivalry of Austria or of France and the peasant soldiery of Switzerland or the English yeomanry, the inferiority of feudal organization, feudal discipline, feudal arms, had been signally displayed. But experience, however long and uniform, of the evils attending any system or practice which has grown out of the general habits or social arrangements of a people seldom avails for its removal. It was not adopted by way of experiment, and it cannot, unless by a giant's hand, be lopped off in a course of experimenting. It must be left to dwindle as the roots decay. We shall not even assert — though the statement has been often made — that feudal warfare received its final blow from the flagrant failures of its last great upholder and representative, Charles of Burgundy. Its rapid decline is to be dated from the period of his fall — because at that period the ideas and institutions on which it was based were visibly hastening to their end. As the whole constitution of society ceased to wear a military aspect, war began to be examined as a distinct subject, and to be cultivated as a distinct pursuit. Then principles could be studied, experiments tried, and new methods introduced, without deranging the fabric of social life, nay, in consonance with the renovation which that fabric was itself undergoing. Early in the 16th century a great writer — the first perhaps in modern times who has treated scientifically of military affairs — was able to lay it down as an incontrovertible maxim, that the bulk of every army ought to consist of infantry; that cavalry, not infantry, was the proper subsidiary force, to be employed in minor operations or in completing successes already achieved. He showed by examples from both ancient and contemporaneous history, that deep battalions of disciplined foot, with three distinct rows of pikes projecting beyond the foremost rank, and with four or more thinner ranks behind, from which any casual gap in front could be instantaneously filled, were impervious to the assaults of the heaviest and best appointed horse. But he also showed (and this was the conclusion which an adventurous and original genius in the position of Charles the Bold might have been led to anticipate) that the force thus resistless and invulnerable by cavalry was suited to such encounters only, — for which it had been specially designed, — and had its own appropriate opponent in a force then just beginning a memorable career; that as the Macedonian phalanx had succumbed to the Roman legion, so the Swiss "hedgehog" with its bristling spears must be pierced and torn by the fierce tusks of the Spanish columns; that the greater mobility of the latter enabled them to distress such an enemy as the former by rapid evolutions and impetuous attacks; that their better defensive armor rendered them more daring without much impeding their agility; that their shorter weapon — the straight sword, not exceeding three feet and a half in length, adapted both to cut and thrust — was manageable under all circumstances, whereas the spear, in close conflict, or as soon as the mass was penetrated, became merely an encumbrance, which the bearer was compelled to drop before he could have recourse to his side-arms in preparation for the death-struggle.[62] Thus, a revolution having once begun, new methods and new instruments had no sooner been adopted than they were superseded by others. States that at first were obliged to borrow troops from other states were able at length to copy

[62] See Macchiavelli, Arte de Guerra, passim.

and perfect the systems and usages of other states. The armies of Europe were again nationalized, but were more closely assimilated than ever before. Bows, halberds, pikes, and swords, all gave place to the musket, which, invented early in the 15th century, had long *hung fire* for lack of some slight but essential improvements; and war became a trial of valor and of strategy between forces nearly alike in composition and material.

The early successes of the duke of Burgundy, while they had doubtless had the effect of inspiring him with self-confidencc, had not blinded him to the defects characteristic of feudal armies, though he either failed to detect the radical causes or felt himself powerless to remove them. His claims to the title of a military reformer, notwithstanding his retention of a faulty method of organization and of tactics, rests upon his efforts to combine — though not with a due regard to proportion, or to their proper relative adjustment — troops of various descriptions; to drill them more thoroughly than had before been common in the manœuvres suited to their respective capabilities; above all (and with such an army this was as difficult as it was important) to habituate them to a common discipline, bring them into complete subjection to a common rule, and imbue them with the consciousness of a single whole. These efforts are attested not only by the pains which he appears to have taken in the choice of his materials, but by the stringent and elaborate regulations embodied, with successive emendations, in a series of ordinances, which throw a welcome light on the details of the military system then in vogue.[63]

It has been said that "in the Middle Ages every man had a slight tincture, and no man more than a slight tincture, of soldiership." This remark, if the requirements of the present age be accepted as a standard, is perhaps not incorrect. Yet we should be much misled by it, were we to imagine a mediæval army as resembling a body of new recruits, partially acquainted with the general routine of duty, but not thoroughly familiarized by practice with the first rudiments. A somewhat nearer comparison might be found in those barbarous but warlike hordes who have excited the admiration of ancient or modern observers by their matchless dexterity in the use of their peculiar weapons and in the execution of their peculiar manœuvres, but from whom neither the precision, tenacity, and patient confidence of regular troops, nor the systematic combinations and skilful dispositions of scientific commanders, could be expected. The bowmen who formed the flower of the English armies were taken from a population among which the national weapon was in as constant use as the far more easily handled rifle now is along the western outposts of civilization. Habitual practice and trials of skill, in all parts of the kingdom, but especially on the northern borders, commenced with

[63] These ordinances may be found in Gollut, in the Schweiz. Geschichtforscher, B. II., and in Chmel, B. I. — The ordinance last cited was prepared and published during Charles's stay at Trèves. A copy with marginal annotations in the handwriting of the Archduke Maximilian, afterwards emperor, is still extant.

childhood; not as mere pastime, but as the indispensable training of a people less exposed to attack but more addicted to invasion than any other, and forever engaged in some grand enterprise of conquest, as well as in a ceaseless predatory struggle with its nearest neighbor.[64] The fiefholders of France, Spain, and Germany were still more assiduous in the cultivation of martial exercises, which formed indeed almost the single occupation of their lives. To manage the war-horse, to support without fatigue or embarrassment a complete encasement of steel, to wield the lance, the mace, the axe, and the sword, with force and address, were arts which required a long preparatory schooling, and in which every youth of noble birth was ambitious to become an adept. In active service, the labors imposed upon the feudal warrior and the exertions demanded of him were not less but more onerous than those of the modern soldier. Badly organized, awkwardly massed, loaded with armor, encumbered with a multiplicity of weapons, it was no easy matter for large bodies of feudal troops to preserve their ranks, to make a change of front or other necessary movement, or to act in general with that entire concert yet individual self-absorption the loss of which converts an army into a mob, rendering every man a terror to his fellows and the helpless prey of an enemy. Hence the bewilderments and panics that so frequently occurred, and the disproportionate slaughter that commonly fell

[64] This fact, well known from familiar sources, is noticed in some of the Venetian Relations of the 16th century.

upon the defeated party. Hence, too, the lack of military genius, which was cramped and stifled by the unwieldy and unreliable character of forces so constituted. The displays of able generalship were confined to petty exploits, or to the exceptional cases in which the bulk of the army was made up of a homogeneous and lightly equipped infantry. The progress of the art of war has been the same as that of other arts in which the coöperation of numbers is necessary for the attainment of a given result. The labor of the common soldier has been rendered more rigid, but at the same time more simple: the labor of the general has been rendered more arduous, but at the same time more definite and feasible.

The full lance (*lance fournie*), which, with varying numbers, constituted the elementary unit of every feudal army, embraced in that of Burgundy eight combatants: viz., the man-at-arms (accompanied by his page, who supplied him, when dismounted, with a fresh steed), the coustillier, two or three archers or crossbowmen, and three or four foot-soldiers. Horses, arms and accoutrements, of a defined description, were provided by the soldiers themselves, the man-at-arms being held responsible for the proper equipment of the whole lance. Five lances—by an arrangement adopted after the trial and abandonment of a decimal system of partition—composed a mess (*chambre*), four messes a squadron, and four squadrons—consequently eighty lances, or six hundred and forty combatants—a company or "band." The "conductors," or commanders of companies, received their commissions from the duke; while most of the inferior officers were appointed, and might be removed,—though not without cause assigned,—by those of a higher grade. Each officer of every rank kept a duplicate list of his men, sent in written reports to his immediate superior, inflicted summary punishment for minor acts of misconduct, and was himself liable to a fine for neglecting to notice or correct them. In camp or on the march the general administration of justice belonged, of course, to the provost-marshal; but in the walled or privileged towns offenders were handed over to the civil authorities, who were warned against any exhibition of remissness or leniency.

The drill prescribed for the men-at-arms included the usual manœuvres and modes of combating practised by this species of force. The rest of the cavalry, being much more lightly equipped and armed with missile as well as other weapons, were trained to act also as infantry, to perform complicated evolutions, and to engage in both distant and hand-to-hand conflicts. Thus, the *coustillier*, in addition to the long dagger and the sword, carried a javelin or short lance, to be hurled at the foe before coming to close quarters. The archers and arquebusiers wore, besides smaller side-arms, two-handed swords,—such as had been used with decisive effect in the battle of Brusten. At the word of command they dismounted, attached their horses together by threes, fastening the bridles to the saddle-bows of the pages, and then either advanced to the charge, if confronted by infantry, or, if menaced by cavalry, rallied behind the pikemen, who formed in rings or hollow squares to receive them, and who knelt while the bolts and arrows were discharged from the centre. These and similar manœuvres were taught at first in small squads, and afterwards in larger bodies, the men being now partially, now fully equipped. Constant drilling for all the troops, especially while in garrison, was enjoined by the regulations. Once in three months reviews were held by commissioners intrusted with the duties of inspecting and paying the army, administering an oath of fidelity and obedience, and maintaining a general supervision.

The banners and ensigns of the companies were distinguishable by their different colors and devices; those of the squadrons and messes, by letters and figures inscribed upon them. When the army was to move, the first trumpet gave the signal for the men to dispose of their baggage, assume their arms, and assemble in front of their several quarters. The second trumpet gave the signal to mount and fall in: the members of each lance ranged themselves behind the man-at-arms, and, with their eyes directed to the front, were by him conducted to the chief of the mess, who, in turn, proceeded with his command to the station assigned it in the squadron. The third trumpet having sounded, the squadrons formed, in the order designated by their respective numbers, around the banners of the companies. The ordinary day's march was not less than three or more than five leagues; in case of necessity every third day was allowed for rest. Pillage was strictly prohibited, in time of war as well as of peace, in a hostile as well as in a friendly country. The manner of dismissing and billeting the troops, and the provisions and conveniences to be furnished at stipulated prices, were carefully specified. If payment were refused or any act of rapine committed, it was the duty of the commissaries to satisfy the injured party, deducting the amount from the wages of the offender, besides reporting him for exemplary punishment. Notice to this effect was given by the public criers, at all halting-places, before the march was resumed. Gambling and profanity were ranked among the violations of the military code. Women, to the number of thirty for each company, — a restriction sufficient, if carried into effect, to have excited a revolt in a convent of monks, — were permitted to accompany the army. The preservation of the inhabitants of the country traversed, and especially of the duke's own subjects, from oppression and outrage, was set forth as the main object of these and other provisions of the like nature; and the constant and rigorous enforcement of them was urged upon the commanders as a matter involving the honor of the sovereign, and one the neglect of which would render fruitless all his efforts and expenditures.

With a small but perfectly appointed and thoroughly disciplined force, Charles might hope to accomplish much. Grand operations — a contest such as he had long waged with a populous and powerful monarchy — did not fall within his present scheme of enterprise. If attacked by the king of France or otherwise menaced with any great and unexpected peril, the means and resources on which he had heretofore relied would still be available for his defence. What he looked forward to was a series of achievements and acquisitions like those through which the Burgundian power had grown to its present proportions. Clearly that growth had yet to reach its natural limits and proper culmination. It would go on, unless arrested by the cross-purposes of Fate, until nations generally had attained their due consistency and their appointed form.

Among the obstacles to national development in the Rhineland and generally in Western Germany, was the temporal sovereignty of so many bishops and other high ecclesiastics, including the electors of Mayence, Cologne, and Trèves. The states thus governed, being neither heritable nor alienable, were subject to none of the casualties and agencies elsewhere so productive of new arrangements and relations, and here also certain to operate were these impediments removed. The common tendency to princely aggrandizement showed itself even where there could be no absorption of territory or permanent enrichment of families. The spiritual electorates might retain their organization, their formal inviolability, their preëminence in the Diet, but they were secularized at the core; they had ceased to represent the domination of the priesthood, and no longer offered to the low-born churchman the prizes of worldly ambition. The chapters were filled from the ranks of the nobility. The electors and bishops were taken from the princely houses, and precisely from those that were the nearest and most encroaching — the destined heirs and conquerors therefore, had inheritance or conquest been possible, of states so situated. Rome itself, far from protesting against this system, found it convenient and even necessary, as insuring to these shadows of a theocratic rule the assistance of the secular arm.[65]

Foremost among the competitors were the two rival houses of Baden and Bavaria. From one or the other of these the spiritual electors were now invariably chosen. Each, in addition to its own strength, relied upon the powerful influence of a still greater house. The house of Baden was allied by marriage with that of Austria. Its members were the stanchest and most trusted supporters of the emperor in the immense sea of troubles in which, without swimming, he yet contrived to avoid sinking. On the other hand, a Bavarian prince, the elector-palatine, Frederick the Victorious, — victorious, namely, over the emperor, — was by him far more cordially detested and feared than the Turk, whose continual and ponderous knockings at the eastern doors of the empire kept the great body of Christendom in a chronic alarm, without disturbing the slumbers of its head.

The alliance between the houses of Bavaria and Burgundy dated, in like manner, from a matrimonial union — that of John the Fearless with Margaret of

[65] See the quotation from Æneas Sylvius in Ranke, Hist. of the Reformation (Eng. trans.), vol. i. p. 68.

Bavaria. It had remained unbroken in spite of the ill treatment which Jacqueline of Holland, a Bavarian princess, had received from her kinsman, Philip the Good. It had been cemented by frequent treaties, leading, as we have seen, to the strenuous but ineffectual and offensive advocacy by Charles the Bold, in the imperial presence, of the rights and interests of the elector-palatine. As a natural corollary, there had been a steady hostility to the Burgundian princes on the part of the house of Baden. That house had given open encouragement to the rebellions of Liége. The electors of Mayence and Trèves, of the same family, had been prominent in thwarting the scheme for elevating the Burgundian states into a kingdom; and the Margrave Charles of Baden was now busily promoting the intrigues carried on at Basel and elsewhere for overturning the Burgundian rule in Alsace.

It will be seen, therefore, that it was at least not from any sudden and presumptuous impulse, without guidance or clew, that the duke of Burgundy plunged into the vast imbroglio of German politics. He was drawn along by entanglements and enticements, not unlike those which had determined his course in the affairs of France. In the one case as in the other he might be denounced as an invader and a disturber; but in neither case could he be considered as a mere stranger or unauthorized intermeddler.

The internal condition of the spiritual electorates was such as naturally resulted from their form of government and peculiar external relations. The two worst systems ever devised have been the union of ecclesiastical with temporal authority, and an elective sovereignty, with its sure concomitants of foreign vassalage and a restricted choice. Either of these systems, much more their combination, is now felt to be intolerable. In the Middle Ages their evils were to some extent neutralized by that which was itself a universal source of perturbation and confusion — the virtual independence of privileged classes and communities and the consequent feebleness of the supreme government.

In 1463, Rupert of Bavaria, brother of the elector-palatine, was chosen archbishop of Cologne. The long wars carried on by his predecessor, of a noble family in Southern Belgium, with an hereditary enemy, the duke of Cleves, had exhausted the ordinary revenues of the electorate and spread a general discontent among the people. In the interval between the death of one prince and the election of another, the chapter, the nobility, and the municipalities entered into an agreement and devised a plan for preventing future mischiefs of a kind to which states thus organized were especially liable. This they effectually accomplished by dividing among themselves, in accordance with their different aims and capacities, all the real powers of government, leaving to the archbishop scarcely a shadow of rule, and not even a sufficient income to support his barren dignity. A shrewd and dexterous politician would have set himself to the task of undermining a league between parties so little connected by any natural affinities. But Rupert, by his open and easily foiled attempts to shake off his manacles, only galled his own limbs and sharpened the vigilance of his jailers. After a long series of squabbles, the chapter, which, conceding to the nobles and the towns whatever immunities they had claimed, had reserved to itself the general care and superintendence of the state, or, more properly speaking, the business of watching and restraining the nominal ruler, took the questionable step of suspending him from his office and appointing a provisional administrator to perform the necessary functions. Matters having reached this crisis, a solution in some shape must be looked for from another quarter. But where was an arbiter to be found? Rome, the proper oracle, seems to have remained mute. The emperor, on his arrival at Cologne after his flight from Trèves, in 1473, received an appeal from the chapter, and thereupon summoned the archbishop to appear and submit to his decision. But that decision would be pronounced, not by the impartial head of the empire, but by the avowed and bitter enemy of the house of Bavaria. Rupert, instead of complying, announced that he had asked for and been promised the support of the duke of Burgundy in the assertion of his legitimate rights.[66]

The case, besides being of no interest or importance in itself, is too obscure in the essential points of character and circumstance for us to venture any opinion on its merits. It involved, no doubt, a two-

[66] Löhrer, Geschichte der Stadt Neuss, s. 132 et seq.

fold question of legal right and moral right; and if we could determine with precision on which side lay the legal right, we might perhaps be safe in assuming that the moral right lay on the other. It had, however, no complexities for Charles. The grounds on which he justified his own intervention might well have seemed sufficient to him, and, if set forth by any one but him, would probably in that day have been deemed so by the world. He was a prince, and interested in maintaining the rights of princes against their rebellious subjects; he was a faithful Catholic, and had been desired by the Holy Father to keep an eye on the affairs of Cologne; he was the kinsman and ally of the Bavarian princes, and was bound to afford them his assistance when required.[67] That he had other and stronger motives for taking part in the quarrel, may be presumed. A new protectorate, a new dependency, a new stepping-stone to the dominion of the Rhineland, would be the sure fruits of success. Of success there could be little doubt, unless indeed the empire should gather itself up and coil its protective folds around the menaced soil. Such a contingency was scarcely to be apprehended. The empire, gigantic but torpid, shrank and bled where pricked, but seemed incapable of active resentment. If at any point signs of life appeared, the force was lost before it could spread throughout the mass and set the whole vast body in motion.

[67] Schreiben H. Karl's von Burgund an den Churfürster von Mainz, Chmel, B. I. s. 120–122.

But Charles had enemies whose dart was as quick as their sting was deadly. While he was thus planning new conquests on the Lower Rhine, his dominion on the Upper Rhine had already fallen.

CHAPTER IV.

LEAGUE FORMED AGAINST CHARLES. — FALL OF HIS DOMINION IN ALSACE. — SIEGE OF NEUSS. — WAR DECLARED BY THE SWISS.

1474.

In the opinion of Philippe de Commines the most sagacious act of the king his master, the grand stroke of policy which, by removing from his path the principal object of his animosity and his fears, enabled him to clear away all lesser obstacles, to crush at pleasure all inferior foes, to seize and secure the prize of a life of unswerving pursuit and restless toil, was the league which he contrived to form against the duke of Burgundy.[1] Yet, strange to say, there is no event of the time respecting which the world has been left so completely in the dark: Commines, who tells us that its importance was little compre-

[1] "Ceste allyance que le Roy conduisit . . . tourna depuis à grand prouffit au Roy, et plus que la pluspart des gens n'entendent; et croy que ce fut une des plus saiges choses qu'il feit oncques en son temps et plus au dommaige de tous ses ennemys: car le duc de Bourgogne deffaict, oncques puis ne trouva le Roy de France homme qui osast lever la teste contre luy, ne contredire à son vouloir: . . . car tous les aultres ne navigeoient que soubs le vent de cestuy là; parquoy fut grant œuvre, . . . et ne se feit point sans grant despence et sans faire maintz voyaiges." Commines, tom. ii. p. 4.

hended by most people, was himself uninformed as to the details and grossly misinformed as to the attendant circumstances; while such has been the general ignorance on the subject that in all the popular accounts the part played by Louis is scarcely noticed, and the explosion is ascribed, not to the combinations of a masterly design, but to a fortuitous concurrence of natural causes — the domineering temper and o'ervaulting ambition of Charles; the tender sensibilities of Austria outraged by the ignominies offered to itself and the oppressions inflicted upon its subjects; and the free, patriotic, and, though humble and pacific, yet dauntless spirit of the Swiss Confederates. Or can there have been a covert malice in this seeming inadvertence or forgetfulness of the narrators — a purpose prepense to defraud the king of the credit that rightly belonged to him, masked under an affected absorption in the work of depreciating and traducing his rival? If so, we delight in the opportunity of repairing this injustice. No duty can be more agreeable to the historian than that of revealing the hand of genius in what has been thought the effect of accident, of reclaiming for the real author of a memorable transaction the honors which his own modesty or the obtuseness of the world has prevented his receiving.

The hostile alliance against Burgundy was the creation of the French king, and of him alone — conceived by his brain, shaped by his plastic skill, set in motion for his peculiar ends. He had not the easy task of dropping a lighted match into a heap of combustibles, inflammable and ready to ignite — of placing a prepared mould for the molten metal poured from another's caldron. The labor and the art were all his own. The furnace and the forge were of his setting up. Nor could the business be brought to perfection without long heating and hard hammering. The Swiss iron was none of the most malleable: the Austrian fagot was of the greenest. Louis himself was no longer the impatient sprite that by dint of fierce blowing had so often scattered about the live coals with damage or danger to his own person.

How great the wrong done to Louis by slighting or ignoring the traces of his agency will appear from his plan of operations — based upon a state of things singularly unlike that in which the affair is commonly believed to have had its origin. His starting-point, the sole projecting ledge from which to hang his web, was the dissatisfaction, not of the Swiss, but of Austria, with the conduct of the duke of Burgundy — the rise of which might have seemed to a less acute and versatile schemer like an ominous blast, threatening the derangement or destruction of his whole plot. For that dissatisfaction had sprung from the repeated refusals of Charles to sanction or assist the projects of his ally against the Confederacy; and therefore, if the connection were severed, the natural result would be the renewal of his cordial relations with the Swiss, and the removal from their minds of every shadow of mistrust, if any had been entertained. Such at first must have been the view of Louis himself. He had shrunk from the contaminating touch of the Austrian pauper; he had rejoiced in the seeming lack of caution with which his rival had entered into so dangerous an intimacy; and he had seen with disappointment that Charles, while submitting to the companionship, had so managed as to avoid defilement. But it was a characteristic trait when he found in the downfall of his old hopes the material for a more solid and elaborate structure, to be presently begun. Since not the alliance between Burgundy and Austria, then the rupture of that alliance should be the means of bringing about the desired collision. Since not Charles, then the Confederacy should become the aggressor. Since not on their own behalf, then in defence of their only enemy, the Swiss should be plunged into a war with their nearest neighbor, their best, their only real friend.

This, it will be acknowledged, was an undertaking of no common order, a feat involving strange transformations and a surprising legerdemain. Let us follow the changes, watching as closely as we may the motions of the conjurer.

In addition to the Diesbachs, whose avocations lay among the boxed-up mechanism the nature of which must chiefly be guessed at from the effects produced, the assistants employed were the envoys whose arrival at his court — being a matter not easy of concealment — Sigismund had found it convenient to announce to the duke of Burgundy, vaunting at the same time their distinguished reputation, the publicity of their reception, the harmlessness of their mission, and the loyalty and discreetness of his own behavior. That Louis, however, had not calculated on any such notoriety in the negotiation, may be inferred from his selection of the persons to conduct it — one of them a native of Lucerne,[2] an ecclesiastic of no high rank; the other a German, probably an Austrian noble, originally an agent of Sigismund himself, sent on a secret mission to France, and there transmuted, by that subtle alchemy of which the king possessed the secret, into a good Frenchman and a member of the royal council.[3]

The opening act of the programme offered no great difficulties. The Austrian prince was himself eager for the dissolution of a partnership which he had found neither profitable nor congenial; and the free cities which had been the first to propose this step, were still ready to make the requisite advances. But who was to compel the consent of the other party if that were withheld? Who was to enforce restitution of the mortgaged territory if refused, or guaranty the safe possession of it when redeemed? The last thought with Louis would have been to take this responsibility on himself. His personal engagements with Sigismund were limited to the grant of a pension of ten thousand francs, in exchange for a promise of service and fidelity similar to that which

[2] Diebold Schilling, s. 108. — Stumpffen's Chronick (Zurich, 1548), B. II. fol. 434 verso.

[3] Zellweger (s. 32, note) notices the identity of name and rank — Graf Johann von Eberstein. That it was the same person appears from a letter of Sigismund himself in Chmel.

had been made to the duke of Burgundy and which was now to be renounced. Yet no one perceived more clearly than he the risk to be incurred, or was more solicitous to guard against it. He was not more intent upon engaging the Austrian prince to deliver the defiance than upon providing him with a proper champion. Sigismund had parted with Alsace in order to gain the support of the duke of Burgundy against the Swiss: to recover Alsace he was now told that he must gain the support of the Swiss against the duke of Burgundy. He had only to acquiesce, and a powerful mediation would be used in smoothing the way for an arrangement. His reluctance may be easily imagined; and the diplomatic art that sweetened the pill was doubtless deserving of honorable record. The process is not described;[4] but in regard to the composition of the specifics employed we have sufficient intimations in the hopes which he was still permitted to cherish, in the claims which he put forth, and in his later repinings and complaints, uttered when the jugglery was over, and heard with the calmest indifference by those who had first raised and then dispelled the illusion.

And now came the real hard labor of the enterprise, two or three months of incessant smiting, twist-

[4] Except indeed that the more obvious inducements held out to him are stated by Edlibach, who seems to have been tolerably well informed in regard to the proceedings of the envoys: "Wenn er die eignossen zu fründen vnd helfer hette, so möcht er die seinen übrigen land behalten vnd uilicht noch mer darzu gewünnen," &c. Gerold Edlibach's Chronik mit Sorgfalt nach dem Original copirt, von J. M. Usteri (Zurich, 1847), s. 139.

ing, tempering, welding — a busy Cyclopean scene, whereof the din was greatly deadened and the sweating figures much obscured by the gloomy depths of the subterranean workshop.[5] In the case of Austria there had been a struggle of feelings, a weighing of interests; and to turn the scale, to bring about a decision, had required at the most but a dexterous nudge, an artful whisper or two. But what motives either of interest or of feeling had the Swiss to offset against a cardinal maxim of state policy of which the wisdom had been attested by their whole experience, against an hereditary national sentiment coeval with their national existence, or against the simple and obvious reasons, founded both on honor and advantage, for respecting their ancient treaties? In what respects were they fitted, by what impulse were they incited, to become the tools of France, the allies of Austria, the assailants of Burgundy?

This was, however, not the form in which the question was submitted. It was only in some of the larger places, only by a purchased faction, — not by the yet unpurchased people, — that the true drift of the manœuvre was apprehended and the ultimate goal discerned. At first, indeed, an inclination was shown to try the effect of a popular excitement — to open all the sluices and send forward at once a volume of turbid water into the destined channel. The old rumors were again propagated; the old phantom was revived. The chief Italian powers — Rome, Naples, Venice,

[5] Of the many secret journeys and conferences we have nothing more than the general account given by Edlibach.

Milan, Savoy — were in league with the duke of Burgundy. The son of the king of Naples was to wed the Burgundian heiress. It had been resolved to impose a master upon the Swiss Confederacy. Great festivities were going on at Milan. There was a bustle and a gathering of princes and soldiers at Geneva. Berne was to be immediately attacked, and, when taken, levelled with the dust. A monument would be raised upon its site, bearing the inscription, "Here stood a town once, whose name was Berne." The council had sent out its spies to observe and investigate, and further information was promised when received.[6] But no demand arising for fabrications of this quality, the supply soon ceased. They were too gaudy and too flimsy for customers addicted to homespun. After the arrival of the French emissaries there was a change of tactics. In their private communications with Berne no reserve was maintained. The final object of the whole negotiation was plainly stated, the means of attaining it were freely canvassed, and plans of the future alliance between France and the Confederacy were sketched and elaborated.[7] A report of this nature, founded either on knowledge or conjecture, reached, as we have seen, the ears of Charles, arousing an alarm, which was speedily allayed by the plausible answers made to his inquiries. But at home the secret was better kept, the body of the

[6] Zellweger, s. 33. — Diebold Schilling, s. 103.

[7] Rodt, B. I. s. 206, 207. — Hence the mistake of many writers who date from this period an alliance not formed or even publicly hinted at till long afterwards.

Swiss nation being left in profound ignorance of the benefits designed for them. The subject presented for their consideration was nothing more than a treaty of peace and amity with Austria; a treaty such as had been often before projected and discussed, such as the Church, the empire, the Burgundian sovereign, and many other powers had repeatedly counselled; a treaty which would abolish all past causes of contention or jealousy, restrain both parties from future usurpations or conquests, and provide for mutual good offices, as well as for assistance, on equitable terms, in defending the rights and possessions to be mutually released. The distinction, it will be observed, between this agreement and that which Charles had formerly striven to effect, was the same as is drawn by the English law between deeds of "quitclaim" and "warranty." But no particular stress was laid upon an engagement of a kind not unusual in alliances of that period,[8] and one which, however opposed to the general principles of Swiss policy, had been adopted by the several cantons in their separate leagues with neighboring communities, which was familiar, therefore, in practice, and admissible in the present case on strong exceptional grounds. Neither does any allusion seem to have been made to the duke of Burgundy, as an ally whose interests would be adversely affected by a measure so nearly conformable with his own previous suggestions. His rule over Alsace was to cease; but the instrument under which he wielded this rule pro-

[8] The project is spoken of by Knebel, a contemporary diarist, and by other writers, as simply one of a permanent peace.

vided for its peaceable termination, the means for giving effect to that provision had been already supplied, and it need not be assumed — at least not openly assumed — that he would hesitate, much less decline, to comply with his sworn obligations. So, too, the Most Christian king was introduced, not as a party concerned, not as a practised stirrer-up of strife, not as the inventor with whom the motion had originated and to whose advantage it would enure, — but as an indifferent though benevolent bystander, a zealous and experienced peacemaker, nay, the umpire specially commissioned by Providence to disentangle a skein which the well-meant endeavors of successive mediators had only helped to tighten. The auspicious conjuncture, the appropriate inspiration, were declared to be the visible work of the Holy Ghost; and it behooved both parties, more especially the Confederates, — who had received from Louis so many messages expressive of a sincere and devoted friendship, — to meet his present offer with a corresponding outburst of gratitude and confidence.[9]

[9] "Dis was ein ordenlich Mittell, ohn allen Zwiffel des heiligen Geistes. . . . Als nun der Fürst von Oesterrich, und auch die Eidgnossen, in disem gutten Willem waren, und doch wenig Gesprechs mit einandern gehebt hatten, . . . wolt der ewig Gott sin Gnade noch witer, in disen Sachen erscheinen; also, das der allerchristenlichest Küng von Franckrich, genant Ludovicus, sich diser Dingen zwüschen der Herschafft von Oesterrich und den Eidgnossen, als ein früntlicher Undertedinger, zu allem Gutten annam. . . . Immassen das beid Teil sinen künglichen Gnaden, all jr Spenne und Irrungen übergaben. . . . Man wolt aber zu beiden Siten, dem Küng der Ehren bas, dann jemand anderm gönnen; und billich, wann er sich in disem allem, allweg sin Lib und Gutt, zen Eidgnossen ze setzen, trostlich erbotten, und mengerlei Warnungen getan hat." Diebold Schilling, s. 108.

There were other and more tangible reasons for embracing so fair an opportunity for a reconciliation with the house of Austria. The present condition of that house was not such as to give its enemies any serious cause of dread. Yet weak as Austria now was, it might hereafter become powerful; or it might — as late events had tended to show — find compensation for its own weakness in an intimate connection with some more powerful house. Its free and full surrender of the pretensions which now constituted its only means of aggression, and the continued assertion of which formed the only remaining ground of quarrel, ought not to be lightly estimated by the Swiss. It would set a seal upon their independence, give a formal validity to their conquests, confer the stamp of legitimacy on their government, relieve them from the frequent controversies arising from alleged provocations to their subjects or allies, and obviate the necessity for keeping a constant watch upon the movements and for seeking to conciliate the good will of foreign powers.[10] There would be a final end to the bickerings and blood-spilling which down to

Schilling was by no means the good, simple, ignorant soul one might suspect from these and other passages. On the contrary, he was a very skilful and well informed scribe, whose talents exactly suited the part assigned to him, that of imposing upon his countrymen such a version of these transactions as might tally with their notions and keep them in the dark as to the true origin of the affair. His suppressions and falsehoods are censured by his townsman and contemporary, Valerius Anshelm.

[10] "Wie gut ein ewiger frid were besunder wen der hertzog von östrich den eignossen die stat sloss länd vnd lüt, so sy vnd jr fordrern jm vun sinnen vordren, abgewunnen vun jngenomen ledenklichen schanckt vun gebe," &c. Edlibach, s. 139.

within a recent period had attended all their intercourse with the inhabitants of a neighboring territory; an end also to the rumors and intrigues which had followed upon the cessation of those more flagrant annoyances. All the advantages derived from the Burgundian occupation of Alsace were to be retained and rendered permanent. Pledges and concessions which could not have been demanded from Burgundy might be extorted from Austria. Moreover — and this, as we shall see, was, on more accounts than one, made an essential feature of the scheme — Basel and the free Alsatian towns proposed to enter the league, which would be not only strengthened by their adhesion, but more deeply infused with the elements of a republican confederation.

This was probably the line of argument mainly pursued. What is certain is, that many arguments were needed and that none were omitted. The strongest persuasion failed to awaken any thing like enthusiasm. Some cantons were well inclined to a union with the free towns, their natural allies, but showed an invincible repugnance to a similar union with the princely house which they regarded as their natural enemy. Some, on the contrary, were willing to see the extinction of an old and troublesome feud, but objected to an extension of the Confederacy by the admission of new members.[11] From the majority a frigid assent was wrung, on condition that others should join. Glarus, Zug, and Unterwalden remained stubborn in their opposition.[12] Without penetrating the disguise

[11] Zellweger, s. 34. [12] Ibid. s. 31, 34, et al.

in which the scheme was enveloped, the popular instinct suggested doubts in regard to its genuineness, which took a natural though erroneous direction. A ruse on the part of Austria was suspected — an attempt to gain by treachery or finesse what it had so often and so vainly endeavored to accomplish by force. The extraordinary zeal manifested by the advocates of the measure was possibly owing to their expectation of private as well as public advantages from its adoption. To remove these fears, it was voted by the Diet that no subject of the Confederacy should accept of any gifts or favors from Austria.[13] Had the prohibition been general and effectual, it might have placed a damper upon the movement. But thus limited in its application, it was not merely useless but superfluous. Sigismund had no money to spend in bribes, and he was quite innocent of any desire to bribe the Swiss.

The resistance of an individual is stronger than that of numbers. In an aggregate composed of several different constituents, the softer portions, as they liquidize, act as solvents upon the harder. If there be still a solid lump or two, they are carried off by the surrounding fluid. Lucerne and Zurich, the cantons which had the closest relations and the strongest affinities with Berne, were the first to promise their coöperation.[14] As soon as one canton had yielded, it was invited to use its influence for the conver-

[13] Ibid. s. 31.

[14] The direct communications of the French envoys were confined to these three cantons. See Edlibach, ubi supra.

sion of others.[15] Thus feeling their way along, the skilful navigators passed in safety the more dangerous shoals, and, when the tide had begun to slacken, hoisted sail, and stood boldly out to sea. In plainer terms, it was resolved to proceed at once with the negotiation, hasten it to a conclusion, and trust to time and the event to overcome the scruples which entreaties and expostulations had been unable to shake.

Accordingly, after one or more informal and tentative conferences,[16] the representatives of France, Austria, the Swiss cantons, and several of the free Alsatian towns, assembled at Constance about the middle of March. The bishop of Constance presided over the deliberations; a papal nuncio had also been engaged for the occasion, and heightened its solemnity by his presence; while Nicholas von Diesbach, who headed the legation from Berne, and Jost von Silinen, provost of Munster, one of the French envoys, had the chief if not the most prominent share in the management and direction.[17]

The discussion was opened by the Austrian orators, in a tone which might have been thought to augur ill for the desired result. An historical statement, going back to the remote origin of the difficulties it was now proposed to settle, was put in: the

[15] Zellweger, ubi supra.

[16] Ibid. s. 30, and Beilage, No. 13. — The Swiss official registrar of the proceedings at one of these meetings seems to have been internally disgusted with them, for he closes his record with the exclamation, "Wie froh ich was, da ich das Ende sach!"

[17] Schilling. — Edlibach. — Zellweger. — Chmel.

Swiss were stigmatized as rebels; their conquest of the Aargau and adjacent lands was declared to have been in violation of truces; and restitution was claimed, as well as an explicit acknowledgment of the Austrian sovereignty. To these offensive and extravagant demands it was answered, on the part of the Confederates, that they had not expected such questions to be again brought forward; that they were a free people, and purposed to remain such; that, whatever the legality of their conquests, they would die sooner than surrender them.[18] Austria, not perhaps feeling itself yet prepared for death, was speedily induced to change the issue, and descend to a less arrogant if not more tenable position. From this also it would have been quickly pushed, had the object not been to allow it to make a show of fight by way of saving its honor, as well as with the purpose to disarm and capture it by an artifice rather than a direct attack or forced capitulation. It was plain that whatever terms the Swiss might insist upon must be granted. Sigismund had long found himself unable to stand alone. He must now choose, if he had not already chosen, between Burgundy and the Swiss. From the former he had nothing more to expect — unless called to a stern reckoning for his part in the present proceedings. The assistance he was to receive from the latter he must purchase at their own price. Or was he to expose himself to the combined enmity of both? He pleaded

[18] Zur Geschichte des Konstanzen Tags, Chmel, B. I. s. 186–199.

for the restoration of at least some roods of territory, — a few small places, such as Schaffhausen and Frauenfeld; for the exercise of at least some form of authority — investiture of fiefs in the discharge of a merely ceremonial function.[19] He resisted stoutly the counter-demand that the four Forest Towns should remain open at all seasons to the passings and excursions of the Swiss — a precautionary measure against any subsequent attempt on his part to slip the noose or resort to further experiments. Various minor questions were likewise agitated. But the point on which the debate centred related to the terms in which the Austrian prince was to renounce all claim to property or dominion in the region actually occupied by the Confederates. He was required to make the declaration to this effect on behalf of his heirs in general. He, on the other hand, contended that it should be made in his own name only, or extend at most to the heirs of his body. He denied, absurdly but pertinaciously, his right to bind other branches of his family or the future inheritors of its possessions. But of what value would be a renunciation thus limited? Sigismund had no lineal descendants, nor the least prospect of any. If his views were suffered to prevail, the house of Austria might, even during his life, by an exchange of territory or some similar arrangement within itself, regain the ground from which it had been wont to proclaim its lofty preten-

[19] See his own account of the matter in his instructions to the envoys whom he afterwards sent to the French court. Ibid. s. 239–245.

sions, to launch its empty menaces, and to summon its opponent before the bar of the empire. It was evidently the design of Austria to avail itself of the asylum now opened to it, as a mere temporary convenience. When sheltered and warmed, it would seek the first opportunity to disclose its sting and pour forth its ancient venom.

The deceit was too transparent to be roughly handled. Let it pass unchallenged; let the self-conceited tyro be encouraged to believe in his own profound calculations and admirable play. More difficult than the task of circumventing Austria was that of securing unanimity among its adversaries. The council of Berne, during the sitting of the conference, kept up a lively correspondence with the other members of the Confederacy, reiterating the inducements offered and urging the importance of timely and concerted action. The still dissentient cantons were invited to send their deputies, even if no instructions were given them to speak or vote. The negotiations were reported to be drawing to a close, and the precise day was named on which the treaty would be signed.[20] Nor was this information incorrect. A single wire remained to be adjusted — that which the contriver himself was to pull when the moment had arrived to set the machine going. A proposition was made and readily accepted that the points on which no agreement had been reached should be left to the arbitration of the French king,

[20] Zellweger, s. 34, 35.

the treaty to be concluded in other respects but left inoperative until sent back by him in its amended form. In the mean time Sigismund was to break off his engagements with Burgundy and demand the surrender of Alsace. This would bring about a crisis in which the course to be taken would become plainer to all parties. It had in fact been determined from the first that Austria should commit itself by this irrevocable step before receiving any pledge from the Swiss.[21] They too would feel the necessity for union and decision when disturbances were threatened or already raging on their frontiers. Sigismund, on his part, was well content with what he regarded as the postponement of a disagreeable alternative which might not, after all, be the only one open to him. Meanwhile he could flatter himself with the notion that, while others were bound, he still remained free. The treaty was in his eyes simply the project of an alliance, to be ratified or rejected by him when he had seen the full extent of his difficulties and could better judge whether any sacrifice were called for. Besides, in the worst event, he had the most satisfactory private assurances in regard to the disposition of the French king and the mode in which the disputed points would be decided.[22] By the Swiss, on the other hand, or at least by their leaders, no assurances on this head were needed.

[21] Ibid. s. 31, 32.

[22] "Oratores vestri . . . proposuerunt, . . . annectentes etiam si in articulis concordie . . . grauamen uel difficultatem haberet quod majestas vestra velit illud mittigare in fauorem principis Austrie." Letter of Sigismund to Louis, Chmel, B. I. s. 262.

They were acquainted with the motives and the whole design of Louis;[23] they knew that in his hands Austria was but a chance-caught implement to start the wheels, and to be cast aside when they were fairly in motion.

The treaty was signed on the 30th of March. In its present shape, it stipulated for a perpetual peace between the contracting parties and the reference to umpires of any subsequent disagreement; for the conservation of existing territorial limits; for the abrogation of tolls and complete freedom of traffic; and for military aid to be rendered to Sigismund, in case of need, by the Swiss, at their own standard rates of payment.[24] The last clause, although the most important in view of the great object with which the negotiation had been set on foot, was far too loosely worded to bear the full construction intended to be put upon it. By a memorandum, however, contained in the original draft, but struck out before the treaty was submitted for ratification by the separate cantons, it appeared that the steps to be taken in the redemption of the mortgaged lands and in the contingencies dependent on that measure formed the subject of a verbal contract, which it was unnecessary to reduce to writing, the honor of both parties being pledged for its fulfilment.[25] No time was lost in giving notice to the French king of the

[23] See the boast of Diesbach to this effect in Rodt, B. I. s. 261.

[24] Zellweger, Versuch, &c., s. 35, and Geschichte des Appenzellischen Volkes, Urkunden, No. 369.

[25] Zellweger, Versuch, &c. s. 37, 38.

success which had crowned his laudable endeavors. There was, however, a marked discrepancy between the communications addressed to him. The council of Berne, in a business-like message confined to essentials, treated the whole affair as happily concluded, informed him that Alsace was to be immediately reclaimed, and promised on behalf of the Confederates prompt and vigorous action for enforcing the demand.[26] In the voluminous instructions carried by the Austrian ambassadors, the topics exclusively dwelt upon were the series of improprieties in demeanor and in act of which the Swiss had been guilty during the past hundred years, and the wrong that would be done to Sigismund if the *proposed* agreement were not modified in accordance with his wishes and with the promises made to him when, at the solicitation of France, he had condescended to overtures of peace.[27]

Whether the treaty were valid or not, was a question however to be settled, not by a continuance of the discussion, but by the practical test to be forthwith applied. Openly the whole negotiation had proceeded on the supposition that the duke of Burgundy would give up possession of Alsace in compliance with the terms of the mortgage. But this would frustrate all the plans and render abortive all the exertions of Louis and his fellow-conspirators. They, at least, would then have little interest in

[26] Ibid. s. 38.—A more formal notice, written in the name of the Confederacy, and giving no intimation of the real object of the treaty, was also sent. Chmel, B. I. s. 173, 174.

[27] Chmel, B. I. s. 239–248.

upholding the treaty, which they valued only as the foundation stone of an ampler edifice. It is even questionable whether the ransom money would have been so easily raised had there seemed to be any probability of its being accepted.[28] Yet it was matter for uncomfortable reflection that, with all his eagerness for dominion and the retentiveness of his gripe, Charles was known to hold peculiar notions in regard to the sanctity of compacts, and to be subject to attacks of squeamishness which had commonly withheld him from any gross violation of his plighted faith. The matter must be so conducted as to obviate all embarrassments from this source. Here was the hinge on which the whole manœuvre was to swing; and it was here that the assistance of the free towns would be especially useful. At Basel the tributary branch of the intrigue had been carried forward with the same activity and skill as had characterized the management of the main trunk at Berne. There had been the same complete understanding with the French agents, the same denials of any hostile intention to the Burgundian envoys, the same sending around of messengers among friends and allies, with more frequent and open meetings for consultation and preliminary action.[29] A train had

[28] So at least we may infer from the alacrity with which it was afterwards redistributed. "Die Hinterlegung desselben," remarks Ochs,—whose researches first dispelled some of the mist that had enveloped these affairs,—"war im Grunde nur ein Spiegelfechten . . . Man wusste wohl, das Karl nicht der Mann war, Aufkündung, noch Pfandschilling, anzunehmen, und dass die Waffen allein entscheiden würden." Geschichte von Basel, B. IV. s. 260.

[29] Wursteisen. — Knebel. — Ochs.

also been laid for the overthrow of the Burgundian government in Alsace, the conspiracy embracing both subjects and neighbors, nobles and towns, all equally chafed by a system so stringent, a presence so austere. Every thing was finished up in readiness for the conclusion of the treaty between Austria and the Swiss, that being the point of junction for the two lines. No sooner had it been reached in the manner just described, than, by distinct instruments, an alliance offensive and defensive was concluded between Austria on the one hand, and the Swiss on the other, with the towns of Basel, Strasburg, Colmar, and Schlettstadt.[30] The latter league, afterwards enlarged by the admission of other places, became known as "the Lower Confederacy," in distinction from the original union comprising the eight cantons. These arrangements, unlike the more difficult achievement which had preceded them, were hampered with no reserves, clogged by no scruples, to prevent their going into immediate operation. While the Swiss people were puzzling and murmuring over the strange device that conflicted with all their old ideas and customary methods, — wondering to what it tended, and still suspecting a trap of the arch enemy's contrivance; while the partisans of France were suppressing premature disclosures and leading, or slyly stimulating the pursuit on a wrong

[30] Ochs; Chmel; Zellweger; &c. — The bishops of Basel and Strasburg were parties to these treaties; but not, as Zellweger absurdly supposes, the elector-palatine, who was a firm ally of Burgundy. The margrave of Baden wished to be included, but was refused. Schilling, s. 111.

scent;[31] while Austria was maundering over its long list of grievances, affecting to consider all that had been done as mere initiatory proceedings, and playing its prodigiously artful game of fast and loose, the streets of the free towns blazed with bonfires, the bells rang joyful peals, and it was publicly announced that the people of Alsace, already in open revolt, were to be liberated from the hellish tyranny to which they had been subjected, and restored to the mild and benevolent sway of their rightful sovereign.[32]

Sigismund — whose connivance in this movement had proceeded not so much from his eagerness to recover his dominions as from his belief that if it were done without the help of the Swiss, he could assume a loftier tone, throw back the treaty on the hands of its framers, and himself dictate the conditions of peace — stood ready to take immediate possession, in person or by deputy. Some previous notice of his intention must be given to Charles; but no delay need follow in the execution of it. A violent resumption would forestall or supersede the necessity for a peaceable resignation. The letters

[31] At a diet held in Lucerne on the 18th of April, it was deemed necessary — or judicious — to repeat the prohibition against accepting presents from Austria. Many objections were made to the treaty. How they were satisfied — or stifled — we can only conjecture. Zellweger, s. 39.

[32] "Darauf hin liess Basel einmüthiglich in seinem Jubel der ganzen Stadt Glocken ertönen, zum Lobe Gottes, und Freudenfeuer aufflamen. Man hob Augen und Hände gen Himmel Gott zu danken; ja Viele weinten vor Freuden, dass das ganze Land von der Tyrannenwuth erlöst werde." Knebel, 1ste Abth. s. 49.

sent to the duke of Burgundy bear date the 6th of April; but it was not until the 17th that they were presented at Luxembourg by the heralds charged with the conveyance of them and the notary appointed to attest the delivery.

The style of these documents, though dry and formal, is vicious and confused. There is a visible embarrassment in the tone; and the brazen assumptions demanded for the task of justifying the course to be pursued are veiled in unintelligible allusions and an ungrammatical phraseology. Charles is told that, for certain strong and legitimate causes not unconnected with his own proceedings,[33] the Austrian prince has determined to renounce the alliance and to redeem the mortgaged territory. Certain other cogent reasons oblige him to enter and take possession without waiting for any formalities.[34] He does not, in fact, consider himself bound to offer previous payment.[35] He has, however, deposited at Basel the sum of eighty thousand florins (comprising the forty thousand received by himself, ten thousand paid on his behalf to the Swiss, and thirty thousand understood to have been expended in releasing claims in other quarters). He likewise abjures the service of the duke of Burgundy, and sends back the letters of protection given him by that sovereign,

[33] "Certis ex causis tum legittimis, tum etiam necessitatem quandam in se continentibus vestri ex parte, non ab re moti sumus."

[34] "Etiam propter nonnullas alias urgentissimas causas prefatis dominiis ac subditis nostris appropinquare et quantocius poterimus ad manus nostras reducere et recipere."

[35] "Quamquam tamen ad hoc minime fuissemus asstricti."

adding an intimation that his future bearing towards his late ally will be governed "by the disposition of things."[36]

Here was an opening for refutation and caustic rebuke which Charles would have been the last man to let pass. His logical mind showed a torpedo-like resentment when it encountered any fraudulent sophism or baseless allegation. He began his reply with some satirical strictures on the incomprehensible jargon employed by his cousin of Austria. He made a full and exact statement of the circumstances under which the alliance had been formed and of the stipulations which it embraced. Sigismund had come, uninvited though not unwelcomed, to the Burgundian court; had exposed his poverty and his perils; had craved assistance, and himself proposed certain engagements. Confessing that he was hard beset by the Swiss, he had asked to be protected against them. Acknowledging that, in his embarrassed state, he derived no profit from his dominions on the Rhine, and that he was even unable to hold them, he had offered them in pawn. His proposals had been accepted, relief granted, security against further molestation promised. With his own free will, at his sole instigation, a covenant had been framed which became thenceforth a law to both parties, irrevocable by either without the other's consent or just cause alleged. Otherwise of what use were any treaty between states or any contract between

[36] Chmel, B. I. s. 92 et seq.

private persons? What, then, were the grounds on which he now undertook to rescind the agreement and depart from his obligations? In regard to the promise of protection, it had been amply redeemed. He had never from that time sustained the slightest injury, or proffered a single complaint; while Charles, by affording the protection, had fallen under the suspicion and exposed himself to the hostility of those with whom he had always lived in friendship. Nevertheless, since Sigismund thought himself able to dispense with that protection and desired to have it withdrawn, he should not be compelled to retain it. This was optional with himself. But his promise of service and fidelity could be revoked only with the assent of the party to whom it was given. From *that* obligation he should *not* be released; and he was bidden to beware how he attempted any infraction of it.

As to the mortgage, given for a consideration which had been duly received, it could be cancelled only in the mode and according to the conditions prescribed. Safe and peaceable possession had been guarantied. Not only the sums advanced, but such as might appear, by the declarations of the Burgundian officials, to have been laid out in necessary works and repairs, were to be refunded. The reckoning was to take place at Besançon. Through what proceedings, on the part of Charles, had the Austrian prince been discharged from compliance with these stipulations? What, above all, did he mean by asserting that he was not even bound to proffer payment before reëntry? The instrument had been his own free act and deed. By his allowance and express authorization, possession had been transferred, and the oaths and homage of the inhabitants rendered, to the Burgundian sovereign. During the latter's occupation of the territory, all possible care had been taken for its security and defence. It had been preserved from the incursions and ravages which had before been so incessant. The routes, never before traversable without an expensive escort, had been rendered perfectly safe. both for natives and foreigners. Charles's just title had not been impaired by any abuse or defalcation; nor, until this moment, in all the communications that had passed, had the least pretext of the kind been set up. Let the Austrian ministers, who but a few months ago had visited him at Trèves and at Dijon, say whether, amidst their profuse assurances of friendship, they had once hinted at the existence of any causes on his side, or indeed of any reasons on the other side, for annulling the contract. Since then he had certainly done nothing to give occasion for regarding it as void; yet now he was suddenly informed that an immediate seizure was to be made, and that even before the notice would reach him. The undeclared causes must therefore have arisen out of Sigismund's own proceedings. It was plain that these embassies and lavish professions of good will had been a mere blind, to hide the conspiracy forming against the Burgundian power and the rebellion instigated for the overthrow of the Burgundian rule. "But we," concluded the writer, "desiring in all our affairs to follow the path of justice, truth, and honor, do hereby engage, when you shall send your commissioners — for whom, on application, safe-conducts will be furnished — to Besançon, empowered to join with ours in a proper and regular settlement (having previously restored us to the peaceable possession in which you were bound to maintain us, and which you have interrupted), to perform faithfully our part of the agreement. If, on the contrary, you shall adhere to the purpose you have announced, in violation of the terms of the contract and of your princely word and honor, we shall make resistance, trusting, with the help of God, that our ability in defence shall prove not inferior to that which you have heretofore seen displayed in the attacks of the Swiss — attacks from which you sought and have received our protection." [37]

This report had at least one consequence — of no moment as regarded the march of events; of much for determining their true character and origin. Two rejoinders, in vindication of the Austrian prince, were prepared. Which was sent, or whether either was sent, is uncertain and unimportant.[38] In one — intended evidently for circulation and popular effect in case the real purport of Charles's answer, contrary to what was desirable, should have taken wind — the defence is based upon his own maladministration of

[37] Chmel, B. I. s. 103–108. — We have conformed to the exact language of these documents as far as a necessary condensation would permit.

[38] Most probably neither. See Knebel, s. 61.

the trust reposed in him. He had been blind to the illegal and tyrannical acts of his lieutenant, deaf to the cries and complaints of the people confided to his charge. At length they had risen against the oppressor, and had sought redress from their natural prince. His intervention had been necessary to rescue the country from impending ruin. Anticipating a refusal, he had not judged it advisable to prefer his demand in the mode stipulated by the agreement.[39]

Whatever color there may have been for the counter accusation now first brought forward, Sigismund's right to avail himself of such a plea had been effectually estopped by his own uniform silence and indifference. In all his intercourse with Charles he had uttered no word of remonstrance or entreaty on this score.[40] His own eyes, his own ears, his own lips, had remained shut in regard to the afflictions of his former subjects, until the futility of his appeals on a quite different matter had become apparent. Moreover, there was a palpable anachronism in his present statement. The outbreak in Alsace, instead of preceding and excusing, had followed and been caused by, his known intention and evident preparations to reassert his own

[39] Chmel, B. I. s. 109. — The delicious non sequitur of this conclusion need scarcely be pointed out. If he had any reason for expecting the non-fulfilment of the agreement on Charles's side, it was surely the more incumbent on Sigismund (who boasts that he too desires to pursue the path of justice and honor) to comply with all the stipulations.

[40] The single complaint which he had made against Hagenbach related to the acceptance by the latter of offers from Austrian nobles to enter the Burgundian service — a proceeding which Charles had contended was perfectly legitimate.

authority. And why, if such were the provocation, had it not been openly and plainly proclaimed in the former letters? Why even now were no particulars set forth? Why, lastly, was there no offer of proof in support of the impeachment?

But Sigismund shall himself testify to the falsity of these pretences. In his other letter — written in a more impulsive mood and in a more genuine strain — he makes a frank exposition of his own motives, and brings a strong and to some extent well-substantiated complaint against Charles. After recapitulating the statements of the latter as to the first formation of the alliance and impliedly admitting their correctness, he proceeds to give an account of his own views in seeking and embracing it. He does not pretend that any thing was ever said or done by Charles to encourage such views; and he overlooks their consequent irrelevancy. He forgets, too, that in point of fact they were an afterthought even with himself[41] — the benefits actually secured to him by the alliance suggesting the hope of a still greater advantage, though one neither promised nor contemplated. In utter contempt of his own express declarations at the time, he avers that he parted with his dominions, entered the service of Burgundy, and accepted its protection, with the sole idea of recommencing the war against the Swiss, and in the full belief that he should receive all the assistance he

[41] This is apparent from his omission of any such statement in the letter in which, soon after his return from Saint-Omer, he gave an account to the emperor of his agreement with the duke of Burgundy and of his motives for entering into it. See Chmel, B. II. s. 131 et seq.

might need in the prosecution of his enterprises. What he wanted, he now boldly avows, was *not* a mediation for the purpose of concluding a peace with his enemies, but a sufficient army to enable him to subdue them. He vehemently reproaches Charles with his failure to answer these reasonable expectations. All his solicitations, all his costly embassies, had been entirely fruitless. Instead of hurling defiance at the Swiss, Charles had treated them with a constant courtesy and tenderness, sent them offers of service and friendship, courted their favor and their alliance. And what had been the end of all this? "Perceiving your total disregard of our sentiments and interests, we have ourselves been compelled to enter into negotiations with our inveterate enemies and to sanction a treaty prejudicial to our honor and subversive of our rights." [42]

Let us be fair to Sigismund; let us not deal harshly with his self-contradictions and inconsequential reasoning. This was not an argument he was putting forth to confute an opponent or convince an impartial world. It was a wail of anguish, a cry of reproach, designed to wring the conscience and the heart of an ungenerous prince — "the only prince," as he frequently boasts, "to whose service he had ever stooped." [43] — who might so easily have grappled him to his breast with hooks of steel, instead of leaving him to fall into despair, exposed to the wily blandishments of the French king and the brutal obstinacy of the hated Swiss. After reading this pathetic lam-

[42] Chmel, B. I. s. 110–114. [43] Ibid. B. I. s. 245 et al.

entation, who can doubt that, if it was for the part he had taken in their disputes with Austria that the duke of Burgundy became a mark for the animosity of the Swiss, he was rightly punished?

The publication, however, of such a document would have been a doubtful aid in calling down the retribution. Had it been sooner brought to light, the most recent and in many respects the best informed writers would scarcely have continued to talk of "the conquests contemplated by Charles in concert with Austria." [44] Its promulgation at the time might have produced a sensation far from favorable to the cordiality of the new alliance. But the whole correspondence was studiously kept from the sight of the Confederates. It was enough for them to know that the money had been tendered to the duke of Burgundy, and that he, in defiance of his engagements, had refused to receive it and release the mortgage.[45]

Was there, then, no way of rebutting the calumny, of unveiling the deceit? Was it too late to interpose a hinderance upon the successful action of the conspiracy, to wrench out the sham bolts with which, in default of better, it had been so cunningly riveted? Or

[44] "Eroberungen die er mit Hülfe von Oesterreich zu machen hoffte." Zellweger, s. 34.

[45] Schilling, s. 110. — And such is the statement of nearly all contemporary and subsequent writers. It has even been said that Sigismund's messengers were detained as hostages. Knebel, however, writing at Basel, where there was much less occasion than in the Swiss cantons for secrecy on this point, gives correctly enough the substance of Charles's answer. Some later historians have also been aware that he insisted that the money should have been tendered at Besançon, but, being unacquainted with the details of the agreement, they have regarded his objection as a mere quibble.

did Charles — insensible to his danger, indifferent to the chances of escape — propose to indulge his pride and display his superiority by vain recriminations with Austria and empty denunciations of France; making no attempt to influence those whom alone he could hope to influence; leaving those with whom he had no quarrel to espouse, under a sheer delusion, the quarrel of a common enemy; not seeking to detach from the league against him those who were themselves reluctant to join it and ignorant of its scope, but without whom it must fall to pieces? Not so. Despise them! Plot against them! It may rather be said that he stood in dread of the Swiss, that he knelt to avert their mistaken hostility. Not with the fear of cowardice, not with the fawning of the betrayer or the parasite; but as one who knew and respected their strength, who valued their good opinion and reciprocation of good offices, who foresaw that their opposition would unhinge all his schemes and make futile all his purposes, who would gladly have cemented his alliance with them and enlisted their coöperation, but who, at the same time, confident in himself and deferring to their decision and established policy, had been content with their assurances of a continued comity and neutrality. On the wriggling and impotent Sigismund he would have set his heel with a pitiless contempt. Against the venomous and crafty Louis he was preparing a gigantic counterplot, of which we shall hear anon. But towards the Swiss he laid aside, not indeed his native boldness in self-assertion and self-vindication, but the haughty air with which he commonly repelled accusation, and the defiant tone in which he was wont to answer any intimation of hostility.

He lost no time in despatching a new embassy, to proclaim the truth in regard both to his own position and to that of the Confederates. Thoroughly acquainted with their internal politics, and now well informed as to the mode in which the intrigue had been carried on and the state in which it rested, he confined his present appeal to those cantons where alone a sentiment adverse to himself had taken root and where the power of giving effect to that sentiment chiefly lay. Again he besought the citizens of Zurich, Lucerne, and especially Berne, to recollect the ties by which they were bound to him, and their own frequent promises and declarations. Let them contrast his conduct towards his allies with the hollow professions and tortuous policy of the French king. Let them weigh the treatment they had uniformly experienced from the house of Burgundy against that which they had received from the house of Austria. Could they prefer the alliance of one who had been an enemy from choice, who would become a friend only through compulsion, to that of one whom his own choice had made their friend, whom nothing save compulsion could make their enemy? He conjured them to tell him what fault he had committed, by what act he had forfeited their regard. Even against Sigismund he had been guilty of no wrong. It was false that he had refused to cancel the mortgage. He had offered, he was still prepared, to give a legal release and to make a peaceable surrender. Hagenbach's proceedings could afford no excuse for a forcible entry. If there had been any real cause for complaint, there was a proper mode of seeking redress. He would be found amenable to pacific representations; he was ready for an equitable settlement. But he could not so degrade himself as to become the willing victim of violence and fraud; and if Austria were bent upon pursuing these methods, he, too, could take but one course, leaving God to be the judge between them.[46]

While Charles was addressing this solemn adjuration to the Swiss, accompanied with proposals so fair to Austria, events in Alsace had reached a consummation for which he seems to have been wholly unprepared. Let us turn, then, from his ineffectual efforts to arrest the current at its fountain-head, and see how it had fared with one who, caught in the rushing waters, was left to buffet them alone. Precisely because he had to deal with facts, not words, modern research is unable to do for Peter von Hagenbach what it has done to some extent at least for Charles of Burgundy. We cannot rescue him from the hands of bitter and furious partisan chroniclers. We cannot scrape away the mire with which they have covered, and, as we may suspect, disfigured his features. The portraiture is still theirs, though the scrutiny and recognition be ours, if something human,

[46] Valerius Anshelm, ap. Rodt, B. I. s. 210, 211.

something even not unheroic, pierce through the hideous incrustation.

His profligacy and his fierceness, kept in abeyance during Charles's visit to the landgraviate, broke out, they tell us, with all the more virulence after the latter's departure.[47] He had obtained from the duke a small reënforcement of troops, and now openly boasted that he would no longer hear of opposition or censure. "Henceforth," he raved, "I am lord, emperor, pope!"[48] Later in the same month he celebrated his second nuptials with a Suabian countess, a woman of high birth and of breeding suitable to her rank. Contributions were levied to defray the expenses; a great company composed of both sexes was collected and entertained with a succession of orgies too frightfully and unutterably indecent to be paralleled by any abominations imagined or enacted outside the walls of a convent.[49] What too often, in

[47] It is reported as among his ordinary habits that "wo er ein hübsche jungfrau sach die muste man jm bringen es were jr liebe oder leydt; . . . und wan vatter und muter jm soliches nit wolten gestatten so liesse er sy töten (!) . . . So er in ein stat kam, so schicket er nach den jungen hübschen burgerin die in der stat waren die mustent ouch komen es were jn lieb oder leit, sie mustent sich ouch nacket ussziehen, und mustent vor jm nacket tanzen." Königshoven, s. 370.

[48] Edlibach, &c.

[49] M. Gachard, the only critic whose practised and scrutinizing glance has questioned the evidence on this subject, remarks, in reference to the story told by M. de Barante, on the authority of Specklin, of the "femmes mises nues en leur couvrant la tête, pour voir si les maris les reconnaîtront."—"Nous ne pourrions croire à de telles infamies, que si nous les voyions attestées par des témoinages irrécusables. Les chroniquers ne sont pas toujours exempts d'exagération; il faut quelquefois se defier de leur récits." The peculiar propriety of this caution, which no one has hitherto heeded, in the present instance, will be seen when we come to notice the origin of Hagenbach's unpopularity.

those days, went on inside such walls we know on good and abundant testimony.[50] Nor should it be forgotten that not only were these holy places desecrated by scenes that would have shamed a brothel, but they were the repositories of tales and traditions the rehearsal of which might have set blushes on the cheeks of a libertine.[51] Is the present story a mere invention from the same prolific source? At all events the pens that revel in the transcription of the beastly details, sparing no grossness either of language or idea, were professedly pointed in the service of religion;[52] the spectators cited by the authors as their informants were brother ecclesiastics;[53] not only nobles, but burgomasters and other civic functionaries, prelates and other dignitaries of the Church, are reported as present; and the festivities, whatever their nature, proved apparently to the taste of these

[50] Nothing need be said as to the convents of Italy at this period. That those of Germany were not much better may be proved from such examples as the following. The Bohemian tourists from whom we have before quoted, when relating their passage through Neuss, — a town in the electorate of Cologne of which we shall have much to say hereafter, — describe the inmates of the great religious houses for which the place was famous, as practising the most open licentiousness. Every nun had her chosen gallant, with whom she went publicly about. See the Ritter-, Hof-, und Pilger-Reise, 1465–1467.

[51] These were the storehouses drawn from, with moderation no doubt, by Rabelais, Boccaccio, and similar *raconteurs*.

[52] Königshoven, Knebel, Specklin, and other narrators, were priests or monks at Strasburg and Basel.

[53] Knebel, whose description, entirely different from others, is at the same time the most indecent, — so indecent that the German translator not only excludes it from the text, but curtails (though on what principle we are unable to perceive) the passages from the original Latin which he gives in an appendix, — says he had the particulars from certain chaplains and ecclesiastical prothonotaries who were eye-witnesses.

sober and illustrious guests, since we find that the invitations — some of which, politely and decorously worded, are still extant in Hagenbach's own handwriting — were issued afresh after a short interval, and were again accepted.[54]

We do not desire, for the sake of sparing criticism or avoiding discussion, to perplex the reader with puzzles. That Hagenbach was a man of corrupt morals we shall not deny or pretend to doubt. What there was in him of finer and gentler feeling lay hidden beneath the coarse manners and fiery passions of a Rhine knight of the 15th century, undiscernible by any but a friendly eye until it glimmered forth starlike through the folding shadows of death. But, in view of certain facts, we may be permitted to retain our self-possession, the attitude of cool and dispassionate inquirers, even when the din of invective, caught up and reproduced from time to time, finds or renders us incapable of making a reply. We cannot forget the total silence of the chroniclers on matters of greater moment. We cannot forget that Hagenbach's vigor and ability in putting down and keeping under the distractions and confusions of a constitutional anarchy — his sole title to the confidence of a sovereign in whose mind, with all its faults, the ideas of "order" and "justice" were always present and generally uppermost, and no ill-judged favoritism ever found a lodgment — had been certified by the unanimous and unimpeachable admissions of the

[54] Stöber, Neuj. Stollen, 1850, s. 15, 16. — Rodt, B. I. s. 214. — Schreiber, s. 22. — Knebel, s. 36, 40.

Swiss cantons. He had made "a new land" of Alsace — that old Alsace, so greatly needing to be made new — What shall we say to this? What but that this alone would go far to explain the clamor of which he was the object? No doubt his aptitude for the task imposed upon him lay not in any fine adroitness or special administrative capacity, but in the same qualities he had manifested in former scenes of action — in the bold promptness and ardor with which, in defiance of custom, he had planted his artillery in open daylight, himself holding the bridle of the leading horse, before the walls of Dinant; — in the simple, dog-like obedience to the commands or caprices of his proper master, and indifference to whatever stood in the way of their execution, with which he had caught the young Flemish nobles in the streets of Bruges and clipped off their dainty lovelocks. In the confused jumble of anecdotes that forms the chief substitute for the full and authoritative sources of information from which we should desire to draw, the image that unfolds itself is not that of a crafty or bloodthirsty disposition, — often as these epithets are used in garnishing the narration, — but that of a sharp-sighted, keen-scented, swift-running nature, guided only by instinct, impatient of plausibilities, easily inflamed by contradiction; not a feline or a vulpine nature, as the chroniclers would make it, but a canine one, with quick perceptions and eager appetencies, pugnacious, loud in quarrel, but fearless, trusty, and sagacious. A long, lean figure, a gaunt countenance deeply caved between the jaw-bones, restless, searching, blood-shot eyes, indicated his temperament.[55] A sheep-dog he, with the qualities proper to the race — put in charge, let it not be forgotten, of a flock little accustomed to be folded, worried from time immemorial by packs of hungry wolves. That his bark was fierce, that he was ready to fly at any interloper real or supposed, may be admitted. Yet here, too, we have good reasons for questioning the accuracy of the reports — for suspecting them not only of exaggerations, but of more faulty suppressions. If the skin of some persons be morbidly sensitive, the faculty of others lies in the quiet application of irritants. It has been already seen how his pretended offences against the Swiss dwindled away before a direct inquiry; and from what has since been disclosed of the secret and long-continued practices of the smooth-faced Diesbachs and their associates at Berne, we may guess whether the insults complained of by them had or had not been designedly provoked. Erelong, too, it will be seen what specific charges his Austrian and Alsatian enemies were able to adduce against his public rule and private conduct, and how these charges were supported. On the whole, therefore, if unable to offer a direct contradiction to the scandalous and declamatory statements of the chroniclers, we may at least waive a mute gesture of dissent. The groans and maledictions of a persecuted people are sacred through all time; but there have

[55] This, the only description we have been able to find of his personal appearance, is taken from the Vita SS. Gervasii et Prothasii, Argentine, 1506.

been noises, loud and general enough in their day, of which the echo need not absolutely deafen or appall us, after the lapse of centuries.

The truth is, these chroniclers — monks and municipal scribes at Basel and Strasburg — recorded simply from day to day, without personal cognizance or investigation, whatever rumors had currency and a special interest in their own localities. The animus, the excessive acrimony, with which they wrote, is the faithful reflex of a popular sentiment which found its usual concomitants and supports in wholesale lying and a boundless credulity. The free cities of the Rhineland had from the first looked askance at the establishment of the Burgundian dominion in their vicinity. Their jealousy was natural, and no doubt to some extent well founded. But it was quite independent of the manner in which that dominion was exercised. No government so situated could have borne the scrutiny of such neighbors. Had Hagenbach been pure as snow, he should not have escaped calumny. Nevertheless, this feeling first acquired its peculiar intensity when the negotiations between Charles and the emperor had begun to attract public attention. For in those towns which called themselves "imperial" as well as "free," the emperor was the primary and abiding object of distrust;[56] and it was his projected partnership with Frederick that had first inflamed their suspicions in regard to the duke of Burgundy. Then it was that they had be-

[56] This disposition towards Frederick was sufficiently manifested during his passage through the Rhineland in 1473.

gun to agitate for the redemption of Alsace, to sympathize with its down-trodden inhabitants, to appreciate the mild virtues of the once hated and contemned Sigismund. It is a curious fact, and one which has been singularly overlooked, that in the writings to which we are constantly referred for the particulars of Hagenbach's administration, the longer portion of it is a complete blank. The stories told to his disadvantage, such at least as have a time and place assigned to them, date from the year 1473 — that "hot summer" when all was in ferment and flame, when many things were set blazing besides the forests, and many things were turned acid besides the wine — the year of the interview at Trèves, and of the hubbub and alarm throughout the Rhineland, anticipative of as well as consequent upon it.[57] Throughout the four previous years no commotions had been witnessed, no utterances of popular discontent had been heard, in Alsace.[58] The Swiss traders, in their frequent visits, had found the country in a condition that contrasted with all their past experience — industry flourishing, justice regularly and impartially administered, and tranquillity every where prevailing. How then, it may be asked, are we to account for the combination and general rising by which the Burgundian government,

[57] As usual at periods of excitement, new chronicles are found starting from this date. Knebel, for example, begins his diary *in mediis rebus* with the year 1473. How little attention Hagenbach's career had previously attracted may be judged from the fact that Königshoven and other writers suppose his whole administration to have extended over only three years.

[58] The revolt at Thann did not occur till 1473. How long previously the tax which occasioned it had been established we are not informed.

unprovided for such an emergency, was brought to a sudden standstill? We do not, however, deny that the yoke was distasteful to those who bore it; we seek only to determine with exactitude why and where it galled them, and from what impulse it was shaken off. Devoutly believing in the "sacred right of revolution," we may still discriminate between the various causes that have given birth to revolutions. Submitting with proper deference to the "will of the majority," we may still recognize the fact that the larger the majority, the more complex have been the motives and the influences at work, and the greater is the difficulty of discovering any single and adequate principle of agreement or of action. The most popular revolution in English history, that which was the most easily accomplished, that in which the nation was most nearly unanimous, was the overthrow of the Protectorate, and the restoration of the Stuarts. The once plausible explanation of that reaction — the grinding tyranny of Cromwell — is now generally abandoned.[59] The present case offers not indeed a parallel, but some analogies to that.

Let all the circumstances be considered. The Burgundian government had no roots in the soil. It had not grown there from the seed; it had been transplanted thither, and that but recently. No man owed it love or reverence because his forefathers had helped to rear it or had sat beneath its shade. No man was even led to expect that it would afford shel-

[59] Thanks to the profound insight of the greatest of England's prose writers, the wisest and most influential of modern thinkers.

ter to his descendants. It had been placed there, not with the active concurrence, but with the mere passive acquiescence, of the living generation. Who, then, but would grudge any trouble in the cultivation of it? Who would not resent any inconvenience or encroachment from it? Who would think himself bound to speak gratefully of the fruit it yielded? A new, strange, temporary rule could have few hearty friends: a strict, just, orderly rule must have many bitter enemies. The towns were called upon to contribute to the support, the nobles were compelled to endure the curb, not of an ancient and legitimate authority, but of one which was acting merely as its *locum tenens.* True, there had been little real attachment to the Austrian prince. There had been no complaints, no regrets, no tender leave-taking, at his departure. But after years of absence and oblivion, nothing was easier than to invest him with a sentimental interest, to construct out of the commonplace materials at hand an affecting interlude, a *volks-drama,* with Sigismund as its hero. He was the rightful lord, the true heir, whose misfortunes had resulted from the failings incidental to a generous nature, and whose heart was touched with sorrow and compunction at the sufferings he had thus entailed upon his old tenants and servants.[60] His wars with the Swiss,

[60] "Die armen leüt nit mehr möchten erleiden, und schickten zu hertzog Sygmundt von Osterich gohn Yszbruch, und clagten ihm gröszlichen, . . . und enttbotten do seiner fürstlichen gnadt, das er in zu hülff keme, seytte mol er ihr rechter herr were. Do ward hertzog Sygmundt sehr erbarmet, . . . und vereiniget sich mit denn eydtgnossen," &c. Straszburgische Archiv-Chronik, Code hist. et dip.

which had finally reduced him to such painful extremities, had been altogether repugnant to his own amiable, pacific, and unambitious disposition, forced upon him by circumstances and bad advisers.[61] Charles, on the other hand, was the alien creditor, the heartless mortgagee, who had taken advantage of his necessities, had sought by involving him in the meshes of legal chicanery to rob him of his patrimony, and had even striven to embroil him still further with his hereditary enemies. Intent upon new schemes of gain and aggrandizement, he had left Alsace to the mercies of a tyrannical steward, the minor villain of the piece, in whom the vices of his principal were mixed with others still more odious, whose cruelty and craft had no false lustre, no redeeming trait. Could a people so commiserated remain insensible to its grievances,[62] or, when a mode of relief was pointed out, refuse to embrace it? The nobles, with their natural yearnings for riot and misrule, pining under enforced habits of quiet and subordination, were ready, with few exceptions, at a sign from Austria, to throw off their newly-sworn allegiance to Burgundy. The towns, with their republican notions of local independence, their instinctive

tom. i. deuxième partie, pp. 185, 186. And to the same effect, Stettler, Edlibach, &c.

[61] Bussierre, p. 10. — See also the contemporary *volks-lied* in Schilling, s. 120.

[62] "Seufzte alles Volk im Sundgau und Elsass und schrie zum Himmel: 'wann werden wir befreit! wann wird uns Gott Gnade schenken, dass er uns aus dieser höllischen Tyrannei des burgundischen Herzogs und des fluchwürdigen Peters von Hagenbach erlöst und wir wieder Unterthanen unseres Hernn Siegismund, des Herzog von Oestreich sein könnten.'" Knebel, 1ste Abth. s. 46.

hostility to every thing that savored of a strong and centralized authority, were not less amenable to the influence of the free cities, which they looked up to as models, as the grand embodiments of all their own ideas and aspirations. When, therefore, the glints and sparkles began to fly from the now rapidly revolving wheels of intrigue in the busy factories of Basel, Strasburg, and Berne, — when it was blazed abroad that Sigismund, out of pure compassion for his former subjects, had determined to reclaim his rights;[63] that his neighbors, from the like sympathetic motives, were to provide him with the means of discharging his liabilities; that, to insure success, he had consented to bury his old antipathies and place himself under the patronage of the Swiss;[64] that on these foundations a great league was being reared under

[63] "Die wil nun die lantschaft anders gehalten ward den sy aber verpfent wz, ward der hertzog von östrich bewegt über sinne armen lütt widerumm losung zu thun." Edlibach, s. 139.

[64] "Als nun der genant Fürst von Oesterrich, dis alles geriett erschowen, und innen werden, das alles, so ihm der Hertzog von Burgunn, zugeseit und verschrieben hat, unwarhafft was, und das auch er die armen Lüht als hartiglichen beschwert, . . . do wart er als ein frommer Fürst zu Miltigkeit bewegt, . . . und begonde da ze þetrachten, nit nützers noch bessers sin, dann das er mit den Eidgnossen, und sy mit ihm in Friden und Richtung kemend." Diebold Schilling, s. 107.

These and similar representations, put forth with that consummate art which has all the appearance of artlessness, have so pervaded the whole field of inquiry that it demands a searching examination and a vigorous effort to disentangle one's self from the meshes. Popular errors in regard to the direct transactions between the duke of Burgundy and other parties have been to some extent and in some quarters dissipated by recent revelations. But no defence has been offered for Peter von Hagenbach — Schreiber's apology, though suggested by a just instinct, containing no refutation of the common falsehoods and no elucidation of their origin.

the benign auspices of France, — what wonder if the effect was universal and electric?

Hagenbach had not been blind to what was going on, or tardy in taking such precautions as were practicable with the scanty means at his disposal. He had but a handful of troops, — two thousand at the outside, — the major part of them Germans, recently recruited and of doubtful fidelity. Leaving a small garrison at Thann, he swept together his remaining force, and threw himself into Breisach, — "Old Breisach," across the Rhine, — the so-called "key of Germany," the key at all events of Hagenbach's position, the point where it was most exposed, yet most defensible.[65] Here he began to provision and fortify. His enemies in the free cities were not a little disconcerted by this manœuvre.[66] Hitherto there had been no overt act on their part; but they had laid their plans, the execution being only suspended until the signal should be given by the negotiators at Constance. These plans might be disarranged were Hagenbach allowed to complete his preparations — to make all secure while he summoned his master to the rescue. There was a consequent disposition in some quarters to precipitate matters. A surprise was planned in concert with the disaffected inhabitants of Breisach; and an expedition was sent out, on the night of the 13th of March, from the neighboring town of Freiburg, — Freiburg in the Breisgau, — an Austrian place,

[65] Stettler, B. I. s. 214, 215.

[66] See the correspondence between the allied towns in the Urkundenbuch der Stadt Freiburg, B. II. 2te Abth. s. 531 et al.

which had served of late as a centre of communication for the conspirators.[67] But over haste brought with it the usual untoward accidents. Every thing went wrong; the attempt was abandoned, and having been abandoned it was of course denied or repudiated on all sides.[68] Sigismund, to whom a formal complaint was addressed, indulged himself in more than his due quota of falsehoods, ending with the customary asseverations of his friendship for Charles and his resolution to stand by the alliance.[69] Two days before the message was delivered he had signed, though not sent, his letters renouncing the alliance.

Having thus closed and fastened the door at which the prowler had proposed to break in, Hagenbach betook himself, as before mentioned, to the duke of Burgundy, in Lorraine. He went to represent the danger and procure succors proportioned to its magnitude and urgency. If Charles were minded to hold Alsace, let him send forward at once all the forces within his reach, and lose no time in collecting more. The application was rejected. Troops were sent into Franche Comté, to be distributed along the frontier, but no direct assistance was granted in this time of extremity. For what reason? Not — we may safely assert — for that which was assigned by the muddle-headed newsmongers in the Rhineland,

[67] Rodt, B. I. s. 216.

[68] Conf. Knebel, 1ste Abth. s. 45 et al., and consolatory letters on the failure from Strasburg and Berne in the Urkundenbuch der Stadt Freiburg, B. II. 2te Abth. s. 530, 531.

[69] See the letter of Hagenbach giving an account of the messages sent him by Sigismund, in Schreiber, s. 41, 42.

whose knowledge of affairs abroad seems to have been on a par with their veracity. The dethroned and imprisoned duke of Gueldres had *not* made his escape into France; consequently, he was *not* leading a French army to invade the Netherlands; consequently Charles was *not* hurrying homewards in trepidation on that account.[70] His motives were at least germane to the matter, and may be deduced from his declarations and line of conduct throughout. If nothing more were intended than the legal redemption of Alsace, he had no occasion, for he had no purpose, to make resistance. That an illegal and forcible dispossession was intended he could not believe. No such step, he felt assured, would be ventured upon without the concurrence of the Swiss; and from the Swiss he had just received the most explicit and emphatic disclaimers of any hostile sentiment or project. The protestations of Austria he had learned to estimate at their true value; but the honesty of the Confederates was in general little liable to suspicion, and in the present instance their policy — that traditional policy to which they had been constant under all temptations — offered an additional voucher for their honesty. It would afford a doubtful commentary on his own professions, it could only expose him to fresh misconstructions, it might plunge him into that gulf which he had so sedulously and resolutely shunned, were he at this delicate conjuncture to send an army into Alsace.

[70] Knebel, 1ste Abth. s. 46.

Let Hagenbach go back to his post, maintaining his accustomed watchfulness, but doing and saying nothing that could furnish the enemies of Burgundy with the handle for which they were so eagerly seeking and without which their machinations would come to nought.

He went back — downcast, chopfallen; like one who has met with a rebuff where he expected approval; like one who, closely pursued, arrives at a port of refuge, but sees himself suddenly shut out.[71] His disappointment and dejection were a source of infinite glee to the malicious onlookers. But they had never more maligned him than in ascribing this momentary depression to craven fears for his own safety. Having left his wife at a castle in Lorraine, he felt no anxiety or chagrin but such as arose out of solicitude for his trust. Nor were his faculties benumbed by the hopelessness of his situation. His motto was still "I spy!" his instinct was as sharp, his heart as courageous, as ever. Starting away from Breisach with a picked band at his heels, he set out on a tour of inspection. The Forest Towns along the Rhine frontier of Switzerland, forewarned and instigated from Berne,[72] refused him entrance. After some vain attempts in this quarter, he proceeded on the 6th of April to Ensisheim. Here too he found the gates

[71] "Viele, die er früher fluchend von sich gestossen, hört er bereits geduldig an, denn er fürchtet jene evangelische Wahrheit: die Thüre ist zugeschlossen! — Es bangt ihm, es möchten ihm alle Wege vermacht werden, und er müste zu den Ausgeschlossenen gehören müssen." Knebel, s. 48. We have chosen a less pious but more natural illustration.

[72] Urkundenbuch der Stadt Freiburg, ubi supra.

closed and guards stationed in anticipation of his coming. Leaving his troops at a little distance he went forward and demanded entrance. Admitted within the outer gate he stopped in front of the inner one to parley with the watch. "What fool's work is this you are carrying on?" he asked. "Have you forgotten that it rests with me, on behalf of the duke of Burgundy, to provide for your defence?" The guard, suspicious of a ruse, bade him either enter or depart, and prepared to close the gates. Striding in, he went straight to the market-place in front of the church, where he found the citizens under arms and the banner of Austria displayed. After a mute survey of the scene, he accosted the principal persons present, and inquired the object of their assemblage. "The safety of the town," was the curt explanation vouchsafed. Turning away with affected unconcern, he bent his steps towards the citadel, regardless of the observation of a party sent in pursuit. On the way he was met by the officer whom he had left in charge, who reported that the keys had been taken from him and the drawbridge removed. Having put some questions and reconnoitred for himself, Hagenbach retraced his steps. As he again passed through the square, he called out derisively, "Keep good watch, friends!" A night or two after he returned and attempted to carry the place by escalade; but his men, after mounting the walls, were overwhelmed by numbers and forced back with heavy loss.[73]

[73] Knebel, s. 52–54.—Urkundenbuch der Stadt Freiburg, B. II. 2te Abth. s. 538–540.

Meanwhile the excitement in the Rhineland had risen to the highest pitch, and there was hot galloping by night as well as day between the allied towns. Strasburg, whose spies had dogged the duke of Burgundy in his march through Lorraine to Luxembourg, reported his movements, his preparations, and his intentions. One story contradicted another; but all breathed the same spirit and served the same purpose. Basel at length announced the conclusion of the treaty so impatiently awaited and the steps about to be taken by Sigismund. From Berne came confirmatory tidings, with the wished-for assurances and promises in its own name and in that of its sister cantons. Mutual congratulations, exhortations, admonitions, were exchanged on all sides.[74] Troops were got ready for service, and a camp was formed in the neighborhood of Freiburg. The country people around Breisach were encouraged in refusing Hagenbach's requisitions for supplies. Officers in the Burgundian service and persons friendly to the Burgundian rule were entrapped, maltreated, and in some instances put to death. Appeals were brought to Hagenbach; but he, powerless to afford redress and already baited beyond endurance, listened with impatience or turned his rage upon the supplicants. "What matters it?" he exclaimed. "My lord of Burgundy leads thirty or forty thousand men to battle, and leaves perchance six thousand on the

[74] Correspondence in the Urkundenbuch der Stadt Freiburg, B. II. 2te Abth. s. 535–541. — Rodt, B. I. s. 216–219.

field; and thou comest whining about *one!* Go help thyself!"[75]

Yes, these were times when each must help himself. For Hagenbach there was no help or hope of help. Flight would have been easy; but he had no thought of flying. He thought only of a desperate defence, of standing at bay and meeting death sword in hand, of baffling as long as possible the efforts of his assailants, and making them pay dearly for their triumph. Such was not, however, the end reserved for him. He was to pass through a sharper trial, through hotter and more purifying flames. He had conceived, among other measures, a plan for converting Breisach into an island, by means of a canal, or wet ditch, to be connected at each of its extremities with the Rhine.[76] On the 10th of April, Easter day, he made proclamation of his intention, and ordered that, on the following morning, the inhabitants, male and female, should assemble to labor in the trenches. He trusted to his armed force, as well as to his own imperious will, for compelling the obedience of a hostile population. But his announcement that the German foot-soldiers were to take part in the work, while the foreigners, of whom they were bitterly jealous, would be reserved for military duty, raised a mutinous spirit among the former. The whole town was soon in a tumult, and the wildest bruits were greedily credited. The object of the scheme was said to be a general massacre: while the young and the helpless were butchered within the

[75] Knebel, s. 43. [76] Stettler, B. I. s. 215.

walls, the waters of the river would be let loose on those who had gone forth. Certain nobles who were present strove to allay this absurd alarm, and to restore quiet. They wished, apparently, to consummate the revolution without the disorders of a popular outbreak. They were in part successful. No conflict took place; but after nightfall the Burgundian troops, few in number, taken unawares, and little inclined to offer a hopeless resistance, were disarmed and driven from the town. At dawn the citizens again assembled and raised the Austrian standard. The seizure of Hagenbach was clamorously demanded; the nobles, exempt from the passions of the populace and susceptible to scruples which the populace was incapable of feeling, uttered a vigorous remonstrance. It would be derogatory to the honor of the prince whose insignia now waved over the place, were violence offered to the representative of the sovereign with whom he had been so closely connected, whose friend and client he had so long professed himself, and against whom, even yet, he had put forth no hostile declaration. In the midst of the dispute, a rush was made towards the burgomaster's house, where Hagenbach had fixed his residence. He was soon in the hands of the mob; but again the nobles interfered, and it was finally agreed that he should be suffered to remain at large in his present quarters on passing his word that he would make no attempt to escape. As an additional precaution, but also with the view of averting any further outrage, a guard of twelve persons, comprising an equal number of nobles, citizens, and soldiers, was posted in and around the building.[77]

Thus strangely and abruptly the crisis had been brought to a conclusion. Environed by foes, abandoned by the master to whom he had looked wistfully for aid, Hagenbach had struggled, vainly but defiantly, until the caving soil no longer afforded him a footing. His conduct at this period has seemed to us capable of a different interpretation from that which was put upon it by inimical contemporary narrators. It denoted, in their view, the foaming desperation of a curse-laden, terror-stricken, but hardened and impenitent wretch, clutching frantically at the empty air while he sinks into the abyss that has opened to swallow him.[78] But it was the vocation of these artists, or of those from whom they copied, to minister to malignant passions and to satisfy a voracious curiosity. Not an actual mortal, but an ideal demon, was to be depicted—fit object for the vengeance and execrations of all human kind. The likeness would have been deemed imperfect if sacrilege and impiety had not been superadded to a cynical sensuality and an untamable ferocity. Accordingly, in the delineation of the final scenes, the pencil is steeped in the blackest colors, and the murky flames of opening hell alone

[77] In this account, which differs much from the ordinary versions, we have followed almost exclusively the letter addressed by an eye-witness, Dr. Johann von Durlach, the "stadtschreiber" of Breisach, to his friend Knebel at Basel. See Knebel, s. 56, 57.

[78] "So zieht dieser Fluchbeladene in seiner Wuth durchs Land, nicht wissend, was er anfangen soll, er wird zuletzt in sein eigenes Schwert stürzen!" Knebel, s. 51 et al., and similar passages in Schilling and other writers.

irradiate the canvas. Hagenbach is represented as crowning his career of infamy by the violation of nuns and the profanation of churches; as scaring priests from the altars and horrifying the worshippers by libidinous interruptions of the adorable mysteries; as mocking at the voice of reproof, and driving away the shuddering remonstrants with the audacious announcement, "While I live I will do whatever pleases me; when I am dead the devil may have both body and soul!"[79]

Happily, at this point, we emerge from the mists, if not of prejudice and rancor, yet of ignorance and lying rumor. Hagenbach had now fallen into the hands of his enemies. The monster had been caught and caged, and was henceforth to be exposed to the common gaze. His qualities and disposition might be as little comprehended as they had before been; but the treatment he underwent and the demeanor he exhibited would be matters of public knowledge and authentic record.

In the cities the first tumult of joy to which the tidings gave rise was succeeded by a fluttering of alarm lest the prey so opportunely captured but so insecurely guarded, should again get loose or be suddenly snatched away. The reputed cunning of Hagenbach himself, the doubtful sentiments of some among his jailers, above all the unstable character and sinuous policy of the Austrian prince, formed the

[79] Ibid. s. 49, 50, 57, et al.—"'Ohoho omnia quecunq. michi occurrunt animo que possum facere faciam quia postq. moriar dyabolus recipiet meum corpus et animam.' Sich, welch schreckliche Antwort!"

grounds of apprehension. Warnings to this effect were sent from Strasburg and Basel. They entreated that more efficient steps should be taken for the safe-keeping of the prisoner, representing it as a matter of the utmost importance that he should be made to suffer the full penalty of his misdeeds. The authorities of Strasburg were especially anxious lest delays should be allowed which might give an opportunity for the duke of Burgundy to interpose by an embassy or other means of negotiation. This, as they wrote, would be embarrassing in many ways.[80] So alive to the chances of rescue or escape were those who had taken no ostensible part in the pursuit! So keen was the thirst for vengeance in those by whom no wrong had been sustained, no complaint preferred! So fearful of a pacific issue, so urgent for extreme measures, were those who had hitherto affected merely a secondary and sympathetic interest in the quarrel! Could any thing more plainly indicate the scope and spirit of the whole transaction — its source in the combinations of a political intrigue, its intended effect in the violent and definitive rupture of an obnoxious alliance?

Already, on the day following his arrest, Hagenbach, in contempt of the agreement made at the time, had been bound with cords. Three days later,

[80] "Besorgen wir, das er durch sin listigkeit es daran bringe, das er vss Brysach gelassen werde, oder aber mit seinen behenden fründen sich mit worten vffhalte, bitz das der Hertzog von Burgund, durch botschafft oder geschrifft trefflich anzöygung tüge inen liddig zu lassen. Solt nu das geschehen, das wer swere in manigerley wege." Urkundenbuch der Stadt Freiburg, B. II. 2te Abth. s. 541, 542.

when these messages were received, he was removed to a dungeon in the public prison, his body was loaded with chains, his wrists were secured with handcuffs, and his legs set in the stocks.[81] Three strong men were appointed to watch him day and night. Unless Satan should come in person to release him, he might now be considered safe. Further action was therefore suspended until the arrival of Sigismund, whose participation was necessary, not only as a means of giving some shadow of legality to the proceedings, but in order that he might be debarred from hereafter disavowing his own responsibility for the acts of his subjects and allies, or seeking to emancipate himself from the inevitable consequences. From Constance, whither he had gone during the sitting of the conference, the Austrian prince had passed into the Helvetian territory, with the object of displaying his confidence in the Swiss and giving a visible proof of the change in his sentiments towards them. His visit seems, however, to have awakened but a faint enthusiasm; and he speedily quitted a soil where his presence had probably tended to revive, rather than efface, ancient and bitter recollections. On the 20th of April he reached Basel. Here he was greeted as a deliverer and a saviour by the magistrates with fulsome addresses, by the rabble in the streets with a doggerel parody on the hymns chanted during the Easter festival:—

"Christ is arisen, the landvogt is in prison;
Let us all rejoice, Sigismund is our choice, Kyrie eleison.

[81] Knebel, s. 57.

Had he not been snared, evil had it fared ;
But now that he is ta'en, his craft is all in vain, Kyrie eleison."

Having appointed a new governor and taken other measures for the reëstablishment of his authority in Alsace, he proceeded to Breisach, instituted a commission for the trial of Hagenbach, and being then no longer wanted, retired to Freiburg to spend the ensuing weeks, with general approbation, in a round of convivial and amatory pleasures.[82]

The first step in the pretended judicial inquiry now set on foot was to subject the prisoner to the torture. The examination, conducted by deputies from the allied cities, shows how little the alleged tyranny of Hagenbach had to do with the agitation which led to his fall, and confirms the view we have already presented in regard to its real origin. Not the acts of the accused himself, but the plans and purposes of his master,—not the mode in which the government of Alsace had been carried on, but the secrets of the Austro-Burgundian alliance,—formed the chief subject of investigation.[83] Wonderful revelations seem to have been anticipated. All the communications and transactions between the two houses, from the original transfer of Alsace down to the abortive conferences at Trèves, were believed to have had but one motive and one aim. The whole Rhineland was to have been handed over piecemeal or entire to the duke of Burgundy, in order that its free communities

[82] Schreiber; Knebel; Rodt; Schilling; &c.

[83] Knebel, s. 59, 61, et al.

might be enslaved and an imperial despotism planted. It cannot be denied that the tendencies of the scheme which had been actually proposed and so nearly accomplished were such as to give some color to these ideas. The main object of that scheme had been to secure a firmer support for the supreme authority; and if this result were attained, there must be a corresponding decline of all inferior pretensions and conflicting rights. Nor can we wonder that the cities, although as members of the empire they might join in the general lamentations over its disorganized condition and in the periodical demands for its reform, should have failed to perceive that their own immunities, so validly intrenched and so regularly exercised, constituted, for this very reason, an impediment even more insuperable than the ambition of the princes or the lawlessness of the nobles. They were not to blame for resisting any project which would have the effect of exposing institutions founded and reared, with painful efforts, amid the convulsions of past ages, to the shock and destructive forces of a reorganization. Yet the narrow, violent, and unscrupulous spirit which characterized their course was itself an evidence of the unfitness of the municipal system to become the sole and sufficient pillar of a national polity. If the design which they suspected had indeed been entertained from the first, it was obvious that Sigismund must be regarded as its author. It was he who had first made application to Charles, and who had initiated the proposals of the emperor. It was therefore against him that the storm should have been directed, and from him that information should have been extorted. Frederick also was guilty, either as a principal or an accessory. It was, however, more convenient, under existing circumstances, to consider Sigismund as an irresponsible instrument, and Frederick as himself an intended victim, of the plot. The projectors would no doubt be found among the nobles of the Rhineland, the natural enemies and constant assailants of civic independence. They, from the motives by which they were commonly swayed, had sought the coöperation of the duke of Burgundy, which he, with similar sentiments and from still stronger inducements, had readily promised. Hagenbach, as the confidant and factotum of his master, the principal medium in negotiating the arrangement and the agent selected to carry it into effect, must be acquainted with the parties and conversant with all the details; and such disclosures as he might make would be all the more precious and convincing that they had been wrung from unwilling lips — distilled, drop by drop, by a process the most searching and eliminative.

Basel, with great alacrity, supplied the necessary apparatus, as well as a qualified and practised manipulator. From lack of accommodation in the prison, the torture-chamber was prepared in a building called "the Water Tower," at the opposite side of the town. On the morning of the 5th of May, Hagenbach was brought from his cell. His condition testified to the adequacy of the arrangements for preventing his escape, and furnished a grateful opportunity for the infliction of fresh indignities. Being wholly unable to walk, he was laid on a wheelbarrow, and trundled along the streets, a stream of people of both sexes and of all ages running on either side, and showering him with insults and menaces. "Hagenbach, thou Judas! Thou cursed Judas! May God damn thee! May he punish thee a thousand years!" was screamed forth in chorus, with appropriate looks and gestures, by old and young, — the latter as brutal as the former, the former, we may safely conclude, as ignorant as the latter. Hagenbach smiled![84]

On reaching the tower, all who could force an entrance squeezed in, to feast their eyes upon a spectacle pleasing to devils and to men. After a series of questions had been put, Hagenbach, who had made no response, was stretched upon the rack, and the zealous tormentors put forth all their strength and skill in the performance of their fiendish task. For a long time the stoicism of the sufferer defied their utmost efforts, and occasioned a painful suspense in ears impatient for the music of groans and shrieks. When a half-smothered cry of "Death! death!" gave a partial intimation of the intensity of his agonies, the excitement of the spectators burst forth in loud vociferations. "Pull, pull! Finish him, finish him!"[85] they shouted, their passions inflamed to the point where a tantalized desire overleaps all bounds and seeks to annihilate its object. At last he was released, and again interrogated. But he still preserved an obstinate silence; and after an interval, the opera-

[84] Ibid. s. 61.— Schreiber, s. 50. [85] "Zieh', zieh'; expedire ihn!"

tion was repeated with the same vigor, but also with the same result. Twice more he endured, without flinching, the worst that it was found possible to inflict. It was not until, for the fifth time, his hands had been tied behind his back and the chains attached to his feet, that his constancy shrank from a further repetition of the fiery test. "Let me loose," he said, hoarsely; "I am ready to confess."[86] Yet his confession seems to have amounted to little in comparison with the expectations which had been raised. To all the accusations brought against himself he assented, indeed, without the slightest demur. But when required to implicate others as having suggested or devised the alliance between Sigismund and Charles, the only names he could be induced to mention were those of persons who had been openly concerned in the business, and most of whom were already deceased. Not a single fact respecting the negotiations with the emperor, in which Hagenbach had borne a principal part, is stated to have been drawn from him. Lest, however, the popular faith should be weakened by an unsatisfactory report, it was given out that astounding discoveries had been made, though, in respect to the details, a prudent reserve must be maintained.[87]

Monday, the 9th of May, was the day appointed for the public trial and its predetermined conclusion. An announcement to that effect brought together an immense multitude of people from the cities, towns, and villages of the surrounding territory. Large

[86] Knebel, s. 61, 65.

[87] Schreiber, s. 50, 51.—Knebel, s. 61.

scows, and other flat-bottomed vessels, with hundreds of passengers, ascended the Rhine from Strasburg, and descended it from Basel. "Every one," says the chronicler, "wished to be present at the death of the tyrant, traitor, sodomite, and ravisher."[88] At eight o'clock in the morning the court assembled in the open space fronting the mansion of the burgomaster. It was composed of twenty-seven members, including eight from Breisach, two from each of the allied places, and the residue from other towns, of which one only, it may be observed, had been subject to the Burgundian rule. Of the Swiss cantons, Berne alone was represented. In fact the Confederacy, in answer to an invitation, had declined to join in the prosecution.[89] The chief magistrate of Ensisheim was chosen to preside, Hermann von Eptingen, the newly-appointed Austrian landvogt, appeared as the nominal prosecutor, but deputed the duties of that office to Heinrich Iselin, one of the commissioners from Basel. The charges adduced were four. The first related to the executions at Thann, which were vaguely declared to have been in violation of justice and right; the second to certain changes recently made in the municipal government of Breisach, contrary to the charters which Hagenbach had sworn to respect. The third charge was a repetition, with several new embellishments, of the ridiculous story in regard to his murderous designs against the inhabit-

[88] Knebel, s. 62.

[89] "Die Eydtgenossen wolttent iñ an dem end nitt verclagen, die wil sy ze gericht ze sitzen da hin erbetten vnd erfordert, warend sy geneight in witter nit anzeclagen." Etterlin, s. 86.

ants of Breisach;[90] and the fourth contained some general averments, without the specification of a single act, as to the immoralities of his private life. On these grounds the accuser demanded that Hagenbach should be adjudged worthy of death, as a murderer, a perjurer, and a general transgressor of the laws both of God and man.

It would be idle to comment upon the flaws and absurdities which, even in that age, would have led any regularly constituted and impartial tribunal to reject an indictment so framed. What alone deserves notice is a circumstance tending to elucidate the question in pursuit of which we have entered into these details. Was the overthrow of the Burgundian government in Alsace, as history still continues to repeat, the work of a popular insurrection, provoked by oppression and tyranny?[91] or was it, as the duke of Burgundy himself asserted, brought about by a conspiracy, the product of extraneous causes and the vehicle of extraneous influences? In these formal and public allegations against Hagenbach, there is the same singular defect which we have found in the gossip of the chroniclers. They make no allusion to any of his acts during the four years preceding the first movement for the recovery of the mortgaged territory. Nay, they are mostly restricted to the

[90] According to this improved version, he had prepared a number of vessels, with holes bored and plugged, in which the women and children were to be all drowned after the men had been massacred by the soldiery.

[91] The prevalent notions on this subject will be found concisely stated in Henri Martin's Histoire de France (tom. vii. pp. 85–88), one of the latest and most authoritative works on French history.

short period which had elapsed since that movement had become active and successful. Could it be presumed that, after strict inquisition, no stronger or earlier pretext for the present proceedings had been discovered, we should be driven to the conclusion that Hagenbach's administration had been all but immaculate. It is, however, clear that no such inquisition had been made. To secure his condemnation an evil reputation had been manufactured for him by the easiest methods and from the readiest materials.

After Iselin had sat down a pause ensued. No one, apparently, had been empowered to speak on the prisoner's behalf; and he himself remained silent, either from physical debility, or more probably from contempt for a procedure so farcical. At length one of the judges, John Irmy, a citizen and merchant of Basel, and a man whose enlightened views and honorable character are known to us, not only from his conduct on the present occasion, but from letters of his own still extant,[92] volunteered to conduct the defence, while he craved the assistance of others better qualified for such a task. Having taken time for consultation, Irmy began by demurring, very naturally, though uselessly, to the competency of the

[92] These letters, written in the spring of 1475, while thoroughly patriotic in their tone, breathe a desire for peace which strongly contrasts with the rabid feeling then dominant at Basel. They were addressed to the duke of Milan, — with whom Irmy seems to have maintained confidential relations, — and have been published by the Baron Gingins-la-Sarra in the first volume of the Dépêches des Ambassadeurs Milanais sur les Campagnes de Charles-le-Hardi (Paris, 1858).

court to adjudicate upon the matter in hand. His client, as the servant of a foreign sovereign, was responsible to none save his master for acts done in his official capacity. He then proceeded to answer the accusations in detail, contenting himself, it would seem, with a simple denial of such as were manifestly and utterly fictitious, while he showed the insufficiency or disputed the substance of others, which had a basis of admitted fact. The persons executed at Thann were rebels against a lawful authority. Moreover the case had been previously referred, not only to the duke of Burgundy, but to the emperor, — then on his passage through the Rhineland, — and both had given their sanction to Hagenbach's course. His innovations at Breisach were justified by similar though less adequate explanations. As to his treatment of women, he had never employed force; he had purchased his gratifications; his habits in this particular had been no worse than those of many others. "It may be," said the advocate boldly, "that there are among the judges themselves some who have been guilty of the like misconduct, without thereby incurring or expecting to incur the forfeiture of life or freedom."[93]

The discussion thus opened was kept up for many hours. Iselin acknowledged his inability to rebut the pleas which had been set up for the defence, and retired from the arena.[94] His place was supplied by

[93] Knebel, s. 62–64. — Schreiber, s. 53–56.

[94] "Jetzt hielt . . . H. Iselin mit den Seinen über das Vorgetragene eine Berathung und kam mit dem Bemerken vor das Gericht zurück:

a less diffident or less scrupulous disputant, an officer of Sigismund's household, who took the ground that the emperor's warrant, if really obtained, afforded no justification for the proceedings at Thann. The head of the empire could never have intended that its laws and constitution should be violated; and it was an act of *lèze-majesté* on the part of the accused to demand that such a supposition should be entertained. But his evasions and subterfuges were now of no account. The only matters for the court to look at were his notorious offences and infamous life. Irmy requested that on these points evidence might be produced, declaring at the same time his own disbelief of much that had been alleged. "Proofs," it was answered, "were unnecessary; the facts were known to all. Nevertheless evidence should be produced —the strongest possible evidence; the declarations, namely, of the prisoner himself." "Declarations," retorted Irmy, "extracted by the rack!" "No," replied the unblushing orator; "they were made freely, while the prisoner was undergoing neither torture nor constraint;" and several witnesses were introduced to corroborate this statement by a narration of the circumstances—Irmy exclaiming loudly, but in vain, against the hollowness of such a distinction.[95]

No further testimony was brought forward, and the approach of night put an end to the discussion, as profitless on the one side as it was dishonest on

er sei zur Replik nicht geschicht. . . . Da ward ihm der weitere Vortrag erlassen." Knebel, s. 64.

[95] Ibid. s. 65, 66.

the other. The judges cast their votes, all, with the exception of Irmy, who had resumed his seat amongst them, concurring in a verdict of guilty and sentence of death. A herald advanced, and, standing in front of Hagenbach, pronounced his degradation from the order of the Knights of Saint George's Shield. Another functionary followed, who, with a glove of mail, struck him a blow upon the right cheek. It remained to decide in what manner the sentence should be carried into effect. When this question was put, the prisoner, apprehensive of a doom which would reflect disgrace, not upon his reputation as a man, — in regard to which he was justly if unconsciously careless, knowing that his life was about to be weighed in nicer scales than those of human opinion, — but upon his memory as a noble and a soldier, lost, for the first time, the firmness and composure which he had manifested throughout the day, and which had been rendered the more conspicuous by the contrasted spectacle of his enfeebled and emaciated frame. His head sank upon his chest. His red eyes, instead of their customary flashes of menace and derision, sent forth from their deep recesses a glance of timid supplication. "Have pity," he whispered, "and execute me with the sword!" Strange to say, the appeal was not disregarded. Each member of the court, as he was called upon by name, gave his voice that Hagenbach should die by the sword. When, however, it came to the turn of Irmy to vote, he refused to participate further. "Hagenbach," he said, "is not a private person, but a public functionary — the agent of a regular and rightful authority. The actions for which he has been condemned were dictated by his own sovereign and approved by our lord the emperor. This statement I have already offered, if a sufficient interval were granted, to substantiate by proof. Even now it is not too late to allow of an adjournment for that purpose."[96]

To this last and solemn protest there was no reply. Preparations were hastily made for finishing a business which had proved perhaps of a less agreeable nature than had been anticipated. A procession was formed; the judges, on horseback, leading the way. Hagenbach was dragged along in the centre of the cavalcade, a confessor striding beside him and holding up before his eyes the image of the crucified Redeemer. A long line of torches guided the march to a field outside the town. Seven executioners, from as many different towns, contested for the honor of officiating. The choice fell on the headsman of Colmar — "a short man, with a short sword." On the scaffold Hagenbach spoke a few words — words that may well have sounded strangely in the poisoned ears to which they were addressed. "I am not concerned," he said, "about my life; I have risked it often enough upon the field of battle. But I lament

[96] "Was Herr Peter von Hagenbach gethan hat das hat er nicht nach seinem eignen Willen gethan, sondern auf Befehl unsers Hernn des Kaisers und seines eignen erlauchten Herrn, des Herzogs von Burgund. Ich habe mich anerboten, das zu beweisen und dafür um eine gehörige Frist gebeten. Dieses kann jetzt noch beschlossen werden." Ibid. s. 68.

that the blood of many an honest man should be shed on my account. For assuredly my noble master, the duke of Burgundy, will not suffer this deed to go unavenged. But do you, in the name of God and of his Virgin Mother, forgive me" — *me*, who when the storm breaks shall be safely sheltered from its rage, — *me*, who, if not guilty as ye deem, know myself truly to be far from guiltless! "Pray for me, all!" He bequeathed his gold chain and his stud of sixteen horses to a religious house at Breisach, expressing to those near him a hope that this provision would be respected by Sigismund, from whose rapacious hand he probably foresaw that his legal representatives would be unable to rescue any portion of his slender property in the Sundgau. His hands were then tied; he knelt; and the short executioner of Colmar acquitted himself in a manner to justify the selection which had been made. The spectators, however, overawed by the singular deportment of the victim, made no demonstrations of applause.[97]

Nor was the impression thus produced as fleeting as might have been anticipated. It is true that subsequent events could not fail to deepen and perpetuate prejudices which had been called into existence with the express design of stirring up animosity and strife. Hagenbach is commonly remembered as "the

[97] Knebel; Schreiber; Rodt; Schilling; &c. — Schilling confesses that a general sympathy was excited by Hagenbach's Christian-like demeanor ("dadurch menig Mensch zu Erbermd mit ihm bewegt," s. 119); though he and other chroniclers, with their accustomed mendacity, twist the request for forgiveness — a request which would have been more properly construed as a granting of forgiveness — into a confession of the justice of the sentence.

Gessler of Alsace:" his evil fame has been handed down in chronicles and ballads still recited at the fireside of the burgher and the peasant; the mention of his name is still coupled with a malediction; and till very recently a hideous head, preserved in a glass case, was exhibited at Colmar as that of "the Burgundian tyrant." But there was an under-current of tradition which, though smaller and feebler, long ran counter to the popular belief. Among those who had witnessed, perhaps connived at, Hagenbach's trial and execution, were some who underwent a reaction of feeling which, strengthened perhaps by further inquiry, remained permanent with themselves and was communicated to their descendants. Care was taken that his remains should be decently interred in the burial-place of his family. A monumental statue was erected over his grave; and for many years afterwards the spot continued to be visited, on anniversaries and fête days, by those who came not to curse, but to pray—to offer not insults, but honors—to commemorate his death, as that, not of a detested criminal, but a benefactor and a martyr.[98]

It is stated by the writers, whose accounts of these occurrences we have been forced to accept, that the duke of Burgundy, when the report was brought to him, fell into a paroxysm of rage.[99] The authority is doubtless bad; but the statement itself must be acknowledged to have an appearance of probability.

[98] Schreiber; Barante; Rodt; &c.

[99] Schilling; Knebel; Königshoven; Archiv-Chronik; &c.

In fact, the murder of his officer — a murder rendered all the more revolting and atrocious by the affectation of legal forms under which it had been thinly veiled — was the crowning act in a series of outrages that might well have exasperated a temper more patient or phlegmatic than that of Charles.[100] To him the last words of the victim, however otherwise intended, must have sounded as a cry for vengeance. That cry was more plainly and imperiously uttered in the living voice of the victim's brother. Was he to reject the appeal? Not unless he was prepared to cover himself with dishonor, or had become keenly ambitious of a reputation for hypocrisy.

The course which he pursued was, however, far from satisfying those who had fired the match and calculated upon the explosion. Neither has it escaped the censure of those who still persist in believing that, if not the actual aggressor, Charles had all along cherished aggressive designs, and had only awaited an opportunity to put them in practice. "He undertook," they exclaim, "no retaliatory measures against either Austria or the Swiss Confederacy, but, with his

[100] The earliest, indeed the only, writer to appreciate that combination of circumstances which fully accounts for Charles's indignation is Ochs, the impartial historian of Basel. "Eine vertragswidrige Hinterlegung des Pfandschillings; eine einseitige Einnahme des verpfändeten Landes; die Begünstigung einer Empörung; die Gefangennehmung eines der ersten Beamten; die Errichtung eines illegalen Gerichts; die unbefugte Hinrichtung eines seiner Unterthanen, die einer Mordthat gleich sahe, und durch das Spiegelfechten einer vermeinten und überstossenen Criminalprocedur weit gefehlt, gerechtfertigt zu werden, nur beleidigender wurde; diess alles musste ihm also so viele Verletzungen des Völkerrechts, und schnöde Eingriffe in seine Hoheitsrechte und Würde vorkommen."

usual lack of reflection and of foresight, went on plunging into new bewilderments." [101] Nor is such criticism from such a quarter altogether unnatural; for had Charles, desisting from all other enterprises, eagerly seized upon the provocations offered, accepted the hostile league as an accomplished fact and most opportune event, and rushed into a war with all the parties composing it, he would not only have fulfilled the expectations of those who had been active in forming the alliance, but he would have furnished his modern assailants with a gratifying corroboration of their preconceived views, and enabled them to preserve some degree of consistency in their attacks under the special disadvantages of a copious and accurate knowledge of the circumstances. By refraining from any such step; by declining to open, and still striving to avoid, if possible, a conflict which he had no cause to embrace, and which, once begun, must be waged to desperation; by continuing his efforts so to widen and consolidate his power that the worst perils of the future might be silently overborne or confidently faced, — he imposed upon his enemies, as we shall see, more arduous labors than they had already undergone, while he left to the hostile criticism of a later day the difficult task of convicting him of intentions undiscoverable either from his acts or from his words, and reduced it to the necessity of accounting for this variance by a charge of undue

[101] Zellweger, s. 40. — Other modern writers have expressed themselves similarly.

slackness where he had been hitherto accused of exhibiting an obstinate rashness.

His conduct at this juncture, if it did not meet the views or harmonize with the theories of others, was at least accordant with the principles and the habits of his own career. The deep fires of his anger found a present vent in the reprisals to which, in that age, an injured state or sovereign commonly resorted. He seized the person and estates of the count of Montbelliard, a prince of the house of Würtemberg, who, though educated at the Burgundian court, had taken an active part in the negotiations between Sigismund and Louis.[102] He issued a proclamation interdicting all trade and intercourse between his own subjects and those of Austria and the allied cities, besides confiscating whatever merchandise or property of the latter might be found in his dominions.[103] The troops in Franche Comté and the contiguous territory, amounting to six or eight thousand, were placed under the command of Stephen von Hagenbach, with order to enter Alsace, and there to waste, plunder, and destroy, after the most approved fashion of mediæval warfare. Accordingly, throughout the summer and autumn of 1474, Alsace, after a comparatively long period of unaccustomed quiet and security enjoyed under the Burgundian protectorate, was once more subjected to the scourge with which it had been so often and so heavily smitten.

[102] The circumstances that justified this step have not been noticed by any of the writers who have denounced it as unwarrantable and odious.

[103] Gachard, note to Barante, tom. ii. p. 442.

The invaders entered at intervals, sometimes in a body, sometimes in detached bands, striking at every assailable point, burning and ravaging wherever they passed, slaying without pity or distinction, and carrying off children to be sold and enslaved.[104] As Hagenbach had predicted, the blood of many innocents was shed on his account. When at last the inhabitants found courage to rally and congregate in their own defence, they were seldom able to make a successful stand against their skilled and organized assailants, while they received but little aid from those whose intrigues had brought the calamity upon them. If, even, under the conduct of a noble, or with the help of the civic militia, they at times repelled and chased the depredator, such successes on their own soil afforded a poor requital for the ruin with which it was seared.

But was this a meet or sufficient revenge for the insults offered to the Burgundian authority — a means of obtaining an equivalent for the loss and the wrong which had been sustained? Obviously not. Neither was it so considered by the Burgundian prince. It was but the resentful spark that flies from the struck shield — the announcement of his determination not to be aggrieved with impunity. But if his wrath was quick, it was not less enduring. No need to give it instant way, lest it should grow cold and expire! No fear that he would fail to seek an ampler satisfaction,

[104] Strobel, B. III. s. 318 et al. — Archiv-Chronik, Code hist. et dip. tom. i. p. 192. — Knebel, s. 75–79, et al.

or that he would cease from the demand and pursuit of it to the end!

Whether his chance of obtaining satisfaction would lose or gain by delay was a question not easy to solve beforehand — a question which even his ultimate failure does not enable us to solve. At all events, it would be neither imprudent nor dishonorable to find out first with whom he had to deal. He had taken up the glove — a glove thrown from the midst of a throng; but before drawing his sword it were better to pick out the challenger than to run a muck against the bystanders. With respect to the Swiss (since, the ground being changed, we are now called upon to apologize for Charles, not in that he attacked, but in that he did not attack, the Swiss), the manœuvres or even the acts of isolated individuals or of a small faction did not bind him to treat the Confederacy as a foe. The Confederacy had not joined, the Confederacy had refused to join, in upsetting his government in Alsace. From no member of the Confederacy had he yet received any but the most pacific and friendly messages. If it was true that a treaty had been framed between Austria and the Swiss, its purport and intent, so far as one of the parties was concerned, was still doubtful, nor had the treaty yet been ratified by either party. Even if the ratification should follow, it was far from certain that the principal object would be attained. Where there was so little desire or cause for quarrel, the interval might be wide between words and deeds. Charles might await the result of his last embassy —

might, if that were ineffectual, send a new embassy, invite mediation, trust something to the influences of time. He had declared that from compulsion only could he become the enemy of the Swiss; and it still remained to be seen whether any inducements short of compulsion would make the Swiss his enemies.

As for Austria, *its* sentiments, *its* purpose, were evident enough. But whether its enmity was a thing to be openly or warily met must depend upon the issue of the contingencies just stated. Austria, before spitting forth its venom, had crawled under the embankments of its ancient foe. Let it be drawn or driven thence, and the subsequent work would be easy and short. But whether sheltered or exposed, whether publicly denounced or apparently disregarded, Austria would know on what terms it now stood with its former protector, and would understand the meaning of his attitude towards it. Not even at the price of renewed amity with the Swiss would he ever consent to have peace and reconciliation with Austria, without the fullest reparation and atonement for the past. So, too, in respect to the hostile action of the free cities — Basel, Strasburg, and the rest. That Charles should have been insensible or indifferent to the gross and wanton injuries he had received from that quarter would indeed appear a strange contradiction to the tenor of his earlier career. It would, however, have been equally uncharacteristic had he quitted the prosecution of the object with which he was immediately engaged, and started in pursuit of another which had newly risen into view. His native tenacity of purpose neither permitted nor demanded such a sacrifice. Nor in fact was the diversity between his present aims and those which the occasion seemed to suggest so wide as has been supposed. The fall of his dominion on the Upper Rhine presented not an objection, but a fresh stimulus, to his projects for pushing forward his dominion on the Lower Rhine. It had demonstrated the insecurity of his distant and outlying possessions — the necessity for an ampler base, for safer and shorter communications. Otherwise his Burgundies also, now in danger of becoming enveloped by enemies, might be cut off and lost beyond the hope of redemption. But let him secure the pivot of which he stood in need, and he should be able not merely to strike and to seize, but to occupy and to hold, to reëstablish and to preserve. In keeping to the road on which he had already set out, he was not turning his back upon, he was not losing sight of, he was — so at least he hoped — advancing by the most secure if not the most expeditious route towards, the point where he had been so suddenly and unexpectedly threatened and assailed.[105] Throughout the continuance of the operations on which he was now entering, extending over a period of eleven months, he looked forward with unwavering

[105] This connection between projects which modern writers have regarded as altogether inconsistent with each other was so obvious at the time that Basin supposes Charles's expedition against the electorate of Cologne to have been undertaken simply with the view of establishing himself in a better position for his operations on the Upper Rhine. See his remarks on the feasibility of this project, tom. ii. pp. 332, 333.

purpose to their successful termination as the avenue to fresh undertakings and achievements. "Let us finish in this quarter," he wrote in all his official letters, "and we shall be ready to march against *the Germans*;"[106] for by that name—a name grown detestable to his ears—he designated the free communities by whom he had been insulted and despoiled. It was the same resolved and deliberate spirit in which, ten years before, he had persisted, in spite of his father's summonses and entreaties, in bringing the king of France to submission and compliance before returning to chastise the rebels of Liége.

Instead therefore of postponing, he pressed forward with greater urgency, his preparations for the invasion of Cologne. The first, the most difficult, and most necessary step would be the capture of Neuss, the second town of the electorate in population and commercial importance, but the first in military strength and the nearest to the Netherland frontier. Maestricht, in the territory of Liége, was consequently named as the point of departure and the *dépôt* of troops and supplies. The army began to assemble in June, and Charles arrived on the 16th of July, having previously visited Brussels and other places and presided at the opening of the Parliament of Malines. On the 21st he set out from Maestricht, and nine days later encamped in the neighborhood of Neuss. He was attended in this expedition by a train of unusual splendor, comprising, among other persons of

[106] See the series of letters appended by M. Foisset to an article in the Mém. de l'Acad. de Dijon, 1851, p. 127 et seq.

rank and distinction, the archbishop of Cologne and his brother the elector-palatine; the duke of Juliers and his eldest son; the heir of the house of Cleves; representatives of the princely families of Orange, Luxembourg, Egmont, and De la Marck; the marquis of Ferrara; the counts of Nassau, Aremberg, Meghen, Chimay, and Campobasso; the lord of Gruthuse, now a peer of England with the title of earl of Winchester; the Scottish earl of Arran; and ambassadors from Denmark, Venice, Naples, and other foreign states.[107]

His army, though commonly reported to have been three times as numerous, did not in reality much exceed twenty thousand men, of whom two thousand or more were mere laborers and artisans designed for employment in the trenches and mines and in the construction of bridges and machines.[108] Yet, small as was this force, the materials composing it were almost as many and as diverse as were found commingled in the vast hordes of Asiatic conquerors. It included a portion of the *bandes d'ordonnance*, consisting of noble cavaliers, with their followers, from the various Burgundian provinces; bodies of pikemen and other

[107] Ancienne Chronique, Lenglet, tom. ii. pp. 213, 214. — Meyer, fol. 361 verso. — Pauli, B. II. s. 325. — Haynin, tom. ii. p. 249. — Molinet, (ed. Buchon), tom. i. p. 35.

[108] The enumeration of Meyer (fol. 362 recto), which seems the most exact, gives a total of 20,500, exclusive of women and camp-followers; that of Fugger (Ehrenspiegel des Hauses Œsterreichs), 23,050, without counting the laborers. Wierstraat, the contemporary *stadt-secretarius* of Neuss, makes the number of the combatants actually engaged in the siege amount to 13,200. Later writers give in round numbers 60,000, and even 80,000.

infantry, collected from Picardy, Brabant, Holland, Liége, Gueldres, and several of the German states; eight thousand Italian troops, chiefly cavalry, under Campobasso and another Neapolitan captain, Jacopo Galeoto; six thousand English archers, with a few knights and men-at-arms of the same nation; and even, we are told, a party of Moors, or Turks, whose reputed skill in engineering had probably suggested the motive for engaging them. The battering-train consisted of thirty bombards and fifty large serpentines, some of them intended for throwing stone balls of a hundred pounds weight and upwards, besides more than a hundred pieces of smaller dimensions.[109] Fifteen hundred women, four hundred priests, clerks, and civil functionaries attached to the ducal household, and a vast multitude of purveyors, sutlers, and menials, followed the march.

Neuss, still a manufacturing and fortified place, but now greatly diminished in population, owed its establishment as a Roman military station and its flourishing condition as a member of the Hanseatic League to a site favorable alike to the purposes of trade and of frontier defence. It had originally stood on the left bank of the Rhine, on a solitary eminence from which the descent was accomplished by a succession of terraces and steps to the marshy plain below. As early, however, as the 14th century, the main arm of the river had receded some distance to

[109] Archiv-Chronik, Code hist. et dip. tom. i. p. 187. — According to Herzogen (fol. 125), the siege guns amounted to 138, and the whole of the artillery to 350 pieces.

the eastward; but the vacated bed having been converted into a canal navigable for vessels of considerable draught, Neuss retained for two centuries longer much of its former prosperity as a market and *entrepôt*. This canal, leading from and to the Rhine, received also the waters of the Erft, which, flowing from the south-west, girdled the town, turning its mill-wheels, and filling the capacious ditches with which it was environed. The natural capabilities of the position had been turned to the fullest account by that skill in fortification in which, considered relatively to the means and methods of attack, the military architects of the Middle Ages have not been surpassed by their successors. A double line of wall, — high and broad, with ditches between and without, — lofty towers, massive bastions, thick gates, intricate passages, covered ways, and outworks at different points, protected three sides; while on the east side, where the defences were less imposing, the deep canal, the winding Rhine a mile or two distant, and two swampy islands which formed the only intervening land, offered no slight obstacles to investment or assault. In thirteen sieges — so tradition said — Neuss had maintained its reputation as a virgin fortress.[110]

Timely warnings of the present danger had been received, not only through reports of the enemy's motions and intentions, but through the formal notice long before given by the Burgundian prince that he had taken the deposed elector under his protection

[110] Molinet, tom. i. pp. 28–30, 36, 37. — Magnum Chronicon Belgicum, p. 413. — Löhrer, s. 144 et al.

with the design of reinstating him in the possession of his rights. Good use had been made of the interval thus granted. The administrator of the see, Hermann of Hesse, brother of the reigning landgrave, came in person to superintend the defence, and showed himself now, as in all his subsequent career, a man well qualified to bear rule, whether in ordinary cases or in times of trial and great emergency. Under his direction the walls had been thoroughly repaired, new outworks added, the suburban buildings destroyed and the serviceable materials brought into the town, and the groves and plantations which might have screened the approaches of the foe, levelled and cleared away. Surrounded by rich and expansive meadows, with a region fruitful both in corn and wine spreading out on every side, Neuss had not far to seek for the needful supplies. Great numbers of cattle had been slaughtered and salted down; wheat and other grain had been abundantly stored; munitions of all kinds still continued to arrive from the neighboring towns and territory.[111] In addition to the burghers — themselves not less familiar with the duties of the occasion than any soldiery of the time [111] — there was a garrison of three

[111] Löhrer, s. 144–146. — Basin, tom. ii. p. 335.

[112] "Peuple qui estoit comme demi gendarme, nourri en feu, en fer, en sang, en souffre et en salpètre, berchié au cri des armes et endormy au son impétueux de serpentines, culverines et harquebucies, dont il estoit si juste et amesuré, que à deux doits de descouvert il rendoit mortelle attaincte." Molinet, tom. i. p. 30. Molinet, who had received permission from Charles to join the expedition in the character of its historiographer (or "our special correspondent"), must be accepted as an authority for facts when he condescends to give them, although

thousand Hessian infantry and five hundred cavalry, while, as soon as the enemy's approach had been announced, bands of volunteers and other auxiliaries came pouring in, not only from Cologne and other places in the electorate, but from the cities on the Upper Rhine. To a discerning eye, cognizant of the preparations on both sides and of the spirit that animated the contending parties, it might from the outset have been apparent that the question of the relative powers of attack and defence — a question called up afresh by each succeeding age — was once more about to be thoroughly debated.

The flourishing prelude customary in mediæval sieges was given by the advance of a body of Italian cavalry several thousand strong, magnificently armed, each man enshelled in a marvel of workmanship sumptuously overlaid with ornament, their horses barbed and garmented in sweeping cloths of gold and silk, their lances upreared and glittering like stalactites, their banners gorgeously flaunting, their trumpets braying forth menaces and vaunts. Deploying and wheeling, they made the circuit of the land front, drawing the fire of the bastions, and skirmishing with the cavalry of the garrison, while their leader, the count of Campobasso, reconnoitred the works, with the view of reporting on the fittest disposition of the troops and the quarters and distances from which the siege might best be opened.[113]

his style — an execrable parody on that of his great model, Chastellain — makes the perusal of his work peculiarly fatiguing.

[113] Molinet, tom. i. p. 32. — Des Stadt-Secretarius Christianus Wierstraat Reimchronik der Stadt Neuss zur Zeit der Belagerung, nach dem

Soon tents were pitched, and the different corps began to take up the positions assigned to them. Five principal stations were occupied each by a mixed body of archers, pikemen, men-at-arms, and other troops,[114] with similar bodies so posted as to constitute their supports and reserves. At each of these stations a few bombards and many smaller pieces were mounted on platforms; and the communications between the several posts were protected by intrenchments, except where the Erft or some tributary rivulet crossed the line and required to be spanned by a bridge. Campobasso, and under him Galeoto, held command on the north side of the town, in the proximity of the Rhine. The largest body of troops, intended for repelling any attempt to raise the siege, was disposed on the south side, opposite the principal gate and near the road leading to Cologne. Here too the duke's quarters were fixed—at the Oberkloster, a community of regular monks of the order

Original-Druck von 1497, herausgegeben von Dr. E. von Groote (Köln, 1855), s. 7, 8.—Mag. Chron. Belg. p. 414.—Löhrer (s. 143) absurdly describes this movement as an attempt to carry the town by a *coup-de-main*. Molinet says expressly that it was a reconnoissance ordered by Charles "pour impertorer les fors, et imaginer par quel moyen, à moins de perte et plus de gaigne, le siége pourroit prendre pied ferme et fondement durable." The notion that Charles expected to take Neuss without any expenditure of labor or time is shared by the modern narrators generally. Yet it is contradicted by all the details of his proceedings, and is based simply upon an erroneous idea of his character, coupled with the taunts of hostile chroniclers and the misconceptions of Commines.

114 Wierstraat and the author of the Mag. Chron. Belg. (a contemporary and a native of Cologne) represent the besieging force as divided according to the nationality of the soldiers composing it. A somewhat different account is given by Molinet, whose authority on such points is of course to be preferred.

of Saint Augustine. The buildings had been vacated by most of the inmates, and partially burned and unroofed by the towns-people; but the authorities, on consideration, had decided against their entire destruction. Charles, who in the field disdained any habitation not appropriate to war, had his portable house set up in the convent gardens. Around were the tents and pavilions of his suite, distinguishable by the different banners that surmounted them.[115]

Before the place could be considered as invested it would be necessary to occupy the two islands on the east side. Boats with provisions and reënforcements were still constantly descending from Cologne and Bonn; while in the low ground beneath the walls, and close to the edge of the canal, pits had been dug, from which a number of coulevriniers gave much annoyance to such parties of cavalry as came within range while watering their horses. The first effort to overcome these embarrassments was made in the early morning of the 6th of August, when, by order of Campobasso, a soldier swam to the larger island, carrying one end of a rope, with the help of which two or three small boats were drawn across. About six score men had been thus passed over when the rope, by some mischance, was carried away. Meanwhile the watchmen on the towers of Neuss had given the alarm; and three hundred pikemen crossed the channel higher up to the smaller island, from which they waded to the

[115] Die Cronica van der helliger Stat vā Coellē, fol. 323 recto. — Mag. Chron. Belg. pp. 448, 450, 451. — Molinet, tom. i. pp. 34, 35. — Löhrer, pp. 149, 150.

larger one and fell upon the unlucky invaders. The Italians fought courageously, but were soon pent up between their assailants, the water, and the swamps. The cannon-balls from their own camp fell indiscriminately among the crowd. Most of them were slain or drowned. Several, who fled to the shallows, were enticed back by promises of safety and then put to death. The remainder, about a dozen in number, among them a gigantic Moor, who had won the admiration of his foes by a prodigious defence, were carried off as prisoners, and, after being paraded through the streets, were let down by cords into a subterranean dungeon.[116]

Emboldened by the result of this affair, a strong party of the garrison, three days later, made a vigorous sortie. They inflicted some damage and captured two guns, but were soon driven in with considerable loss, leaving their dead in the hands of the enemy.[117]

In his premature attempt with inadequate means to effect a lodgment on the islands, Campobasso had disregarded the injunctions of Charles.[118] The latter, meanwhile, had been making more ample preparations with the same object; and on the 11th, five hundred pikemen of the *bandes d'ordonnance*, under Josse de Lalain, were swiftly and securely ferried over in a number of large boats collected along the Rhine. Intrenchments were thrown up, batteries planted, and an enfilading fire having been opened on the pits, the

[116] Wierstraat, s. 10, 11.—Molinet, tom. i. pp. 36, 39.—Mag. Chron. Belg. pp. 453, 454.

[117] Löhrer, s. 154.—Mag. Chron. Belg. p. 456.

[118] Gachard, note to Barante, tom. ii. p. 443.

coulevriniers were dislodged and forced to take refuge within the walls. Both islands were soon in complete possession of the besiegers. In order to complete the cicumvallation two bridges were laid, one from the larger island to the ground in the vicinity of Galeoto's camp, the other from the smaller island to a meadow occupied by a party of English under Sir John Middleton, and separated by the Erft from the Burgundian head-quarters.[119]

No resistance was offered to these operations by the besieged. But from Cologne a fire-ship, followed by a fleet, was sent down, under cover of night, in the hope of burning the upper bridge and throwing in fresh reënforcements. The experiment, however, proved unsuccessful. To prevent its repetition, Charles gave orders for damming up the canal at its southern extremity — a matter of no slight difficulty, for the current was swift, the channel thirty feet wide and more than a spear's length in depth. Earth, timber, old boats, straw, whatever could be heaped together or made to adhere, were used in the construction. Not only the laborers and pioneers, but pages, women, and even men-at-arms, shared in the task, and were protected against the interruptions offered both by the garrison of Neuss and the people of Cologne by tiers of wine-casks filled with earth. The whole was carried on under the personal supervision of the duke. Finally, a fleet of fifty vessels,

119 Mag. Chron. Belg. pp. 454–456. — Wierstraat, s. 15, 16. — Molinet, tom. i. pp. 39–41.

moored in the main arm of the Rhine, prevented any surprise in that direction.[120]

Neuss was now beleaguered on all sides. No further succors were to be expected from its sister towns. The besiegers were beginning to threaten and exult;[121] the inhabitants contemplated their own situation with gravity and in silence, but without dismay.

In fact, the difficulties of the siege had as yet only begun to disclose themselves. Apart from the enormous strength of the defences, their commanding situation gave to their fire a great superiority over that of the besiegers, at a time when the art of intrenchment and the cognate branches of military engineering were still very imperfectly comprehended. The vast extent of marshy soil formed another obstacle to the approaches, to obviate which Charles conceived the plan of diverting the Erft from its course and draining all the adjacent regions.[122] The work was accordingly begun; but even if practicable, it must prove a gigantic and tedious undertaking. Meanwhile the bombardment was kept up with more or less vigor, one of the batteries on the island proving the most efficient. Two gates were demolished; but they were strongly retrenched, and the flanking fires were still unsubdued. Nevertheless an assault was determined

[120] Molinet, tom. i. pp. 141–144.

[121] Mag. Chron. Belg. p. 455.

"'Syet naber, ghy moyt blyuen,
nu moeghdy nyrgent vyt!
wy wyllen naerre drijuen
ind cloppen v dye huyt!
naber, gy moyt oick hangen,
v wijff behalden wy,
gheen nemen wy gefangen,
ghy syt eyn vuyll parthij!'
Wierstraat, s, 16.

[122] Löhrer surmises, oddly enough, that this was undertaken with the vain idea of depriving the town of water.

upon. By Campobasso's advice, a tower thirty feet high was erected in front of the proposed point of attack, and manned with couleyriniers and arquebusiers for the purpose of pouring a fire into the adjoining bastions. On the 10th of September a storming party, composed of Italians and English, advanced from the shelter of the tower, and having cleared the open ground, planted their ladders against the wall. They were met with a cross-fire from the casemates, and with showers of missiles, blazing fagots, and streams of scalding oil from above. Their ladders proving far too short, they were unable to reach the parapet and hurl themselves upon the foe. Yet they maintained the attempt for more than two hours, trusting to the effect of the fire from the tower and from the island battery for opening a favorable chance. But the defenders, though greatly exposed and severely galled, were too numerous and too resolute to give way for a single moment. The assailants retired, with a loss of more than three hundred dead, but bearing off their wounded.[123]

A later attack in another quarter was attended by a like result; and the citizens, judging from their own experience and from the general practice of the age, believed that the siege would now be abandoned. The time had long passed when armies were content to lie

[123] Molinet, tom. i. pp. 44–47.—Wierstraat, s. 20–22.—The wounded English, comprising fifty-four archers, thirteen men-at-arms, and three captains — Stanley, Ebringhem (?), and Talbot—received liberal guerdons from the duke. See the Ancienne Chronique (Lenglet, tom. ii. p. 214), where, however, there is a mistake in the date, unless an earlier assault be referred to.

for months, and even years, before a fortified place; intrenching themselves between lines of circumvallation and countervallation; spending long periods in constructing new machines and devising new expedients for forcing an entrance; hurling huge rocks, and piling mount upon mount, after the manner of the Titans; and at length either starving out the besieged or fighting their way in through some ruined portcullis, from passage to passage, and from chamber to chamber. The invention of artillery, without giving any exclusive advantage to the attack, had shortened the contest, alike by the greater loss of life inflicted, by the greater and more rapid consumption of resources which it entailed, and by developing at an earlier stage the probable issue. As an earnest of their expectation, and also as a means of securing its fulfilment, the authorities of Neuss caused the bones of Saint Quirinus to be carried in solemn procession; and the church bells, which at the commencement of the siege had ceased to ring, in order that the warnings of the alarm-bell might be at all times audible, sent forth a congratulatory peal.[124]

But if their dependence on their patron saint was not misplaced, they had assuredly mistaken the character of their enemy. Unlike his modern critics, Charles "the Laborious," did not conceive that it was the part of a general or of a statesman to abandon an enterprise simply because it had begun to appear arduous.[125] He had not expected it to prove easy; and

[124] Wierstraat, s. 23, 24.

[125] Even Von Rodt (B. I. s. 247, 257) censures Charles for his persistency in struggling "mit den

the more arduous it appeared, the more necessary was success, and the more certain to bring with it the results for which he hoped. He had reached that crisis in his career which must test his possession of the power and capacity requisite for attaining the position he aspired to hold. Unless he were able to exalt by some notable feat the reputation he had already acquired, his triumphs in the past would have served only to awaken envy and hostility. Let him retire in confessed impotence from his present undertaking, and not only must he forego the great and immediate object of his ambition, but he must prepare himself for the treatment that commonly befalls those who are at once aggressive and weak. Let Neuss, on the other hand, after a conspicuous defence, exhibiting all the resources of nature and art, of valor and skill, succumb to his superior strength, and the subsequent resistance to be apprehended would have lost its chief moral as well as its chief material support. Ancient history, his favorite source of inspiration, furnished encouraging examples. It was by their successful prosecution of protracted and what had seemed to others impracticable sieges that Alexander and Cæsar had laid the foundations of their conquests. If the difficulties in the present case were such as had not yet been surmounted, this supplied an additional motive for persevering in the attempt. The proper mode

unerwarteten Schwierigkeiten einer unzeitigen Unternehmung," and considers that it would have been well for him if he had been called off by attacks from other quarters. Yet it was precisely because he was not then exposed to such attacks that his undertaking was not an unseasonable one.

of surmounting them could be discovered only through practical trial and endeavor; and an achievement of this nature was precisely what was needed for the impression which he wished to produce. Not Cologne merely, but Strasburg, Mühlhausen, Basel, would recognize their future master in the conqueror of Neuss. Nor did the conjuncture appear such as to render a further continuance of the struggle impolitic or hazardous. He was not now, as at Beauvais, hampered by engagements, surrounded by hostile territory, dodged and harassed by a nimble foe, unprovided for a long campaign, or liable to be summoned back for the defence of his own provinces. His communications were unimperilled, his dominions were unmenaced. The single danger to be foreseen lay in a general arming of the empire; but this was a danger which it would be time enough to guard against, when it should have assumed a more determinate shape.

Evidently, however, the siege would be of long duration, involving the necessity for strenuous exertions and a heavy expenditure of means and material. It presented, therefore, in Charles's view, a conjuncture that entitled him to make fresh demands upon his subjects. Accordingly, he despatched letters to the Estates of Flanders, with a requisition for an additional number of pikemen and pioneers, and a large quantity of munitions. Meantime his own efforts were unrelaxed. New drains were cut, new dikes were formed, new batteries were raised. A town constructed of wood and clay, and regularly laid out in streets and squares, rose outside the walls of Neuss, and announced his resolution to keep the field, if necessary, through the ensuing winter.[126] Experiments looking to a more speedy reduction of the place were also tried, and whoever had any suggestion to offer found a ready hearing. Galeoto received permission to erect a "cat," or movable castle, resting on twenty-four wheels; and a somewhat similar machine, called a *grue*, with accommodation for three hundred troops, and an exterior ladder sixty feet long, depressible by chains and pulleys to the proper incline for ascending the walls, was constructed on the plans of a Castilian knight.[127] But as great ships are sometimes more easily built than launched, and are found, when launched, to suit no particular purpose beyond that of testing the force of the winds and waves, so both the cat and the *grue* proved incapable of being rolled to the positions intended for them, and, probably, had it been otherwise, would have served merely as targets for the enemy's bombardiers. "Villanous saltpetre" had put an extinguisher on all such contrivances.[128] Somewhat better fortune attended an attempt to set fire to the town by means of blazing arrows and similar missiles. On the 3d of October the flames, fanned by a strong wind, broke out at once in several different quarters; and while the

[126] Mag. Chron. Belg. pp. 450, 451.

[127] Molinet, tom. i. pp. 47, 48.

[128] "Depuis le temps que le feu, le plus actif des quatre éléments, s'est adjoint avec le soulfre, pour répugner au salpêtre son contraire, . . . tels engins et semblables béfrois de bois, apts et susceptibles de combustion véhémente, sont hors de usaige maintenant, par subtilité d'artillerie qui se multiplie chacun jour." Molinet, tom. i. p. 49.

citizens were busy in saving their dwellings, the trumpets sounded, the alarm-bell rang, and they were called away to defend the works against another assault. It was nightfall before they had triumphed over these opposite dangers. Then a new conflagration burst forth; but this time without the walls, in the Italian camp, where the inflammatory materials had been collected. Some five hundred huts or tents were consumed, besides horses, equipments, ammunition, and stores of all kinds. The guns were, however, safely removed, and a new camp, at no greater distance from the walls than the old one, was speedily pitched.[129]

On the same day, the 25th of October, on which the Estates of Flanders assembled to consider, with their habitual gravity and phlegm, the message received from their sovereign,[130] another representative body, more remote from the scene of operations, but more deeply interested in the issue, was sending *to* the Burgundian prince a message calculated to produce a profound sensation and eventful results.

It was observed in a former chapter that, with many strongly contrasted features, there existed between the Swiss and Burgundian governments certain points of resemblance, which might have been expected, under the circumstances of their increasing propinquity, to exert a disturbing influence upon the relations they had hitherto maintained. Such was in fact the common expectation at the time, and we

[129] Molinet, tom. i. pp. 53, 54. — Wierstraat, s. 27–30.

[130] Gachard, Doc. Inéd., tom. ii.

have seen the plans that were built upon it and the purposes they were intended to serve. France, Austria, Baden, Milan, and the cities of the Rhineland, had all labored, either singly or in concert, either with some special gain in view or from apprehensions common to all, to bring about a collision between the two foremost military powers of the age.[131] But we have seen also how long this expectation remained ungratified, how futile seemed the labor, how ineffective the schemes. For, as if by mutual agreement and for the purpose of disconcerting the hopes and efforts of their neighbors, these two powers, each so sensitive, each so overbearing, in its dealings with the exterior world, had manifested in their demeanor towards each other a studious forbearance and reserve. The alliance between Burgundy and Austria had failed to give offence to the Confederates. Communications and treaties between the Confederates and France had drawn nothing more than a friendly remonstrance from Burgundy. All the tuggings and pushings of Sigismund had found Charles immovable as a rock. All the blandishments and enticements of Louis had found the body of the Swiss people as cold and insensible as ice. Even when the perfidy of Austria, the manœuvrings of France, and the violence of the free towns had brought about a conjuncture that seemed to make a rupture unavoidable, continued amity and a cordial understanding was

[131] "Wie zu disen Zyten disen Herzog und die Eydgenossen allein über all Tütsch und Welsch Nation Kriegs halb hochgeachtet und geforchtet waren; also ward von Tütschen und Welschen flyssig gesucht, sie . . . aneinandren zu hetzen." Valerius Anshelm, B. I. s. 113.

still the avowed object of Charles, neutrality and an adherence to old engagements was still the real purpose of the Swiss.[132]

How, then, was the aim of the conspirators at length accomplished? On this point the reader will have been prepared for a rectification of the common statements of history; and the whole truth may now be told without concealment or disguise. It was not for the protection of their territory or in defence of their liberties against aggression or menace; it was not in revenge for slights and indignities offered to their government, its subjects, or its allies; it was not because they shared in the disquietude and the fears awakened by the encroachments of a formidable neighbor; that the Swiss people made war upon Charles of Burgundy. It was not from any feeling of jealousy or hostility; it was not from any views of national policy; it was not on their own behalf, or in support of any principle or cause in which they were personally interested. It was simply as the strong, intelligent, hired bravoes of a foreign potentate — too weak, too timid, or too crafty to strike with his own hand.

It is generally known that during the 16th century, and even in more recent times, the Swiss Confederacy was regularly subsidized by France. Open and stipulated pensions were paid to the several cantons; secret and variable pensions were paid to the

[132] See the remarks of Valerius Anshelm (who fully comprehended the whole situation, and, if he has gone too little into detail, was without doubt intimately acquainted with all the particulars), Berner-Chronik, B. I. s. 100–123.

leading citizens. In return for the gold thus constantly, but not too lavishly, not always punctually, distributed, Swiss blood was freely poured forth in defence or for the aggrandizement of the French monarchy. In the armies of France there were no troops so valiant, so skilful, so reliable, as the Swiss, whose audacity in the most desperate encounters, and fidelity in the darkest trials, gained a peculiar and well-merited renown. This renown was, however, of a somewhat different kind from that which the same nation had acquired by its primitive achievements, on its own soil, and in its own battles. The praise so readily bestowed was such as is accorded to the trusty domestic, to the zealous attorney, to the blood-enamoured gladiator. Now the popular error in reference to the war with Burgundy is merely in the nature of an anachronism. In that war the Swiss displayed the same qualities, and earned as high a fame, as in earlier and in later wars: but they fought not, as in earlier wars, for freedom, but, as in later wars, for hire.[133]

[133] This is stated with the utmost plainness by Valerius Anshelm, who describes the alliance with France as "den rychen, aber an Ehr und Lyb verderblichen Bund" — the beginning of a system, introduced by Berne, and since deeply infixed throughout the Confederacy, by which favor and disfavor, friendship and enmity, peace and war, ay dear blood and noble freedom, had become marketable commodities. He contrasts this period with the former history of the nation. "Where," he asks, "were the pensions, when our fathers won their liberties, and exalted themselves above every other German people? But Berne," he remarks, "thought good to depart from the ancient customs, and from its own precedents." See Berner-Chronik, B. I. s. 82, 118, 126, 127, 134, 151–153.

Anshelm's outspoken rebukes are explained by the fact, that, at the time when he was appointed historiographer of Berne, the Reformation had given an impulse to the

Of the consequent effects upon their social condition and their standing among states, we may speak hereafter. It behooves us now to notice the steps through which this change in their relations and position took place. For, as may easily be supposed, it was not with a sudden and single leap that a people proud of its antecedents, rigid in its notions of fair-dealing, and firmly attached to a simple and well-considered line of policy, descended to such a depth of degradation — bartering away their manhood, their honor, and the precepts of their ancestors, receiving from a whilom enemy and restless schemer the dagger which it plunged into the heart of a confiding and consistent friend.[134] As happens alike with nations and with individuals, the fall was gradual, unpremeditated, almost insensible — induced by deceptions, impelled by urgings, consummated before the full and conscious intention had been evoked.[135] With the plans of the tempter, and with the earlier arts and seductions employed,

efforts of a patriotic party, desirous of shaking off the corrupting influences of the French alliance, and its debasing tribute. Their hopes were, however, doomed to disappointment, and hence perhaps the reason why so important a chronicle remained unpublished until the present century.

[134] "Charles," remarks Valerius Anshelm, "coveted nothing so much as the friendship of the Swiss, and especially of Berne, dreaded nothing so much as their hostility." After noticing one of Schilling's lies in regard to the duke's course, "There was no prince, no lord, no people," he remarks, "to whom he behaved so worthily as to the Confederacy." B. I. s. 109, 113.

[135] Even after every thing was settled, we are told by Valerius Anshelm — and his statement is confirmed from other sources — there was a general dissatisfaction among the Swiss, who were only reconciled to the arrangement by its prosperous issue. Berner-Chronik, B. I. s. 122.

the reader is already acquainted; and the final struggle shall be related with the conciseness which his instinctive distaste for the spectacle will prompt him to require.

The treaty of Constance was carried for approval to the French king by the two persons whose energy and tact had overleaped or smoothed away the obstacles to its adoption — Nicholas von Diesbach and Jost von Silinen; while Sigismund's messengers followed as fast as the preparation of their more voluminous despatches and the greater weight of their saddle-bags would permit. There was, however, no real necessity for speed. For the delay which ensued, Louis was himself responsible. No doubt it was a source of satisfaction to have in his grasp the bolt that had so long been forging; but the moment was not convenient for discharging it. His last truce with the Duke of Burgundy was now running out. Until it had been renewed — until he had withdrawn to a safe distance and secured his own person from any risk of mischief — it would scarcely be prudent to give the signal for the fray. Accordingly, it was not until the 11th of June — a week or more after the truce had been extended for a year — that he found leisure to examine and confirm the treaty between Sigismund and the Swiss.[136] The clauses insisted upon by the latter were inserted without hesitation. The arguments of the other party made no visible impression on the mind

[136] The treaty of Senlis — so called from its having been there ratified by Louis — may be found in Lenglet, tom. iii., Chmel, B. I., and other collections.

of the royal arbitrator. Subsequent remonstrances were swept aside with a brusque impatience. "Let it hang as it hangs," he interrupted, in very tolerable German,[137] — a language for which he had formerly professed an abhorrence, calling it a Burgundian tongue,[138] but which had lost much of its harshness in the smooth accentuation of his friends the Diesbachs, while on the present occasion it gave to his decision a greater emphasis and plainness.

Meanwhile the council of Berne, now filled with the partisans of Diesbach to the almost total exclusion of every other faction, had grown alarmed at the long absence of its head,[139] as well as at the silence of the Most Christian King, and the rumors touching his negotiations with Burgundy. The council had itself been neither dumb nor inactive in this interval. Persuasive letters had been addressed to the reluctant members of the Confederacy. Agents had been sent to Basel to concert plans for a military expedition. Troops had been actually raised in Berne and its dependent territory. Some special grievances, which stood in the way of the Austrian alliance, were settled by arbitration. An energetic, though unsuccessful, effort was made to induce the acceptance of new offers of alliance from Milan.[140]

But of what use would be all this zeal and indus-

[137] "Dixit in vulgari Alamanico — 'Er lässt in hangen als er hangt.'" Chmel, B. I. p. 264.

[138] Ludwigs von Diesbach Selbtbiographie, Schweiz. Geschichtforscher, B. VIII. s. 171.

[139] Diesbach had been re-elected to the office of schulteiss — apparently without opposition.

[140] Zellweger; Rodt; Tillier; Stettler, &c.

try on the part of the subordinates, if indifference or a change of purpose had crept over the instigator? The fainting hearts of the council were at length gladdened by a letter from Diesbach, bearing date the 24th of June. They were not to listen to any rumors affecting the loyal intentions of their patron. His extension of the truce need give rise to no uneasiness. There had been excellent reasons for it, which the writer would explain on his return. The king had no secrets from him or his coadjutor the provost. His own protracted absence had been highly advantageous to the common interests. He should bring back a most satisfactory report. Let Berne continue its preparations. A watchful eye must also be kept upon Savoy, and precautions taken for the security of Montbelliard and other neutral places exposed to the treacherous attacks of the Duke of Burgundy.[141]

The return of Diesbach, a month later, was followed by several abortive conferences at Lucerne. The agents of Sigismund and of the allied towns, strenuously backed by the deputies of Berne, pressed in vain for immediate hostilities against Burgundy, alleging the necessity, for the preservation of Alsace; the obligations under the treaties with Austria and the free cities; the propitious opportunity, seeing that Charles had found full employment for his forces in a distant quarter; above all, the great advantages to be derived from the support of France, which, if rejected now might be withheld when applied for in some fu-

[141] Rodt (from the archives of Freiburg), Book I. s. 160.

ture emergency. The only point which seems to have received much attention was the demand for aid in repelling the incursions into Alsace. Six cantons had now ratified, from the various motives and under the specious representations before described, the treaties on which this demand was grounded. But, with the exception of Berne, they all — like Charles of Burgundy in answer to similar appeals — contended that the case had not arisen in which aid was to be furnished. It was not for them to guard the frontiers of Alsace or to save it from inroads and devastations. This was a duty incumbent on the ruler and the inhabitants. When walled towns were closely besieged, when the enemy had begun to occupy the country, and Sigismund was in danger of losing possession, it would be time enough to call upon the Swiss. Consent was, however, given for the admission of Montbelliard into the Lower Confederacy ; and ambassadors from Savoy, sent with proposals for a mediation, were somewhat sharply bidden to remind their mistress of the responsibilities she incurred by granting a passage to recruits from Lombardy for the Burgundian service — an intimation which drew forth the not unreasonable rejoinder, that the duchess had not been made aware of any measures or intentions on the part of the Confederacy which rendered this proceeding inconsistent with her neutrality.[142]

Unpromising as was the aspect of affairs, the conspirators did not allow themselves to be disheartened. The time had come for a determinate effort ; if the

[142] Tillier, B. II. s. 215, 216. — Rodt, B. I. s. 161.

present conjuncture were let slip, none similar could be expected to present itself. Soon a diet was again convoked, to receive the gracious overtures of the French king, who had sent a new embassy, headed by Gratian Dufaure, president of the Parliament of Toulouse, with proposals for an alliance offensive and defensive.[143] The ambassadors arrived at Berne on the 26th of August, and on the 30th were introduced to the council and burghers. If this was the same assembly as that to which the Burgundian envoys had addressed their appeal a few months previously, a change, which it might not be difficult to account for, had in the mean time passed over its sentiments. And in fact its composition was not precisely the same. The Diesbachs were now present, while Adrian von Bubenberg and his friends absented themselves. Bubenberg had given his assent to the Austrian treaty, provided it should not be so construed as to impair the obligations of the earlier treaties with Burgundy. His insistance on this latter point proved his unmanageable character; and finding himself all but alone, he yielded to that hopelessness which is inspired by the unequal conflict between reason and destiny, ceased to resist a tide which, contrasted with the ordinary course of action at Berne, might be termed a revolutionary movement, and was finally driven into a retirement, from which he did not emerge until summoned by his countrymen, in a season of danger, to take command in the field.[144]

[143] Pouvoir, &c., Lenglet, tom. iii. pp. 337, 338.

[144] Valerius Anshelm. B. I. s. 118, 119.

There were consequently no expressions of dissent on the present occasion. The message delivered was highly characteristic of the source from which it emanated. With professions of unbounded admiration and regard, and commendations of their bravery and rectitude, Louis made an offer to the Confederates of his counsel, assistance, and "undivided friendship." To gain time for an arrangement with them, he had consented to a further truce, in which he had caused them to be included as his allies. The Duke of Burgundy had offered him a peace for a term of years, on condition that he should give no help to the Swiss; but this, from his love for them, and his resolution to place his life and his possessions at their disposal, he had refused. He had already posted fifteen thousand troops on the marches of Burgundy The truce formed no obstacle to immediate hostilities, since a justification might easily be found in the proceedings of the opposite party. As a contribution towards the expenses, and as an earnest of his sentiments, he would pay to each of the eight cantons, and also to Freyburg and Solothurn, a "friendly pension" of two thousand francs. On his side he would carry on the war entirely at his own cost. If, however, it seemed more agreeable to them that he should refrain from taking an active part, then, "out of true friendship," he would make them a yearly grant of eighty thousand francs as long as the war continued.[145]

In conformity with a vote passed at this meeting, commissioners, of whom Diesbach was one, empowered

[145] Zellweger, s. 43, 44.

to open the matter to the other cantons, accompanied the French envoys to a diet at Lucerne. All the arguments so often repeated were again reiterated, and fortified by the offers of France. War, sooner or later, was unavoidable. Austria and its allies were arming, and it would be impossible for the Swiss to hold themselves aloof. A foreign prince stood ready to defray the cost. Was it not better to embark in the contest, thus aided and supported, than to run the chances of sustaining alone the charges and the risk? That private persuasion was used, that personal inducements were held out, we may reasonably conjecture. The pension scheme had not yet been publicly unfolded in all its details. At all events, while the deputies, with few exceptions, shrank from reporting the business to their constituents, and declined to make it a transaction of the diet, permission was given for Berne, and for Nicholas von Diesbach by name, to carry on the negotiations.[146]

Of this concession Diesbach and his associates availed themselves to the fullest extent. On the 19th of September the executive council, enlarged by the admission of twenty-two burghers, met for deliberation. An oath of secrecy, similar in form and tenor to that with which the sessions were yearly opened, was administered. It was further charged upon each of the persons present that he should never hereafter reproach another for his share in the resolves.[147] With

[146] Rodt, B. I. s. 267. — Tillier, B. II. s. 218. — Tillier (from the Rathmanual of Berne), B. II. s. 217, 218.

[147] Valerius Anshelm, B. I. s. 120.

the discussions of a meeting thus packed and thus silenced, we can neither be acquainted nor concerned. The result was the formation of a treaty in accordance with the wishes of Louis, including a supplementary declaration, to be hereafter noticed, on the part of Berne, the full virtue of which was not perhaps appreciated by the signers.

But could this treaty, surreptitiously authorized, secretly framed, be regarded as the act of the Confederacy? Manifestly not. To have sent it for ratification to the cantons would have insured its rejection. To have treated it as binding would have demonstrated its invalidity. When Berne disclosed to Freyburg, its particular ally, the benefits of which the latter was to be made a partaker, the answer received was to this effect: "Freyburg has too few people to send any away for gold; it wants no alliance with France or with any foreign power; it is content with that of Berne and the Confederacy; it now regrets even its treaty with Burgundy."[148]

The arrangement with France was not, however, meant to go into immediate effect. It did not professedly bind the Swiss to embark in a war with Burgundy; it contemplated the case of their being already involved in such a war. When this crisis had occurred, there would be no fear of its rejection; let the relative parts of the contrivance be adjusted, and the clasp would shut with a snap, and hold them firmly together.

The alliance with Austria was still, therefore, the

[148] Valerius Anshelm, B. I. s. 128.

only string on which to pull. To that alliance all the cantons, save Unterwalden — which still proved incorrigible — had now consented. The propriety of exchanging the ratifications furnished a reason for again convoking the diet, which was attended by Sigismund in person, by the French envoys, by the agents of Basel and the allied towns, and by an imperial embassy. For the convenience of the Austrian prince — perhaps also in order that all the parties might feel a greater freedom from constraint — Feldkirch, beyond the boundaries of the Swiss territory, was chosen as the place of meeting. There the proceedings were opened on the 9th of October.

The deputies were doubtless the same that had attended the last diet; and it is plain that the manipulation employed on that occasion, and since, had so softened the material that it might now be moulded into the destined shape. The French money might not yet have been handled; but it had not been carried back. The treaty could not yet be enforced or published; but it was ready for production, and would take effect, without further parley, when the preliminary movement had been made. In a word, the real motive for action had been presented and embraced, and all that remained was to discover a pretext. Sigismund was told that, although the Swiss cantons would not on their own account undertake a war against Burgundy, yet they were ready to send a stated force into Alsace for the purpose of clearing it of the invaders, provided he would defray the estimated expenses, amounting to eight thousand guilders.[149] To have taken the money directly from France would, under the existing circumstances, have been the palpable acceptance of a bribe.[150] But it was a stipulation of the treaty with Sigismund that the troops raised for his defence were to be paid by him; and where he procured the means was a matter of indifference to all parties. As usual, even at this late moment, he would fain have played the part of a marplot. He was still prating of his grievances, and demurring to the objectionable clauses in the treaty. To quiet him, Diesbach and the French envoys gave him a written assurance that the opening of the Forest Towns should not be turned to his prejudice; while he was left to refer the other questions to the further consideration of Louis, from whom he received the answer already mentioned.[151] After all these matters had been settled, it was voted by the diet that an agreement with France on the basis proposed should be concluded—"seeing that it had become a thing of necessity."[152]

149 Zellweger, Geschichte des Appenzellischen Volkes, B. II. s. 90 et seq.

150 Zellweger, however, objects to this view of the transaction. "The stipulated pensions," he observes, "were regarded by the cantons merely as a payment of wages for services rendered; and this was agreed to by the people, which was nevertheless as firmly set against corruption as ever." (Versuch, &c., s. 49, note.) He warns us, also, that Anshelm judges every thing in the spirit of his own time. This is true, and Schilling also, we may presume, judged the matter in the spirit of *his* time, which was that of the transaction itself. He at least has nothing to say about "wages." It is all about the "gracious bounty" of the French king (Die Burgundischen Kriegen, s. 124). Flunkey!

151 Chmel; Zellweger; Rodt; &c.

152 "Dann es denn grosse Nothdurft ist." Zellweger, s. 48.

The main point had now been gained. Yet it was felt to be desirable that every possible addition should be made to a pile formed of so questionable a substance and still much in lack of cement. The imperial envoys supplied the desideratum. They produced a missive from their master calling upon the Confederates, as members of the empire, to aid in defending it against the aggression of the Duke of Burgundy.[153] True, such a summons had never before taken effect in this quarter; but was it not a natural consequence of the change in their relations with the house of Austria that the Confederacy should begin to recognize its duties towards the head of the empire?

An adjournment of the diet, some days later, to Lucerne, left the deputies at liberty to finish the business among themselves. Yet it was still judged best to remit to Berne the task of preparing the requisite instruments, as well as of making such communications as were desirable to all the parties concerned. The French treaty, consented to as a thing of necessity, had already begun to radiate and dazzle. Berne was instructed by the diet to procure the immediate payment of the first instalment.

Diesbach accordingly prepared himself for a new journey to the French court. He was to inform the king of the great obstacles which had been overcome; to present him with the treaty, bearing the seal of Berne, and obtain the royal duplicate in exchange; above all, to bring back without delay the money both for Sigismund and the Swiss. Berne, in

[153] Rodt, B. I. s. 270.

the mean while, would discharge itself of the responsibilities it had assumed by procuring the ratifications of the cantons. Troops were already in motion, in full reliance on the purpose of Louis to make good all his engagements.[154]

Five days before Diesbach's departure, on the 24th of October, a message to the Duke of Burgundy was prepared in the Council. On the following day, it was secured in the usual manner to the herald's staff, by insertion in a split at one extremity, and despatched to the commander of a Burgundian garrison at Blamont, by whom it was courteously received, for transmission to his sovereign. On the ground of their obligations to Sigismund, whose territory had been invaded, and of a command from the emperor, whose subjects they acknowledged themselves, the magistrates and people of the communities constituting the Great Confederacy of Upper Germany, with the allied states of Freyburg and Solothurn, proclaimed themselves the enemies of the Burgundian prince, with purpose to execute this declaration, whether in attack or defence, in the day or in the night, by slaying, by burning, by plundering, and by all other customary methods — whereof he was required to take notice.

Such was the message brought to Charles in the midst of his labors outside the walls of Neuss. As he listened to it a deep gloom overspread his features. It was not alone his perception of the blight that had suddenly fallen upon his prospects which

[154] Zellweger, s. 49, 50, and Beilage.

gave its poignancy to the blow. It was the sense of injury, the consciousness of his own innocence, the recollection of his misplaced trust. As his eye fell upon the seal affixed to the document, a single exclamation showed that the arrow, so winged, so pointed, had gone home. "Berne! Berne!" he muttered through his clinched teeth.[155]

[155] Diebold Schilling, s. 135, 136. — Stettler, s. 219. — Rodt, B. I. s. 271–273.

END OF THE SECOND VOLUME.